The Christopher Bolla

This reader brings together a selection of seminal papers by Christopher Bollas.

Essays such as 'The Fascist state of mind', 'The structure of evil' and 'The functions of history' have established his position as one of the most significant cultural critics of our time. Also included are examples of his psychoanalytical writings, such as 'The transformational object' and 'Psychic genera', that deepen and renew interest in unconscious creative processes. Two recent essays, 'Character and interformality' and 'The wisdom of the dream' extend his work on aesthetics and the role of form in everyday life.

This is a collection of papers that will appeal to anyone interested in human experience and subjectivity.

Christopher Bollas PhD is a Member of the British Psychoanalytical Society, the Los Angeles Institute and Society for Psychoanalytic Studies, and Honorary Member of the Institute for Psychoanalytic Training and Research (IPTAR) in New York.

Arne Jemstedt MD is a psychoanalyst in private practice in Stockholm. He is a member and training analyst of the Swedish Psychoanalytical Association and its current President.

The Christopher Bollas Reader

Christopher Bollas

Introduction by Arne Jemstedt
Foreword by Adam Phillips

Routledge
Taylor & Francis Group

LONDON AND NEW YORK

First published 2011
by Routledge
27 Church Road, Hove, East Sussex BN3 2FA

Simultaneously published in the USA and Canada
by Routledge
711 Third Avenue, New York NY 10017

Routledge is an imprint of the Taylor & Francis Group, an Informa business

© 2011 Christopher Bollas and Arne Jemstedt

Typeset in Times by RefineCatch Limited, Bungay, Suffolk
Printed and bound in Great Britain by TJ International Ltd, Padstow, Cornwall

Cover design by Andrew Ward
Cover image: *Venice 2*, painting by the author
Cover photography by Suzanne Bollas

British Library Cataloguing-in-Publication Data
A catalogue record for this book is available from the British Library

Library of Congress Cataloging in Publication Data
Bollas, Christopher.
  The Christopher Bollas Reader / by Christopher Bollas ; introduction
  by Arne Jemstedt; foreword by Adam Phillips.
    p. cm.
  Includes bibliographical references and index.
  ISBN 978-0-415-66460-8 (hbk.: alk. paper)—
  ISBN 978-0-415-66461-5 (pbk.: alk. paper)
  1. Psychoanalysis.   2. Subconsciousness. I. Title.
  BF173.B6354 2011
  150.19'5—dc22

                                                      2010053802

ISBN: 978-0-415-66460-8 (hbk)
ISBN: 978-0-415-66461-5 (pbk)
ISBN: 978-0-203-58107-0 (ebk)

Contents

About the authors

Arne Jemstedt MD is a psychoanalyst in private practice in Stockholm. He is a member and training analyst of the Swedish Psychoanalytical Association and its current President. He edited the Swedish translation of Christopher Bollas's book *Being a Character* and has published articles and chapters on Bollas's work in Swedish and international psychoanalytic journals and books. He is a member of the International Editorial Panel for the *Complete Works of D. W. Winnicott* and editor of Swedish translations of Winnicott's work. He is a member of the 'nomenclature group' for the Swedish translation of Freud's *Standard Edition*.

Christopher Bollas PhD is a Member of the British Psychoanalytical Society and of the Los Angeles Institute and Society for Psychoanalytic Studies, and Honorary Member of the Institute for Psychoanalytic Training and Research (IPTAR) in New York.

Foreword

Adam Phillips

How can psychoanalysis stop itself becoming a version of the very thing it seeks to cure? How can it avoid being a narrowing of the mind, a simplifying of the self, when each of the psychoanalytic schools has an essentialist story to tell about what a person is, and what a person should be? Psychoanalysis is 'about' the unconscious, and yet psychoanalysts themselves seem to be all too conscious of what they are supposed to be doing. The cost of such knowingness has been what Christopher Bollas called in an interview 'the devastating failure' of psycho-analysis, 'the failure to comprehend the unconscious creativity of the analysand'. This is the predicament addressed in these inspired and inspiring essays.

Once Freud encouraged people to freely associate he was so daunted by the prospects opening up – by what people were able to say, by the glimpses he was getting of what people were alive to, by the sheer complexity of psychic life – that a great deal of theoretical containment was mobilised both in himself and his followers. Over time the inevitable uncertainties of the treatment were apparently resolved in the stated aims and the militant competence of the respective schools ('the worse your art is', the poet John Ashbury said in an interview, 'the easier it is to talk about'). But psychoanalysis, as an account of how and why modern people were divided against themselves, was itself excessively divisive. In its brief history, outsiders have always been sceptical or dismissive, insiders have always been territorial. Psychoanalysis, it seems, began as a panic from which no one has been able to recover.

We have to consider the possibility, as Christopher Bollas intimates, that it was not 'infantile sexuality', or the idea of the death drive, that was so explosive (or implausible) about psychoanalysis; it was the idea of people being encouraged to speak freely. The essentialisms of psychoanalysis – the concepts of cure, the accounts of human nature, the developmental theories – have been an attempted self-cure for what the 'method' of free association keeps revealing: our unfathom-able unconsciousness of ourselves – what Bollas refers to, alluding to King Lear in one of his many winning titles, as the mystery of things. To speak freely, with someone freely listening, is a radical act, at once historically unprecedented and uncanny, and by definition unpredictable (when it comes to the unconscious, one might say, outcome studies are unpromising). As Freud discovered and resisted acknowledging, free association – 'free' as an adjective and a verb – was the eye of the storm.

So it is not exactly a return to Freud that Christopher Bollas proposes in these extraordinary papers – though in virtually every one he has written something original and often slightly startling about Freud – but a return to free association. That is, to the unfolding unconsciousness of the psychoanalytic opportunity, to what he calls 'the fact of living as an unconscious being'. And this involves, in Bollas's view, all of the available psychoanalytic approaches, as points of view, perspectives, ways of seeing. It is only a more inclusive vision – not, it should be said, an eclectic one – that can do justice, so to speak, to the unconscious (the unconscious refers to all possible language-games). But writing in 'the American Grain', rooted in the ordinary and the everyday – in the tradition of Emerson, Melville and Whitman – Bollas never takes refuge in earnestness, in the mandarin or the dogmatic; nor, indeed, in the portentous moralism that psychoanalytic writing is prone to. It is what he has called 'the surprisingly widespread disinterest on the part of therapists and analysts about what the analysand is actually saying' that has absorbed him. And kept him humorous.

The last thing analysts have wanted to think about, Bollas suggests in his unusually eloquent and evocative writing, is the unconsciousness of the psycho-analytic process itself; that, as he puts it, 'the greater part of psychic change occurs unconsciously, and need not enter consciousness, either in the analyst or in the analysand'. Ironically, analysts have gone on wanting to know too much what they are doing, when it is precisely this knowledge that pre-empts the possibilities of psychoanalysis. Bollas's work shows us that when it comes to psychoanalysis there may be other things to want. 'We hate', Keats wrote in a famous letter, 'poetry that has a palpable design upon us.' After reading Bollas it is clear why a psychoanalysis that has a palpable design on us is a contradiction in terms. And why we might hate it.

Acknowledgements and permissions acknowledgements

Christopher Bollas and Arne Jemstedt wish to thank Kate Hawes and the editorial staff at Routledge for their invaluable assistance in assembling this Reader.

Thanks to Sarah Nettleton for her editorial contribution to this Reader.

Permissions acknowledgements

Various chapters in this reader have been previously published, and acknowledgement for kind permission to reproduce them in this volume is given as follows:

Chapters One, Two and Three (respectively) in this volume were originally published as 'The Transformational Object' (Chapter 1, pp. 13–29); 'The Extractive Introjection' (Chapter 9, pp. 157–69); 'Normotic Illness' (Chapter 8, pp. 135–56) in C. Bollas (1987), *The Shadow of the Object: Psychoanalysis of the Unthought Known*. London: Free Association Books. © 1987 Christopher Bollas. Reprinted with kind permission of Free Association Books.

Chapter Four in this volume was originally published as 'The Destiny Drive' (Chapter 2, pp. 23–49) in C. Bollas (1989), *Forces of Destiny: Psychoanalysis and Human Idiom*. London: Free Association Books. © 1989 Christopher Bollas. Reprinted with kind permission of Free Association Books.

Chapters Five, Six and Seven (respectively) were originally published as 'Psychic Genera' (Chapter 4, pp. 66–100); 'The Fascist State of Mind' (Chapter 9, pp. 193–217); 'Why Oedipus?' (Chapter 10, pp. 218–46) in C. Bollas (1992), *Being a Character: Psychoanalysis and Self Experience*. London: Routledge and in the USA by arrangement with Hill & Wang, a division of Farrar, Straus and Giroux, LLC, New York. © 1992 Christopher Bollas. Reprinted with kind permission of Routledge and Farrar, Straus and Giroux, LLC.

Chapters Eight, Nine and Ten (respectively) were originally published as 'The Functions of History' (Chapter 5, pp. 103–45); 'Cracking Up' (Chapter 8, pp. 221–56); 'The Structure of Evil' (Chapter 7, pp. 180–220) in C. Bollas (1995), *Cracking Up: The Work of Unconscious Experience*. London: Routledge and in the USA by arrangement with Hill & Wang, a division of Farrar, Straus and Giroux, LLC, New York. © 1995 Christopher Bollas. Reprinted with kind permission of Routledge and Farrar, Straus and Giroux, LLC.

Chapters Eleven and Twelve (respectively) were originally published as 'Mental Interference' (Chapter 8, pp. 88–105); 'Creativity and Psychoanalysis' (Chapter 15, pp. 167–80) in C. Bollas (1999), *The Mystery of Things*. London and New York: Routledge. © 1999 Christopher Bollas. Reprinted with kind permission of Routledge.

Chapter Thirteen was originally published as 'Architecture and the Unconscious' (Chapter 2, pp. 47–77) in C. Bollas (2009), *The Evocative Object World*. London and New York: Routledge. © 2009 Christopher Bollas. Reprinted with kind permission of Routledge.

Chapter Fourteen was originally published as 'What Is Theory?' (Chapter 4, pp. 71–83) in C. Bollas (2007), *The Freudian Moment*. London: Karnac Books Ltd. © 2007 Christopher Bollas. Reprinted with kind permission of Karnac Books Ltd.

As Chapters 1–14 are taken from previous works, which were published by a variety of publishers, every effort has been made to include a comprehensive Reference listing in this Reader. In a small number of instances it has not been possible to locate accurate Reference data for the listing for this Reader and in those cases the text citations are published exactly as they appeared in the original works.

Introduction

Arne Jemstedt

This book contains a selection from the work of Christopher Bollas, one of the most creative and inspiring writers in the history of psychoanalysis. He is the author of eleven psychoanalytic books, three novels, five plays and numerous essays.

Surprisingly, Bollas says[1] that until well into his thirties he never thought of himself as a writer: 'I wrote an essay on Plath with Murray Schwartz, one on *Bartleby*, one on character but I never felt any need to write.' What happened? J.-B. Pontalis invited him to write for the *Nouvelle Revue de Psychanalyse*, a scintillating literary psychoanalytic journal, which prompted Bollas to write. These essays, published in French, have not all been translated into English, but they inspired him to embark on what has been a notably rich and prolific career as an author.

After his paper 'The Transformational Object' received wide acclaim when it was published in the *International Journal of Psychoanalysis* in 1978, he settled at first for writing one essay every year or so. Publication of his first book, *The Shadow of the Object*, in 1987, was not his idea but that of a friend and colleague who suggested he collect his essays from the previous decade, add a few more, and submit them to Free Associations Books. When the book was celebrated inside and outside the psychoanalytic world, Bollas finally turned seriously towards writing.

Why such a long gestation period?

Bollas says that working ten-hour days with patients in five times a week analysis left him with no time to write, apart from his notebooks which were not intended for publication. He also felt throughout the 1970s that what he was learning from his analysands and the mutual experience of psychoanalysis still seemed deeply unconscious and inaccessible.

'I wrote in my notebooks to find out what I thought', he says. The notebooks are composed of brief entries – a page, maybe two – that are dated and given a title. An idea would pop into his mind, he would add other entries over the years,

---

1 These comments and some others in this Introduction derive from conversations with Christopher Bollas.

and then if it formed a gestalt in his mind he might proceed to write an essay. 'I had been developing the concept of "the transformational object" in my notebooks since 1975. I came to a point where I felt ready to write it, not because I had reached a final conclusion, but because I knew that if I wrote it over the course of one day, then what I had been thinking over the years would come into its own unity and it felt the right moment to do this.'

His readers often feel they have been given a deep and compelling access to his mentality, one by which they feel moved and inspired. Bollas's work is a form of inner disclosure – a paradoxical act – because although these are publications, they seem private musings into which the reader is invited.

The range of his interests is impressive. His deep knowledge of psychoanalysis, literature and other art forms enriches his texts, and he extends his thinking to wider issues of culture and society. One of the central threads is his appreciation, and defence, of the complexity of the human mind, especially the creativity and intelligence of the unconscious and how this richness can potentially be nurtured or obstructed, both in the individual and in the group.

It has not been easy to select the chapters for this collection, and inevitably many important and innovative essays have had to be left out. This selection is aimed at all those who are interested in the complexities of inner life. It is not assumed that readers will necessarily be well acquainted with psychoanalytic literature in general, and most of Bollas's more specifically technical texts have not been included. Nevertheless, in several chapters the reader will find him discussing central psychoanalytic issues, often illustrated with clinical examples from his work with patients.

After a brief biography, I shall give an overview of the chronological development of Bollas's theoretical contribution, followed by a more detailed introduction to some of his key ideas.

Biography

Christopher Bollas was born in Washington, DC in 1943. His father, Sacha Lucien Bollas, was French and raised in Paris until his early adolescence when the family moved to Argentina and later to England. He emigrated in his mid-twenties to the United States.

His mother, Celeste Wilde, a native Californian, was a classical pianist and an aspiring actress before she married at 21 and became the classic 1950s housewife. Two brothers were born after Christopher. Until he was 4 years old the family lived in Glendora, a small rural town in the foothills of the San Gabriel Mountains south of Los Angeles. They moved first to South Pasadena and then, when Christopher was 8, to Laguna Beach, an artists' colony on the Californian coast.

Laguna Beach figures prominently in his writings and clearly influenced his sense of the environment's evocative play upon self-experiencing. To get to his high school, he walked two miles along the beach, from cove to cove, gazing at the remarkable universes of small tide pools full of hidden life. He loved free diving and exploring the reefs and kelp beds. He was an outstanding baseball player, and for a time he thought his future might be in sport and not in the academic world.

He graduated from high school in 1962 and went to the University of Virginia, where he studied political theory and constitutional law and became involved in the civil rights movement. In 1964 he transferred to the University of California at Berkeley where he majored in American History.

During this time he began psychotherapy with a psychoanalyst at Berkeley, an experience he describes as life-changing. He took courses on 'Anthropology and Psychoanalysis' (with Alan Dundes) and 'Psychoanalysis and Literature' (with Frederick Crews), and he was gripped by Carl Schorscke's lectures on 'Intellectual History' which were informed by a psychoanalytic vision of the history of Western ideas.

From 1967 to 1969 he worked at The East Bay Activity Center for autistic and schizophrenic children. At the same time, while working in a bookstore in San Francisco, he read a review of Guntrip's book *Schizoid Phenomena, Object Relations and The Self*, and he went on to read Guntrip, Winnicott, Fairbairn and Klein who between them opened up entirely new ways of thinking about the children with whom he was working. He decided that he wanted to train as a psychoanalyst, but he did not want to study medicine or psychology to get there. Instead, he decided to study for a doctorate in English literature at the University of Buffalo, concentrating on 'psychoanalysis and literature'.[2]

Buffalo's English Department was renowned for its tradition in phenomenology and psychoanalysis, and it was staffed by some of the most interesting writers and critics of the day, including Rene Girard, Michel Foucault, John Barth, Robert Hass, Robert Creeley, Angus Fletcher and Charles Altieri.

At the same time as studying for a PhD in the middle novels of Herman Melville (*Moby Dick* and *Pierre*), Bollas trained in adult psychotherapy and co-founded with Lloyd Clarke MD a training programme in psychotherapy and the humanities that was in the process of being approved for a PhD in psychotherapy. Unfortunately the state of New York then froze all new PhD programs, and Bollas spent a year at Smith College earning an MSW so that he could be licensed to practise in the United States. However, his sights were set on training at the Institute of Psychoanalysis in London. He was accepted there in 1972, and he left for England in September 1973.

Relieved to leave the Nixon-era America behind, he looked forward to Europe as a potential space. He was struck initially by the differences he perceived between British and American analysts. 'The English analysts were', he says, 'by comparison highly spontaneous, imaginative, freewheeling interpreters, and decidedly eccentric.'

---

2 The program in psychoanalysis and literature was chaired by Norman Holland and included prominent psychoanalytic critics: Murray Schwartz, James Swann, Robert Rogers, Mel Faber, Leslie Fiedler, and visiting scholars such as Kenneth Burke.

He began a training analysis with Masud Khan which lasted from 1973 to 1976. Khan was a highly gifted and complex analyst who by the end of the 1970s was deteriorating, both physically and psychically. Although Bollas's work with Khan was complicated, it reached him on a deep level and led to important inner changes. In the late 1970s he began a third analysis, with Adam Limentani who was then the president of the International Psychoanalytical Association.

From 1974, he took seminars with Betty Joseph, Donald Meltzer, Eric Brenman, Joseph Sandler, Nina Coltart, Herbert Rosenfeld, Hannah Segal, Harold Stewart and the incandescently inspiring Henry Rey, as well as other well-known British analysts. Having been so impressed at first by the free-thinking writings of British analysts, he was surprised by the lack of tolerance he encountered for differences of opinion, especially among Kleinian analysts. Overall, however, he found the training very rewarding, and he remembers with particular appreciation his supervisors Paula Heimann and Marion Milner. Milner and Bollas would become life-long friends.

He qualified from the Institute of Psychoanalysis in 1977, after which he worked as a full-time analyst in private practice in London, apart from his stay at the Austen Riggs Center in Massachusetts, where he was Director of Education from 1985 to 1987. He was also Professor of English at the University of Massachusetts from 1983 to 1987.

It was Paula Heimann who recommended that he develop his analytic career outside the British Society in order to avoid the impact of Kleinian orthodoxies, which she thought would hamper his creativity. In the mid-1970s he was, as mentioned above, asked by J.-B. Pontalis to contribute to the *Nouvelle Revue de Psychanalyse*, which led to many trips to Paris where he would visit with J.-B. Pontalis and André Green and discover a new world of psychoanalytic thinking that he regards as transformative.

At this time he was also invited by the Italian psychoanalyst Adriano Giannotti to become Visiting Professor of Psychoanalysis at the University of Rome, a post that Bollas fulfilled for the next twenty years. His early papers were first delivered to the staff and students of the Istituto Neuropsichiatria Infantile of the University of Rome, and it was, therefore, to an Italian 'other' that he first presented his ideas. In 1983 he began a life-long affiliation with psychoanalysis in Sweden, which continues to this day with a small annual conference, and from 1993 until 2009 he led workshops in Chicago that met three times a year for intensive study of the psychoanalytic process. He was part of the formation of the European Study Group on Unconscious Thought (ESGUT) which met several times a year in either Zurich, Tubingen or Stockholm for ten years.[3]

Bollas has a special talent as a lecturer and supervisor. His capacity to engage his audience is obvious and remarkable, and he is frequently invited to speak and

---

3 The ESGUT met in groups of 15 analysts from Sweden, Germany and Switzerland to study highly detailed process notes of individual sessions, with the original aim to gain a better understanding of how analysands think free associatively.

teach at psychoanalytic institutes and other institutions all over Europe, North and South America, Australia and Asia. His books have been published in French, German, Italian, Danish, Swedish, Hebrew, Portuguese, Spanish, Japanese, Korean, Romanian and Greek.

In his spare time Bollas devotes himself to painting, something that he began out of the blue in 1998. Some of his paintings may be seen on the covers of his last three publications. His wife, Suzanne, is an English architect, and they have three children.

Overview

Bollas's first book, *The Shadow of the Object: Psychoanalysis of the Unthought Known* (1987), is a collection of essays most of which had been written in the 1970s. Proclaimed by the *International Journal of Psychoanalysis* as 'one of the most important books of the last decade', it introduces the readership to his concepts of 'the transformational object' and 'the unthought known', terms that have now become widely disseminated and used by psychoanalysts, academics and artists.

Forces of Destiny: Psychoanalysis and Human Idiom followed in 1989, when his post at the Austen Riggs Center allowed Bollas two years in which to focus on writing. In this volume he introduces his concept of 'idiom', which grew out of Winnicott's theory of the 'true self'. He also considers the ways in which the analysand uses the differing elements of the analyst's personality, and he explores the idea that people live their lives governed either by 'fate', in reaction to an environment that fundamentally determines them, or by 'destiny', the free articulation of the self's idiom through the creative use of objects.

In *Being a Character: Psychoanalysis and Self Experience* (1992), Bollas presents a series of remarkable free-standing essays. As well as developing threads from the earlier works, he returns to Freud, considering certain crucial ideas that were implied in Freud's writings but not explicitly explored by him. In offering a new theory of unconscious perception, creativity and communication, Bollas's prior immersions – in existential psychoanalysis, ego psychology and object relations theory – come together to form a new Freudian-based exploration of self-experience. His concepts of 'the evocative object' and 'psychic genera' are linked to a revised theory of free association and to his model of 'the receptive unconscious'.

In *Cracking Up: The Work of Unconscious Experience* (1995), Bollas extends Freud's radical notion of free association as a process that takes place between patient and psychoanalyst – something that has, he argues, been repressed by the psychoanalytic world. In addition, he further evolves his theory of the unconscious, of how our internal world is composed of evocative as well as endogenous objects, and of ways in which we communicate unconsciously.

The present volume includes several papers from the early books in which Bollas uses psychoanalytic ideas to explore non-clinical subjects that should appeal to anyone interested in human experience and human mind. 'The Fascist State of Mind' (Chapter 6) delineates the structure of 'intellectual genocide', and 'Why Oedipus?' (Chapter 7) argues that mental life can exceed our ability to bear it and that we find a cure in group psychology. 'The Functions of History' (Chapter 8) proposes a new theory of historiography – that it transforms the dead facts of the past into new life; and 'The Structure of Evil' (Chapter 10) argues that evil is a serial process that exposes a horrifying logic.

Also published in 1995, *The New Informants*, co-authored with lawyer David Sundelson, is a coruscating critique of the abandonment of patient confidentiality by psychoanalysis and psychotherapy, at a time when clinicians were increasingly finding themselves pressurised into handing over clinical notes to insurance companies, lawyers and courts. It proposes a way through this ethical morass and was hailed by law reviews, medical journals and the *New York Times* as a seminal work in the field. Bollas and Sundelson go as far as to advocate civil disobedience, if necessary as a last resort, in order to protect patient–analyst privilege.

Next, Bollas produced *The Mystery of Things* (1999) and *Hysteria* (2000). Like his earlier volumes, the first of these consists of individual essays that further develop his view of various aspects of unconscious life. Two of these are included in the present volume: 'Mental Interference' (Chapter 11) and 'Creativity and Psychoanalysis' (Chapter 12). *Hysteria* was the first of his books to be presented as a through-composed entity. It is certainly one of the most important contributions to the topic since Freud's and Breuer's *Studies on Hysteria* (Freud, 1895).

After a condensed and thought-provoking monograph on *Free Association*, published in 2002, Bollas turned to fiction. Over a period of three years he produced a series of three novels – *Dark at the End of the Tunnel* (2004), *I Have Heard the Mermaids Singing* (2005) and *Mayhem* (2006a) – and a volume of five plays, *Theraplay* (2006b). He creates a psychoanalyst as the hero (or anti-hero) of his novels, and by placing him in various absurd situations Bollas skilfully explores aspects of the psychoanalytic world.

It is clear that these novels are predicated on the idea that psychoanalysis is a form of contemporary theatre. On the private stage of the analytic consulting room are to be found all the character types and bizarre issues that have plagued humankind from the beginning of time. In these dire, sometimes tragic, and hair-raising experiences Bollas finds a dark and compelling existential humour. His five plays – 'Theraplay', 'Old Friends', 'Apply Within', 'Your Object or Mine?' and 'Piecemeal' – clearly hark back to the Theatre of the Absurd as the characters are presented with meaningless encounters and the precious themes of our life-times are presented on stage like mental props.

Included in the present book are two papers from his more recent theoretical publications: 'What Is Theory?' (Chapter 14) from *The Freudian Moment* (2007), and 'Architecture and the Unconscious' (Chapter 13) from *The Evocative Object World* (2009a).

Throughout his work, Bollas includes clinical vignettes that give intriguing glimpses of the way he works in the consulting room. However, in *The Infinite Question* (2009b) he provides for the first time an extensive demonstration of his searching use of all aspects of the technique of free association. Through extensive clinical material and detailed commentaries, Bollas illustrates the deep unconscious work that takes place in the ordinary analytic session.

Also included here are two new essays, not previously published: 'Character and Interformality' (Chapter 15) and 'The Wisdom of the Dream' (Chapter 16).

Bollas is currently completing *China on the Mind*, a book on how psychoanalysis bridges the Eastern and Western mind, and *Catch Them Before They Fall*, an account of his work with analysands in mental breakdown. He is also midway through a book on character analysis, and he is transcribing his notebooks, which now consist of twenty-four volumes spanning the period 1973 to the present.

Key ideas

Idiom

The work of the British psychoanalyst D. W. Winnicott has been a major source of inspiration for Bollas. Obvious especially in his early works, it is also there as an undercurrent in his later writings. A central and elusive idea in Winnicott's theories is that of the 'true self'. He writes:

> At the earliest stage the True Self is the theoretical position from which come the spontaneous gesture and the personal idea. . . . Only the True Self can be creative and only the True Self can feel real. . . . The True Self comes from the aliveness of the body tissues and the working of body-functions. . . . It is closely linked with the idea of the Primary Process, and is, at the beginning, essentially not reactive to external stimuli, but primary. . . . It is important to note that . . . the concept of an individual inner reality of objects applies to a stage later than does the concept of what is being termed the True Self.
>
> (Winnicott, 1960: 148–9)

In *Forces of Destiny* and in *Being a Character*, Bollas develops and refines his own thoughts on the true self, for which he gradually substitutes the term 'idiom'. He does this partly because he feels that 'overusage of a term . . . [leads to loss of] meaningfulness through incantatory solicitation, devaluing any word's unthought potential' (Bollas, 1992: 64), but also, I think, because he wishes to find his own way in this elusive area.

In his paper 'The Psychoanalyst's Multiple Function' (*Forces of Destiny*, 1989), he writes:

> The true self cannot be fully described. It is less like the articulation of meaning through words which allow one to isolate a unit of meaning as in the

location of a signifier, and more akin to the movement of symphonic music. . . . Each individual is unique, and the true self is an idiom of organization that seeks its personal world through the use of an object . . . the fashioning of life is something like an aesthetic: a form revealed through one's way of being.

(1989: 109–10)

In 'The Transformational Object', the early seminal paper that forms Chapter 1 of the present volume, Bollas explores the beginnings of the infant's elaboration of this individual aesthetic, something that is fundamentally dependent on a facilitating early environment. If the mother does not respond sensitively to the infant's spontaneous gesture, his/her early idiomatic expressions will be blocked and replaced by false adaptations. But if she is attuned with the infant's emerging self she will have the capacity, through subtle conscious and unconscious interactions with her baby, to transform his/her inner state. Bollas suggests that the 'mother is less significant and identifiable as an object than as a process' and he adds that 'not yet fully identified as an other, the mother is experienced as a process of transformation, and this feature of early existence lives on in certain forms of object-seeking in adult life, when the object is sought for its function as a signifier of transformation'.

In *Forces of Destiny* Bollas formulates a crucial difference between 'fate' and 'destiny'. He links fate to the concept of the false self and reactive living and destiny to the fulfilling of one's own inner potential. In 'The Destiny Drive' (Chapter 4, this volume), he writes: 'I believe that this sense of destiny is the natural course of the true self through the many types of object relations, and that the destiny drive emerges, if it does, out of the infant's experience of the mother's facilitation of true self movement.'

As we go through life, our idiom continues to be articulated through our choice and use of objects. Bollas writes:

If idiom is, then, the it with which we are born, and if its pleasure is to elaborate itself through the choice of objects, one that is an intelligence of form rather than an expression of inner content, its work collides with the structure of the objects that transform it, through which it gains its precise inner contents. This collisional dialectic between the human's form and the object's structure is, in the best of times, a joy of living, as one is nourished by the encounter.

(1992: 59–60)

The evocative object

In ordinary language the word 'object' usually denotes an inanimate thing, a physical article in the external world. Psychoanalysis sometimes uses it in this way, but more often it employs the word to refer to an 'other' – a person who is 'not-me' – with whom the subject exists in some kind of emotionally charged relationship. The separate, objective quality of this object is complicated by the subject's projections, which will colour the subject's experience of the object. Through these intricate projective and introjective mechanisms the individual builds a complex inner world of diverse relationships to many kinds of object. The British Object Relations School of psychoanalysis has developed very creatively the idea of this inner world of object relations, and the influence of projective mechanisms has been well understood by many theorists, especially in relation to the transference relationship to the analyst.

Bollas expands the psychoanalytic understanding of object relations, contributing in particular an appreciation of what he calls 'the integrity of the object'. By this he means the object's intrinsic quality of being fundamentally itself, outside the sphere of projective mechanisms.

There is an echo here of Winnicott's seminal paper 'The Use of an Object' in which he describes the child's joyful discovery of the object's authentic realness, outside the realm of the child's omnipotence, as a result of the object's survival of 'maximum destructiveness (object not protected)' (1969: 91).

In the introduction to *Being a Character*, Bollas writes:

> Thus I have found it rather surprising that in 'object relations theory' very little thought is really given to the distinct structure of the object, which is usually seen as a container of the individual's projections. Certainly objects bear us. But ironically enough, it is precisely *because* they hold our projections that the structural feature of any one object becomes even more important, because we also put ourselves into a container that upon re-experiencing will process us according to its natural integrity.
>
> (1992: 4)

In the same volume, he first elaborates in detail what he terms 'the evocative object', the object with 'high psychic value' (to use Freud's term) that touches us on a deep level and sets inner creative processes in motion. The evocative object might be a person, a landscape, a poem, a piece of music, or something else that we encounter significantly in our everyday lives. We may consciously search out such objects, but often we seek them intuitively, led by some unconscious idea or wish, and sometimes they arrive by chance. The evocative object might, of course, also come from our inner world, a memory or feeling that surfaces from deep inside us, maybe in the course of the psychoanalytic process. Such objects 'release the self into being' (1992: 42) and facilitate the articulation of our idiom.

Psychic genera

In 'Psychic Genera' (Chapter 5), Bollas develops an original theory about the formation of new psychic structures. He describes receptive areas in the unconscious that attract processes and phenomena, both from the internal world and from the self's encounter with external reality. These develop into matrices that in turn generate a further search for evocative objects.

In Bollas's theory of genera there is a deep appreciation of the intelligence of the unconscious, of creative processes that – unknown to the conscious mind – select items and events from the outer and inner world to form networks of ideas and images linked to each other in complex ways. These networks may become dense enough to precipitate into a dream or, after a period of condensation, to create a new perspective on oneself and on life.

With a kind of inherent wisdom, the unconscious will steer away from premature intrusion by the logic of consciousness in order that these creative matrices may have space to grow and develop. With words such as 'proto-nucleations', 'generative chaos' and 'psychic gravity', Bollas conveys a picture of an unconscious, dynamic *cosmos*.

He writes:

> In many respects the theory of genera is inspired by the theory of repression. . . . But the theory of repression points only to the banishment of the unwanted, and I am convinced that other types of ideas are invited into the unconscious. To complement the theory of repression, we need a *theory of reception*, which designates some ideas as the received rather than repressed, although both the repressed and the received need the protective barrier provided by the anticathexes of preconsciousness.
>
> (this volume: 61–2)

The psychoanalytic situation, with its open-ended and non-directive conscious and unconscious communication between analysand and analyst, enables the formation of new psychic genera. For this to happen, both participants need to be able to respond intuitively, to perceive subtle inner shifts and unexpected links in the flow of associations. It is significant that Bollas frequently compares these psychoanalytic processes with descriptions given by both artists and scientists of their experiences of creativity.

Bollas contrasts the concepts of 'genera' and 'trauma' in ways that connect with Freud's theory of the life and death instincts. The inner freedom and creativity needed for the formation of genera is initially founded on the parents' sensitive receptiveness to the child's unique personality and his/her spontaneous expressions. 'Children', he writes, 'whose parents are impinging or acutely traumatizing collect such trauma into an internal psychic area which is intended to bind and limit the damage of the self . . . and the subject who contains such anguishing complexes will usually not seek to symbolically elaborate them.' Thus, genera are the outcome of symbolic elaborations, while the effects of trauma are symbolic repetition and stagnation.

Dreaming

Each night we are immersed in the mysteriously creative process of dreaming. We feel that our lives are enriched if we have conscious contact with our dream life

– it gives us a sense of depth, resonance and communication with inner sources. For Freud, the dream was crucial to the task of getting in touch with processes and structures in the unconscious, and he found that the technique of associating freely to the manifest elements in the dream allowed the emergence of latent dream-thoughts – ideas and feelings that, because of their anxiety-laden quality, had previously been repressed from consciousness.

Freud's ground-breaking book *The Interpretation of Dreams*, published in 1900, was a fundamental contribution to modern Western culture. Bollas is deeply appreciative of its genius, and he works with, and elaborates, Freud's dream theory in many of his texts. What he emphasises continually is the *creativity* of the dream, which involves the *aesthetic intelligence* of the unconscious.

In *Being a Character* Bollas writes that 'the capacity to be the dream work of one's life, to devolve consciousness to the creative fragmentations of unconscious work, is evidence of a basic trust in the reliable relation between such dreaming and the consciousness that results in our reflections' (1992: 53). A main thread in his paper 'The Wisdom of the Dream' (Chapter 16) is that dreaming, together with the experience of recollecting, recounting and exploring dreams in analysis, increases and deepens the communication between conscious and unconscious selves. Bollas claims that it fulfils a 'phylogenetic need', one that is of increasing importance in these days when superficial and focused effectiveness dominates the social and psychological fields. He writes:

> Everyone dreams. And people often think about their dreams. But psycho-analysis establishes a partnership (the Freudian Pair) that extends the dream and communicates with it. The ego now grasps that it has a partner, and we discover another pairing: between the ego that offers the matrix of its own creativity in the form of the dream and the analysand who transforms the material into a new form of unconsciously worked-upon meaning. Over time, the Freudian Pair becomes structuralised and sets up a new paradigm within the ego that proceeds to generate more sophisticated forms of unconscious work. . . .
> . . . [T]he structuralisation of the Freudian Pair creates a tension between the curiosity of consciousness and the creativity of the unconscious. It concerns not so much the psychopathology of everyday life as the *psycho-creativity* of everyday life.
>
> (this volume: 257, 258)

The Freudian Pair

Bollas begins the last chapter of his book *The Mystery of Things* with the following words:

> Theories of mental life and human behaviour will come and go much as they have since the beginning of psychoanalysis. Only the passing of time will

determine the value of any particular theory and some models which seemed assured of perpetuity ... will be abandoned, even by their most avid supporters. What will not change is the deeply evocative effect of the psycho-analytic situation and its method.

(1999: 181)

In 'Two Encyclopaedia Articles', written in 1923, Freud issues instructions to both participants in what Bollas terms 'the Freudian Pair'. Freud describes the task of the analysand thus:

The treatment is begun by the patient being required to put himself in the position of an attentive and dispassionate self-observer, merely to read off all the time the surface of his consciousness, and on the one hand to make a duty of the most complete honesty while on the other not to hold back any idea from communication, even if (1) he feels that it is too disagreeable or if (2) he judges that it is nonsensical or (3) too unimportant or (4) irrelevant to what is being looked for. It is uniformly found that precisely those ideas which provoke these last-mentioned reactions are of particular value in discovering the forgotten material.

(1923: 238)

It should be noted here that it is ideas that seem to be unimportant or irrelevant that turn out to be of particular value. If the analysand talks freely and spontaneously in this way – articulating the events from the previous day, remembrances from child-hood, associations to a dream, thoughts and feelings towards the analyst – patterns will emerge that give a new perspective on emotionally important issues in his life. In 'Creativity and Psychoanalysis' (Chapter 12), Bollas states that '[it] may be a measure of Freud's genius that this discovery [of free association] which would have been sufficient for many people, was only the first of many. For me, however, this is his greatest accomplishment. In a few years of work with his patients ... he settles on free association and in that moment Western culture is changed forever.'

'It is strange', an analysand told me many years ago, 'that so much can happen just because you lie down on a couch and talk.'

After his explanation of free association, Freud continues with advice for the clinician:

Experience soon showed that the attitude which the analytic physician could most advantageously adopt was to surrender himself to his own unconscious mental activity, in a state of *evenly suspended attention*, to avoid so far as possible reflection and the construction of conscious expectations, not to try to fix anything he heard particularly in his memory, and by these means to catch the drift of the patient's unconscious with his own unconscious.

(1923: 239)

This fundamental state of mind in the analyst has been discussed by many theo-rists, most notably Wilfred Bion who uses the term 'reverie' to capture its essence. Elusive and difficult to put into words, Bollas explores and elaborates this medita-tive state in a way that illuminates the complex and non-logical inner processes that it facilitates. In 'Psychic Genera' (Chapter 5), he emphasises its intuitive nature: 'Perhaps', Bollas writes, 'the sense of intuition is our preconscious experi-ence of the ego's intelligent work, leading us to consciously authorise certain forms of investigation in thought which are not consciously logical but which may be unconsciously productive.' He adds, however, that 'the fact that intuition seems to be an immediate knowing should not obscure the fact that it is the outcome of sustained concentration of many types of unconscious and conscious thinking'. This point is illustrated with a statement by Stravinsky, quoted by Bollas in 'Creativity and Psychoanalysis' (Chapter 12):

> This foretaste of the creative act accompanies the intuitive grasp of an unknown entity already possessed but not yet intelligible, an entity that will not take definite shape except by the action of a constantly vigilant technique.
>
> (this volume: 198)

Bollas develops this theme elsewhere. In a paper from *Cracking Up* entitled 'What Is This Thing Called Self?', he writes:

> As analyst and patient shape one another . . . the analyst's self works with an inner, intuitional ear . . . the analyst's perception may enable him to learn something at a deeply unconscious level about the nature of the other's forming intelligence, and just as the aesthetics of literature or music have much to do with timing, pausing, and punctuational breathing, it may well be that he, too, works technically – knowing when to make a comment, what diction texture to choose, when to remain silent, what image to pick up at what moment, when to use his feelings as the basis of an interpretation, or when to scrutinise a word presentation. These decisions are aesthetic choices, and should be in tune with the analysand's self – namely, his aesthetic presence and its articulation. Such 'technical decisions' involve work at the level of self to self, of the analyst's self sensing the patient's self. . . . There is a feeling there of one's being, of something there, but not a something we can either touch or know; only sense and it is the most important sensed phenomenon in our life.
>
> (1995: 171–2)

In these dense lines Bollas captures qualities of intuitive perception and subtle inner processes that characterise the interaction between the two participants in the Freudian Pair. There is an echo here of Freud's crucial statement in his paper 'The Unconscious': 'It is a very remarkable thing that the *Ucs.* of one human being can react upon that of another, without passing through the *Cs.* This deserves closer investigation . . . but, descriptively speaking, the fact is incontestable' (1915: 194).

Listenings

The analyst listens to the analysand from many different perspectives, and these lead to different kinds of activities on the analyst's part. Two perspectives in particular can be seen to contribute complementary elements to the clinical situation.

In the first, the analyst *receives* the analysand's chains of associations, not knowing where they might lead, listening to them with dreamlike attentiveness. He may remain silent for a long time until something in the analysand's communications alerts him: a word with a special ring, maybe, or a link to a dream from yesterday or from several months ago. The analyst does not have to be overly explicit: he may simply repeat the word (what Bollas calls the 'Freudian echo') or point to the link in order to facilitate the process.

A second and different way of listening focuses more directly on the relationship between analysand and analyst. The analyst listens with an ear tuned especially towards conscious and unconscious references to him/herself in the analysand's narrative. In other words, he pays particular attention to transference material. The analysand's problems and pains are linked to inner object relations derived partly from early experiences, and the analysand will often project these into the relationship with the analyst. The task for the psychoanalyst will then be to catch and analyse these transferential processes as they appear, providing what are often referred to as 'here-and-now interpretations'. This is a technique that has been developed very extensively by the British School of Psychoanalysis, stemming from the work of Melanie Klein.

These different ways of listening are both invaluable to psychoanalytic work. One or the other may predominate with different analysands, and the analyst will also oscillate between them at different moments with the same analysand. 'It would be a sad misconception indeed to see these differences as incompatible in the conduct of an analysis', writes Bollas in *The Mystery of Things* (1999: 189).

What concerns him, though – and more and more so during the last ten years – is that the object relational way of listening with the focus on the transference has come to dominate the scene in many psychoanalytic quarters at the expense of a 'Freudian way of listening'. The constant attention to the transference and 'here-and-now interpretations', Bollas claims, diminishes the openness of the psychoanalytic situation and forecloses the flow of free association. Bollas has developed his arguments on this issue in various texts, and most vigorously in 'On Transference Interpretation as a Resistance to Free Association' from *The Freudian Moment* (2007).

Anti-life

So far I have concentrated predominantly on Bollas's writings on creative, life-promoting processes. This is certainly not without reason: through his theories of psychic genera, destiny drive, and evocative objects he has decisively deepened our understanding of and perspective on such processes. However, both explicitly and implicitly in these texts Bollas also considers the internal and external obstacles to such progressive and expansive psychic movements, and there are other papers in which he focuses specifically on destructive processes and phenomena, both on an individual and on a social level. Several of these are included in the present volume.

At the beginning of 'Normotic Illness' (Chapter 3), Bollas writes: 'I believe we are witness . . . to the emergence of a new emphasis within personal illness . . . [that is] a particular drive to be normal, one that is typified by the numbing and eventual erasure of subjectivity in favour of a self that is conceived as a material object among other man-made products in the object world.' This tendency is perhaps even greater today than when Bollas wrote this chapter in the 1980s.

He continues: '[the] presence in contemporary literature and film of the human who is revealed to be a robot is a recognition of this personality type emerging in our culture. Such representations are less descriptive of the future of robots than they are accurate prognostications of a personality disorder that is already with us.' This state of mind is characterised by a deadening of the complexity of inner life and a flight to material objects in the external world. It is akin to the workings of the death instinct in Freud's original sense: the drive to rid the psyche of tension and to undo psychically meaningful connections. Bollas ends this chapter on the normotic personality thus: 'Such a person suggests that mind itself, in particular the unconscious, is an archaism, a thing to be abandoned in the interest of human progress.'

Again in 'The Fascist State of Mind' (Chapter 6) there is in the background an echo of Freud's theory of the death instinct. In this chapter Bollas explores the driving forces behind totalitarian movements of various kinds and the horrifying atrocities for which they are accountable. He states that a fundamental feature of the Fascist state of mind is 'a special act of *binding* as doubts and counter-views are expelled, and the mind ceases to be complex, achieving a simplicity held together initially by the bindings around the signs of the ideology'. The totalitarian ideology 'freezes up the symbolic order' (in the Lacanian sense) and '. . . the elimination of the symbolic, or polysemousness, is the first murder committed by this order, as the symbolic is the true subversion of ideology'. The denial of complexity and doubt and the blind striving after certainty create a moral void: 'at this point the subject must find a victim to contain that void, and now a state of mind becomes an act of violence. On the verge of its own moral vacuum, the mind splits off this dead core self and projects it into a victim . . . [and] the Fascist mind transforms a human other into a disposable nonentity.'

At the beginning of this chapter Bollas warns us that: 'there is a Fascist in all of us and that there is indeed a highly identifiable psychic profile for this personal state' and at the end he describes 'the genocide of everyday life', where subtle distortions, caricature and denigration of opponents, groups or people might pave the way for Fascist movements.

Form and content

It is clear, I think, that in Bollas's writings 'form' is, in a sense, as important as 'content'. 'How' is as important as 'what', and he frequently emphasises the 'intelligence of form' in human articulation and communication. When discussing the elusive essence of idiom he states that 'a person's idiom is . . . an implicit logic of form', and when examining psychoanalytic technique he asserts that: 'inevitably we must turn to the aesthetics of form – the particular way something is conveyed – as an important feature of unconscious communication' (1995: 41).

This appreciation of the importance of form is also embodied in his style of writing. Bollas's style is more literary than that of most psychoanalytic writers, not only because of his knowledge of and references to poets, painters, composers, but because there is a sort of idiomatic musicality to his words and phrases, with simple statements of high density interspersed with meandering trains of thoughtful associations, subtle cadences and rich underlying resonances.

One thing that has always impressed me about his work – and this has to do with content rather than form – is his capacity to penetrate into diverse fields of thought and experience, as it were writing himself into them in order to develop and extract intriguing ideas and conclusions. In the essay 'Why Oedipus?' (Chapter 7), Bollas immerses himself in a close and intelligent re-reading of Sophocles' drama *Oedipus the King*, discerning hidden themes and patterns that provide a challenging new perspective on Freud's theory of the Oedipus Complex.

'The Structure of Evil' (Chapter 10) is another – and very different – example of this. In this chapter Bollas rigorously examines the *process* of evil, using biographies of serial killers, sadomasochistic interactions, political tyranny and Othello's murder of Desdemona to distinguish a common pattern. This involves the presentation to the other of a perverted form of good, the creation of a false potential space and the victim's catastrophic shock when this is reversed into evil. Bollas suggests that underlying this there is a drive in the perpetrator to master his own psychic death.

Bollas's works are not textbooks; he does not set out to teach. Instead he invites the reader to take part in a fascinating exploration of the mind, of the complexities of our interaction with the world around us, and of what it means to be a human being. In this sense his essays are themselves 'evocative objects' that allow us to create our own links with ideas that are truly mind expanding.

Stockholm
November 2010

References

Bollas, Christopher. (1987). *The Shadow of the Object: Psychoanalysis of the Unthought Known*. London, Free Association Books.

—— (1989). *Forces of Destiny: Psychoanalysis and Human Idiom*. London, Free Association Books.

—— (1992). *Being a Character: Psychoanalysis and Self Experience*. London, Routledge.

—— (1995). *Cracking Up: The Work of Unconscious Experience*. London, Routledge.

—— (1999). *The Mystery of Things*. London, Routledge.

—— (2000). *Hysteria*. London, Routledge.

—— (2002). *Free Association*. London, Icon.

—— (2004). *Dark at the End of the Tunnel*. London, Free Association Books.

—— (2005). *I Have Heard the Mermaids Singing*. London, Free Association Books.

—— (2006a). *Mayhem*. London, Free Association Books.

—— (2006b). *Theraplay*. London, Free Association Books.

—— (2007). *The Freudian Moment*. London, Karnac.

—— (2009a). *The Evocative Object World*. London, Routledge.

—— (2009b). *The Infinite Question*. London, Routledge.

—— and David Sundelson. (1995). *The New Informants*. London, Karnac.

Freud, Sigmund. (1915). 'The unconscious'. *Standard Edition* 14.

—— (1923). 'Two encyclopaedia articles'. *Standard Edition* 21.

Freud, Sigmund (with J. Breuer) (1895). *Studies on Hysteria. Standard Edition* 4 & 5.

Winnicott, D. W. (1960). 'Ego distortions in terms of true and false self', in Winnicott: *The Maturational Processes and the Facilitating Environment*. London, Hogarth, 1965.

—— (1969). 'The use of an object and relating through identifications', in Winnicott: *Playing and Reality*. London, Routledge, 1971.

Chapter 1

The transformational object

We know that because of the considerable prematurity of human birth the infant depends on the mother for survival. By serving as a supplementary ego (Heimann, 1956) or a facilitating environment (Winnicott, 1963a) she both sustains the baby's life and transmits to the infant, through her own particular idiom of mothering, an aesthetic of being that becomes a feature of the infant's self. The mother's way of holding the infant, of responding to his gestures, of selecting objects, and of perceiving the infant's internal needs, constitutes her contribution to the infant–mother culture. In a private discourse that can only be developed by mother and child, the language of this relation is the idiom of gesture, gaze and intersubjective utterance.

In his work on the mother–child relation, Winnicott stresses what we might call its stillness: the mother provides a continuity of being, she 'holds' the infant in an environment of her making that facilitates his growth. And yet, against this reciprocally enhancing stillness, mother and child continuously negotiate inter-subjective experience that coheres around the rituals of psychosomatic need: feeding, diapering, soothing, playing and sleeping. It is undeniable, I think, that as the infant's 'other' self, the mother transforms the baby's internal and external environment. Edith Jacobson suggests that

> when a mother turns the infant on his belly, takes him out of his crib, diapers him, sits him up in her arms and on her lap, rocks him, strokes him, kisses him, feeds him, smiles at him, talks and sings to him, she offers him not only all kinds of libidinal gratifications but simultaneously stimulates and prepares the child's sitting, standing, crawling, walking, talking, and on and on, i.e., the development of functional ego activity.
>
> (1965: 37)

Winnicott (1963b) terms this comprehensive mother the 'environment' mother because, for the infant, she is the total environment. To this I would add that the mother is less significant and identifiable as an object than as a process that is identified with cumulative internal and external transformations. I wish to identify the infant's first subjective experience of the object as a transformational object, and this chapter will address the trace in adult life of this early relationship. A transformational object is experientially identified by the infant with processes that alter self experience. It is an identification that emerges from symbiotic relating, where the first object is 'known' not so much by putting it into an object representation, but as a recurrent experience of being – a more existential as opposed to representational knowing. As the mother helps to integrate the infant's being (instinctual, cognitive, affective, environmental), the rhythms of this process – from unintegration(s) to integration(s) – inform the nature of this 'object' relation rather than the qualities of the object as object.

Not yet fully identified as an other, the mother is experienced as a process of transformation, and this feature of early existence lives on in certain forms of object-seeking in adult life, when the object is sought for its function as a signifier of transformation. Thus, in adult life, the quest is not to possess the object; rather the object is pursued in order to surrender to it as a medium that alters the self, where the subject-as-supplicant now feels himself to be the recipient of enviro-somatic caring, identified with metamorphoses of the self. Since it is an identification that begins before the mother is mentally represented as an other, it is an object relation that emerges not from desire, but from a perceptual identification of the object with its function: the object as enviro-somatic transformer of the subject. The memory of this early object relation manifests itself in the person's search for an object (a person, place, event, ideology) that promises to transform the self.

This conception of the mother being experienced as transformation is supported in several respects. In the first place, she assumes the function of the transformational object, for she constantly alters the infant's environment to meet his needs. There is no delusion operating in the infant's identification of the mother with transformation of being through his symbiotic knowing; it is a fact, for she actually transforms his world. In the second place, the infant's own emergent ego capacities – of motility, perception, and integration – also transform his world. The acquisition of language is perhaps the most significant transformation, but learning to handle and to differentiate between objects, and to remember objects that are not present, are transformative achievements as they result in ego change which alters the nature of the infant's internal world. It is not surprising that the infant identifies these ego achievements with the presence of an object, as the failure of the mother to maintain provision of the facilitating environment, through prolonged absence or bad handling, can evoke ego collapse and precipitate psychic pain.

With the infant's creation of the transitional object, the transformational process is displaced from the mother-environment (where it originated) into countless subjective-objects, so that the transitional phase is heir to the transformational period, as the infant evolves from experience of the process to articulation of the experience. With the transitional object, the infant can play with the illusion of his own omnipotence (lessening the loss of the environment-mother with generative and phasic delusions of self-and-other creation); he can entertain the idea of the object being got rid of, yet surviving his ruthlessness; and he can find in this transitional experience the freedom of metaphor. What was an actual process can be displaced into symbolic equations which, if supported by the mother, mitigate the loss of the original environment-mother. In a sense, the use of a transitional object is the infant's first creative act, an event that does not merely display an ego capacity – such as grasping – but which indicates the infant's subjective experience of such capacities.

The search for the transformational object in adult life

I think we have failed to take notice of the phenomenon in adult life of the wide-ranging collective search for an object that is identified with the metamorphosis of the self. In many religious faiths, for example, when the subject believes in the deity's actual potential to transform the total environment, he sustains the terms of the earliest object tie within a mythic structure. Such knowledge remains symbiotic (that is, it reflects the wisdom of faith) and coexists alongside other forms of knowing. In secular worlds, we see how hope invested in various objects (a new job, a move to another country, a vacation, a change of relationship) may both represent a request for a transformational experience and, at the same time, continue the 'relationship' to an object that signifies the experience of transforma-tion. We know that the advertising world makes its living on the trace of this object: the advertised product usually promises to alter the subject's external environment and hence change internal mood.

The search for such an experience may generate hope, even a sense of confi-dence and vision, but although it seems to be grounded in the future tense, in finding something in the future to transform the present, it is an object-seeking that recur-rently enacts a pre-verbal ego memory. It is usually on the occasion of an aesthetic moment, that an individual feels a deep subjective rapport with an object (a painting, a poem, an aria or symphony, or a natural landscape) and experiences an uncanny fusion with the object, an event that re-evokes an ego state that prevailed during early psychic life. However, such occasions, meaningful as they might be, are less noteworthy as transformational accomplishments than they are for their uncanny quality, the sense of being reminded of something never cognitively apprehended but existentially known, the memory of the ontogenetic process rather than thought or phantasies that occur once the self is established. Such aesthetic moments do not sponsor memories of a specific event or relationship, but evoke a psychosomatic sense of fusion that is the subject's recollection of the transformational object. This anticipation of being transformed by an object – itself an ego memory of the ontogenetic process – inspires the subject with a reverential attitude towards it, so that even though the transformation of the self will not take place on the scale it reached during early life, the adult subject tends to nominate such objects as sacred.

Although my emphasis here is on the positive aesthetic experience, it is well to remember that a person may seek a negative aesthetic experience, for such an occasion 'prints' his early ego experiences and registers the structure of the unthought known. Some borderline patients, for example, repeat traumatic situations because through the latter they remember their origins existentially.

In adult life, therefore, to seek the transformational object is to recollect an early object experience, to remember not cognitively but existentially – through intense affective experience – a relationship which was identified with cumulative transformational experiences of the self. Its intensity as an object relation is not due to the fact that this is an object of desire, but to the object being identified with such powerful metamorphoses of being. In the aesthetic moment the subject briefly re-experiences, through ego fusion with the aesthetic object, a sense of the subjective attitude towards the transformational object, although such experiences are re-enacted memories, not recreations.

The search for symbolic equivalents to the transformational object, and the experience with which it is identified, continues in adult life. We develop faith in a deity whose absence, ironically, is held to be as important a test of man's being as his presence. We go to the theatre, to the museum, to the landscapes of our choice, to search for aesthetic experiences. We may imagine the self as the transformational facilitator, and we may invest ourselves with capacities to alter the environment that are not only impossible but embarrassing on reflection. In such daydreams the self as transformational object lies somewhere in the future tense, and even ruminative planning about the future (what to do, where to go, etc.) is often a kind of psychic prayer for the arrival of the transformational object: a secular second coming of an object relation experienced in the earliest period of life.

It should not be surprising that varied psychopathologies emerge from the failure, as Winnicott put it, to be disillusioned from this relationship. The gambler's game is that transformational object which is to metamorphose his entire internal and external world. A criminal seeks the perfect crime to transform the self internally (repairing ego defects and fulfilling id needs) and externally (bringing wealth and happiness). Some forms of erotomania may be efforts to establish the other as the transformational object.

The search for the perfect crime or the perfect woman is not only a quest for an idealized object. It also constitutes some recognition in the subject of a deficiency in ego experience. The search, even though it serves to split the bad self experience from the subject's cognitive knowledge, is nonetheless a semiological act that signifies the person's search for a particular object relation that is associated with ego transformation and repair of the 'basic fault' (Balint, 1968).

It may also be true that people who become gamblers reflect a conviction that the mother (that they had as their mother) will not arrive with supplies. The experience of gambling can be seen as an aesthetic moment in which the nature of this person's relation to the mother is represented.

Clinical example

One of the most common psychopathologies of the transformational object relation occurs in the schizoid self, the patient who may have a wealth of ego strengths (intelligence, talent, accomplishment, success) but who is personally bereft and sad without being clinically depressed.

Peter is a twenty-eight-year-old single male whose sad expressions, dishevelled appearance, and colourless apparel are only mildly relieved by a sardonic sense of humour which brings him no relief, and by an intelligence and education which he uses for the sake of others but never for himself. He was referred by his general practitioner for depression, but his problem was more of an inexorable sadness and personal loneliness. Since his break-up with a girlfriend, he had lived alone in a flat, dispersing himself during the day into multiple odd jobs. Although his days were a flurry of arranged activity, he went through them in a style of agitated passivity, as if he were being aggressively handled by his own work arrangement. Once home, he would collapse into the slovenly comfort of his flat, where he would prop himself before the TV, eat a scanty meal of packaged food, masturbate and, above all, ruminate obsessively about the future and bemoan his current 'bad luck'. Every week, without failure, he would go home to see his mother. He felt she lived in order to talk about him and thus he must be seen by her in order to keep her content.

Reconstruction of the earliest years of his life yielded the following. Peter was born in a working-class home during the war. While his father was defending the country, the home was occupied by numerous in-laws. Peter was the first child born in the family and he was lavishly idolized, particularly by his mother who spoke constantly to her relatives about how Peter would undo their misery through great deeds. An inveterate dreamer about golden days to come, mother's true depression showed up in the lifeless manner in which she cared for Peter, since she invested all her liveliness in him as mythical object rather than actual infant. Soon after Peter's analysis began it became clear to me that he knew himself to be primarily inside a myth he shared with mother; indeed, he knew that she did not actually attend to the real him, but to him as the object of her dreams. As her mythical object, he felt his life to be suspended and, indeed, this was the way he lived. He seemed to be preserving himself, attending to somatic needs, waiting for the day when he would fulfil her dream. But because it was mother's myth he could do nothing, only wait for something to happen. He seemed to empty himself compulsively of his true self needs in order to create an empty internal space to receive mother's dream thoughts. Each visit to the home was curiously like a mother giving her son a narrative feeding. Hence he would empty himself of personal desire and need in order to fulfil mother's desire and he would preserve himself in a state of suspension from life, waiting for the myth to call him into a transformed reality.

Because his mother has transmitted to him his crucial function as her mythic object, Peter does not experience his internal psychic space as his own. Inner space exists for the other, so that in reporting inner states of being Peter does so through a depersonalized narrative as this region is not the 'from me' but the 'for her'. There is a notable absence in Peter of any sense of self, no quality of an 'I', nor even of a 'me'. Instead his self representation bears more the nature of an 'it' on an existential plane. Being an 'it' means for him being dormant, suspended, inert. Peter's free associations are accounts of 'it' states: ruminative reports on the happenings of his body as a depersonalized object. His mother's primary concern was for him to remain in good health in order to fulfil her dreams for him. He was consequently obsessed with any somatic problem, which he reported with almost clinical detachment.

Gradually I recognized that the mythic structure (existing in a narrative rather than existential reality) disguised the secret discourse of the lost culture of Peter's earliest relation to his mother. His ego-states were an utterance to mother who used them as the vocabulary of myth. If he was feeling like a casualty because of ego defects and the failure of id needs, it was because he was her knight errant who had fought battles for her and must rest for future missions. If he felt depleted by his personal relations it was because he was a cherished god who could not expect to mix successfully with the masses. If he spoke to his mother with a sigh she responded, not by discovering the source of the sigh, but by telling him not to worry, that soon he would make money, become famous, go on TV, and bring to the family all the wealth that they deserved.

His existential despair was continually flung into mythic narrative, a symbolic order where the real is used to populate the fantastic. On the few occasions when he tried to elicit from his mother some actual attendance to his internal life, she flew into a rage and told him that his misery threatened their lives, as only he could deliver them. He was to remain the golden larva, the unborn hero, who, if he did not shatter mythic function with personal needs, would soon be delivered into a world of riches and fame beyond his imagination.

In the transference Peter spoke of himself as an object in need of care: 'my stomach hurts', 'I have a pain in my neck', 'I have a cold', 'I don't feel well'. He spoke to me in the language of sighs, groans, and a haunting laughter which served his need to be emptied of agitated desire and to elicit my acute attention. He rubbed his hands, looked at his fingers, flopped his body around as if it were a sack. As I came to realize that this was not obsessive rumination which served as a resistance, but a secret discourse recalled from the culture of his earliest relations to his mother, he found my attention to his private language an immense relief. I felt that he was trying to share a secret with me within the transference, but it was a secret utterance that was prior to language and masked by its enigmatic quality. I could only 'enter' this sequestered culture by speaking to him in its language: to be attentive to all groans, sighs, remarks about his body, etc. Above all, I was to learn that what he wanted was to hear my voice, which I gradually understood to be his need for a good sound. My interpretations were appreciated less for their content, and more for their function as structuring experiences. He rarely recalled the content of an interpretation. What he appreciated was the sense of relief brought to him through my voice.

Peter's language, which I shared in the beginning of the analysis, reflected the terms of a minimally transformative mother. Later, when Peter would invite me to become a simple accomplice in the mother's transformational idiom, I would refuse such transformations (such as the golden larva myth) in favour of achiev-able transformations. As I analysed this transformational idiom, it gave way to a new culture of relatedness. The constellation had to be broken down through analysis before a new idiom of relatedness could be established.

Peter's sense of fate, his remaining a potential transformational object to the other, suggests that not only does the infant require separation and disillusion from the transformational mother, but the mother must also suffer a 'let-down' brought on by the real needs of the infant, which mitigates the mother's uncon-scious wish for an infant to be her transformational object. Peter's mother contin-ually refused to recognize and attend to him as a real person, though admittedly there was a quality of what we might call covetous mothering. She possessed him like an alchemist guarding dross that was her potential treasure. His real needs went unmet, as mother insisted that Peter fulfil her sense that destiny would bring her a deliverer-child.

Discussion

The search for the transformational object, in both narcissistic and schizoid characters, is in fact an internal recognition of the need for ego repair and, as such, is a somewhat manic search for health. At the same time their idiom reflects a minimally transformative mother, a factor that becomes clear in the often meagre way they use the analyst in the transference.

To be sure, one of the features of such patients is their comparative unavail-ability for relating to the actual other – their obtuseness or excessive withdrawnness – but I think such characteristics, reflective of psychodevelopmental arrests, also point towards the patient's need to assert the region of illness as a plea for the arrival of the regressive object relation that is identified with basic ego repair. In analysis this can result in the patient's almost total inability to relate to the analyst as a real person, while at the same time maintaining an intense relation to the analyst as a transformational object. What is the patient trying to establish?

As other authors have pointed out (for example, Smith, 1977), such patients seek a special ambience with the analyst, where the analyst's interpretations are initially less important for their content and more significant for what is expe-rienced as a maternal presence, an empathic response. Indeed, so-called analytic neutrality of expression – ostensibly to mitigate the hysterical or obsessional patient's dread of feeling criticized and to facilitate the analysand's freedom of association – actually works in a different way for narcissistic or schizoid patients: they can become enchanted by it, and may appear oblivious to the actual content of the interpretation so long as the song of the analytic voice remains constant. Now, we may look upon this as a complication in the path of analysability, or we may recognize that the analytic space (the provision of the holding environment) facilitates a process in such patients that leads to the evocation of a deeply regressed state which may be a part of this patient's necessary path to cure. Indeed my experience with such patients is that a regression to this form of object relating often takes place in the first session of analysis, as the ecology of the analytic room (analyst, analyst's interpretations, couch, etc.) becomes a kind of asylum.

As I view it, the patient is regressed to the level of the basic fault, but as each regression points to the region of illness within the person, it also suggests the requirement of a cure. What is needed is an initial experience of successive ego transformations that are identified with the analyst and the analytic process. In such moments, the patient experiences interpretations primarily for their capacity to match his internal mood, feeling or thought, and such moments of rapport lead the patient to 're-experience' the transformational object relation. He appreciates the analyst's fundamental unintrusiveness (particularly the analyst not demanding compliance) not because it leads to freedom of association, but because it feels like the kind of relating that is needed to become well. The paradox is that as the patient regresses into need, searching for a miraculous transformation, the analyst's ordinary work of listening, clarifying and interpreting introduces a different idiom of transforming psychic life.

Some clinicians might regard this use of the analyst as a resistance, but if so, I think we overlook the undeniably unique atmosphere we create for relating. The very offer of treatment invites regressive longings in many patients. Placing the patient on the couch further induces a sense of anxious expectation and dependency. Our reliability, our unintrusiveness, our use of empathic thought to meet the requirements of the analysand, are often more maternal than was the actual mother's care. And in such moments, the patient's identification of the analyst as the transformational object is not dissimilar to the infant's identification of the mother with such processes. Indeed, just as the infant's identification of ego transformations with the mother is a perceptual identification – and not a desire – so, too, the patient's identification does not seem to reflect the patient's desire for us to be transformational, but his adamant perceptual identification of the analyst as transformational object. In the treatment of the narcissistic, borderline and schizoid characters, this phase of the analysis is both necessary and inevitable.

This stage of treatment is very difficult for the clinician since, in a sense, there is no analysis of the patient taking place, and interpretive remarks may be met by a gamut of refusals: from indifference to polite contempt to rage. One such patient would often nod politely, say that yes he did see what I meant, indeed was impressed with how accurate my remark was, but invariably he would end by saying: 'But of course, you know what you have said is only technically correct. It doesn't help me with life experiences, so, as such, as correct as it is I don't see what you think I can do with such a remark.' He was convinced I knew how to take care of him, and even if it was only for an hour a day, he wanted me to soothe him. Analysis proper was regarded as an intellectual intrusion into his tranquil experience of me, and I was for him a kind of advanced computer storing his information, processing his needs into my memory banks. He was waiting for an eventual session when I would suddenly emerge with the proper solution for him, and in an instant remedy his life. I have come to regard this part of his analysis as that kind of regression which is a re-enactment of the earliest object experience, and I think it is folly for an analyst to deny that the culture of the analytic space does indeed facilitate such recollections. If such regressions are a resistance to the analysis of the self, they are resistances only in the sense that the patient must resist analytic investigation as premature, and therefore not to the point. In the transference – which is as much to the analytic space and process as it is to the person of the analyst – the patient is relating to the transformational object, that is, experiencing the analyst as the environment-mother, a pre-verbal memory that cannot be cognized into speech that recalls the experience, but only into speech that demands its terms be met: unintrusiveness, 'holding', 'provision', insistence on a kind of symbiotic or telepathic knowing, and facilitation from thought to thought or from affect to thought. In these sessions, then, the primary form of discourse is a clarification which the patient experiences as a transformative event. Interpretations which require reflective thought or which analyse the self are often felt to be precocious demands on the patient's psychic capacity, and such people may react with acute rage or express a sudden sense of futility and despair.

Perhaps because psychoanalytic theory evolved from work with the hysterical patient (who interpreted the analytic space as a seduction) or the obsessional patient (who adopted it willingly as another personal ritual) we have tended to regard regressive reactions to the analytic space as resistances to the working alliance or the analytic process. Yet the hysteric's sexualization of the transference and the obsessional's ritualization of the analytic process (free dissociation?) may be seen as defences against the very 'invitation' of the analytic space and process towards regression. Thus, in the analysis of such patients, psychic material was readily forthcoming and one could be relatively pleased that there was considerable grist for the analytic mill, but treatment often continued endlessly with no apparent character change, or was suddenly intruded upon by archaic or primitive material. In such cases I believe the analyst was unaware that the failure of the patient to experience the analytic situation as a regressive invitation was a resistance. Indeed, the analytic process, in emphasizing the mechanics of free association and interpretation of the patient's defences, could often result in a denial of the very object relation that was 'offered' to the patient. If the analyst cannot acknowledge that in fact he is offering a regressive space to the patient (that is, a space that encourages the patient to relive his infantile life in the transference), if he insists that in the face of the invitation 'work' must be carried out, it is not surprising that in such analyses patient and analyst may either carry on in a kind of mutual dissociation that leads nowhere (obsessional collusion), or in a sudden blow-up on the part of the patient, often termed 'acting out'.

As I view it, then, the analyst functions as an evocative mnemic trace of the transformational object, because the situation will either induce a patient's regressive recollection of this early object relation or the variations of resistance to it: either denial by sexualization or obsessional ritualization, for example. Indeed, the transference from this point of view is first and foremost a transference reaction to this primary object relation and will help us to see how the patient remembers his own experience of it. There may be a deep regression to an adamant demand that the analyst fulfil the promise of the invitation and function in a magically transformative manner. Or the patient may have enough health and insight into regressive recollections to carry on with subsequent work in the analysis while remaining in touch with more archaic aspects of the self. Indeed I believe that much of the time a patient's passivity, wordlessness or expectation that the analyst knows what to do is not a resistance to any particular conscious or preconscious thought, but a recollection of the early pre-verbal world of the infant being with mother. Unless we recognize that psychoanalysts share in the construction of this pre-verbal world through the analyst's silence, empathic thought and the total absence of didactic instruction, we are being unfair to the patient and he may have reason to be perplexed and irritated.

The transference rests on the paradigm of the first transformational object relation. Freud tacitly recognized this when he set up the analytic space and process and, although there is comparatively little about the mother–child relation within Freud's theory, we might say that he represented his recognition of it in the creation of the analytic set up. The psychoanalytic process constitutes a memory of this primary relation, and the psychoanalyst's practice is a form of countertransference, since he recollects by enactment the transformational object situation. What Freud could not analyse in himself – his relation to his own mother – he represented through his creation of the psychoanalytic space and process. Unless we can grasp that as psychoanalysts we are enacting this early paradigm, we continue to act out Freud's blindness in the countertransference.

The search for transformation and for the transformational object is perhaps the most pervasive archaic object relation, and I want to emphasize that this search arises not out of desire for the object per se, or primarily out of craving or longing. It arises from the person's certainty that the object will deliver transformation; this certainty is based on the object's nominated capacity to resuscitate the memory of early ego transformation. In arguing this, I am maintaining that though no cognitive memory of the infant's experience of the mother is available, the search for the transformational object, and nomination of the deliverer of environmental transformation, is an ego memory.

In a curious way, it is solely the ego's object and may, indeed, be to the utter shock or indifference of the person's subjective experience of his own desire. A gambler is compelled to gamble. Subjectively, he may wish he did not gamble, even hate his compulsion to do so. In Melville's *Moby Dick*, Ahab feels compelled to seek the whale, even though he feels alienated from the source of his own internal compulsion. He says:

> What is it, what nameless, inscrutable, unearthly thing is it; what cozening, hidden lord and master, and cruel, remorseless emperor commands me; then against all natural lovings and longings, I so keep pushing, and crowding, and jamming myself on all the time; recklessly making me ready to do what in my own proper, natural heart, I durst not so much as dare? Is Ahab, Ahab? Is it I, God, or who, that lifts this arm?

(1851: 444–5)

There is something impersonal and ruthless about the search for the whale, and indeed for all objects nominated as transformational. Once early ego memories are identified with an object that is contemporary, the subject's relation to the object can become fanatical, and I think many extremist political movements indicate a collective certainty that their revolutionary ideology will effect a total environmental transformation that will deliver everyone from the gamut of basic faults: personal, familial, economic, social and moral. Again, it is not the revolutionary's desire for change, or the extremist's longing for change, but his certainty that the object (in this case the revolutionary ideology) will bring about change that is striking to the observer.

Conclusions

In work with certain kinds of patients (schizoid and narcissistic) who exaggerate a particular object-seeking, and in our analysis of certain features of culture, I think we can isolate the trace in the adult of the earliest experience of the object: the experience of an object that transforms the subject's internal and external world. I have called this first object the transformational object, since I want to identify it with the object as process, thus linking the first object with the infant's experience of it. Before the mother is personalized for the infant as a whole object, she has functioned as a region or source of transformation, and since the infant's own nascent subjectivity is almost completely the experience of the ego's integrations (cognitive, libidinal, affective), the first object is identified with the alterations of the ego's state. With the infant's growth and increasing self-reliance, the relation to the mother changes from the mother as the other who alters the self to a person who has her own life and her own needs. As Winnicott says, the mother disillusions the infant from the experience of mother as the sole preserver of his world, a process that occurs as the infant is increasingly able to meet his own needs and requirements. The ego experience of being transformed by the other remains as a memory that may be re-enacted in aesthetic experiences, in a wide range of culturally-dreamed-of transformational objects (such as new cars, homes, jobs and vacations) that promise total change of internal and external environment, or in the varied psychopathological manifestations of this memory, for example in the gambler's relation to his object or in the extremist's relation to his ideological object.

In the aesthetic moment, when a person engages in deep subjective rapport with an object, the culture embodies in the arts varied symbolic equivalents to the search for transformation. In the quest for a deep subjective experience of an object, the artist both remembers for us and provides us with occasions for the experience of ego memories of transformation. In a way, the experience of the aesthetic moment is neither social nor moral; it is curiously impersonal and even ruthless, as the object is sought out only as deliverer of an experience.

The aesthetic space allows for a creative enactment of the search for this transformational object relation, and we might say that certain cultural objects afford memories of ego experiences that are now profoundly radical moments. Society cannot possibly meet the requirements of the subject, as the mother ymet the needs of the infant, but in the arts we have a location for such occasional recollections: intense memories of the process of self-transformation.

Although all analysands will experience the analytic space as an invitation to regress in the care of a transformational object, and although it may be essential for the analyst to allow the patient a prolonged experience of regression to dependence, many patients will invite the analyst into a pathological transformational relation. For example, some analysands create confusion in order to compel the analyst to misunderstand them. This is a negative transformation and may represent the transfer of a pathological mother–child relation. Of course this must eventually be analysed, but even here, in the analyst's vigorous interpretive 'work' I think the patient unconsciously experiences the analyst as a generative transformational object.

Transformation does not mean gratification. Growth is only partially promoted by gratification, and one of the mother's transformative functions must be to frustrate the infant. Likewise, aesthetic moments are not always beautiful or wonderful occasions – many are ugly and terrifying but nonetheless profoundly moving because of the existential memory tapped.

Chapter 2

Extractive introjection

Generative mutuality in human relations depends, amongst other things, on an assumption that the elements of psychic life and their different functions are held in common. If A talks to B about his grief over the loss of a parent, then he should be able to assume that B knows what grief is and will 'share' A's problem with him. If A confides in B about her sexual frustration with her husband who is no longer interested in her, then A should assume that B knows about the need for sexual gratification and can understand what frustration would be like.

In an ordinary life, if it is possible to speak of such, couples and families share the elements of psychic life and their functions through a division of labour. In a marriage, a wife may tend to process the element of comforting physical care in relation to her children, while the husband may process the element of 'management' of the outside world. In contemporary life, partners pass the functions of these elements back and forth between themselves. The healthy wife and husband value and understand the elements being processed by the other.

In the modern child-guidance clinics, psychiatric hospitals, and in the secluded space of a psychoanalysis, however, the psychoanalyst is more likely to be aware of failures in mutuality, particularly breakdowns in the sharing and understanding of the common psychic elements and their functions

Kleinian psychoanalysts, in particular, have focused on one way in which a person may rid himself of a particular element of psychic life. He does so by putting it into someone else. If a father feels guilty over impulse buying or the pressure created internally by the urge to be impulsive, he may break psychological contact with this impulse and its inspired guilt by criticizing his child's ordinary impulsiveness. As the parent unconsciously rids himself of this unwanted part of himself, his overly censorious relation to the child's impulsiveness creates the 'desired' effect. Unable to bear the father's censorious approach, the child becomes even more impulsive. In studying human relations, whenever we note that one person compels another to 'carry' an unwanted portion of himself, then we speak of 'projective identification'.

I believe there is a process that can be as destructive as projective identification in its violation of the spirit of mutual relating. Indeed, I am thinking of an inter-subjective procedure that is almost exactly its reverse, a process that I propose to call extractive introjection. Extractive introjection occurs when one person steals for a certain period of time (from a few seconds or minutes, to a lifetime) an element of another individual's psychic life. Such an intersubjective violence takes place when the violator (henceforth A) automatically assumes that the violated (henceforth B) has no internal experience of the psychic element that A represents. At the moment of this assumption, an act of theft takes place, and B may be temporarily anaesthetized and unable to 'gain back' the stolen part of the self. If such extraction is conducted by a parent upon a child it may take many years of an analysis before B will ever recover the stolen part of the self.

Some examples

A common event. B is a five-year-old child and is seated at a table with his parents. He reaches for his glass of milk and spills it on the floor. A parent yells: 'You stupid idiot, why don't you watch what you are doing!' In the fraction of a second prior to that comment, B has felt the shock of his mistake and has been cross and upset with himself. But A's comment steals from B the expression of shock, of self-criticism and of reparation to the group. These elements have in a sense been stolen by A. At this point B is likely to be further stunned by the parent, who assumes furthermore that B is not upset, critical or wishing to make it up to the family. It is this assumption and its expression that represents the violence against B and constitutes an extractive introjection, as A arrogates to himself alone the elements of shock, criticism and reparation. These can, of course, be quickly restored to B if A were to say something like, 'oh, I'm sorry, B, I know this is upsetting to you, and we all do this sort of thing, so don't worry: here, have another glass of milk'; whereupon B might then say, with relief and also in contact with himself, 'I'm sorry, A, for being clumsy', having in that moment processed the elements of shock, criticism and reparation. Later I will explore how extractive introjection which is maintained alters the intra-subjective function of a psychic element. The victim could radically dissociate himself from the element of criticism because its function is to isolate him from the family world. He might willingly allow himself in such a circumstance to be the family fool in order to be part of the group, thus giving up his own contact with important psychic elements.

B is a four-year-old at play. He is moving small figures about and is engaged in a private drama that is nonetheless realized through actual objects. The space is entered by A, who creates such distraction that B loses his playfulness. This is a common enough occurrence, particularly if we say that A is also four. But let's imagine that A is the mother or father, and that each time B sets up a small group of objects to play with, the parent enters the scene and appropriates the playing by telling the child what the play is about and then prematurely engages in playfulness. B might continue to play, but a sense of spontaneity would diminish and be replaced by expectant gamefulness. If every time B is spontaneously playful the mother or father takes over the play and embellishes it with their own 'play', the child will come to experience an extraction of that element of himself: his capacity to play.

B is a student in a class. This can be as either a five-year-old or a twenty-five-year-old. The teacher, A, is knowledgeable and intense. Ordinarily, B is quite capable of representing his views coherently. But A does not permit this. He continually finds flaws in B's arguments and attempts to present a coherent point of view. B becomes rather confused and perplexed. He is less articulate. The less articulate B is, the more aggressively coherent and knowledgeable A is. Gradually A assumes the total function of critical thought, as B simply provides the material for A's superior thinking. This procedure is in the nature of an extractive introjection, since A takes into himself what was partly B's ability, the capacity to think clearly and to put thoughts into words.

B is an adult working in a setting with quite a few colleagues. One day he says something that is rather insensitive – in effect, he is overly critical of a colleague. He has felt privately unhappy with this and in the course of the hour or two after the event he empathizes with his colleague (C). He feels true sorrow, realizes that his colleague's view is actually essential to the overall view of things, and he plans to apologize. At lunch that day B anticipates that he will apologize to his colleague, but before he has the opportunity to do so A enters the situation and upbraids B for his aggression. B nods and at first agrees that yes, he was too thoughtless. A goes on. He proceeds to go over the situation as if B had not acknowledged what A had said. Indeed, A proceeds to praise the offended colleague, C, and in so doing suggests that C has been wronged. B may have an internal experience of feeling that his own private feelings, recognitions, appreciations and reparations towards C have been extracted from him by A who uses the situation to presume himself the only party capable of such capacities. Again, it is A's assumption and its violent delivery that extracts from B what had been present.

B is alone in his room mulling over certain private internal issues. A arrives in a euphoric mood. What is the matter, A inquires of B. B tells A something of what is on his mind. A extracts the elements of B's concerns and with great speed and intensity organizes B's private concerns into a false coherence. The more A organizes B's state of mind into 'meaning' the less B feels in contact with himself and, if A is a manic personality, B may gradually begin to feel dulled and inert, since he is left to carry the split-off deadness that typifies the other aspect of A's personality. In this example, we can see how extractive introjection and projective identification may work together. As A extracts B's sense of inner workings, he deposits in its place a split-off element of his own personality: a deadness.

It is a community meeting in a psychiatric hospital. Some thirty people are in the room together with a rather loose agenda that permits enough space for the introduction of feelings and thoughts as they arise. One of the unconscious issues of each community meeting is the feeling that no one person will ever have enough time to feel personally attended to. Thus, to some extent, each person is feeling neglected and irritated by the inevitable failure of the meeting. But A will not tolerate this. In a moment of fury, while getting out of his chair, A screams, 'you people don't know what it is to feel frustrated and angry', and he stomps out of the room, banging the door behind him. In that moment A may have successfully extracted from the group the individual experience of irritation, frustration and anger. Through a violent fit of temper he has left the group shocked and speechless. Only much later will individual members compete to have the right of fury returned to them.

Another meeting. This time the executives of a corporation are gathered together to work on a difficult problem. As the members of the group express different views and try to think their way through to a creative solution to the problem, A, who has been silent and perhaps envious of the creative capacities of his colleagues, makes the following speech: 'I think we must take this problem seriously. This is not a matter to be taken lightly, and we have to act with great responsibility and caution.' Up until that moment the group has indeed been approaching the problem with seriousness of thought. No levity or lack of seriousness is present and people are obviously thinking responsibly. By making his morally narcissistic speech, however, A appropriates for himself the elements of seriousness, responsibility and caution. It may be very difficult at this point for any other person to express an idea, as A's position suggests that all ideas up until his speech have been somehow irresponsible. Indeed, it is quite possible – largely depending on A's power in such a group – that the group will become silent or overly cautious in its thinking.

By utilizing a combination of curiosity, charm and quiet persistence, A manages to get B to give intimate details from B's life, so B betrays important feelings, self states and historical material. The necessity of solitude is destroyed. A then organizes B's life and self into a coherent account, assuming a narrative authority and power, dispossessing B of his relation to himself as an object. A's narrative grasp of B is 'greater'; that is to say, more organized, intense, comprehensive, certain. A has violently extracted B's relation to himself as an object. This sort of intersubjective violence is common in so-called encounter groups conducted by leaders who extract patients' relations to themselves as an object.

A and B have recently decided to live together. A is actually quite ambivalent about this because he does not like to share his space with anyone else and, although he quite likes B and is sexually attracted to her, she also infuriates him. A self-styled moralist, A is not comfortable with his irritations over B's existence. He aims to transcend this. One of the most irksome irritations in A's life are B's pets, which B has brought into their shared life together because she loves animals and is a very caring person. Indeed, we can say that one of the reasons why A has persuaded himself to live with B is that she is loving and nurturing. In a short time, A can no longer bear the pets and discovers a device for their removal. He is affectionate and shows intense interest in them, but, after a while and with apparent heavy heart, he tells B that he finds it personally unbearable that such lovely pets should have to be confined to the small flat. Both A and B work during the day, and the pets are alone. This has bothered B. A suggests that if one really loves one's pets this kind of treatment cannot be allowed, and he tells B that he cannot stand it any longer: the pets must be sent to someone who has the time to look after them. As A assumes the function of loving concern, B, who has loved the animals very much, now feels guilt (not love) and anxiety (as she knows something will happen to them). She gives up the animals, now believing that all along she has been cruel, when in fact she has been loving. A has extractively introjected the elements of love and care and appropriated them into himself, leaving B to feel dreadful.

Discussion

I hope the examples given clarify the intersubjective process which I have termed extractive introjection, a procedure in which one person invades another person's mind and appropriates certain elements of mental life. The victim of extractive introjection will feel denuded of parts of the self. When this process occurs in childhood, the victim will not have a clear idea why certain elements of mental life seem not to be his right. For example, a child who is constantly attacked by a critical parent for the child's mistakes will in adult life discount the value of his guilt. He may expect punishment or harsh treatment since the healing value of the structure of guilt has been removed by the harsh parent. The said structure generates a mental process that moderates a potentially destructive error by means of the self-arresting affect of sorrow which leads to identification with the harmed other and sponsors the capacity to repair the damage. When the structure of guilt is removed by a critical parent, the person will feel anxiety but will have little sense of sorrow, empathy and reparation. He will never be able 'to make good'.

When we analyse our patients' projective identifications, we should simultaneously consider both the effects of extractive introjection as an alternative explanation and the interplay of these two defence mechanisms. For example, a patient may be internally damaged because he has evacuated parts of the self via projective identification, leaving him with a certain hollow or empty state of mind. The analyst will eventually come under considerable pressure to bear all the evacuations, as this patient tries to split off and project the psychic contents and mental structures that involve the elements of destruction. There might also be a very different kind of patient who is also rather empty, but who is not emptied by virtue of projective identifications. I refer to the person who has been emptied by the active violation of the other, his internal life having been extracted from him. In an analysis, the analyst will not come under pressure to take this analysand's unwanted parts into himself. On the contrary, this analysand will seem almost incapable of projecting into the analyst. More likely, the analysand will develop a parasitical transference in which he assumes that all that is life-enhancing (including destruction) is inside the analyst, thus inspiring him to live as close to the analyst as possible. It should eventually be possible for us to differentiate kinds of illness by considering the effects of pathological intersubjectivity. For example, a mother and father who projectively identify unwanted split-off elements of their own self into their child will burden this child with a highly

complex and chaotic internal world. In adult life this person might be an uninte-
grated collation of parts of his intrinsic self and unwanted parental introjects. This
is true of the borderline personality. Another mother and father may extract mental
content and structure from a child, denuding the child of the contents and structure
necessary to the processing of mental conflict. In this case the adult would seem
mentally impaired or impoverished rather than overburdened with mental conflict.
It may be that the person I will describe in the next chapter – the 'normotic' individual – suffers from a form of extractive introjection. If so, I do not think the
normotic child is witness to the parents' extraction and identification (by assumption) of the stolen mental element, but is the participant-victim of a process of
extraction followed by vaporization of the psychic structure.

Undoubtedly, each extractive introjection is accompanied by some corres-
ponding projective identification. As a person takes from another person's psyche,
he leaves a gap, or a vacuum, in its place. There he deposits despair or emptiness
in exchange for what he has stolen. The situation is further complicated by the fact
that a child who is the victim of consistent extractive introjection may choose to
identify with the aggressive parent and install in his personality this identification,
which then functions as a false self. He may then act in a similarly aggressive and
greedy manner, subsequently extracting elements of psychic life from others. But
this false self is just that: a false act, an empty theft. This person does not truly
appropriate the stolen elements, he just acts as if he does. One can think here of
certain psychopaths who violate other people's states of mind, but who do not over
time use what they steal to dominate or control a person. The theft is quick, fleeting
and empty. I believe we can differentiate between four types of extractive introjection: the theft of mental content, the theft of the affective process, the theft of
mental structure, and the theft of self.

Theft of mental content. We have our own ideas and mental representations. In
a sense they are our creations, even though we hold ideas and representations in
common with others. These are subject, of course, to correction and alteration,
both by ourself and by others. The theft of ideas is one of the forms of extractive
introjection and is often characterized by an act of assumption. B tells A about his
latest thinking on a topic and A replies 'Yes, of course' or 'exactly' or 'naturally',
and then A proceeds to say 'and furthermore', as if A has already thought B's
ideas and adds many more of his own. This exchange is quite common, and its
effect often relatively harmless, although B is likely to feel some irritation and
perhaps a disinclination to talk much further with A.

Theft of affective process. If a person commits an error he is likely to feel the
following emotional sequence: surprise/shock, anger with the self, sorrow, a sense
of guilt and responsibility, reparation, and restoration of peace of mind. This
affective process is an essential feature of the individual subject's experience in
life. But it can be interfered with by another so that the process is interrupted and
altered. The subject who has had the affective process interrupted has instead the
following emotional experience: surprise, shock, acute anxiety and fear, humiliation, concealment and dread. If A extracts the elements of this process from B,

thereby altering the course of the emotional experience, then the character of B's emotional life may be permanently shifted. The damage here is more serious than with the theft of mental content.

Theft of mental structure. A can assume the function of the structure of that part of the mind we term the superego, so de-structuring B's mind in such a way that B, instead of feeling reproached from within, expects to be humiliated from without and eventually ceases to reproach himself, for he concerns himself with either pleasing or deceiving (or both) the external superego. If this occurs, then there has been an important loss of a mental structure. If A denigrates B's capacity to think issues through for himself and arrogates to himself the function of thinking, then the mental structure that generates rational thought and problem-solving will be dismantled, and B will not feel himself capable of solving a problem. Indeed, he may be left in a stupor with little confidence in thought itself, since he has come to regard thinking as a dangerous enterprise in which he feels anxious and threatened. B may give up secondary-process thinking and instead speak from the primary process, as a kind of fool or idiot savant who utilizes the licence of madness to engage in covert thinking.

Theft of the self. The parts of the self are multifold and, understandably, differ between people. I shall not outline them here. But each of us has a unique and idiomatic history. This sponsors the culture of the self, which is composed of many selves, and is perhaps our most valuable possession. The loss of a part of the self means not only a loss of content, function and process, but also a loss of one's sense of one's own person. A loss of this nature constitutes a deconstruction of one's history; the loss of one's personal history is a catastrophe, from which there may well be no recovery.

Loss, unconscious grief and violence

The person who has consistently had important elements and functions of his psyche extracted during childhood will experience a certain kind of loss. He will feel that a primary injustice has occurred, that he has been harmed by something, and like Captain Ahab he may seek a vengeful solution. Indeed, vengefulness of this kind is a bitter and agitated despair that constitutes a form of unconscious mourning, as if the loss can only be undone by the law of talion: an eye for an eye, a leg for a leg. In this respect, the law of talion is an unconscious act intended to recover the lost part of the self by violent intrusion into the other – to recover what has been stolen from oneself.

We may observe how some children can develop relevant patterns of behaviour if they have been violated by parents who have stolen important parts of their psychic life. A man who burgles may be violating a home to steal the internal objects of a family, and in that moment his act may mirror his own experiences as a child, compulsively reversing his life pattern through violent redress.

When one person invades another's psychic territory he not only deposits an unwanted part of himself, as in projective identification, but in some respect he also takes something. At the very least he steals the recipient's peace of mind. That indeed is one of the functions of projective identification. By putting unwanted parts of oneself into another person the projector enjoys limited peace of mind, a psychic state that is extracted from the recipient who is left in confusion.

Necessary paranoia

One of the most important differential assessments a psychoanalyst can make in working with a severely disturbed person is to determine whether the individual's loss of mind is due fundamentally to projective identifications, that is, acts of expulsion which may reflect defensive manoeuvres against primitive anxieties over annihilation, or whether such a loss is due to the absence of internal integrity because of the other's violent extraction of the essentials of psychic life.

Because the child who has had his mind extracted by the other will have little ability to process the experience of being the victim of extractive introjection, he will in some fundamental way know very little of what has happened to him. Know, that is, in the sense of being able to represent mentally the nature of the intersubjective phenomenon he has experienced. The loss of mind may be stored in the individual's memory only as a life-defining event that is beyond comprehension. He may be either remarkably empty and indifferent to his existence, or he may be quite the opposite: angry, depressed and paranoid. But the paranoid process in this person differs from paranoia that represents the individual's projection of unwanted elements into others, a paranoia that precipitates anxiety in the person's relation to the outside world. For the victim of extractive introjections, the paranoid state is an attitude of mourning, of loss over the 'gone', and constitutes a belief that something hostile 'out there' has taken something valuable from within. Such a person does not live in hiding from paranoid objects, but quite the opposite – like Ahab, he seeks the other. He travels towards it in an effort to bring it back to him, or him to it. He does not identify it in order to expel it, but rather to continue the extractive process.

We may distinguish the paranoia that develops as a result of parental extractions of the child's psyche from the dynamically projective paranoia by examining the nature of the transference and the countertransference. The analysand whose paranoia is a form of anguished grief seeks a repatriation with the elements of the psyche. In the transference he believes that the analyst contains important psychic processes and he is determined to gain these talents for himself. Although the analyst will come under pressure to give the elements of psychic life back to the analysand – this will be the patient's unconscious concept of the transaction – the analyst will not find himself persecuted by the dynamic qualities of the more ordinary paranoid process. Namely, he will not have to carry or to bear unwanted sections of the patient's mind. Quite the contrary. The patient seeks to recover his mind and, as the analyst helps him to think and to repossess affects, mental processes and ultimately psychic structure, the analysand responds to the analyst's transformational function with something like object hunger, and eventually love.

My aim in this chapter has been to explore what I mean by the concept of extractive introjection and to provide vignettes to make the concept clear. I have not considered why some people are more vulnerable to extractive introjection than others, nor have I distinguished between its ordinary and pathological forms. It should be clear, however, that I believe extractive introjection to be a common and indispensable part of intersubjective processes.

I shall also have to postpone a more extensive examination of the interplay between projective identification and extractive introjection, as well as a full discussion of the implications for psychoanalytic technique of working with a patient whose inner emptiness is determined by the other's extraction of mind rather than the subject's projective identifications.

Chapter 3

Normotic illness

When Winnicott wrote that 'it is creative apperception more than anything else that makes the individual feel that life is worth living' (1971b: 65), he was aware that psychoanalysis focuses on those disturbances in human subjectivity that make creative living difficult. As if to gesture towards a different pathway of disturbance, he suggested another axis of illness.

> People may be leading satisfactory lives and may do work that is even of exceptional value and yet may be schizoid or schizophrenic. They may be ill in a psychiatric sense because of a weak reality sense. To balance this one would have to state that there are others who are so firmly anchored in objectively perceived reality that they are ill in the opposite direction of being out of touch with the subjective world and with the creative approach to fact.
>
> (1971b: 66–7)

I believe that we are witness either to the emergence of a new emphasis within personal illness or we are just getting around to perceiving an element in personality that has always been with us. This element is a particular drive to be normal, one that is typified by the numbing and eventual erasure of subjectivity in favour of a self that is conceived as a material object among other man-made products in the object world.

We are attending an increasing number of disturbances in personality which may be characterized by partial deletions of the subjective factor. Therefore, we write of 'blank selves' (Giovacchini, 1972), 'blank psychoses' (Donnet and Green, 1973), and an 'organizing personality' (Hedges, 1983). The effort to explore selected features of these personalities can be found in the work of Masud Khan (1974, 1979), André Green (1973), Donnet and Green (1973) and Robert Stoller (1973, 1976). Such persons are often unsuccessful in their effort to be rid of an intrapsychic life, since they are unable to resolve that psychic pain which derives from the annulment of internal life. They are usually aware of feeling empty or without a sense of self, and they seek analytic help in order to find some way to feel real or to symbolize a pain that may only be experienced as a void or an ache.

There is a certain kind of person, however, who has been successful in neutralizing the subjective element in personality. As Winnicott suggested, some people have annihilated the creative element by developing an alternative mentality, one that aims to be objective, a mind that is characterized less by the psychic (by the representational symbolization of feelings, sensations and intersubjective perceptions) than by the objective. This mentality is not determined to represent the object, but to be the echo of thingness inherent in material objects, to be a commodity object in the world of human production.

In the following account a particular kind of person will be described, one who has for the most part escaped our attention, although Joyce McDougall's intelligent and searching account of what she calls the 'antianalysand' (1980) may very well be a description of the person I term a 'normotic'.

A normotic person is someone who is abnormally normal. He is too stable, secure, comfortable and socially extrovert. He is fundamentally disinterested in subjective life and he is inclined to reflect on the thingness of objects, on their material reality, or on 'data' that relates to material phenomena.

We may speak of a common normotic element when we identify any mental activity that constitutes a transfer of a subjective state of mind into a material external object that results in the de-symbolization of the mental content. If this element is overutilized, if it is a means towards the evacuation of subjective states of mind, then the person may be subtly moving towards normotic illness. If the normotic element is ordinary, then normotic illness develops when the subjective meaning is lodged in an external object, remains there and is not re-introjected, and over time loses its symbolic function as a signifier. Normotically disturbed persons successfully house varied parts and functions of their internal world in material objects, and even though they use these objects and collect them into a familiar space, they serve no symbolic purpose. Such an individual is alive in a world of meaningless plenty.

Normotic personality

The fundamental identifying feature of this individual is a disinclination to entertain the subjective element in life, whether it exists inside himself or in the other. The introspective capacity has rarely been used. Such a person appears genuinely naïve if asked to comment on issues that require either looking into oneself or the other in any depth. Instead, if the evolution towards becoming a normotic personality is successful, he lives contentedly among material objects and phenomena.

By the subjective element, I mean the internal play of affects and ideas that generates and authorizes our private imaginations, creatively informs our work and gives continuing resource to our interpersonal relations. The subjective ability amounts to a particular kind of internal space (Stewart, 1985) that facilitates the reception of unconscious affects, memories and perceptions.

The normotic seems unable to experience evolving subjective states within himself. Without moods he may appear unusually steady or sound. If he is forced by circumstance into a complex situation in which the subjective element is called into play (such as being part of a family quarrel, or discussing a film, or hearing of tragic events), he betrays the absence of a subjective world. He may speak of a phenomenon as an object in its own right, laden with known laws, and thus understandable. A quarrel might lead him to say 'you people are just being unreasonable', or *Hamlet* might inspire him to say 'an unhappy young fellah', or more often than not, he lapses into respectful silence.

This is not to suggest that he does not go to the theatre or the cinema. But he stresses that he is going to a play or that he is in possession of season tickets. He avoids discussing the content of the play by emphasizing the play as something to go to or to possess. He is sincerely incapable of reading and commenting on a poem. The capacity to consider a poem is a sophisticated mental accomplishment and requires a subjective ability which eludes this individual.

Instead, the normotic is interested in facts. But he does not have a passion for factual data in order to establish a common knowledge that sponsors a group's creativity (as in the scientific community). Facts are collected and stored because this activity is reassuring. It is part of a personal evolution in which he unconsciously attempts to become an object in the object world. To collect facts is ultimately to be identified with that which is collected: to become a fact in one's person. It is truly reassuring to become part of the machinery of production. He likes being part of an institution because it enables him to be identified with the life or the existence of the impersonal; the workings of an institution or the products of a corporation. He is part of the team, he is at home in a committee, he is secure in social groups that offer in pseudo-intimacy an alternative to getting to know someone.

The normotic takes refuge in material objects. He is possessed of an urge to define contentedness through the acquisition of objects, and he measures human worth by means of collections of acquired objects. But this kind of appropriation is not passionate, unlike, for example, when a person buys a boat and cherishes it, working on it during weekends and learning about sailing lore. Material objects are accumulated in a wishless manner. They appear in this person's life as if they were logical outcomes and signatures of his personality.

It would be untrue to say that the normotic person is not in possession of a sense of identity. This is not an as-if person or a false self, as defined by Winnicott. It is not easy to describe the nature of his identity, other than to say that an observer may feel that it seems to be an artificial acquisition, as if no mental work has been employed in the historical fashioning of this identity.

It would also be untrue to say that the normotic person cannot fall in love or form a relationship. He is attracted, however, to those of like mind and, since love can come close to some of the addictions, he can be in love with someone without this ever making a claim on his subjectivity.

Is his affect impoverished? Not in the sense that he is affectless. He may have a sense of humour, he enjoys a good laugh, and seems fun-loving. But rather than experience sadness, he slows down. Action is the quality of life for him, so depressions or anxiety states do not appear in a mentally elaborated form: they only slow him down in his otherwise 'faultless' pursuit of happiness, in extreme form, he would strike us as appallingly empty, but this observation is all the more remarkable given that he would appear so only to us, whilst in himself he would seem to be without want. In this sense, the presence in contemporary literature and film of the human who is revealed to be a robot is a recognition of this personality type emerging in our culture. Such representations are less descriptive of the future of robots than they are accurate prognostications of a personality disorder that is already with us.

This person may be a workaholic. He thrives on the structure of life and constructs his future through revised agendas. He often knows what he will be doing every hour of each day. Spaces are appropriated into rituals, thus obviating the possibility of spontaneous choice. He knows where he will eat lunch, or that on Thursday evenings he will be playing cards, or that on every Monday he will have dinner with his wife. Recreation lacks playfulness and is pursued with the same zealousness as any chore.

It is striking that such a person does achieve something of a state of reverie. A female patient wanders from one store to another in the course of her day. She might find herself in a supermarket for an hour or more, not because she is in particular need of any food or other items but because the material aesthetic of the supermarket, resplendent with its vegetables, cereals and canned goods, is soothing.

From the supermarket to the pet shop; from the sportsware store to the large hardware shop; from a lunch with friends in which there is an itemization of actions lived out by each, to the home for a listless cleansing of the kitchen; from a tennis match to the jacuzzi: this person *can* live a life without ever blinking an eye. If his mother or father is dying the normotic does not feel grief, but instead engages in a detailed examination of the nature of the disease, the technology of the hospital treating the person and the articulation of clichés that are meant to contain and launder the experience of death: 'Well, she's very old you know, and we've all got to go some time!'

This person is by no means friendless. Indeed, he may be exceptionally adept at organizing dinners and parties. Topics that require a capacity to tolerate the subjective element in life, however, are rarely raised, and the friendships are characterized by mutual chronicling of life's events, rather than by intersubjective exchanges in which the increasing intimacy that allows for a true sense of knowing one's friend is established. The capacity to speak frankly about one's self, about one's personality and one's feelings, is unknown. While many people need to engage the other in mutual knowing, aware that such intimacy involves both parties in the precarious balance of ambivalence, no such requirement appears in the normotic.

This is not a person without conviction or standards, but both seem to be inherited from somewhere other than the self. Little thought or subjective drive seems to have gone into the workings of the mind. Such a person is in possession of a curious alternative to guilt. He does believe in right and wrong, yet instead of that kind of inner dialogue which takes place in the interchange between ego and superego, a dialogue that is often the articulation of guilt, there is a kind of teutonic legal introject. There are many rules or paradigms that suggest right and wrong behaviour. On careful examination, however, such rules are not really responsive to changing circumstances in life, and they are less reflective of critical acts of judgement than photographic feats of mnemonic recall.

The unborn

It is striking how this person seems to be unborn. It is as if the final stages of psychological birth were not achieved, and one is left with a deficiency. Or, at least this is how it seems, when one is working with such a person who appears to be content and happy, and yet is so like the infant for whom the breast will always be the ultimate solution to distress and the fulfilment of need.

What is lacking is that originating subjectivity which informs our use of the symbolic. The normotic does not see himself other than as an object (ideally smart and spruced up, productive and sociable) among all the objects of the material world. Since he does not perceive himself as a subject, he does not ask to be seen by the other, nor does he look into the other.

Having no interest in subjective states and seeking material objects as things-in-themselves – for functional rather than symbolic purposes – the normotic has only partly developed the capacity to symbolize the self. In Bion's language,[1] there is an impoverished production of 'alpha elements', a term which he uses to represent that mental transformation whereby emotional experiences become a possibility in the first place. 'Alpha elements are produced from the impressions of the experience; these are thus made storeable and available for dream thoughts and for unconscious waking thinking' (1977: 8). This underlying flaw in the person's mental life means that he registers and communicates his being through 'beta elements', which for Bion represent 'undigested facts' or facts in existential life that do not evolve into subjective states of mind. Although I do not believe that the absence of alpha function in the normotic is solely due to hate or envy, Bion's description of the person whose alpha function is chronically deficient comes close to defining the nature of the normotic, and I shall quote it in full:

1 Bion's theory of mental functioning is complex and challenging. Those unfamiliar with his work may wish to read *Second Thoughts* and *The Seven Servants*. They may also wish to consult *Introduction to the Work of Bion*, edited by Leon Grinberg et al.

In a psychoanalysis the analyst will note many kinds of verbal and non-verbal communication between the patient and himself. There are many factors involved and, in Bion's theory, factors are elements of functions.

Each person has sense impressions and emotional experiences. There is a specific function of the personality which transforms sense impressions and emotional realities into psychic elements which are then available for mental work, such as thinking, dreaming, imagining, remembering. This element of transformation Bion arbitrarily terms the alpha element.

Beta elements are untransformed sense impressions and emotional experiences which are experienced as things-in-themselves, and which are operated on by projective identification.

Attacks on alpha-function, stimulated by hate or envy, destroy the possibility of the patient's conscious contact either with himself or another as live objects. Accordingly we hear of inanimate objects, and even of places, when we would normally expect to hear of people. These, though described verbally, are felt to be represented by their names. This state contrasts with animism in that live objects are endowed with the qualities of death.

(1977: 9)

The attack on alpha function means that the person never really comes alive, and is therefore only partially born. Unable to find alpha function, stuck in a primitive communicative exchange characterized by beta thinking and functioning, the normotic solves psychological problems by medicating himself (usually by overdrinking) and living among material objects.

Aetiological considerations

I can make sense of the evolution of normotic illness only by considering such a development within the life of a family. At the most fundamental level the normotic was only partly seen by the mother and the father, mirrored by parents whose reflective ability was dulled, yielding only the glimmer of an outline of self to a child. In spite of his profound study of the nature of mental functioning, Bion places the attack on alpha functioning only within the infant: hence the references to hate or envy. It is a source of puzzlement to me why madness within the mother or the father, or between the parents, or in that atmosphere that is created by all participants in the child–parent interaction, should be eliminated as one of the potential sources of disturbance in the child's development of alpha function. This is all the more bewildering because Bion does acknowledge the vital function of the parent as a container for the infant's psychic life. If so, is it not conceivable that a parent, through projective identification, can lodge an unwanted and destructive part of himself in the infant, leaving the child possessed of a certain confusion and overwhelmed with destructive feelings?

I do not understand why some children give in to such a family atmosphere and become normotic, and why others do not. I am not arguing that normotic adults inevitably produce normotic children. Although those persons who become normotic must have come from normotic families, some children raised in such an atmosphere manage to discover and sustain a private subjective world in striking contrast to the parents' lives. Others become perpetually delinquent, registering subjective life through continual feats of acting out, a testimony to their rebellion against normotic mentality. Perhaps the difference between normotic children and those who emerge into health (or neurosis) is that some children find a way to be mirrored even if the parents are not providing this. By finding their reflection elsewhere they internalize a mirroring function and utilize intra-subjective dialogues as alternatives to interpersonal play. They develop an introspective capacity, and life for them will be meaningful even if incomplete.

Although the subject will have to be studied further and in greater depth, I think it is highly likely that the children who give in to the normotic element perceive in the parents' way of being a form of hate that we might conceptualize as a death instinct. Such a hate does not focus on the personality of the child, so it would be untrue to say that the child feels hated by the parent. It may be more accurate to say that the child experiences the parents' attack on life itself, and that such a parent is trying to squeeze the life out of existence.

It may be, however, that the child's disposition to be emptied of self reflects his own death drive, an activity which can only be successful, in my view, if the parents wish it to be. Parent and child organize a foreclosure of the human mentality. They find a certain intimacy in shutting down life together, and in mastering existence with the unconscious skill of a military operation. Because the normotic person fails to symbolize in language his subjective states of mind, it is difficult to point to the violence in this person's being, yet it is there, not in his utterances, but in his way of shutting life out.

Normotic parents wish to become objects among objects. This striving implicates the child in the evolution towards a certain mentality that could correspond to the child's own death instinct. The drive not to be (human) but to master being facilitates the movement towards the inorganic state of constancy that Freud (1920) considered when writing of the death instinct. The accomplishment of this drive (not to be but to have been) is to rid the psyche of the tensions of being and to transfer the self into external objects which become alternatives to self awareness. This is why the normotic transforms intrapsychic and cultural experience into mnemic excreta: a holiday snap is more important than the actual experience of visiting a new place, a subscription to the opera is more significant than going to see the opera.

If there is a dialectic of 'death work' (Pontalis, 1981) in which parent and child develop a reciprocal preference for maintaining an unborn self, the partnership develops into the child's personality disorder by virtue of the parent's adamant refusal to be alive to the child's inner reality. This is the death work of a certain family 'life', as the child gradually internalizes this partnership and transforms its terms into his relation to himself as an object, which results in his refusal to entertain the inner life of the self.

As the parents of the normotic person were not sufficiently alive to his inner reality, they did not facilitate the creative expression of the inner core of the self. We could say that they were responsive to the child's false self development, in that they responded to the child's adaptation to convention with praise and material reward. It is my view that the parents' transformational object function (see above, chapter 1) was of a particular kind.[2]

---

2 I have used this term – transformational object – to define the infant's experience of the first object. By this I mean that the infant experiences the mother as a process of alteration. She attends to him in a way that changes his external and inner worlds. Infants do not internalize the mother as a person or imago. They do internalize the maternal process which is laden with logical paradigms that contribute to the laws of the child's character. As mother and child are engaged in countless transactions, these become facts of life that contribute to the logic of each person's existence.

I do not believe that anything remarkable takes place in the history of the normotic person. These children are reared in structured settings by parents and are provided with toys and playthings, and certainly do not suffer deprivations of a material kind. But neither of the parents is inclined towards the celebration of the child's imaginative life. If they do enter into play I think it is often designed to terminate the playing, to subtly turn the child towards reality. Above all, they are concerned that their children be normal and they do not wish them to act in a way that could be construed as inappropriate or odd. So the child is rewarded for being good, where good means ordinary, and he is ignored or threatened for being imaginative, particularly if this is expressed in social settings.

It is important to bear in mind that as these parents disown the imaginative element in their child, they offer instead some kind of ritual in its place. An empty structure replaces creative lack of structure. For example, the child who is wanting to play murder with his father is pushed into watching TV. Programme follows programme, day after day, in a predictable manner.

The child might perhaps be encouraged to become an athlete, and the father could decide that throwing a football is the way to go about it. Exercising such ritualized and available activities is another example of the child accommodating to a pre-existing form set up by others. They do not depend on the child's imaginative life, although children may still endeavour to imagine themselves being football heroes, or the like. Such children, although they may engage in sundry outdoor activities, all of which are quite physically and educationally stirring, participate in a life that becomes an alternative to living from the core of the self. In their continuing transformational object function, the parents direct the child's psychological life outward into physical activity or into some structured and ritualized container, such as a television set or a video game. The child's creative invention of life is not encouraged.

Withholding response to the creative element in the child amounts in some ways to a negative hallucination, since important parts of the child's personality are not noticed. As the child lives on, these parts of the self are the not-there elements and, as each of us inherits those basic paradigms generated by the parent's transformational object functioning in our own way of looking after our self as an object, the not-there elements of parental negative hallucination join the child's own intrinsic defences (such as denial) to become the not-there particles of this person's intrasubjective life. When a child enters adolescence, if he does suffer from too much psychological pain, he is in the horrifying dilemma of being unable to symbolize his pain. Instead, he experiences the negative hallucination, which is only a kind of blank, an ellipsis that forms a continuing amnesia. This may be all the more agonizing as the child may appear to have all that he should want, and the parents may be vigorously indifferent to idiomatic behaviour.

Normotic breakdown

If psychotic illness is characterized by a break in reality orientation and a loss of contact with the real world, then normotic illness is typified by a radical break with subjectivity and by a profound absence of the subjective element in everyday life. As psychotic illness is marked by a turning inward into the world of fantasy and hallucination, normotic illness is distinctive as a turning outward into concrete objects and towards conventional behaviour. The normotic flees from dream life, subjective states of mind, imaginative living and aggressive differentiated play with the other. Discharges of mental life are favoured over articulated elaborations that require symbolic processes and real communication. We could say that if the psychotic has 'gone off at the deep end', the normotic has 'gone off at the shallow end'.

A normotic family may be successful for quite some time, depending on material comfort and the availability of personal wealth. As they need a supply of material objects to enrich their personal happiness, they are far more dependent than other sorts of people on the flux of economic life. For example, if one of the parents becomes unemployed, this amounts to more than redundancy: it threatens the breakdown of a mentality. It does not lead to reflection or to affective states that deepen the family members' understanding of themselves and of their life. A father may become absent, either literally, by going off and staying away from home, or he may sit before the TV for long periods of time. We would say that there is a depression there, but from inside the family; it is the experience of 'leave your father alone' whose mental equivalent is 'leave that part of your mind concerned with your father alone'. Such statements abound, and in this way the mind is gradually shut down.

A mother may convert the house into an object that must be exhaustively cleaned. Her somewhat lifeless and compulsive activity would be striking to us, but inside the family this might be described as 'your mother is helping out' whose mental equivalent is 'when you believe you see signs of distress in us, cancel this idea, and replace it with an observation of the action you see before you'. If the father finds work again, this entire episode will be negated and probably only referred to in clichés: 'boy, that was really tough' or 'well, you have your downs as well as your ups'. If matters do not improve, however, strain begins to enter the picture in such a way that a normotic defence cannot successfully endure.

The most common form of breakdown is alcohol abuse. When this person feels psychic pain or when he is invited by fortune to undergo incremental subjective experiences, he refuses to do so and drinks himself into an anaesthetized state. Alternatively, he may throw himself even more exuberantly into his work, staying at the office for inhumanly long hours. He might, along with other activities, become an exercise fanatic, jogging for ten miles a day. If he becomes depressed and is incapable of work or exercise, he will characterize himself in mechanical metaphors. He is just 'shot', or 'kaput', or 'in bad working order'. He may seek a chemotherapeutic solution to his state of being.

Certain psychosomatic disorders and eating disturbances may be forms of normotic breakdown in which the person tries to elude introspective examination of the subjective origins of distress, preferring the focus of a concrete breakdown, such as a pain or dysfunction of part of the body or a preoccupation with taking in food and monitoring the shape of the body.

The above processes are all syntonic with the normotic personality. They are endeavours to remain within the normotic personality and its assumptions. Some homosexual disturbances, however, may be understood as anti-normotic personality formations. The homosexual's adornment in exaggerated representations of the subjective element can be a defiance of the normotic way of life. Where the normotic parent may have stressed 'reasonable' thinking, the homosexual may espouse the superiority of anti-reason. Where the normotic parent never tolerated the controversial, the homosexual may become perversely addicted to collecting controversies. This defence against the normotic element (rather like the compulsive defence against schizophrenic illness) nonetheless contains the trace of its intended antithesis. For the homosexual's creativity may only be artifice: the subjective appropriated for the purposes of adornment. The homosexual may become the material object, as if he is endeavouring to retrieve desire from his past by being that which is compulsively collected. Sexual promiscuity amongst homosexuals has the character of a material phenomenon, and is in part an inverted representation of the normotic illness.

[handwritten margin note: what? seems random and unbalanced heteros could also be ? inverted representations]

The most fragile period in a normotic person's life is during adolescence. It is my view that we can often observe how a child raised in such an atmosphere feels unbearable strain and turns to either drugs or suicide as an alternative to life in the family. We can also witness the family dynamic more clearly, as normotic parents often exorcise themselves of their adolescent child as if they are cleaning house.

Tom

Some time ago I was invited to interview a patient in front of the members of a department of psychiatry in a large hospital. I was not accustomed to this experience and looked forward to it with some reservation and anxiety.

Before the patient entered the room of roughly thirty people, we were told by the family therapist that the patient was an adolescent who had attempted suicide by cutting his arm from the wrist to the elbow. This event had followed a disappointment in school when he felt he had failed people. For several days after the disappointment he had become 'dreamy', a change which had been observable to his friends and apparently to the members of his family, although no one said anything to him about it nor investigated his mood. He then attempted suicide and would certainly have died had he not been discovered. After several weeks in a hospital he seemed much better. He had become attached to a young psychiatrist who was enthusiastic and empathic, if a bit unsophisticated. It was clear that he cared deeply for the boy.

We learned that Tom had been placed on antidepressants, as his dreamy state, which was typical of him at times in the hospital, was deemed evidence of a clinical depression. After less than a month, he was released from the hospital. Within a few days he was re-admitted following another serious suicide attempt.

He resumed his relation to the psychiatrist, and we were to discuss what to do with him. Not the least of the issues, particularly in the mind of the hospital administrators, was the fact that he was about to overstay his allotted time.

Before seeing the patient, I imagined him to be a rather depressed looking and hopeless chap, and I thought the interview would be difficult: how would I be able to get him to speak about himself? I was quite surprised when he entered the room and strode confidently to his chair. Sitting next to me was a handsome, athletic, wholesome looking lad, neatly dressed in cotton trousers, tennis shoes and stylish short-sleeved shirt. He opened the meeting with some appropriately humorous comment about the rather unusual nature of this event. Clearly he knew me for what I was and he meant to be up to any skill on my part.

I think it is accurate to say that although I did interview him, I never overcame the shock of meeting him. This became somewhat apparent in the consultation. For Tom behaved as if nothing was at all unusual in his immediate history. Although he had a ferocious scar visible on his arm, he did not relate to this suicide attempt. After five minutes of chat, I said to him that obviously he must be in great pain or else he would not have attempted to kill himself. He handled this comment as if I had not meant what I said. He politely rebuffed me with an 'OK'. He did respond to those questions I put to him about the events leading up to his suicide attempt, and it was clear that he had felt terribly isolated since moving to his new school, and had entered into athletics in an effort to find friendship. He had never been allowed to mourn the loss of his friends from the previous school, for his father led the family with clichés about how strong people put things behind them. As the interview progressed, we were all moved by the utter failure of Tom's family to think about what they had all been through. Since they had not engaged in any mental work to deal with the distress of such an upheaval, needless to say they did not discuss it with one another.

When I tried to discuss Tom's experience of the move with him, he would inevitably refer me to one or another of his father's remarks: 'It will all turn out for the best' or 'If you want to get ahead in life, you have to get on with life'.

We knew from the family therapist's report that Tom's father was a genial but shallow man who worked as an engineer. He was not oppressive or heavy handed, and spent quite a lot of time with his children, inevitably engaged in outdoor activities: football, water skiing, basketball. He never gave the impression, however, of having sat down with one of his children to discuss any of their problems.

Tom's family, like many such people, appeared ideal. They were civic minded and took part in many local social events. No doubt they were regarded by their friends as steady people with their feet firmly planted on the ground. When Tom tried to kill himself, the response amongst his friends must have been similar to his family's reaction: it was beyond belief and outside the purview of common sense. It was therefore something that could not be considered and should be labelled as an unfortunate event, a 'real shame', which would no doubt end when Tom snapped out of it.

While sitting with Tom, I felt I was confronted with a mentality that admitted of no inquiry or reflection. It was clear after a while that it would be fairly useless to question him further, since he was unable at this point to speak of himself to another person. So I decided to tell him a bit about adolescence as I had experienced it. I said that I had felt dreadfully uncertain at times about how things would turn out in my life. I reminisced about high school sports and recalled how dreadful I felt if I did not do well in competitive games, but how much worse it was if I let the team down, which, I said, I inevitably did. After going on in this vein for a while, I then said that I could not get over how little of the uncertainty and doubt and anger about being an adolescent seemed to be expressed in him. With humour, I said that he reminded me more of one of his father's fifty-year-old colleagues than he did a sixteen-year-old. I said that I reckoned that he was trying to live up to some impossible standard, which made him feel furious and incompetent at times, and that he must be figuring that if this is what he is to be stuck with in life that he might as well do himself in.

When I started to talk about myself, he seemed more interested, but also more anxious and uncertain, as no doubt he was unaccustomed to hearing an adult talk to him about the ordinary fears and uncertainties of adolescence. He remained composed and polite throughout the interview, in contrast to myself. I now realize looking back that I was rather more slovenly than I usually am (I was slouching in my chair, whilst he was sitting quite properly), and I was at a loss for words (while he had an answer for every question). In other words, I was closer to the adolescent experience than Tom was, while he, in turn, was closer to emulating the businesslike orientation to life that he believed characterized normal behaviour.

It is my view that Tom's breakdown constitutes a mute refusal to live within normotic culture, even though at the point of his suicide attempt he had not discovered other avenues for the expression of his feelings. Hopefully that will come with his psychotherapy.

Deflecting the self

As has been argued, the normotic person is nurtured in an environment in which the parent avoids responsiveness to the core of the child's self. In health, a child's play leads the parent to elaborate on this experience through affective participation, imaginative mirroring and verbal comment, so that the child evolves from playing to speaking, to feeling enhanced and enlarged by language. In the normotic family, the child's play goes uncommented upon, except as an object, much as one might point to a chair and say 'there is a chair'. The parent does not interact with the child's imaginative inventions, he does not elaborate any of the child's imaginings by commenting on them, and the child is not reflected by the parent. Instead of being mirrored by the parent, the child is deflected. This is accomplished by diverting the child from the inner and the psychic towards the outer and the material.

Normotic families develop a library of material objects. If a child is working on some inner psychic problem or interest, the family usually has an external concrete object available for the transfer of the psychic into the material. Let us imagine that a four-year-old child is on the verge of enacting in play his interest in his penis as a weapon in heterosexual intercourse. He invents a space game in which he invites a boy or a girl to be his victim while he imprisons them in a capsule which he is determined to preside over with a sword. I say that he is on the verge of this activity because, by the time he begins to set this game up, a normotic parent would already have intervened to direct him elsewhere. He would be told that if he wants to play he should throw the ball or ride his bicycle and that he should be nice to his friends and not act like a monster. He might be told to sit down nicely with his friends and watch TV. This example illustrates the concept of a deflected self, a self that is transferred elsewhere. This is fundamentally different from the act of dissociation that Winnicott (1960) refers to when writing of the schizoid character, for in this case there is a private inner self that goes on living a secret life, hidden and protected by a false self. Schizoid persons do have complex, possibly even rich, inner fantasy lives, but suffer from a lack of spontaneity and liveliness. The normotic person is almost exactly the opposite. He may be quite extrovert (although not truly spontaneous) and a past master at utilizing material objects, but he would have very little inner psychic life.

It is difficult to characterize the atmosphere that prevails in the normotic person's inner world. Indeed, I am well aware that by discussing this issue removed from a particular clinical example, I run the risk of lumping complex phenomena together in a way that can be oversimplistic. Nonetheless, I believe it is possible to discuss certain characteristics of these persons' inner lives.

Because the normotic individual is not known and reflected by the other, he is deficient in his own techniques of insight. He is also relatively unable to introject an object and is therefore both unable to identify with an other and hampered in the ability to empathize. His inner object world is strangely objectless. This individual does not think about others. He does not delineate the nature of an other to himself. One patient seen in analysis rarely spoke of any person, or any distinguishing traits of such a person. Instead she listed her daily happenings, all of which seemed to take place in a void. As she chortled on session after session about what had happened that day, I struggled to define the quality of her inner life. She was not empty, that was for sure. She bubbled over with accounts of events, often striking for their sheer meaninglessness. If I was unable to define the quality of her inner life, I was nonetheless able to characterize it, as it reminded me of certain radio talk-ins, when we find ourselves listening to the host and someone on the end of the telephone engaging in animated meaninglessness, artfully trivializing complex and significant issues. My patient's inner world seemed like a background noise, full of trivial observations and listings.

If such a person really does not introject objects, nor indeed project herself into objects, what mental mechanisms do characterize her internal life? In my view, she incorporates rather than introjects, and excorporates (Green, 1981) rather than projects. If for the moment we think of the difference between incorporation and introjection in the clinical setting, this distinction as it is used here should be clear. If a patient takes in the analyst through the senses, he is incorporating the analyst not introjecting him. The sight of the analyst and his consulting room is diet enough for such a person, as is the smell of the analyst and the room, as is the feel of the couch and the sound of the analyst's voice and other sounds that characterize the consulting room. Incorporation in and of itself is non-representational, and the analyst as an internal object is relatively meaningless. If a patient thinks about what the analyst has said, if he imagines his analyst and develops an internal relation to him, then we can speak of introjection. As the term is used here, introjection refers to the internalization of the object's personality (or part of it) in a dynamic relation to some part of the patient's self. The patient who incorporates takes in only sense presentations and keeps them at a non-representational level. This is the equivalent of Bion's beta level of functioning.

An excorporation is an act of expulsion of an object that is roughly equivalent to the terms of incorporation. Again, it is useful to consider Bion's formulations, in particular his concept of the 'reversal of function' (1958). We not only take in an object through the eyes, we also eject objects through the eyes. The same is true of hearing, of smelling, of touching. In the clinical situation, some of the more common forms of ex-corporation are the occasions when a patient coughs, or yawns, or taps the couch or sighs.

What is the nature of normotic communication? I do not think that it follows the laws of Bion's theory of beta functioning – specifically, objects are not manipulated via projective identification. Almost the opposite happens. It is as if language 'transformers' are used that launder a communication of all meaning, thus enabling the person to vaporize conflict and appear perfectly normal. This takes place by incorporating phrases that are in themselves meaningful, but that are used so repetitively that they eventually lose their originating subjectivity. I am referring to the use of familiar phrases by a person, indeed to the constriction of vocabulary, a foreclosure of language that would be observable only over time in the knowing of any one individual. So, for example, a person who has a normotic personality disorder would be found to use a vocabulary of phrases that laundered the self of meaning; phrases such as 'that's tragic' or 'uh huh' or 'yeah' or 'wow' that nullify meaning whilst appearing to recognize significance. Or a person might have more complex phrases such as 'gosh, that's really amazing' or 'it's extraordinary what the world is coming to' which deflect meaning away from inter-subjective exchange.

The function of transformation from potential meaning into meaninglessness reflects a process derived from the parents that is installed in the ego to form part of its procedure. This ego function is in the nature of a memory of the early mother and father, who in their functions as transformational objects constantly denuded the child's gestures of their meaning function. This interactional paradigm becomes one of the many laws of the child's character.

As has been suggested, the outcome of such a situation is a person who appears really quite extroverted and able. He seems to be without conflict, even in a troubled world. He manages distress through the use of 'language transformers' that alter significance into insignificance by virtue of the use of a vocabulary of phrases that function as evacuators of meaning.

From subject to object

Normotic children conceive of themselves as objects. Becoming a good object for someone is a worthy enterprise. Nurtured by parents who approve of their behaviour, they, like the parents, develop a concern to appear perfectly normal. This does not result in a schizoid split, at least as we have commonly understood it, because in such children the development along false self lines is materially rewarded, and as children these people are really very pleased to contribute to the population of the norm.

Family members wish to be placed in each other's minds as solid and friendly objects similar to the position of the material objects they all value. These families pride themselves on their articulation of a known and familiar identity (such as being American or English), and they take pleasure in seeing the other recognize himself in them. A normotic person is concerned with being 'a good guy' or a person 'people would like to have around'. The self is conceived of as a material object, much the way any common object is imagined. And valuing the self is determined only by the external functioning of the self, as it appears to the norm: the person's treatment of the self as an object has a quality similar to a quality control department's concern with the functioning quality of a product.

In the person who maintains a normotic personality successfully, a sense of isolation is mitigated by virtue of his ability to mingle with objects and to feel identified with the commodity object world. For instance, driving a car that one is proud of may be an unconscious act of marriage. In this way, products become part of one's family, and the normotic's family of objects extends itself throughout the material object world. The sense of 'family' is revealed when the normotic is in a strange environment. When travelling, the normotic may be quite unhappy because he cannot find any common or family object. In such a world of alien objects there is an increased strain to maintain his familiar internal sense of self and of well-being, so that the simple discovery of a familiar object, such as Coca-Cola, can be greeted with an affection and celebration that other people reserve only for human beings.

Conclusion

There is a personality type that we psychoanalysts have tended to neglect in our writings, because, as Winnicott has suggested, this disturbance lies along the axis of the normal. Yet, if we look closely, we can observe that some persons are abnormally normal. They are unusually rooted in being objective, both in their thinking and in their desire. They achieve a state of abnormal normality by eradicating the self of subjective life, as they strive to become an object in their own being.

In his cultivation of material phenomena the normotic has become an object, both for himself and for his others: an object with no subject, an object alive and happy in a material world. Such a person suggests that mind itself, in particular the unconscious, is an archaism, a thing to be abandoned in the interests of human progress.

Chapter 4

The destiny drive

The psychoanalytic process contains within it two seemingly opposed elements: a deconstructive procedure and an elaborative process. The patient brings a dream, a scrap of narrative, a random thought, and the analyst, by asking for associations, breaks down the manifest text of the material to reveal the unconscious latent content. In some respects this is an act of destruction, and most analysts are well accustomed to the patient's initial distress over having his manifest context (his word) deconstructed in this manner. In time, however, the patient not only accustoms himself to this dismantling of his discourse, but soon joins in the process. Analyst and patient then engage in a mutual destruction of manifest texts to voice the latent thoughts of the repressed unconscious.

Interestingly, such deconstruction is possible only if the analysand elaborates latent thoughts through the semantic migrations of free association. Perhaps such elaborations are themselves deconstructions as the ceaseless waves of displaced signifiers, seeming to represent a vast sea of meanings, leave traces in the sand, to reveal the secrets of this other world. If so, analysis needs the fecund elaborations provided by free association, a movement away from the latent unconscious, in order to suggest the secret sub-text. To dismantle the patient must construct. To find the truth all patients must lie.

Another elaborative feature of the analytic process is the patient's transference.

Psychoanalysis as an elaboration of true self

The patient's unconscious use of the psychoanalyst in the transference is seemingly an elaborative rather than a deconstructive process, as the analysand cumulatively constructs his object world through the person of the analyst. If the dismantling of the dream's manifest text illuminates the analytical side of the psychoanalytic process, the articulating of the transference exemplifies the elaborative factor. A patient begins analysis with some transference idea of the analyst, perhaps an avuncular figure. In the months to follow he experiences the analyst differently according to the varying elements of his personality. Of course, the transference uses of the analyst, like the free association to the dream text, are a deconstruction, a dismantling of the analyst's 'true' or 'manifest' personality.

And the establishments of transference have a constructive logic. Just as dream analysis unveils a chain of signification through free association, so too the analysand reveals through the transference the psycho-logical affiliations between elements of the mother's, father's, and child selves' personalities, engaged as they were in living and creating a life together. As a personality field, the analyst is also used to elaborate the analysand's idiom, but this is less easily objectified than the patient's dream report or transference construction.

In some respects, however, the analyst's mental relation to these two factors – the deconstructive and the elaborative – is different. In breaking down manifest texts, he searches the material to discover important signifiers of meaning. As a transference figure, he is used as an object, and his mental state is receptive rather than analytic. Winnicott wrote of a 'natural evolution of the transference' and suggested that this process should not be disrupted by the 'making of interpretations'. He did not mean that the analyst should not interpret: he meant that the analyst should not be engaged in making interpretations. By stressing the making of interpretation as disruptive, he acknowledged that sometimes we feel obliged to make an interpretation because we imagine this to be our task as analysts. And the 'making' of an interpretation may preoccupy the analyst for the better part of a session, interfering with his more receptive frame of mind.

Clearly, if the transference is viewed as partly a natural and evolving process, then psychoanalysis sets in motion a constructive articulation of the patient's object world. The analyst's task here, at least as Winnicott viewed it, is to give the patient time to establish and articulate his internal world. This, of course, does not necessitate abandonment of the deconstructive procedure in analysis. In fact, mental life is sufficiently complex and sophisticated to embrace such a relatively small contradiction. We can continue to ask for the analysand's associations and break down his manifest texts without disturbing the evolution of the transference which moves in a different category of signification.

But in dwelling on these two different valences of the analytical procedure – deconstruction and elaboration – I think we can say that the deconstruction of the material as an object is part of the search for meaning, and the elaboration of the self through the transference is part of the establishment of meaning. The need to know and the force to become are not exclusive, but the latter element of the analytic process has received less attention that it deserves and is my focus now.

The true self and the use of the object

By allowing the patient to use him as an object in the transference, Winnicott facilitated the establishment of self states, many of which had only been a possibility. He understood the analytic situation to be a potential space. Its potential was largely the analyst's creation. If the analyst was inattentive to the patient's need to create his own transference object, then analytic practice, of sorts, existed, but one could not speak of potential space. Through the illusions of the transference, the patient could bring into life elements of the mother, the father, siblings, and parts of his child self. Bringing to life is an important feature of the nature of the transference. There is a difference between talking about the mother, the father, and former child selves, and *being* the mother or father or a child self. Only by being someone or something is the patient able to establish elements of the self in psychoanalysis.

In his complex and interesting paper 'The use of an object', Winnicott (1969a) wrote that the infant's capacity to use an object followed on his ability to relate to the object. To some this seems a callous reversal of priorities. How can using someone be maturationally more promising than relating to someone? It's a fair question, but relating to the object refers to the depressive position, and the infant's anxiety about harming the object. In the depressive position, the infant realizes his hate could harm the (internal) love object, and reparative work is necessary to repair the internal object although, of course, this also involves actions in the actual world.

The concept of the use of the object assumes that the child has a fairly secure sense of his love of the object so that hate is allowed without decomposing the ego or its objects. This internal work allows for appreciative recognition that the actual object has, in any event, survived its own destruction as an internal object. The survival of the actual object is both a relief and a new beginning. The child knows now that he can assume his love of the object in order to use it (in phantasy and in reality) without concern about its well-being. 'Because of the survival of the object,' Winnicott writes, 'the subject may now have started to live a life in the world of objects, and so the subject stands to gain immeasurably' (1969a: 90).

What does it mean to 'live a life in the world of objects'? Do we not all live in a world of objects? Do we know of anyone who does not? The issue Winnicott addresses can only be understood if we grasp that he does not assume that we all 'live' a life. We may construct the semblance of such and certainly the false self attests to this. But to live a life, to come alive, a person must be able to use objects in a way that assumes such objects survive hate and do not require undue reparative work.

Relationship as a defence against usage can be seen most clearly in the life of sexual couples. In lovemaking, foreplay begins as a act of relating. Lovers attend to mutual erotic interests. As the economic factor increases, this element of lovemaking will recede somewhat (though not disappear) as the lovers surrender to that ruthlessness inherent in erotic excitement. This ruthlessness has something to do with a joint loss of consciousness, a thoughtlessness which is incremental to erotic intensity. It is a necessary ruthlessness as both lovers destroy the relationship in order to plunge into reciprocal orgasmic use. Indeed the destruction of relationship is itself pleasurable and the conversion of relating to using transforms ego libido into increased erotic drive. If a couple cannot assume this essential destructiveness, erotic intensity may not give in to mutual orgasm. Instead, reparation may be the fundamental exchange between such couples with partners entering into prolonged mother–child scenarios, of cuddling, holding, or soothing. This may be because such persons have not been able to experience a good destruction of the object, and reparative work is activated during the arrival of instinctual urges. When this happens, sexual uses of the object may be enacted as dissociated activities. Instead lovers may masturbate each other, with one partner relating to the other's sexual needs and mothering them through it, or at an extreme, in the perverse act, the couple may wear interesting garments and introduce curious acts to entirely split off the destructive side of erotic life, in a kind of performance art.

In some ways the analytic relationship is akin to the above relation of lovers. Some analysands are so frightened by their destructive phantasies, or, by the effect of such feelings, by a fear of being torn to pieces by the analyst, that they cannot bring themselves to use the analyst as an object. This may show up ironically enough in the form of a continuous self-analysis, with the patient rigorously analysing himself in the presence of the analyst whom he seeks, if anything, as a supervisor. Or the patient may simply, as we know, keep silent about the more disturbing feelings and talk about something removed from the person of the analyst.

But there are patients who seem to have an uncanny ability to use us as an object in the transference. By discussing one patient briefly I think I can make this point clear.

Jerome

Jerome was a stocky East European man in his mid-forties when he came for analysis. He had been in psychotherapy for some years and had previously sought analysis, but had been refused because he was considered too paranoid for analytic treatment. When I saw him, it was true that he was harassed by ideas of reference, and many sessions were filled with preoccupations about what other people were thinking about him, or saying about him, and how he was going to gain his revenge. Analytic hours became painstaking reports on how someone had slighted him and what he had done to retaliate, or what he would do to continue his campaign against the person. Whenever possible, I would make an interpretation in the transference, but he insisted that he trusted me and that he was not suspicious of me. Over time he became more critical of me, saying that I lived with certain analytical prejudices which he found unfortunate. One such prejudice was to have in my mind the idea that he suffered a depression; he did not want me to talk about his hate leaving him depleted, because he experienced the interpretation itself as contaminating him with the very affect I described. This led to a useful period of working on how he needed to preserve me as an unreal object in order to protect himself against an imagined revenge on my part.

But the fact was that his narratives were conveyed from the same self state, day in and day out. He was always tentative, anxious, intense, and somewhat irritable. He reported events in the same manner, listened to what I said carefully, usually did not reply, or agreed, and then would proceed to talk about something else. While I could persuade myself that I was analysing the patient's transference to me, that I was putting it into words, including sharing my sense that he was keeping a certain psychic distance from me, the fact is that I became troubled by the rut we seemed to be in.

Then one day Jerome changed the course of his analysis. He came to a session with a smile on his face and chuckled to himself as he lay on the couch. I commented on this, and he seemed anxious and uncertain about what to say. I noted this and said that whatever it was he had thought, it seemed to have left him worried. He then spent some time trying to talk but not talk about what had been on his mind. He told me that he had been thinking about the patient who had preceded him. As he did so, he suggested that he had mixed feelings about the patient and told me about his previous therapist who had interpreted to him often about his sibling rivalry. As he talked about this, the image of the previous patient came to my mind, and the idea of rivalry did too. But these discourses still did not feel right to me. I concentrated on his chuckle and said that nonetheless he seemed to have gained some amusement from the previous patient: did he intend to keep this pleasure to himself? I said this in a playful manner. I am sure that I worded it this way because he was ready for a comment such as this, and then Jerome told me the truth. On the way to his hour, while passing by the door by which patients leave, he had had an impish thought. He wondered what I would do if he knocked on the door. He imagined that I would open the door to find him wearing cowboy boots and a Stetson hat. He would then rather awkwardly peer into the room, introduce himself to the patient (whom he imagined to be a woman) and say in a Texan drawl, 'Well, how de do Dr Bollas! Be seeing you for one of our great meetings just as soon as you're finished with the little lady here.'

And that was it. I found his daydream aptly funny and I laughed. Even in reporting the fantasy, the patient had been quite worried by my response, but he was greatly relieved that I had found it funny. I told him why I found it amusing. Here he imagined something that clever I certainly could not interpret my way through. Yes, it would certainly be an impossible moment for me! I congratulated him on his invention. He then embellished the idea of surprising me and for the next two weeks he would come to sessions with yet another story of putting me in a difficult situation, one that inevitably caused him great humour. And I must say, I found these vignettes funny.

The point is that he quite changed within himself through his imaginary use of me. He was still somewhat hesitant, but he was more confident than I had seen him before, and much more likeable. His paranoid thoughts and revenge plots diminished over the next few months until they completely disappeared. He found his way to create an imaginary me, and then through more direct expressions of feeling, disagreement, anger, and difference, he established different self states in my presence. I do not mean to suggest that these were either unconscious or conscious roles that he enacted. He had rarely forcefully disagreed with anyone. This had left him in a very frustrated and highly mentated world with aggression becoming omnipotent destructiveness. So when he 'abused' me in phantasy by making me ridiculous, which I enjoyed, he discovered a pleasure in aggression.

Eventually, he would disagree forcefully with interpretations that I made and he did so with a clarity and acuity of perception that had been missing.

If we view this from a certain perspective, then it's possible to say that through my willingness to be used as an object, announced in some respects through a very slight though different playfulness in my orientation to his presence, the patient was able to invent me anew in the sessions. As I desisted from interpreting the content of his imagining and instead simply took pleasure in his inventions, I believe I created a certain freedom for him to play without such activity being prematurely moved into the domain of analytical reflection. This seemed to announce to the patient that it was now quite safe for him to change his use of me as an object. Perhaps the months of interpretive work had gained effect. The patient could now play with the analyst, his prior persecutory anxieties having been worked through. The fact that I responded to the slightly different use of me facilitated his spontaneous articulations. He could forget how I felt, he could abandon his worry about whether he was damaging me, and he could forget being serious as a way of forestalling any imagined revenge on my part. He was able to do this because in effect, as the object, I announced, 'I'm capable of a change of use'.

My willingness to be imagined evoked a different unconscious aim in the patient. Whereas before we can say that the aim was to understand his internal object world and to learn something of his mental processes, the new aim in the sessions was to set aside that priority in order to act. Such acting was a means of establishing domains for true self articulations.

For example, many months later, when we had time to reflect on his many imaginings, we could see that the Texan with the Stetson reflected a choice of object determined by his personal idiom. As a boy he played at being a cowboy who strode about the streets of his neighbourhood. I think it signified confidence and phallic capability. In the context of the session, viewed from a transference perspective, it indicated oedipal rivalry with me.

The patient had to be ruthless in his use of me. He had to be beyond concern. In this I think he was assisted by my slight celebration of his right to destroy me. I think that this ability to enjoy destroying me was partly accomplished through interpretive work that had accomplished an internal structural change in the patient. But he was further enabled to destroy me without inner persecution because I enjoyed it. What I did is not dissimilar from what a good enough mother does when she celebrates the infant's aggression. And, of course, my celebration of him was a symbolic act, rather than a literal act of mothering, the paradigm of aggression as acceptable was communicated to him unconsciously, and as soon as he understood this, he changed. It actually occurred within one session.

To be sure, this therapeutic experience would in and of itself be insufficient to effect a lasting psychological change. When the patient was ready for it, we looked back on what had happened and analysed my contribution to the change, his response to it, his use of me, and how this enabled him to be aggressive without persecution. But with this good enough experience inside him, I think the patient had that kind of self that could then work more fruitfully with ordinary analytic interpretation. He did not feel deprived by insight but enhanced by it. Before, even though he rarely alluded to it, he often felt that I somehow diminished him by interpreting his destructiveness, and he felt despair about his future.

On the differentiation of fate and destiny

In considering the elaborative factor of a psychoanalysis, I find it useful to consider the idea of destiny and to distinguish a person's sense of destiny from his sense of fate. In classical literature, fate and destiny tend to be used synonymously, although occasionally we can observe some difference in their use. In the *Aeneid*, Juno calls upon the fates to intervene on her behalf against Aeneas, but her wishes are thwarted because Aeneas' destiny does not permit such an intervention. This brings to mind an interesting distinction between the two concepts. I have not found a single instance in classical literature where destiny intervenes as a capricious or destructive act on the part of one of the gods. The course of destiny can be altered, but this is usually through the epic hero's interpretation of his destiny. On the other hand fate, or the fates, do intervene quite often, and it's possible to speak of capricious fates. Not until the seventeenth century do we observe an increasing differentiation between these terms, when destiny becomes a more positive concept depicting that course that is a potential in one's life. One can fulfil one's destiny if one is fortunate, if one is determined, if one is aggressive enough. Possibly the idea of fate derives from an agrarian culture where people are dependent on the seasons and the weather for their nurturance, thus giving man a sense that his life is very much up to the elements. If this is true, then destiny as a positive factor may be linked with the rise of the middle class as individuals who, through vision and labour, are able to take some control of their lives and chart their future.

Fate derives from the Latin *fatum* which is the past participle of *fari* which means to speak. 'Fatum' is 'a prophetic declaration', and 'fatus' is an oracle. Webster's *New Twentieth Century Dictionary* states that fate is 'The power supposed to determine the outcome of events before they occur'. This is an interesting definition and helps us to differentiate between the meaning of fate and of destiny. If we review the classical literature, I think that we will find that fate is usually announced through an oracle, or the words of a person, as, for example, when Oedipus' fate is spoken by the oracle of Apollo at Delphi. Oedipus' destiny, however, is determined by the chain of events that the oracle announces. Destiny, from the Latin *destinare*, means to fasten down, secure, or make firm, and the word destination is a derivative of this root. Thus destiny is linked to action rather than words. If fate emerges from the word of the gods, then destiny is a preordained path that man can fulfil. I think it is of interest that one of the clearest distinctions between these terms emerges in the twentieth century in *The American College Dictionary* which states:

> *Fate* stresses the irrationality and impersonal character of events: 'it was Napoleon's fate to be exiled'. The word is often lightly used, however: 'it was my fate to meet him that very afternoon'. *Destiny* emphasizes the idea of an unalterable course of events, and is often used of a propitious fortune: 'a man of destiny'; 'it was his destiny to save his nation'.

What place do these terms have in a psychoanalysis? The person who is ill and comes to analysis either because of neurotic symptoms, or characterological fissures, or psychotic ideas and pains, can be described as a fated person. That is, he is suffering from something which he can specify and which has a certain power in his life to seriously interfere with his capacity to work, find pleasure, or form intimate relationships. And we could say that the classical symptom is a kind of oracle: figure it out, unravel it through associations and the discovery of its latent meaning, and one can be free of that curse which its unknownness has sponsored. But along with the fate a person brings to analysis is a destiny which can only be a potential whose actualization depends less on the sleuth-like unravelling of the oracular symptomatology or the dream, than it does on the movement into the future through the usage of the object, a development that psychoanalysts term the transference.

In endeavouring to use these two concepts in a psychoanalytic sense, I must create further distinctions between them. I believe we can use the idea of fate to describe the sense a person may have, determined by a life history, that his true self has not been met and facilitated into lived experience. A person who feels fated is already someone who has not experienced reality as conducive to the fulfilment of his inner idiom. Thus I can link the sense of fate to the concept of the false self and to Winnicott's idea of reactive living. And such a person, frustrated at the very core of his being and relating, will project into his internal objects split-off aspects of this true self, thus giving to internal objects a certain further power to fate his life. Indeed, classical man's fate, mediated through an oracular voice, may be based on split-off parts of the self preserved as hallucinations. The intervention of fate would, then, be a return of a split-off part of the self (or other).

It is to the idea of destiny that I now turn. We can use this concept to address the evolution of the true self, to ask of any individual whether or not he is fulfilling his destiny. There is, as I have said, an urge to establish one's self. This destiny drive is that force imminent to the subject's idiom in its drive to achieve its potential for person elaboration. Through mental and actual objects this idiom seeks to articulate itself through the 'enchainments' of experience.

Idiom and destiny

For classical man, a sense of destiny would refer to the parts of the self that have not been split off and remain 'inside' the subject, giving him a sense of being on the right track. To some extent, then, heredity, biology, and environment are factors contributing to one's destiny. A mother can either be fundamentally a fateful presence or an object through whom the infant establishes and articulates aspects of his destiny. What do I mean by this?

By sustaining the infant's illusion that he creates his world, the mother, from Winnicott's point of view, enables the infant to experience his objects as subjective in origin. Thus object orientation and subsequent object relating emerge from this primary experience that objects derive from one's creativity. Naturally the infant will actually be disillusioned, both by the mother's ordinary failures and by the many lessons culled from reality, but the illusion of primary subjectivity will not completely disappear. In my view, it simply means that the infant, the child, and then the adult will carry an internal sense of creating his own life, even if the structures of society, the laws of one's culture, and the course of events cannot possibly be said to evolve out of the subject's true self. But the maternal provision of an illusion of creativity, which sponsors an experience but not a sense of omnipotence, marries up with the destiny drive which we can think of as an internal sense of personal evolution through space and time. After all, in some ways, this is what developmental theory is about: an evolution that traces the progressive maturation of the individual.

A sense of destiny, then, would be a feeling that the person is fulfilling some of the terms of his inner idiom through familial, social, cultural, and intellectual objects. I believe that this sense of destiny is the natural course of the true self through the many types of object relations and that the destiny drive emerges, if it does, out of the infant's experience of the mother's facilitation of true self movement. The true self, as Winnicott suggested, can evolve through maternal adaptation and responds to the quality of care the child receives from the mother and the father, as well as from the school and the peer world. Does the object world, in other words, provide the right conditions for the child to evolve his idiom, to establish his personality in such a way as to feel both personally real and alive, and to articulate the many elements of his true self?

Destiny

When Freud wrote of endopsychic perception – an ability to visualize the inner workings of the subject's mind – he argued that such perceptions were projected into objects to form, for example, the structure of myths. In *Totem and Taboo* (1913) he said that myths partly described the structure of the human mind.

We may certainly wonder if those factors in the ego that make endopsychic perception and projection possible also work on the true self, to, as it were, perceive the potential idiom that we are, and to project it in dreams, personal myths, daydreams, and visions of the future. Endopsychic projection of our idiom means that we are ever so slightly led by our projections, that we have a sense of direction built into our existence. (This loss of a sense of direction might help us to understand psychotic patients who often project the loss of an inner sense of direction.) Perhaps if the child is living from the true self, if his right to *jouissance* is sustained by the parents, he will feel inclined to receive endopsychic perceptions of his idiom and to project them into objects, as early formations of the path of desire. A child of three, receiving such a bit of idiom urge, may imagine himself swimming the crawl. This could be an endopsychic projection of a personality potential which objectifies its possibility in the image, and perhaps the eventual action, of swimming. Another child will imagine playing the piano, another playing football, etc. If all goes well, a child will develop passionate interests in objects, many of which project the child into the future. The destiny drive, then, makes use of unconscious projections of idiom potential into objects which are organized by the child and set up for true self experiencing. If so, then the urge to elaborate has the assistance of an ego capable of endopsychic projection of the figurations of idiom, imagining objects which are projections of idiom, and through the use of the actual object, the child comes into passionate expression of himself.

What are the implications of this idea of a sense of destiny in the clinical situation? In what ways can the psychoanalyst use this concept?

It should be clear that I think that one of the tasks of an analysis is to enable the analysand to come into contact with his destiny, which means the progressive articulation of his true self through many objects. The analytic process, then, becomes a procedure for the establishment and elaboration of one's idiom rather than simply the deconstruction of material or the analytic mapping of mental processes and the fate of internal objects. By introducing an element of play in my work with Jerome, I signified myself as an object available for a particular use, in order to facilitate the patient's elaboration of a part of himself that he had yet to experience.

This view of analysis holds that the patient's provision of material should at certain times be treated as if it does not as yet yield a latent content which could be found tucked away in the slips of language. In some respects, the latent content, if we think of the true self, can only be discovered through object usage, as otherwise it could not be established, and therefore could never be found.

The analyst destroys the patient's manifest texts in order to reveal unconscious meanings, and the patient destroys the analyst through that particular object usage we call transference. Each transference use of the analyst is in some respects a destruction of the analyst's true personality, and this ruthless employment of the analyst is essential to the patient's articulation of his early environment, representations of his psychic life, or elaboration of his true self through experience.

I suggest that for a good destruction of the analyst to take place, one that is not constituted out of the death instinct, but is part of the life instinct, the analyst must indicate to the patient, at the right moment, that he is ready for destruction. The 'to be destroyed' analyst has a different function – indeed is a different object – from that analyst who deconstructs the material. And I am quite sure that when I concentrate on interpreting some aspects of the material or the transference that I announce to the patient that I am the thinking or reflecting object. In some respects I would then be that object that is a mental process, part of the reflective procedure established by both patient and analyst. As the object who is somewhat playful, I am the object of play. The technical aspect of when the analyst should function differently in order to provide a different object for the patient is obviously a crucial issue, and one that makes analytic work challenging and creative.

Some analysts will immediately object to the idea that the analyst should aim to be any object for the patient. This smacks of an active technique. But one of the flaws to this kind of objection, it seems to me, is the thoughtless assumption that ordinary or classical technique is not active. We know in fact that it is. The analyst asks the patient to lie on the couch. That's an action. He remains silent and does not engage in socially conventional forms of behaviour. That's an action. He does not answer questions. These actions form part of the psychoanalytic praxis.

Part of Winnicott's (1947) conceptualization of the countertransference is that in part this amounts to an act of provision. The analyst provides the patient with his silence, his absence of socialization, his evenly hovering attentiveness. This provision elicits a certain kind of self state in the patient, one that is conducive to analysis. Within the same spirit of provision one can talk of the analyst's use of humour as provision. It is a way of announcing to the patient that the analyst is at play and in that moment the analytical situation shifts slightly from a space which potentializes reflective consideration of unconscious contents to a place that is a potential for the imaginative use of the analyst.

Changing in one's use to a patient is not, however, an applied act. The analyst has no choice. As the analysand uses the analyst, so too is the analyst affected. A funny remark inspires a humorous response in the analyst, who is used as a bearer of that which is conveyed in humour. Often a patient will diminish the analyst evoking an increased irritation in the analyst, which may eventually change the analyst into a challenging object. Jill is a case in point.

Jill

Jill had been in analysis with me for two years, and I knew from her accounts of relations with men that when she felt slighted, she would give a bloke the cold shoulder. I knew, of course, it would be my fate to be the object of such coldness, and, sure enough, this happened. Initially she would leave a session, wordless, her head virtuously erect, her movements reminiscent of Boadicea sallying forth, her gaze fixed straight ahead. This started as a Friday session phenomenon and I commented on it, saying that she was upset and cross over our relationship being interrupted by the weekend. When she would go silent, as in 'stony silent', during a Friday hour, I would say that she had just experienced the separation and that it felt awful. These comments did not enable her to talk about her state of mind other than to inspire a strange sort of strangled speech as she suffered to speak to me. 'Well, I *suppose* you could put it that way, couldn't you?' she would say, and, if I would follow up with, 'You might put it differently?' she would reply 'Pardon me?' I would repeat myself and she would say 'Possibly', or 'I don't know; you are the analyst, *aren't you?*' in a witheringly sarcastic manner. In the early stages of this enactment the patient would emerge from such moods to tell me how she had been feeling, and even laugh at how awful she had been to me. But as time passed these moods increased both in frequency and duration. It was no longer organized around a weekend; it could, and eventually did, last all week – or even for ten days. Each session I would take this up as an expression of her cold fury with me that I was such a disappointing analyst, because I would not be with her all the time. She was going to eject me (as she felt cast off) to make me suffer. Sometimes an entire session would pass, and she would say nothing. At other times she would say 'You *are* right, I am going to punish you'. Occasionally with transcendental effort she would rise above me and glutted with reluctance tell me some episode from her work or life that had upset or pleased her.

We all know what it's like to get up in the morning and draw the curtains to have our first look at the day's weather. It can be a good moment of anticipation. But walking into the waiting room to greet Jill reminded me of those rather dreadful mornings in London when it had been raining and overcast continuously for six weeks, so that in drawing the curtain, one more or less knew what to expect.

I worked with a determined variation of one essential interpretation: that she felt rejected and in turn aimed to give me the cold shoulder. As abandonment by the mother was an important theme in her life, I said that she aimed for mother–me to have a dose of abandonment, a 'shared' experience that brought us closer together as victims of sorts.

After a while I actually thought to myself that I didn't think I could stand to be with this patient one moment longer. In particular I found the extremely cold and dead partings unspeakably awful, and even though I interpreted from counter-transference that she was recreating an early experience of being cast off by the mother, this did not alter her self state.

Then one day, after ten minutes of her killing silence, I said, 'You know, *you* are a monster'. I said it quietly and matter of factly. She inhaled and in a kind of sepulchral cough said 'Why do you say that?' 'Because you are a monster', I replied. She said nothing and lapsed back into silence. 'I suppose', I said, 'that you are now going to be silent for the remaining twenty minutes?' She was silent. 'Well of course you intend to; I can see that', I said and then I went on: 'But you are being monstrous, and this is inhuman behaviour on your part'. At this point she clenched her fists, burst into tears of fury and said, 'I cannot help it. There is nothing I can do about it. That's all.' She reached for her handbag, fumbled about in it and produced a mighty white cloth which she blew into with extraordinary force. 'You certainly can help it', I replied. 'Well, I'm not', she said. A longer silence, the session ended, and the next day she walked ahead of me to the consulting room like the Statue of Justice irately compelled by necessity to assume human form in order to punish the more inaccessible criminals such as psycho-analysts. 'How *dare* you call me a monster!' she cried out. She went on for some minutes saying that I had no right to say something like that to her. I was meant to tell her what I thought was behind her conflicts, to help her, not to assault her like I had. I said, 'I am not sorry that I said you were a monster, because you are being one, but I do regret that it had to be said to you in that way'. Again she went into a fury, and then I said, 'Do you have any idea what it's like to sit with you day in, day out, with you an absolute ice maiden of rage? Do you? Well, let me tell you. It's dreadful. We have analysed why you do this, but I think understanding is not what you want. You insist that I suffer! Well, let me tell you, it's monstrous, and you had better do something about it if you ever expect to rid yourself of your terrible moods.' It is difficult to recreate my state of mind. I do have to emphasize that I was actually suffering, and that I had decided to combat my patient's use (abuse) of me in the transference rather than simply to interpret it.

To my surprise and relief, Jill said, 'Well, I have been very cruel to you, I know, but you have hurt me' – referring to my failure to provide her with actual love. In the months following this session, whenever she would resume a period of killing silences, I would combat her, 'Ah! The deadly silence again!' and she would leap into fury, but eventually this shifted to more aggressive encounters with the patient being counter-combative in a specific way, occasionally spelling out how something I had said, or not said, had upset her. I supported her right to 'quarrel' with me, and in my view these experiences in her analysis were important to her accomplishment of new self experiences. By quarrelling with me she engaged in reciprocal aggression with an object, an experience previously unknown to her. This illustrates another way in which an analyst's status as an object (in this instance a combative one) enables the patient to move into new self experience through the course of such use.

Jill's experiences of her primary objects, through which she could not elaborate her true self, biased her to deaden herself and others, thus identifying with her fate and imposing it in the analysis upon me. As I am a psychoanalyst, meant to have unending supplies of patience, and as Jill was a very angry and negating patient, just being herself, it was simply my bad luck that my interpretations of the patient's negative transference had no mutative effect. My professional demeanour obliged me to remain strictly analytic and patiently and calmly to analyse the negative transference, while Jill's transference intent was to turn this demeanour against myself, to turn it into a fateful attitude. To some extent, 'You are a monster', broke the customs of analysis and emerged from another part of me, perhaps expressing the need of my true self to destroy a pathological object relation, and in order to find and use those psychoanalytic objects (including the analytic process) that form my professional identity.

My destruction of the negative transference, which had already been analysed, but remained intact, enabled the analysand to use the field of analytical objects available to her. To some extent, then, this destruction of an imposed fate enabled the patient to rediscover her true self within the psychoanalytic context. If the analysand can employ the analyst to multiple effect then an analysis is destiny, as the patient uses the analyst and the analytic process to articulate the terms of their personality.

A psychoanalysis then is a means of providing different objects for the patient who uses the objects to experience and accomplish varying self states which are derivative of the idiom of the person. Such an elaboration proceeds through the use of the analyst as a transference object where usage precedes thinking and then knowing. As I have said elsewhere (Bollas, 1987a), we could say that personal idiom is known but has not yet been thought and that it is part of the unthought known. So one of the features of a psychoanalysis is to think the unthought known, which is part of the core of the individual, and to do so through object usage and the drive to unfold the self through space and time.

Futures

A person who is fated, who is fundamentally interred in an internal world of self and object representations that endlessly repeat the same scenarios, has very little sense of a future that is at all different from the internal environment they carry around with them. The sense of fate is a feeling of despair to influence the course of one's life. A sense of destiny, however, is a different state, when the person feels he is moving in a personality progression that gives him a sense of steering his course. 'How amusing it is', writes Alice James (1979), 'to see the fixed mosaic of one's little destiny being filled out by tiny blocks of events – the enchainment of minute consequences with the illusion of choice weathering it all.' Such an enchainment also forms a basis for the subject's projection of himself in the future. Any person who is partly living from the true self will project idiom possibilities into the future, and I shall term such projections 'futures'. If we can say of most people that they have memories, so too they have futures. Of course this term is popular in economic theory. When a person buys a future, he invests in the future as favourable to his well-being. Interestingly, Freud referred to the organizations of futures in his paper on 'The uncanny' (1919): 'There are also all the unfulfilled but possible futures to which we still like to cling in phantasy, all the strivings of the ego which adverse external circumstances have crushed, and all our suppressed acts of volitions which nourish in us the illusion of Free Will' (p. 236). People who have a sense of destiny also invest psychically in the future. This involves a certain necessary ruthlessness and creative destructiveness, of the past and the present, in order to seek conditions necessary for futures.

For example, let us think of the selection of a partner. Let us imagine that I am young again and single. I see a woman whom I like and enjoy knowing, but I do not find her sexually attractive. Now let us say that a question emerges: 'Should I marry her?' What right have I to refuse to do this if we add that this person would like to marry me? Now let us add that if I do not marry this person, she will feel terribly upset by my refusal. Should I not marry her, because I know her to be a very decent, intelligent, and creative person? Well, of course, we know that some people would marry under these conditions and, indeed, it is one of the interesting facts of life that in the course of the marriage the man might become sexually attracted to the woman. Or we know that he might marry out of unconscious reparative needs. But I am referring to the essential ruthlessness that is a factor in the refusal to marry, a ruthlessness that in effect amounts to the following statement, 'No, I am not going to marry you, because I am not sexually attracted to you'.

The choice of partner, of vocation, of city or country, can be made for similarly ruthless reasons – an essential ruthlessness, which is part of the destiny drive. There is an urge to invest in futures which to the true self are potential spaces not yet immediately at hand. Many people who live from the true self, relatively unhindered by conflict, may have a sense of destiny which generates futures, or visions of the self in a temporal progression beyond the present. That 'inner sense' that people rely upon to choose an object is a sense of destiny, and some individuals may root about amongst present objects in order to select a suitable object to fulfil a future. Imagine that I have a sense of the man I feel myself to be, and that this self is contingent upon my choice of partner. If I choose the right partner who knows the essence of me, then I shall be freer to be my self than otherwise might be the case. Or imagine I am at university, and I have a choice: do I study psychology, literature, history, or social anthropology? These disciplines will, to some extent, overlap. But as I imagine myself in the future, working in these areas, which one do I feel to be the evolution of my idiom? Where shall I find experiences of myself?

The person who lives from this inner sense of destiny will have an intuitive knowledge of object choice based on the need to express the idiom of the true self, and will in turn have imaginary objects (futures) that are visions of potential use. Such objects, yet to be met, nonetheless collect interest, as the subject will explore objects related to this future object, and perhaps acquire a 'skill' that is meanwhile quite useful and eventually of further use in the time to come. One of my children, for example, developed a passion for BMX bicycles. He decorated his bicycle handsomely, tinkered with it endlessly, and drove it mercilessly. It was clear to him that although it was a bicycle, it was also an intermediate object that was intrinsically linked to a future. In this respect, it was also a car. Indeed, its decorations, his freely supplied sound effects, his fascination with its speed, meant that he was really driving a Porsche. Present objects are often pregnant with futures and a person who has an inner sense of his or her destiny will, if conditions present, choose objects that facilitate access to futures.

A person who feels fated may imagine futures that carry the weight of despair. Instead of feeling the energy of a destiny drive and of 'possessing' futures which nourish the person in the present and creatively serve to explore pathways for potential travel (through object use), the fated person only projects the oracular. A glimpse into the future, a vision from fate, only echoes the voice of the mother, the father, or the socio-cultural context which oppresses the self. There is, then, no wish to call up futures, as the person does not wish to evoke painful memories. Indeed we can speak of the repression of futures, in the same way as we speak of the repression of memories. If they contain too much distress, futures are as liable to be repressed as painful memories.

The loss of futures for a child is a very particular kind of loss. A simple and obvious example is the child who, when losing a parent, loses the future relation to the object. Each child unconsciously invests in the parent as a future object, and has an unconscious sense of the potential uses of the object throughout development, a use that is inextricably linked to the elaboration of the true self. Thus the loss of a parent forecloses, in some respects, the use of the parental object, the articulation of self via the object, and therefore those futures that derive from the successful use of objects. A sense of fate, the projection of the present terms into the future, will prevail, and the drive to fulfil one's destiny, to drive the true self into being and relating, will not be accomplished.

What is that grief that occurs when a child or adolescent loses futures? In a certain respect it is a loss of potential selves, a mourning for what could have been and now will not be. The acute anguish, if not rage, of such a person is extraordinary – and understandable. Rage over being fated, rather than destined, may result in the negative celebration of fatedness, as in *Richard III*, when Richard tries to make his fate into a destiny by assuming a pseudo-joyful 'control' over his future by being monstrous. But for those of us who watch or read the play, his futures are projected forms of grief and encapsulated states of pain.

It may be an essential part of analytic work to help a patient transform fatedness into destiny and to gain futures. Nancy comes to mind.

Nancy

Nancy is an intelligent, thoughtful, punkish young woman who contacted me for analysis, or, rather, who used a friend to contact me. A colleague called me and said somewhat apologetically that his son knew a young woman who was training to be a solicitor and who wanted analysis. Would I give a consultation? I said I would be pleased to do so. My colleague paused and then said somewhat ill at ease, 'Well, I should tell you that she can be rather difficult'. He said that Nancy had expressed interest in seeing me (she knew of me through the analyst's son) but had said she had 'no idea' when or if she would ever contact me. Would it be possible for me to remember her name and see her in the future, even if I did not at that time have a vacancy? I agreed.

Over a year went by, and one day a very charming voice on the phone said, 'Is this *Christopher* Bollas?' in a way that I quite liked my name being used. 'This is Nancy X. You won't know me but . . .' and she narrated the account of her contact with my colleague. I said, 'Yes, I do remember. I have been expecting to hear from you.' We set a time for her to come and see me.

I will not describe the first meeting, except to say that I found her mischievous and depressed at the same time. She said she wanted to begin analysis but could only come at hours completely determined by her, changing week to week, but she would call me each day to tell me when she would come. I was astonished that she seemed to be serious, and, after saying that this was impossible, I stressed that she seemed determined to put me in a situation where it would appear that I had failed her. We parted, and another fifteen months passed before I saw her again.

The analysis did eventually begin and was interesting and worthwhile – for both of us. I will only focus on one element – the element of fate. For Nancy had, as I had seen, this remarkable knack of making extraordinarily arbitrary and silly statements which sealed actions. I learned about this from her narration of life with her boyfriend. While they were both relaxing in the living room, Nancy would say, 'We are going to the opera!' This would come completely out of the blue. She did not say, 'I would like to go to the opera', or indicate that it was a wish. She said it as if announcing the evening's fate. This sudden oracular voice typified her in other relations as well and would have seriously jeopardized her career had she not been in some ways remarkably responsible when working on a task. She was only this way with colleagues in a social situation, and the rest of the time she had an impish smile playing across her face: a reminder that she could and would announce sudden action that would alter the course of life at any moment.

Once I knew of Nancy's early life, it was not difficult to understand this characteristic, for her parents had treated her similarly. They periodically intervened fatefully in her life by commanding her (and one another) into certain drastically alternative actions, such as suddenly changing schools, clothing styles, houses, friends, or vacations. Everything was topsy-turvy. What would mother or father declare next? And these declarations were fateful, as they directly affected the life of the children, who found themselves continuously cast into new situations.

At the beginning of her analysis, Nancy simply enacted the familiar environment, but in time she 'calmed down'. From this position, it was possible for us to listen to her own wishes and for her to grasp that wishing could be an internally fruitful act. She had never known what she had wanted to do. For some time she leapt into outrage whenever I made an interpretation that felt to her like an oracle. I very carefully indicated how I associated to what she said, thus helping to derive our future from her comments. In this respect, we can see how ordinary analytic attentiveness, supplemented by the analyst's associative comments, facilitates the right of the patient to live from the core of the self, and for the destiny of associations in the analytic hour to be determined from and by the true self.

On reflection, Nancy's impulsive announcements were somewhere between fateful commandments and destined actions. An impulse could be seen as an expression of true self movement, so when Nancy declared 'We are going to the opera', she was partly espousing a future to give course to an element needing some particular experience at that moment. But Nancy's seeming spontaneity always occurred in relation to, and at the immediate cost of, the other, for whom her apparent destiny was the other's fate. In parodying the destiny drive in this way, I think Nancy demonstrated her experience of parents who followed their destinies at the cumulative expense of their children. The other then had to carry the burden of the self's action.

If there is a ruthlessness essential to object selection and use, such an element should obviously not become a rationale for thoughtless and egocentric action at the dynamic cost to the other. A dynamic cost is an act committed by the subject that is intrinsically destructive to the other and recurs, if not behaviourally, then intrapsychically. If Jack is at a party, sees Betty whom he courts, Mary may feel disappointed, but Jack's ruthless choice (acting only for himself) will not cause Mary dynamic harm. If, however, Jack initially courts Mary, then 'chucks' her upon seeing Betty, this is somewhat harmful. Some form of reparative work may be essential to help Mary deal with the after-effects of such an experience, as Jack has elicited her desire, engaged himself with her, then discarded her. He has been in dynamic relation to her.

Nonetheless, we often act out of self-interest, in a form of ruthlessness that we feel to be essential to the evolution of our idiom. And to varied extents, this will affect the other. As an undergraduate I studied history, and several of my professors wanted me to continue with graduate studies in that field. I chose instead to study English literature. This disappointed my professors, but I made my choice because I knew I could find more of what I was searching for through literary studies. To my mind, this is ruthlessness of a non-dynamic kind, as it is a form of object selection which does not have destruction either as its aim or as its primary effect.

Of course, we are always involved in necessary compromises between our inner drive to articulate our idiom through experiences of objects and the contexts in which we live. The internal world is the arena in which the claims of the drive and the context of our lives are objectified, particularly when the needs of the other suggest to us the necessity to restrict, delay, displace, or transform a destiny aim.

In 'A Theory for the True Self' (Bollas, 1989), I have argued that imaginative projections of true self idiom are likely, and I have used Freud's theory of endopsychic perception to argue this. I think we project our idiom into imaginary objects which then partly serve as precursors of more direct lived experience. There is an imaginative forerunner of true self action, although I think imaginative acts are already articulations of one's idiom, as the subject expresses very precise idiom features through the choice and use of imaginary objects.

In this respect, then, the dream is an even more unique event than we already know it to be. For in this special place the subject partly creates the object of his future. Is this an argument for the prophetic character of dreams? In a way, yes. 'By picturing our wishes as fulfilled', Freud wrote, 'dreams are after all leading us into the future' (1900, p. 621). Although he rightly dismissed the idea that the subject foretells the future through the work of a special part of the mind, Freud believed that as the past recreates itself in the future, the dreamer can, to an extent, correctly foretell such futures. 'Who could deny that wishes are predominantly turned towards the future?' he asks.

We may agree with Freud that a dreamer creates his future insofar as it is determined by a past, but we may add that the dream also constitutes a fictional forerunner of reality, in which the idiom of the self is played. My stress is less on the repetition of past events, than it is on a prior knowledge coming into thought through the formation of dream thoughts as an early 'playing about' with reality before the imaginary becomes the actual.

At the very least, then, the dream creates futures, visions of the self in transformed states that are nonetheless articulations of the individual's unique person. It does not simply generate futures, it is vital to the subject's formation of the future. It is where some futures are hatched. It is the origin of vision, the place where the subject plays with objects, moving through potential patterns, setting up fields of imagined persons, places, selves and events – to be there as potential actuals for future use. If we think of this in Bion's terms, when the dream produces thoughts, alpha funcion transforms idiom potential into imaginary realizations, converting personality preconceptions into imaginary realizations.

The destiny of any of us then is more than slightly determined in advance. A *déjà vu*, the sense of having lived precisely this event before, may be an existential signature of the recurring resonance between the dream and the future, as some of our action experiences will have been dreamt before.

'The greatest things that man has done, he owes to the painful sense of incompleteness of his destiny' muses Madame de Staël (quoted in Seldes, 1985: 397). This incompleteness that we must all endure is a special sense of loss, as each of us is only ever a part subject, an incomplete sample of our potential. But we are mercifully free of the ideal of completion. As it has never been accomplished, it does not form a part of our ordinary ego ideals, and many of the differing theologies of an after-life accept the impossibility of completion on earth while posing different places (a heaven) or forms (reincarnation) where presumably we continue to elaborate our potential. But we don't. We are stopped by our deaths and usually long before then – in what we modestly phrase a mid-life crisis – we have an inkling of how we shall not be destined after all to fulfil our urge to be fully present in our own existence.

The fashioning of a lifetime

In the course of a day, a week, a year, or a lifetime we are engaged in successive selections of objects, each of which suits us at the moment, 'provides' us with a certain kind of experience, and, as our choice, may serve to articulate our idiom, recall some earlier historical situation, or foreclose true self articulation.

In the last week I have read certain books. Why have I read what I have? Why have I rejected certain possibilities? When I listen to a record why do I select certain pieces of music and reject others? When I go for a walk, where do I go? When I seek a night out, which form of entertainment do I choose? Do not these choices provide textures of self experience that release me to articulate some idiom move on my part?

Sometimes we are conscious of why we choose what we do. More often than not, however, we choose our objects because we seek the experience potential of the choice. We need the object to release our self into expression. And now and then we will be quite transformed by the uncanny wedding of our idiom and an object, meeting up at just the right time. One late afternoon in the summer of 1972, I heard a performance of one of Hindemith's viola sonatas in a small church in New England. It immediately served to process a feature of my idiom, and this occasion sponsored vivid and intense feelings and ideas which lifted me into the next moments of my life. Shall we ever have the means to analyse that? Why that particular work?

When we have lived all there is of our lifetime, our families and friends will at some point look through and sort out what we call 'personal effects'. What an interesting way to describe what we leave behind. Effects. Articles of use? What I have caused to come into my existence as expressions of the very particular life I have lived? Why not borrow this ceremonial phrase and apply it to living? What are my personal effects? Where are they? As psychoanalysts we have, of course, to include the persons we affect and what we create in them of ourself and former others. Aside from this psychological establishment, we create a field of objects which serve to express our idiom and are its signature. Each of us establishes a private culture, and personal effects are those cultural objects we generate.

In health the true self continuously establishes its idiom and the fashioning of a life is the work of the destiny drive, as our urge to elaborate this idiom partly results in our creation of personal effects. As the psychoanalyst tills away, interpreting the roots of free association, identifying the branches of transference expression and reconstructing the family trees in a patient's life, he must find some way to catch glimpses of the forest. Does he have a point of view that enables him to see the analysand's culture? If he is useful as a multiple object, if his presence is the object of the patient's true self, then he will, in time, carry many of the patient's personal effects, and the destiny of the analysand will have been partly fulfilled: to establish a cultural life from the idiom of the true self.

Chapter 5

Psychic genera

Although the child's first response to a severe environmental impingement is an important part of the formation of a trauma, it is with its 'second' occurrence, upon a reawakening in consciousness, that its truly disturbing nature is revealed. Not only burdened by memories of the actual event, the person now feels inhabited by it from within the psyche–soma. Originally an externally sponsored shock, it becomes intrapsychically organized and incessantly reasserts itself. Intrapsychically sponsored eruptions of emotional turbulence emphasize the true helplessness, confusion, and isolation of the traumatized, echoing something of the child's original aloneness.

A victim of child molestation at the age of thirteen, however, may report this to a friend and be helped by the cohesive effect of narrative, even though this will not end the trauma. It is liable to an overwhelming reappearance later on, often 'triggered' by a nonmolesting event, perhaps in the course of lovemaking. At least when the thirteen-year-old becomes an adult he is likely to have a memory of turning to someone for help, and the memory of the environment's response and the therapeutics of the talking cure will be an important part of self recovery.

If a molested child of five is unable to speak of this to someone, then his problem will be compounded in adult life when an event may evoke it; for, as the child did not speak the molestation to someone in the first place, it will not have been narratively objectified. There will be no memory of having told someone about it and thus there will be no generative side to the recollection, only the trauma.

This may be one of the reasons why some adults will be confused upon experiencing an uncanny feeling that they have been the object of some abuse. Did it actually happen or is it imagined? Psychic confusion is part of the full effect of trauma because, unable to narrate the event in the first place, the person now re-experiences isolation, this time brought on by the aloneness of mental confusion. The feeling that it might not have happened, that it could be invention, underscores this person's increased lonesomeness, particularly as he is disinclined to report such feelings. A prominent feature of the original impingement is the child's felt separation from his family and fellow kind, as he is made different by the action, isolated by it, and rendered speechless.

In this chapter I shall put forward the view that trauma has an opposite – genera[1] – which is the psychic incubation of libidinal cathexes of the object world. The sense of how to gather psychic investments to an inner area of work derives from the individual's experience of elaborating his own idiom, a process that involves the selection of specific objects which release idiom to its expression. As we are born with our idiom and as it is elaborated through parental provision, the individual develops a belief in psychic dissemination, which leads him to assume that he can articulate his idiom through the psychic freedom of object representation and the liberty of object choice.

Naturally, as this freedom to evolve the self is facilitated and influenced by the mother and the father, any sense a person has of the nature of personal elaboration will bear the marks of maternal and paternal provision. In fact, what we might think of as primal genera – specific nascent factors of the infant's idiom that sponsor early aesthetic cohesions of the object world – are met by another organizing intelligence: the logics of parental provision. The question is, can the idiom of the child elicit generative parenting so that the articulations of subjectivity use the materials of reality to promote elaboration?

If genera develop through the successional elaboration of idiom, trauma leads to the person's binding of the self, which sponsors a type of psychic pain and leads to a very different kind of unconscious work. Thus these two principles, of trauma and genera, begin as fundamental ego dispositions toward reality, derived from the infant's and child's experience of the mother and the father. Children whose parents are impinging or acutely traumatizing collect such trauma into an internal psychic area which is intended to bind and limit the damage to the self, even though it will nucleate into an increasingly sophisticated internal complex as

---

1 Heretofore 'genera' has been the plural form of the noun 'genus,' which means class or kind. But a different noun structure has always been hidden within it, based on the Latin origin of the word, 'gignere,' which means to give birth. The Aryan root, 'gen,' also means to beget. In *Creative Evolution* Henri Bergson almost transformed 'genera' into a verbal noun when he linked it to reproductivity and to his concept of vital energy. In the late nineteenth century, perhaps 'genera' still carried within it the notion of a dynamically moving structure, but twentieth-century thought has denuded the word of its dynamic origins, and it is now used only to refer to classes of objects, although it would be allowed that such classes do evolve. I think it is within the spirit of the original base of this word (to give birth, to reproduce) to use 'genera' as both a singular and a plural noun, simply because the word 'genus' – its theoretically proper singular form – now definitely refers to a a single class or species, and does not contain in English a sensible verbal noun meaning. I also find that I cannot say 'a genus' when referring to the dynamic organization of an evolving psychic structure. So I suggest that we create a contemporary, though restricted usage, in which 'genera' also refers to a particular type of psychic organization of lived experience that will result in creative new envisionings of life, either in psychoanalysis or in other walks of life. In the psychoanalytic context it matches exactly with trauma. The plural noun was 'traumata,' but this is rarely used. Sometimes writers use 'traumas' for the plural form, but increasingly 'trauma' is used for both singular and plural noun forms. As the entire aim of my neologistic use of 'genera' is to pair it with 'trauma,' in order to clarify complex issues having to do with the nature of mental development, I feel justified in this small act of linguistic violence.

resonant trauma are unconsciously 'referred' to such an area for linked containment. Children who experience parents as contributing to the elaborative dissemination of their personal idiom will subsequently develop an open-mindedness to the contributing effects of the object world.

Some interpersonally derived psychic trauma are enforced mental labors in which the subject processes the other's unconscious projective identifications, which necessarily become part of oneself but which are contained and limited. If the trauma is subsequently symbolically elaborated (in discourse, painting, fiction, etc.), the aim may be to evacuate its disturbing effect through the work of repetition and displacement, while symbolically elaborated genera create intensified re-envisionings of reality which, however anguishing, are the pleasure of the ego's creativities. Psychic genera are wished-for psychic workings which reflect the subject's introjective choices as he feels free to follow the unconscious articulations of his own idiom and are part of the eros of form. The child who is binding a psychic trauma into a collection of ideas aims to minimize contact with the external world and to nullify the ideational, affective, and interpersonal effect of traumatic psychic complexes. The child who nurtures his own genera seeks novel experiences that will bring him into renewing contact with his ideational and affective states, often within an enriching interpersonal environment.

A trauma is just that, traumatic, and the subject who contains such anguishing complexes will usually not seek to symbolically elaborate them, not have them, as it were, spawn newer, more radical perspectives on life; but a trauma is represented, in actings-out, in creative works, in human relations. It is important to make clear here that the effect of trauma is to sponsor symbolic repetition, not symbolic elaboration. Nonetheless, certain writers, painters, musicians, and so forth only ever repeat themselves, and their works are valued as significant symbolizations of human life – which they no doubt are. A subject whose principle of engagement with reality is generative will seek to work unconsciously on specific issues that will enable him to re-envision his reality and in turn sponsor new ways of living and thinking. But again, it is important to qualify this: the incubation of genera can be, and usually is, the work of great personal struggle, as any change of one's status quo involves emotional turbulence.

In essence, genera are, first, the inherited proto-nucleations of any child's idiom, so that if he is free to elaborate himself, then life will be punctuated by inspired moments of self realization, deriving from the instinct to elaborate the self, which I have termed a destiny drive (Bollas, 1989b). If we look upon infants as embryonic characters and early childhood as a form of germinal settlement (which includes parental unconscious contributions), then subsequently the child and adult will be elaborating different areas of the self at different times, with differing paces of articulation, under differing circumstances. The relatively successful expression of particles of personality idiom, a movement from deep structure to the surface engagements of life, gives the adult an inner knowledge of the development over time of deeply private, as yet mentally inaccessible areas of the self.

Although this chapter focuses on how genera are formed in psychoanalysis, each of us possesses unconscious knowledge of how this is accomplished; a person's idiom is itself an implicate logic of form – partly inherited, partly acquired – which generates visions of self and object. The unconscious skill involved in selecting objects that will release this form to its realizations derives from the infant's innate ability to fashion a psychic reality from lived experience. The sense of vision that most people possess is energized by the destiny drive, the very particular urge to develop the form of one's private idiom through the articulating and elaborating experiences of object usage. 'Form, after all, is nothing but content-as-arranged,' writes Vendler (1988: 3), and in thinking of personality as form, we can say that each person's idiom is the peculiar manner each individual possesses of shaping the contents of life. Given the urge to find objects through which to come into one's shape – and to fashion the object world at the same time – I think of personality as an erotic aesthetics, an intelligence of form that desires to come into existence. This dissemination of our personality suggests principles of creativity which we may follow, the cultivation of genera being one such outcome.

Perhaps it is possible to see how trauma-developed psychic processes will be conservative, fundamentally aiming to control the psychic damage, desensitizing the self to further toxic events. Thus, trauma can be seen as allied to the indigenous inner principle of the death instinct, which aims to preserve a constant state by ridding the subject of excitation; only in the beginning trauma is the effort to rid the self of excitation sponsored by the external object (or actual other) rather than in the more classical and Kleinian formulations which emphasize the death work's effort to rid the subject of the disturbing effects of instinctual urgency. The trauma-evolving child is already a self developing along very particular lines, such as those conceptualized by Fairbairn in his theory of the infant's internalization of the bad object, where the aim is to control the negative effect of bad parenting by taking the negating objects into oneself.

The child who internalizes fundamentally generative parents – who contribute to the evolution of his personal idiom – aims to develop such inner processes and to seek excitation and novelty as means of triggering personal growth. As such, genera link up with the life instincts which aggressively seek the procreative combinings of self with object.

The child who establishes inner psychic holding areas for the containment of disturbed parental communications or shocking events seeks to break links between the referred contents and their preconscious derivatives. To use Bion's language: he attacks the linking function that is vital to K (knowledge) and works to devitalize the pain of its meaning by transforming it into −K, thereby giving to such inner experiences an empty or vacuous feel. Pain is thereby transferred into nothingness. In the child's cultivation of internal possibilities for creative revisioning of self and reality, links between inner areas of such work and the data of life that seem related to it are sought, thereby establishing a valorization of unconscious work informed by the K function.

Genera and trauma are broad principles, and psychoanalysts will be aware of the countless exceptions to the rule. A child raised by impinging parents may partly fend them off and defiantly preserve a part of himself capable of wresting contributive factors from the parents and their substitutes. He would then have his particular sense of how to be contributed to and, in turn, how to subsequently hatch intrapsychic areas for the work of genera. Alternately, a child who has facilitative parents may, as a result of the birth of a sibling, embark on a prolonged bout of unconscious hate that will convert facilitative parental endeavors into mnemic traces of parental procreativity, which is therefore envied and so the continuous source of trauma.

We can view genera from another psychoanalytic model: the topographic point of view. Freud's theory of repression identifies a crucial pathway of mental conflict, when an individual preconsciously represses unwanted feelings, ideas, and experiences to the unconscious, where such banished contents immediately constitute a nucleus of interlocking ideas. Consciousness has been denuded of a part of its contents and repression signifies a diminution in the person's self awareness. However, as such ideas are, according to Freud, instinctually driven, there is an intrinsic energy to find expression, to return to consciousness for fuller mental realization, a procedure that can only be done by changing the nuclear ideas through displacement, substitution, etc., to achieve some derivative expression. When the repressed ideas fail to find adequate escape from banishment to the system unconscious, they tend to collect to them further ideas and affects that occur in subsequent moments of consciousness as these ideas disappear from the mind like refuge seekers in the now increasing colony of banished ideas – a group that paradoxically gains in strength as it is oppressed. Psychoanalysts accept the clinical validity of this theory. They see how patients present gaps in conscious contents that point to repressed or withdrawn ideas and feelings, and how such unwanted ideas are maintained by anticathexes, by forces or mental energies opposing their return to consciousness. They can hear in the parapraxes, or detect in the symptom, or unravel in the dream the effective ability of repressed states of mind to re-enter consciousness in disguise.

In many respects the theory of genera is inspired by the theory of repression. At the heart of the matter is my view that there is a collecting psychic gravity to unconscious clusters of ideas that are organized, dynamic, and representationally effective in consciousness. But the theory of repression points only to the banishment of the unwanted, and I am convinced that other types of ideas are invited into the unconscious. To complement the theory of repression, we need a *theory of reception*[2] which designates some ideas as the received rather than the repressed,

---

2 The idea of a receptively derived unconscious, as partner to a repressed unconscious, suggests the possibility of a maternal type of unconscious work that collaborates with paternal action. The metaphors I use – to conceive, to impregnate, to incubate, to give birth – consider a certain type of unconscious creativity differing from the paternal metaphors which stress repression, domination, and disguised representation.

although both the repressed and the received need the protective barrier provided by the anticathexes of preconsciousness. But if the aim of repression is to avoid the censoring or persecutory judgments of consciousness, the aim of reception is to allow unconscious development without the intrusive effect of consciousness.

Thus with reception the ego understands that unconscious work is necessary to develop a part of the personality, to elaborate a phantasy, to allow for the evolution of a nascent emotional experience, and ideas or feelings and words are sent to the system unconscious, not to be banished but to be given a mental space for development which is not possible in consciousness. Like the repressed idea, these ideas, words, images, experiences, affects, etc., constellate into mental areas and then begin to scan the world of experience for phenomena related to such inner work. Indeed, they may possibly seek precise experiences in order to nourish such unconscious constellations. The contents of the received are then the nuclei of genera which, like the repressed, will return to consciousness, but in the case of genera as acts of self enrichment rather than paroled particles of the incarcerated.

In this chapter I shall allow the work of repression to become part of a broadened view of trauma, insofar as repressed contents denude the self of representational freedom, bind unwanted ideas, and feel endangering to the self. Quite rightly, the analyst will work with shrewd tact and analytical cunning to designate affects, words, memories, etc., that will serve to release such contents into bearable consciousness just as he will analyze the resistance to such experiences. The clinician working with the analysand's receptive unconscious activity will sense that the patient is withdrawing ideas, feelings, or memories from narrative representation and selectively from consciousness in order to work upon them from within the unconscious, without the premature expression in consciousness that would foreclose deep unconscious work. In such moments the analyst may let the patient be, understanding that the receptive process needs unconsciousness to be effective.

In the rest of this chapter I discuss what I mean by the principle of genera, which is intended on the one hand to define a form of internal work that results in an important new way of seeing the world – one which would apply to people working on scientific, artistic, or vocational problems or tasks – and yet on the other hand one precise enough to enable the clinician to see how psychoanalysts and patients unconsciously collaborate to construct psychic structures that change the analysand's view of himself and his world. I shall conceptualize this phenomena, in turn, from the axis of three different psychoanalytic models of the mind: topographic, ego-psychological, object-relational. I hope thereby to indicate the value of a theory of psychic work that is distinct from the exclusively pathologic models, although genera formation is born of conflict and promotes emotional turbulence.

Combinatory play

The unconscious play work that a subject devotes to any set of received 'issues' incubates an internal organization derived from and devoted to such effort. A scientist working on a scientific task, for example, plays with many ideas; years may pass before he has an inspired idea that heralds an important discovery, one that will change his outlook on handling his future work. A composer is at work on a symphony. Perhaps, like Aaron Copland, he is asked to write on Lincoln, and, like Copland, he asks himself how Lincoln sounds.[3] It could be that an idea will come to mind immediately, but more likely the symphonic idea will derive from intensive unconscious play work until something announces itself. A psychic nucleus derives from the many moments of distinct consideration brought to bear on the task. Such a generative structure will now sponsor many new ideas that ultimately will constitute the symphony, eventually achieving a semi-autonomous status, and in the process changing the composer's conscious intentions, and possibly altering his way of composing future works.

Ordinarily, then, genera are produced after a period of play work and, once established, transform the subject's outlook on life, generate new questions and new works, and contribute to the formation of new genera.

Einstein wrote of his 'rather vague play with the . . . elements' in his mind's eye, which he also described as a form of 'combinatory play' that he believed to be 'the essential feature in productive thought – before there is any connection with logical construction in words or other kinds of signs which can be communicated to others' (1952: 43). This play with the elements, prior to logical construction, is the receptive process that occurs inside each of us as we form genera: a combinatory play that leads to the eventual establishment of a new perspective. It is not irrelevant that Einstein twice refers to this as play, which brings to mind Wordsworth's description of the infant's aggressive receptivity: 'Hence his mind, / Even in the first trial of its powers, / Is prompt and watchful, eager to combine / In one appearance all the elements / And parts of the same object' (Wordsworth, 1799: 67).

One cannot overemphasize the long hours of effort devoted to the work of reception. Any psychoanalyst and his analysand know how many hours of analytical labor are precursor to a psychic discovery. He would sympathize with the mathematician Henri Poincaré's description of the effort that goes into discovery:

> For fifteen days I strove to prove that there could not be any functions like those I have since called Fuchsian functions. I was then very ignorant; every day I seated myself at my work table, stayed an hour or two, tried a great number of combinations, and reached no results. One evening, contrary to my custom, I drank black coffee and could not sleep. Ideas rose in crowds; I felt them collide until parts interlocked, so to speak, making a stable combination. By the next morning I had established the existence of a class of

---

3 In her lyrical and intelligent book *Notebooks of the Mind* (1985), Vera John-Steiner explores the many types of creativity, and I have used her work to support my own clinical findings. However, were one to study the conviction in creative persons of what I term genera, then Vera John-Steiner's book would be an excellent point of departure.

Fuchsian functions, those which come from the hypergeometric series. I had only to write out the results, which took but a few hours.

(1952: 36)

Poincaré would not have reached his discovery without many hours of labor. Nor would he have achieved this breakthrough if he had not tolerated his ignorance, which I liken in the psychoanalytic situation to the capacity to tolerate not knowing what one is doing, so that uncertainty becomes a useful feature to the private work of the receptive process.[4]

Poincaré's illustration of that internal combinatory process describes the inner *sense* that one has of the embryonic form of a generative structure, which in his case resulted in his discovery of Fuchsian functions, and which for the psychoanalyst announces itself as a particular type of interpretation that becomes a psychically seminal vision: a condensation of many trial ideas and explorations of thought now cohered into a germinal point of view that generates new perspectives.

Trauma and the search for negative qualia

A psychoanalyst and his patient could cumulatively construct traumatic psychic structures if they collected material to support a perspective that only repeated itself. Analytic work may sometimes have to be this way for a while; for example, in the case of interpretive work about certain patients' grandiosity in which the analyst must repeatedly confront the analysand. At least the psychoanalyst will be aware that such interpretations may be recurrently traumatic to the patient and relentlessly resisted, before nucleating, if ever, into genera. Certain analysands are for a long time only traumatized by psychoanalysis, a fact which must be respected and which inevitably invites us to continuously rethink technique.

Psychic genera worked on in a psychoanalysis are the outcome of the mutual contribution of analyst and patient – a reflection of the patient's life instincts such that, in spite of resistances, he can unconsciously specify a complex of work that must be accomplished in order to achieve a significant new perspective that will enhance living. Unconscious recognition of the areas of such work motivates receptive action. Memories, instinctual representations, self experiences, and dreams that relate to the inner complex gravitate toward it in unconscious and preconscious holding areas. Their diverse but specific structure gives each potential genera its feel.

'Wordsworth had to grope along the grains of the language,' writes Seamus Heaney, 'to find the makings of a music that would render not so much what Hopkins called the inscape as the instress of things, known physically and intuitively at such times' (1980: 47). Incubating genera creates, in my view, such an

---

4 See *The Shadow of the Object* (Bollas, 1987a) for a discussion of the receptive process, and also the work of Peter Thomson.

'instress' which can be felt and which guides the subject's graspings among objects as he intuitively shapes his own spirit out of receptive intelligence.

The 'work' of trauma will be to collect disturbing experience into the network of a traumatic experience (now a memory and unconscious idea) while the play work of genera will be to collect units of received experience that interanimate toward a new way of perceiving things.

An individual may, however, struggle with traumatic inner constellations and, by transformations of the trauma into works of art, achieve a certain mastery over the effect of trauma. The view that the artist transforms trauma and psychic pain into an artistic object is a common psychoanalytic perspective on the nature of creativity. And an individual may indeed work on a trauma to transform its psychic status by developing from it a new psychic structure that establishes a new perspective. Thus genera can and do emerge from the play work devoted to the transformation of psychic pain and traumatic perspectives.

But in psychoanalysis we find many persons who collect negative qualia around traumatized areas of the self, just as we find patients who seek experiences that though psychically painful are nonetheless essential to the formation of genera. A trauma-evolving person, or an individual living episodes of experience from this position, will seek negative qualia in objects and experiences. He will either find unpleasant or disturbing objects and experiences or he will transform potentially positive qualia into negatives. Hence, the object relations of each action will partly reflect the nature of the unconscious work being employed. A person who unconsciously develops a first-stage impingement into a full trauma will collect negative qualia into an ever-nucleating condensation that may intensify until the point of conscious emergence, when the subject is deeply disturbed by the erup- tion of the accumulated disturbed contents. The full trauma may be released into experiencing by a dream, an event, or a person. An individual who cultivates genera seeks objects and experiences that yield positive qualia, although positive here does not mean optimistic, good, or conflict-free, but something that will link with and possibly elaborate the psychic material that is incubating into a new vision.

Indeed, genera have no moral value, as it were, and a person could cultivate inner psychic structures and visions that others would find aesthetically, politi- cally, or socially repellent. To distinguish genera from trauma one must ask only if the individual is free to organize the data of life into new visions that change the meaning of existence, a continuing process of discovery, or, as in the case of trauma, whether the person is organizing the material of life in a repetitive way, one aim of which is to denude the ego of a creative play upon the stuff of existence.

A trauma-seeking patient will unconsciously sabotage the analytic work by seeking negative qualia, either by distorting the analyst's remarks, by turning the generative comments into destructive ones, or by spoiling some of the analyst's internal states. For example, a patient 'abused' as a child by parents who prema- turely involved him in their conflict and in their sexual life – by inappropriately disclosing things to him – was afraid of his own capacity to destroy the other's peace of mind by attacking the other's mental life, thus feeling ultimately rejected because the other would depart in hurt or horror, leaving the patient guilty and furious. This only became clear after some time in the analysis when I examined certain countertransferences I had and linked them to the patient's transferences. I found that the patient, who knew some people I also knew in the analytical world, would often – in passing – say nasty, gossipy things about these people, for a moment affecting my internal representations. Did X really do that to his wife? I wondered. Did Y really say that about Z to W? I puzzled. Such slight shocks were not lasting, but one day the patient came to the hour and mentioned a play about psychoanalysis which he knew I was interested in: he also knew that I was to review it, but that I had not yet seen it. 'Well, I have seen the play and it was just awful and my friend, A, who reviews for *The Times*, thought it was an intellectual sham and bogus drama. I wonder what you will make of it when you view it.' For the moment I felt as if this play had been spoiled in advance of my seeing it. I was mildly irritated. In a separate moment in the same session, the patient reported an irrational fear that I was going to peremptorily end the analysis. I said that he was unconsciously inviting me to have my internal representation of the play damaged just as his internal world was spoiled by envy and rivalry.

The patient understood the interpretation and spoke of his inclination to damage his relationships by isolating features of the other person or by remembering only unpleasant experiences, thus collecting part experiences into a traumatic gestalt. As he did this he was aware of an inner sensation, associated with such spoilings, linked to anal mental contents that found expression through certain interactional processes.

From this perspective we may argue that the inner mental sensation associated with spoiling is the emotional climate of his traumatic thinking: specifically the feeling image derived from the search for damaging experiences. The individual who contributes to genera, however, seems to have a different psychic library, generated by the mental feeling derived from the creative effort of thought. Such an internal object may be associated by the person with the search for meaning or truth or beauty, and perhaps it is simultaneously an objectification of a frame of mind and its internal presence.

Indeed, a person who is at play with a life issue is constantly contributing to the generative internal object. The scientist at work on a task contributes new data and new observations to the generative internal object each day of his life, adding to the compositional shape of such an internal structure. No contribution to solving a scientific problem, to the final product of a poem, or to the designing of a car engine is lost on the unconscious.

The 'feel' of genera

Scientists, poets, composers, and other people involved in creative efforts of thought have mental representations of the singular effort of mind brought to bear on their tasks. Most of them 'see' an abstraction of the problem and its solution, even though it has not yet arrived. I wonder if this internal abstract picture – more an endopsychic graph – is the presence of an internal object, as defined by Hinshelwood: an internal object (rather than an internal representation) is the presence of a structure that is mentally sensed. An individual who is at play work on a genera would, then, have a 'sense' of an internal object's 'constitutional evolution,' formed by the psychic gravity of multiformal processings of units of experience cohering into a nucleus of potential meaning movements. Heaney writes: 'It is that whole creative effort of the mind's and body's resources to bring the meaning of experience into the jurisdiction of form' (1980: 47). This 'coming together' of many separate factors, a condensation building around a convergence of issues in life, would naturally sponsor a sense of itself as a psychic numen. One would feel this as a kind of familiar force of psychic gravity attracting ideas, questions, and play work and constituting a place of creativity. A person who is concentrating the issues of life, or some of them, into a trauma, on the other hand, might well have an internal object that is the place of such work, to which he turns for traumatic networking, and the psychic sensation involved would be disturbed, as if one were playing a mad internal drum.

Einstein's conceptualization of creativity is perhaps the best-known description of the internal object as inner reference point. 'The words or the language, as they are written or spoken, do not seem to play any role in my mechanism of thought,' writes Einstein. 'The psychical entities which seem to serve as elements in thought are certain signs and more or less clear images which can be "voluntarily" reproduced and combined' (1952: 43).

Sometimes a single word or phrase may serve as a locational sign of this internal object to which one may turn. Hart Crane writes: 'It is as though a poem gave the reader as he left it a single, new *word*, never before spoken and impossible to actually enunciate, but self-evident as an active principle in the reader's consciousness henceforward' (1979: 182). This is a kind of evocative psychic genera, achieved through the work of the poem (a structure) and changing the poet's vision of reality. I shall, however, not be exploring this interesting aspect of the formation of genera, when – as with Hart Crane – we encounter an evocative object that is apparently not the result of our own inner labor, but which nonetheless is inspiring and seemingly introjected as a psychic structure that sponsors important new visions. The best moments in any person's formal education are composed of just such evocative occasions when an object (a theory, another perspective) radically alters one's way of imagining reality. I think it is highly likely, however, that such introjective epiphanies are the outcome of substantial unconscious work that preceded them.

'My own experience of inspiration,' writes Stephen Spender, 'is certainly that of a line or a phrase or a word of sometimes something still vague, a dim cloud of an idea which I feel must be condensed into a shower of words' (1952: 118). This 'dim cloud of an idea' which Spender condenses into 'a shower of words' brings to mind Freud's theory of the dream work, as a condensation of all the elements relevant to psychic life (instincts, affects, memories, existential experiences) which may be the prototype of all creative discoveries. The construction of a genera is somewhat akin to dream work, as we unconsciously labor to receptively condense many phenomena into a psychic structure that will eventually disclose and disseminate itself. It is less an effort of representational thought, more an act of *operational intelligence*. Lyotard reminds us that Freud says the dream work 'does not think, calculate or judge in any way at all; it restricts itself to giving things a new form' (1989: 20). To Lyotard the thoughtless movement of condensation is desire, desire in its essence, prior to any derivative representation. By collapsing words into things, condensation becomes a thing of sorts – an inner thing – that is the inchoate movement of desire. 'The "language" of the unconscious is not modeled on articulated discourse, which, as we know, finds utterance according to a language. Rather, the dream is the acme of the inarticulate deconstructed discourse from which no language, even normal, is entirely free' (p. 33). So too with the receptive process, those inner workings, prearticulate yet gravitational, compelling yet silent, until the day when suddenly the mind is inspired to new visions.

Perhaps genera are what Wordsworth means by a 'fructifying virtue.' 'There are in our existence spots of time/Which with distinct preeminence retain/A fructifying virtue' (1979: 51), a creative force emanating from a very particular moment in one's ontology. 'There exists/A virtue which irradiates and exalts/All objects through all intercourse of sense' (p. 67), such a virtue the disseminative spirit of a generative part of the self. If the theory of repression embraces a concept of ultimate expression, in the ideas of the return of the repressed and in sublimation, the received unconscious finds expression through the development of psychic structures that come into consciousness in a shower of disseminative energy. The ego is not working to disguise genera; it is using displacement, substitution, and symbolization as part of the *jouissance* of representation.

I think of imagist theory, which Heaney believes yields a 'sense of that which presents an intellectual and emotional complex in a moment of time' (1980: 89). Baudelaire, Poe, Rimbaud, Pound (and one could go on) believed that the image concentrated life into it. Wordsworth's 'spots of time,' Einstein's 'signs,' Spender's 'dim clouds,' or anyone's inner image of psvchic procreativity serves as a kind of internal point of reference of that highly complex protean vision waiting to be born, raised, and articulated.

Each of us will, then, refer ourselves to particular inner images that indicate the psychic gravity of work taking place at a deeply unconscious level. Note how Henry Moore describes his inner place of psychic labor:

> This is what the sculptor must do. He must strive continually to think of, and use form in its full spatial completeness. He gets the solid shape, as it were, inside his head – he thinks of it, whatever its size, as if he were holding it completely enclosed in the hollow of his hand. He mentally visualizes a complex form from all round itself: he knows while he looks at one side what the other side is like; he identifies himself with its centre of gravity, its mass,

its weight; he visualizes its volume, as the shape that the shape displaces in the air.

(1952: 74)

Although Moore's internal object seems concrete, like a sketch of a particular piece of sculpture, it is in fact the representation of sculptural form itself. It is a way of collecting in a psychic place the individual sculptor's nascent shaping of an actual object, a process that begins with a dynamic inner form.

Moore's object for the psychic location of inner creative work is somewhat unusual; many creative people depict their inner creatings as taking place in a less than lucid space. No doubt each person chooses a metonym that ultimately signifies the place of genera even though it does not depict the process itself.

The poetics of psychic structure

Few writers have described the anguish of constructing a generative internal structure as well as Paul Valéry. Like many creative people, he says that chaos, or 'disorder in the condition of the mind's fertility' (1952: 106), is the internal feel of this phase of work, something which may correspond in the psychoanalytical situation to the bewildering intersections of the patient's and analyst's free associations.

Valéry says that we wish for an inner experience that assembles disorder into structure. I do not think he believes it is only a wish, but a recurring fact which, perhaps because of its comparative rarity, elicits our desire: 'Sometimes what we wish to see appear to our minds . . . is like some precious object we might hold and feel through a wrapping of cloth that hides it from our eyes. It is and it is not ours, and the least incident may reveal it. . . . We demand it, being faced with some peculiar combination of elements all equally immanent to the mind' (p. 101). Are these wrappings layers of preconscious membrane that protect unconscious workings from premature consciousness, thus heightening Valéry's sense that the internal object in question is both his and not his?

Even while rooting about among pregenerational ideas, we sense which image, sound, movement, or feeling promises to become part of a generative conceptualization as we 'grope along the grains' of experience. In conversation with Aaron Copland, Harold Clurman asked if composers played a measure over and over, testing out ideas. Copland replied that it might seem dull, but even if you repeat an idea 'you have a different idea of where it will go. It is the process of saying, how will this first idea inspire me toward the next one.' John-Steiner writes: 'Composing thus emerges as a process which demands – as do other forms of creative endeavor – an ability to synthesize germinal ideas into elaborative structures' (1985: 157). This description of musical structure is a useful illustration of how genera work, involving elaborations which continue throughout a lifetime. Always 'there' for use, genera, like a composer's protean visions, remain in mind for re-usings.

Germinal ideas may only make themselves felt in the process of articulation. Picasso writes: 'The picture is not thought out and determined beforehand, rather while it is being made it follows the mobility of thought' (1952: 57). It is a commonplace for artists to state, quite sincerely, that the work seems to arise of its own accord. As Amy Lowell writes: 'A common phrase among poets is, "it came to me." So hackneyed has this become that one learns to suppress the expression with care, but really it is the best description I know of the conscious arrival of a poem' (110). Perhaps this is an additional reason why the writer, musician, or painter consciously feels that the created object is its own creator.

'In the very essence of poetry there is something indecent,' writes Czeslaw Milosz in *Ars Poetica*. 'A thing is brought forth which we didn't know we had in us, / so we blink our eyes, as if a tiger had sprung out / and stood in the light, lashing his tail' (1979: 3). As we contain many generative structures, often conceived through long hours of labor, the moment of original impregnation unknown to us, it is little wonder that such inner resources should seem so surprising, and yet our unconscious commitment to producing them – or, more accurately, to their production of us – remains undaunted. This containment of so many semi-autonomous psychic workings may be one of the reasons why writers or philosophers are disenchanted with the notion of a unified self. This view is not simply a postmodernist position. It was well put in 1915 by the Portuguese poet Fernando Pessôa: 'I feel multiple. I am like a room with innumerable fantastic mirrors that distort by false reflections one single pre-existing reality which is not there in any of them and is there in them all.' We can imagine what it is like if a person does not have a sense of an integrated self, as genera then might be cultivated by split-off portions of the personality, leading toward a powerful sense of fragmented multiple personalities. Pessôa continues: 'I feel myself living alien lives, in me, incompletely, as though my soul shared in all human beings, incompletely, through a sum of non- "I's" synthesized in an afterthought "I" ' (1979: 5).

But perhaps these alien lives are the seemingly independent creatures of genera, that unconscious that 'lives' inside us, is part of us, but sponsors ideas, images, and feelings which 'we' often find disturbing and wish we didn't have. These are the 'dark embryos' of thought that T. S. Eliot described as 'a something germinating in [the poet] for which he must find words' (in Heaney, 1980: 70). Why are they alien? Perhaps because psychic structures feel mysterious. More akin to what René Char termed the 'increate real,' genera cannot be found in the external world and possess no material actuality, although paintings, poems, musical compositions, and other forms of art express such internal processes. But such psychic gravities are profoundly real to us.

Steps in the formation of genera

1. The conception of an inner space devoted to the formation of a generative psychic structure is likely to be the outcome of an unconscious protean moment when lived experience evokes intense psychic interest that constellates initially around the evoked ideas, feelings, and self states and gels into a form of unconscious desire for 'its' evolution.

2. The nascent unconscious ideas, feelings, or self states constitute a psychic gravity that draws to it relevant data.

3. The unconscious collection of hundreds of links to the psychic complex gives rise to inner senses of generative chaos.

4. Chaos is tolerated, indeed facilitated, as the subject knows it is essential to the process of discovering new concepts about living.

5. Gradually chaos yields to a preformative sense of emergent nucleation. It is important to stress that this is only a sense, but it does reflect a process of structural cohesion.

6. Suddenly the person discovers a fundamentally new perspective that generates many derivatives. This new vision is not the genera, but it is the first manifestation of its presence in consciousness and it will sponsor many new ways of seeing oneself, others, and one's work.

7. This moment will often feel revelatory, and although it is a special experience it is not an occasion for a new theory of the sacred, but it does describe those seminal visions created by unconscious processes pushed by the life instincts, and is an erotics in form.

Intuition

Is it surprising that a generative internal object should provide us with a heightened mental capability? As we construct the skeleton of such an internal process, doesn't it enhance our perception as we go along? As the dreamer finds his first dream images to represent his dream thoughts, doesn't the dream content crystallize further imaging as its narrative structure becomes more plausible, bringing to it further condensation?

This seems obvious to me. A poet or scientist or musician begins with a notional sense of an undeveloped and inarticulate task. At first the ideas generated are trials, some seeming about right, others not so. In time, a set of ideas or representations feels more correct and as these ideas set in, they give back to the scientist, poet, or musician an increasingly specific vision of his object world, attuned to seeing things now with an enhanced eye.

What is this ability that derives from the incremental cohesion of a mental structure set up to think an as yet inarticulated idea? Is this not what we mean by a sense of intuition: the sense we have of where to look, what to look at, and how to look at it? Derived from the Latin *intuitus*, the past participle of *intueor*, to look at, its root suggests that intuition is a looking at or viewing of a phenomenon. Webster defines it as 'the direct knowing or learning of something without the conscious use of reasoning; immediate apprehension or understanding.'

What if we look upon intuition as an unconscious skill at least partly derived from the construction of genera? After the filmmaker makes his first film, or the author writes his first novel, comes an increased intuitional sense in the nature of such creations and in time this inner sense assists them in developing a special intelligence for work within this area. Build genera and out of such construction you get a new sense, enabling you to 'feel about for the solution to life problems.' Such feeling about is not an occult or mystical act, but a form of desire derived from the unconscious multimodal work of the different areas of the self acting upon an issue or problem. It is the sense of the pathway toward a revelation in one's perception.

Perhaps the sense of intuition is our preconscious experience of the ego's intelligent work, leading us to consciously authorize certain forms of investigation in thought which are not consciously logical but which may be unconsciously productive. It may emerge as a particularly strong factor in our decision making in ratio to the successful nucleation of a genera. 'Prior to the writing of the poems I tried to have a sense of key areas that I'm watching, that are beginning to evolve as points I must know about,' says Gary Snyder. These points may be similar to preconsciously understood areas of work in a psychoanalysis. 'And poems will flow out of those in time,' he adds, to which we may add that generative interpretations emerge in a psychoanalysis in like manner. An interviewer has asked Snyder if the genesis of his poems arrives from note taking or particular observations of reality. 'I listen to my own interior mind-music closely,' he replies, which may remind some readers of Freud's description of the multi-locular sense, derived from internal perceptions. 'Most of the time there's nothing particularly interesting happening,' he continues, 'but once in a while I hear something which I recognize as belonging to the sphere of poetry. I listen very closely to that.' Isn't there an equally special area in the mind of the psychoanalyst who listens differently, so that now and then he recognizes something that belongs to the sphere of psychoanalysis? (I should add, however, that such recognitions would derive from unconscious play work already long since applied to prior patient communications.) The interviewer asks Snyder if what he hears comes from 'inside,' and the poet replies, 'But it's coming from outside, if you like. Maybe I have a radio receiver planted in my spinal cord' (Snyder, 1979: 284–85). A poet and the founder of psychoanalysis both use the metaphor of a radio receiver to address a particular form of listening, which in my view is the work of the intuitional part of the mind, one that knows how to receive messages (or significations) if it has crystallized points of attraction from a collection of psychic nodes that I term genera.

The fact that intuition seems to be an immediate knowing should not obscure the fact that it is the outcome of a sustained concentration of many types of unconscious and conscious thinking. Perhaps the inclination to differentiate intuition from reason is intended to stress the apparently effortless side to it. Working at an issue diligently in one's laboratory, studio, or consulting room is often hard work. How different intuitions seem, as first we follow an unreasoned hunch or clue, then we become deeply absorbed in it as it feels increasingly correct to us, and then suddenly we discover a new way of looking at, conceiving, or producing something. No wonder this process is subject to our mystifications. Perhaps we would like it to remain unlooked at; intuitive procedures seem so successful because they apparently exist outside of consciousness.

I would argue that intuition is a form of desire associated with the ego's notion of what to look at, what to look for, and how to do both beneficially. This sense is partly derived from the structure that evolves out of a multiformal contributing to the generative internal object from the many different types of self experience over a long period of time and owes much to that intelligence involved in the ego's selection of forms through which the subject's idiom may find its articulation. Our association of intuition with unintentionality and the irrational is testimony to the need for a relaxed nonvigilant effort of integration in the subject. Intuition works as successfully as it does precisely because the subject thinking in this way does not see what he is working on and what he is working with. In this respect, its strength rests upon its hiddenness. It may be so successful, then, because the intuiting person is unconsciously able to explore lines of investigation that would meet with incredulous disapproval if he were fully conscious of what was being considered.

Perhaps in time we will give increased attention to the self experience and mental processes involved in intuition. The fact that such inner proceedings are themselves the object of many convergent projective identifications – to which people assign magical wishes – should not deter us from investigating an important feature of unconscious life, particularly as it is such an important part of psychoanalytic experiencing. For although it is true that the analyst's evenly hovering attentiveness allows him to achieve a type of disciplined dispassion, much of his internal rendering of analysis depends on his intuitive capability.

Composed of the psychoanalyst's capacity to follow internal sensings when listening to the patient's material, such feelings are responsive to the subtle exercise of forms of experience and modes of expression in the analysand. Patient and analyst develop between them internal objects specific to the mutual processing of this self (analyst or patient) with this other (analyst or patient) in this particular place (the psychoanalysis). Just as a ship is constructed for sailors to sail the seas, or instruments are crafted in order to play music, patient and analyst construct internal objects to process the analysis.

As the patient conveys to the analyst the nature of his self (and objects), he uses differing forms of experience and modes of expression to represent his being. If he uses the iconic and verbal categories rather than the gestural, affective, and sonic, he conveys a perceptual structure with a particular character that will usually evoke structurally specific self experiences in the analyst. In this case, the analyst's visual and verbal abilities would be used, and his gestural, affective, and sonic capacities would not be directly played upon by the patient, although, of course, such categories would have their own independent existence. In other words, the analyst would feel his affects, move gesturally, perhaps convey elements of himself in his sound cadences, but not in dialogue with the patient.

Naturally the specific idiomatic contents processed in each category are communicated to the analyst, who builds pictures of, words about, feelings for, and somatic responses to the analysand. In time many factors contribute to a multilectical sensing of the analysand, which forms internal objects in the analyst and the patient that come to constitute core areas for the reception of and mulling over of the many contributions of both persons to the analysis.

An analysis is a creative process involving two subjectivities at work on over-lapping tasks, and analytical genera are formed as shared internal structures. The respective significance of such complexes to the two persons will naturally differ; for the analyst such devotions are unconsciously sought after as part of his creative work with a particular patient, while such internal objects become part of the analysand's mental structure. But the psychic structure that will evolve out of psychoanalysis is the result of such a collaborative effort and its desires.

The dreams of psychoanalysis

The psychoanalyst and the patient construct a complex network of thinkings derived from a sequential multitude of categories of self experience, and over time play work condenses such thinkings into a structure (a complex) that has psychic gravity and desires further data that now serve both persons as a shared internal object. Such a psychic structure in analysis is homologous to the creation of dream content which is the result of a similar play work during the day when the person transforms 'undigested facts' into psychic material. The unconscious scanning[5] occurs before sleep and reflects the dialectic between hermeneutic searching and aleatory evocativeness, as meaning meets up with chance to create psychic news. At night the dreamer nucleates many dream ideas (feelings, memories, day observations, theories, somatic urges) into condensed images which form a complex of ideas that work symbolically to bind the many contributing factors into a structure that may now generate new meanings.

This view suggests that the dream work, the factors working to assemble the dream in the first place, is as significant as either the meaning it yields or the experience it provides, if many different categories of self experience are utilized in the processing of life units, then many different modes of representation will be at work in the collecting of the dream. Dream content expresses a process begun long before the dream event – indeed, well before sleep. During the day a person's experiences are unconsciously assembled into different mental holding areas, incubating associative nuclei that evoke memories, serve to release instinctual drives, and satisfy the person's need to have 'senses' of self. All these factors are none other than overdeterminants converging upon such clusters of assembled experiences to form increasingly condensed (psychically 'weighty') internal states.

As the day proceeds, as new episodes accrue in these inner clusters, the condensed nucleations of experience sponsor a dream potential: psychic material has been gathered for dream experience. Do we need the dream to represent the condensing procedure? Has it become a type of ego excitation that needs discharge? If the individual cannot dream such 'dark embryos,' then such work may need an alternative form of expression. Is the creative act, such as writing poetry, painting, composing music, an alternative means of releasing nucleations

---

5 See Ehrenzweig, *The Hidden Order of Art* (1967).

into representation? Is it also possible that psychotic hallucinations are violently radical means of releasing such internal objects, perhaps because the psychotic cannot use the dream experience to positive effect, and cannot find in creative work, or human relations, equally satisfying representations of the condensations of life gathered into nucleated internal objects?

In a psychoanalysis the clinician uses an intuitive sense to receive, play with, and work upon the patient's transferential actions, narrative contents, and free associations. When he claimed that psychoanalyst and analysand were on mutual wavelengths of the unconscious, transmitter (patient) to receiver (psychoanalyst), Freud suggested that analyst and analysand were in unconscious communication with one another.

This suggestive idea has played a considerable role in the clinical work of psychoanalysts in the British School of Psychoanalysis, who, through the concepts of projective identification and countertransference, have elaborated the methodological implications of Freud's statement. The patient unconsciously acts upon the analyst, as either a direct or a disguised internal object, or upon his actual internal world. If the psychoanalyst is aware of an inner affective and ideational shaping of his internal world which seems specific to clinical work with a particular patient, he may postulate that this shaping indicates his patient's projective identifications. Through a sustained self analysis the clinician works upon his own states of mind to see what object world the analysand is soliciting.

Although some British clinicians overuse the view that all patients' narrative content is an extended metaphor of the patient–analyst relation, this perspective nonetheless contributes to an important psychic capacity within the psychoanalyst. If we take the position that narrative content is a metaphor of the patient's internal state, then when listening to even rather ordinary material we find that it assumes a potential allegorical significance. Common statements such as 'I am going to the cleaner's after the session' or 'I can't stand the rain today' become encoded voices of unconscious states of mind (i.e., 'I am going to have to clean the analytic shit off me after the session' or 'I cannot bear your reigning over me anymore').

To use the metaphoric potential of an analysand's narrative content, the analyst must allow himself an imaginative inner play. His associations elaborate the patient's discourse, as narrative episodes sponsor the clinician's imaginings. Sometimes his associations are further displacements of the patient's latent thoughts. But even if the inner elaboration of a displacement moves the analyst further away from the latent thought, at the same time the derivative suggests its origins. In time, as the analyst elaborates the patient's displacements or defenses through his own inner associations, the structure of this elaboration will sometimes suggest the architecture of the defended latent contents. Unlike the patient, who is often dynamically driven not to discover such latent thoughts, the analyst is professionally motivated to find them, which in some respects he will do by collaborating with the analysand's wishes and defenses through concordant internal associations which allow him to internally 'feel' the outlines of the patient's emotions, internal objects, ego defenses, and unconscious ideas. By internally elaborating a defense or by further articulating a signifier, the analyst follows the clues released through such associations to their points of origin.

It is difficult to describe how I listen to the analysand within the session. The endless slide of words, signifiers that evoke limitless associations just as they suggest specific links that imply precise meaning, the images that bring me to a formed world in that strange intimacy of co-imagining. Often patients indicate through diction texture, hesitation, body state, and expectation those moments in a session that are of particular significance. Most people take five to fifteen minutes to 'settle in' to the hour, a devolution of socially adaptive wishings assisted by analytical silence. Then something happens. The patient is 'in' the analysis. One analysand put it well: 'This is the only place where I can hear myself speak.' When the analysand reaches this place, he brings the analyst into deeper rapport with him, as the core mood of the hour rather naturally casts off prior rationalizations or defensive diversions.

How do we know such moments which Dennis Duncan (1990) calls 'the feel of the session'? Is it possible to gain this understanding through psychoanalytic training? Certainly it helps when we learn how to be quiet and listen. Is knowledge of this ability to be found in the texts on ego psychology or object relations or theories of the subject? How could it be? And yet, knowing how to follow the analysand's moods in the session – dispositions that punctuate the hour with significance – is one of the most important clinical skills the analyst can possess.

I think the ability to move into the meditative state of evenly hovering attentiveness, to receive and articulate projective identifications, to elaborate the narrative contents through inner free associations, and to follow the analysand's mood in the hour contributes to the psychoanalyst's intuitive grasp of the analysand. Certainly this is what Bion means by the analyst's reverie when he takes in the patient's communications, contains them, works unconsciously to transform them into sense, and gradually passes them back to the analysand for consideration.

By containing, processing, and elaborating the analysand through the procedures described above, now and then the clinician is aware of working on something without knowing what that something is or what it might eventually mean. *Analytic work at such a point is in some respects like the dream work before the dream scene.* But the unknown area of work does yield a sense of its presence, and certain thoughts, feelings, object representations, memories, and body states somehow seem to link with the task at hand. Whether the manifest issue is a patient's refusal to sleep with her husband or a fear of traveling on the Underground, these issues eventually signify a very deep form of psychic work that may lead to genera. If so, then the analyst is involved in the construction of a dream not dreamed before, but one that is nonetheless based on the patient's prior self experiencings and the analyst's contributions.

For weeks and months I work with a patient, listening to dreams and associations, dispersed by the polysemous riots of language, gathered by the glue of imagery, attending to sonic punctuations and gestural suggestions, that dense

moving panoply of communicatings uttered by the analysand, and I in turn associate, am moved to discrete affective positions, constitute the analysand and his
objects in my internal world made out of them and yet of my own creation, offer
interpretations, pose questions, and abandon many, many ideas and views along
the way. Yet in the midst of all that I usually feel that this patient and I are at work
on something. Something beyond our consciousness yet unconsciously compelling. Something that seems to draw us to it, so that ideas, interpretations, and
associations that feel off center of this inner pull are discarded. Something we
know but as yet cannot think. Some interpretations, views, questions, feel more in
touch with that unthought known area being worked on, even though they seem
no more plausible than the abandoned ideas. But the objectifying processes available to the analyst and the patient's corrections and associative directedness help
the analyst to follow an unseen path, feeling the way as he goes.

Three years into an analysis, following scores and scores of dreams, thousands
of associations, hundreds of comments from me, a patient discovers the pleasure
of differentiated sexual desire of the other. At this very moment she has also
reached a considerable new peace of mind with her internal mother, whom she
now sees in a different light. Memories are de-repressed. She finds a new sense of
her father. Her work becomes more creative. And so on. A new psychic structure
is secured and the analysand's life is changed. Although she felt that she now had
a new insight, originally expressed as a sense of herself as attractive to men
because she had felt inner peace with her father, this point of view only announced
that a genera was now in place.

In the months preceding this 'discovery' I knew my analysand was at work on
an important internal task. I knew it involved the mother and the father, but her
transferential uses of me (and my countertransferential states) were so subtle,
shifting, and unconscious that I could only sense the workings of a use-movement
that I believed was her form of ego creativity. As she worked upon her disturbed
states of mind, naturally my analytical acumen was involved, and yet the entire
process had an inner logic of its own which I sensed but only partly understood.
Resistances, false self movements, intellectualizations, hypomanic defenses,
projective identifications, were analyzed, yet without the patient's continued
contribution of the psychic truth pertinent to her inner work, the development of
a new psychic structure would never have been forthcoming.

If the dialectic between the analysand's transferences and the analyst's countertransferences, between the patient's narratives and the analyst's associations,
between the analysand's linguistic specifications and the clinician's readings,
between the patient's declarations and the clinician's questions – and one could
go on and on, listing the binary pairs that structure the dialectic – can be viewed
as the labor of two separate yet deeply involved unconscious subjectivities, then
much of the work of a psychoanalysis is a kind of dream work. Mutually agreed-
upon core interpretations are, then, the dreams of psychoanalysis, constructed
more through the interlocking logics of an unconscious dialectic than from the
secondary-process delivery of a white-clothed surgical intervention.

It suggests, furthermore, that the play of two subjectivities at work on the formation of psychoanalytic genera is often as much an act of deception and disguise as it is an effort of understanding. One is not referring to conscious deception but to the evasion of organized consciousness which somehow robs the work of its integrity. Patient and analyst, through the necessary destruction of free association, collapse, conflate, and condense one another's communicatings. Consciousness is casualty to unconscious discourse, which in my view operates through the laws of unconscious distortion, not so much evading censorship as eluding premature consciousness. As I have discussed elsewhere, for example, in 'The Psychoanalyst's Use of Free Association' (Bollas, 1992), the irony is that the analyst's misunderstandings of his patient as well as the analysand's distortions of the clinician's meanings are as essential to the dream work of psychoanalysis as informed understanding.

Chapter 6

The Fascist state of mind

'Our program is simple,' wrote Benito Mussolini in 1932. 'They ask us for programs, but there are already too many. It is not programs that are wanting for the salvation of Italy but men and willpower' (1983: 185). 'What is Fascism?' asked Gramsci some ten years before Mussolini's spartan statement. 'It is the attempt to resolve the problems of production and exchange with machine-gun fire and pistol shots' (82).

Fascism seemed to simplify the ideological, theological, and cultural confusions that emerged from the failure of the Enlightment view of man to comprehend human existence. It was, argues Fritz Stern, a 'conservative revolution' constituting 'the ideological attack on modernity, on the complex of ideas and institutions that characterize our liberal, secular, and industrial civilization' (1974: xvi). Where the Enlightenment had partly emphasized the integrity of individual man, twentieth-century Fascism extolled the virtue of the state, an organic creation driven by the militant will of the masses, a sharp contrast indeed to the federal republic encumbered by checks and balances dividing power so that the people remained individually free to speak their minds in a pluralistic society.

While Freud reconsidered the dark side of man's self, this id never was free as a virtuous agent of the innate will of man. It became part of an internal federation of complex checks and balances, of ego working with superego against id, or id with superego in compromise negotiations with the ego. Freud rethought man and maintained some considerable belief in the power of reason to influence the id, and even if his theory of the death instinct accounts for the possibility of a mass negation of life, he remained a Bismarckian with a sense of real politics: life was to be an endless series of compromise solutions between the parts of the self. At the end of a Freudian life it is possible to be a Montaigne, rendered far too wise by the mayorial negotiations of existence to characterize ontology as a 'pursuit of happiness,' but nonetheless continuously respectful of the individual skills of man to negotiate a good enough life.

Like many Europeans of his time, Freud deferred recognition of a deeply troubling factor in human culture, an element which preoccupies us now with its haunting relevance: the related issues of terror and genocide. In February 1915 the Ottoman government decreed that its Armenian population would lose the privileges of the ordinary civilian, and immediately the slaughter began. In that year 800,000 Armenians were massacred, and although the *entente* nations (Britain, France, Russia) protested to the Ottoman government and Arnold Toynbee collected a volume of essays testifying to the atrocities against the Armenians, this was to be a massacre that could not be inscribed in the symbolic orders of Western thought; references to it were scarce indeed. There is no mention in Freud's work of the elimination of 75 percent of the Armenian population. Nor indeed does he make more than a single reference to the pogroms that preceded it in European history.

Although the genocide against the Jewish population in Nazi Germany – the Holocaust – seems an irreplaceable icon to evil in the twentieth-century mind, we may wonder if its ironic function (the Jew now used once again to serve as a point of projection) is to serve as a continued mental negation of the continuation of genocide. We seem to know this, as citizens of the Western world do try not to eliminate from their thoughts the re-emergence in Cambodia of the Khmer Rouge which put to death millions of people. 'Never forget,' the cry of the Holocaust victim, seems a tellingly apt injunction: we seem all too able to forget.

'Terror is the realization of the law of movement: its chief aim is to make it possible,' writes Hannah Arendt, 'for the force of nature or of history to race freely through mankind unhindered by any spontaneous human actions.' Is genocide, the mass implementation of terror, social license to remake the world according to one's vision? 'Those who are not of my species are not my fellow men . . . a noble is not one of my species: he is a wolf and I shoot' (O'Sullivan, 1983: 49). So spoke a French revolutionary. And from 3 executions a week in 1793 to 32 a week in early 1794, the revolutionaries executed, on average, 196 people a week in the summer of 1794.

But a noble is not man but wolf, so is this the destruction of a lowly creature? In genocide a person is killed for who he is, not for what he does, which prompts Kuper to pose an uncomfortable question: as there is a 'thoroughgoing dehumanization of the bourgeoisie' in the Communist manifesto, is it possible to see this intellectual act as a precondition for Stalin's elimination of such bourgeois elements in his death camps (1981: 95)? In other words, is this famous act of Marxist objectification, the vilification of the bourgeoisie to which thousands of intellects since that time have paid lip service, the 'warrant' for killing some 20 million human beings in the years between 1919 and 1939 (p. 59)?

In the *perestroika* world created by Mikhail Gorbachev it now seems not only possible but equally essential to think not only about what we have done but about who we are, or what we are, when we license genocide. As a psychoanalyst I turn my attention to that frame of mind which is the warrant for the extermination of human beings. I term it the Fascist state of mind, knowing that in some respects this is historiographically incorrect, as Fascism was a particular movement in world history with highly unique features to it, but I justify this license by playing on the double meaning of the word 'state.' There was a Fascist state. The coming into being of that state and its political theory can tell us quite a lot about another state: the state of mind that authorized a Fascist theory. Furthermore, like it or not, 'Fascist' is now a metaphor in our world for a particular kind of person, and I wish to reserve this ironic scapegoating of the Fascist from the convenient movement of its personification of evil, as, like Wilhelm Reich and Hannah Arendt, I shall argue that there is a Fascist in each of us and that there is indeed a highly identifiable psychic profile for this personal state.

Noel O'Sullivan, a political theorist and author of a fine study of Fascism, dismisses the psychoanalytical literature on Fascism as 'dangerously complacent . . . since it merely explains Fascism away by pushing it out of sight into a psychiatric ward.' He disagrees with Martin Wangh's view (O'Sullivan, 1983: 247) that the idealization of Hitler relieved homosexual tensions through submission to the leader, and objects to this and other analytical studies of Nazi pathology as failing to 'explain why other nations whose children were left fatherless in the First World War did not produce successful Führers and Nazi-type mass movements.' Psychoanalytic studies, he continues, 'explain everything, and therefore tell us nothing'; they assume that any sane person would be a liberal, and 'once this hidden postulate is granted, it naturally follows that those who dislike parliamentary institutions, respond to nationalistic appeals, and show a taste for heroism and self-sacrifice, are the victims of some psychological disorder.' The psychoanalytic argument, O'Sullivan concludes, ultimately claims that Fascists are the insane, and liberals and psychoanalysts are the sane (p. 27).

Some analytic studies of the Nazi movement may have suggested that there was an illness peculiar to the Germans, and if such a disorder is regarded as an idiosynchrome of culture and history, then I would join O'Sullivan in regarding such psychoanalytical positions as worryingly simplistic. It is my understanding of a prominent feature of psychoanalysis that the pathology found in the Fascist movement is inside each of us, and that one aim of a training analysis is to provide the analyst-to-be with the evidence of neurotic and psychotic processes within the ordinary self. Indeed I shall argue that it is possible to be both a liberal believing in a parliamentary world and yet capable of developing a Fascist frame of mind. I thus find no contradiction between a belief that a world of checks and balances mitigates genocide and the view that as the Fascist state of mind is ordinary, it can indeed subvert the democratic mind.

There is a view now fairly common in psychoanalysis that the subject is composed of varied parts of the self. These parts are the ordinary functioning parts of the mind (i.e., the workings of the mind according to Freud, Klein, Fairbairn, and Winnicott) and the differing selves and objects represented in this internal world. It is rather like a parliamentary order with instincts, memories, needs, anxieties, and object responses finding representatives in the psyche for mental processing. When under the pressure of some particularly intense drive (such as greed), or force (such as envy), or anxiety (such as the fear of mutilation) this internal world can indeed lose its parliamentary function and evolve into a less representative internal order, particularly as differing parts of the self are projected out into other objects, leaving the mind denuded of its representative constituents.

To see the mind's move to Fascism, we need to consider just how this democratic order is changed. How does one become Fascist? Eric Brenman suggests
that 'the practice of cruelty' is a 'singular narrow-mindedness of purpose' that
when 'put into operation . . . has the function of squeezing out humanity and
preventing human understanding from modifying the cruelty' (1988: 256). In
object relations terms, humanity is presumably represented or representable by
the presence of different capacities of the self (such as empathy, forgiveness, and
reparation) which had been squeezed out of the self.

Kleinian psychoanalysts frequently refer in their literature to the 'killing off' of
those parts of the self, thereby emphasizing the factor of murder as an ordinary
feature of intrapsychic life. Rosenfeld, for example, describes an aggressive
aspect of the narcissistic self state achieved by 'killing their loving dependent self
and identifying themselves almost entirely with the destructive narcissistic parts
of the self which provides them with a sense of superiority and self admiration'
(1987: 248). Compare this psychoanalytic observation to the terrorist credo of
Mikhail Bakunin's *Revolutionary Catechism* written in 1869.

> All the tender feelings of family life, of friendship, love, gratitude, and even
> honor must be stifled in the revolutionary by a single cold passion for the
> revolutionary cause.
>
> (p. 67)

Bakunin's statement is a conscious articulation of what the revolutionary must do
to achieve his cold passion, and perhaps because he knows (has made conscious)
what must be squeezed out, we can feel the horror and sadness of this psychic
movement. Rosenfeld, however, addresses the unconscious equivalent of this
process, and in a passage strikingly relevant to our subsequent considerations of
political genocide, he likens destructive narcissism to the work of a gang:

> The destructive narcissism of these patients appears often highly organized,
> as if one were dealing with a powerful gang dominated by a leader, who
> controls all the members of the gang to see that they support one another in
> making the criminal destructive work more effective and powerful.
>
> (Rosenfeld, 1987: 249)

The death camps of Buchenwald and Dachau come to mind, the training ground
for the SS, a gang dominated by a hierarchy of Hiter clones who watched each
other commit atrocities in order to ensure that no one in the gang stepped outside
the ethos of terror. There could be no internal opposition to the gang's operation
of the death camps, organized by their 'death work' (Pontalis, 1974: 184). 'Terror
becomes total when it becomes independent of all opposition,' says Arendt.
'It rules supreme when nobody any longer stands in its way' (1986: 464).
Other psychoanalysts (e.g., Kovel and Federn) have addressed certain mental
mechanisms that are useful to an understanding of the Fascist state of mind.

It is incumbent to very briefly outline the extraordinary study by Robert J. Lifton, who believes the key to understanding how Nazi doctors committed acts of genocide yet remained ordinary family men lies in the psychology of doubling: 'the division of the self into two functioning wholes, so that a part self acts as an entire self' (1986: 418). Such doubling may be ordinary – for example, when a surgeon needs to be his ordinary doctor self in order to perform operations. Nazi doctors escaped the sense of guilt arising from their evil actions by transferring the guilt from the ordinary to the 'Auschwitz self.' Nonetheless, argues Lifton, the Auschwitz self must become psychically numb to commit atrocities, something partly achieved by refusing to name the act of killing, finding instead many alternative words.

Lifton brilliantly illustrates the link between these Nazi doctors' sense of being inside the atmosphere of death and their increased omnipotence and mechanization of self as they transcended the death feeling. German genocide, argues Lifton, emerged from the sense of death that followed on from the First World War, a war that left Germans with a 'profound experience of *failed regeneration*' (1986: 468). A sense of collective illness pervaded the country, leading to a 'vision of total cure' (p. 470) which the charismatic Hitler provided. The cure that becomes genocide, according to Lifton, must be total, invincible, transcendental. The victim of genocide is designated a disease that could contaminate the self and must therefore be eliminated, sponsoring a 'genocidal necessity' that is a 'fierce purification procedure' (p. 482).

The Fascist state of mind

Whatever the factors that sponsor any specific social act of genocide, the core element in the Fascist state of mind (in the individual or the group) is the presence of an ideology that maintains its certainty through the operation of specific mental mechanisms aimed at eliminating all opposition. But the presence of ideology (either political, theological, or psychological) is hardly unusual; indeed it is quite ordinary. The core of the Fascist state of mind – its substructure, let us say – is the ordinary presence of ideology, or what we might call belief or conviction. Arendt finds the seeds of totalitarianism in ideology because ideologies 'claim . . . total explanation,' divorce themselves from all experience 'from which they cannot learn anything new,' insisting therefore on the powerful possession of a secret truth that explains all phenomena, and operates from a logic which orders facts to support the ideological axiom (1986: 470–71).

Thus something almost banal in its ordinariness – namely, our cohering of life into ideologies or theories – is the seed of the Fascist state of mind when such ideology must (for whatever reason) become total.

To achieve such totality, the mind (or group) can entertain no doubt. Doubt, uncertainty, self-interrogation, are equivalent to weakness and must be expelled from the mind to maintain ideological certainty.

This is accompanied, in my view, by a special act of *binding* as doubts and counter-views are expelled, and the mind ceases to be complex, achieving a simplicity held together initially by bindings around the signs of the ideology. Political slogans, ideological maxims, oaths, material icons (such as the flag), fill the gap previously occupied by the polysemousness of the symbolic order. When the mind had previously entertained in its democratic order the parts of the self and the representatives of the outside world, it was participant in a multifaceted movement of many ideas linked to the symbolic, the imaginary, and the real – Lacan's terms. Specifically, words, as signifiers, were always free in the democratic order to link to any other words, in that famous Lacanian slide of the signifiers which expressed the true freedom of the unconscious (this Other) to represent itself. But when representational freedom is foreclosed, signifiers lack this freedom, as ideology freezes up the symbolic order, words becoming signs of positions in the ideological structure. When Michael Dukakis tried to introduce complex issues in the American presidential campaign of 1988, George Bush made the word 'liberal' a sign of weakness visited upon the certain mind by doubt and complexity. To supplement his destruction of the symbolic order Bush made the American flag the sign of the difference between Dukakis and himself; sadly, it signified the end of discourse and the presence of an emergent Fascist frame of mind.

As the empty binding of the order of signs constitutes an act of de-semiosis, it enables the mind to function in a highly simplified way, cushioned initially by the success of such binding.

O'Sullivan believes there is a 'marshall sense' to Fascism, which I shall define here as a binding of mental forces to create a sense capable of murder. In a way the elimination of the symbolic, of polysemousness, is the first murder committed by this order, as the symbolic is the true subversion of ideology. The slide of signifiers will always dissipate a bound meaning and subvert any act of solidarity, a fact which Freud showed so very simply in his numerous demonstrations of how the parapraxis subverts the position of the conscious subject.

Aware of the pathological functions of certainty, Freud wrote in *The Future of an Illusion*:

> An enquiry which proceeds like a monologue, without interruption, is not altogether free from danger. One is too easily tempted into pushing aside thoughts which threaten to break into it, and in exchange, one is left with a feeling of uncertainty which in the end one tries to keep down by over-decisiveness.
>
> (1927: 21)

Ideological certainty, then, in spite of its binding of the self through simplification and the exile of other views, is threatened by the sudden breakthrough of the pushed-aside thoughts, which now must be dynamically ordered by an over-decisiveness.

This will work for some time, perhaps for a long time. Stuart Hampshire claims that the Nazi movement created 'a dizzying sense in German minds that all things are possible and that nothing is forbidden . . . and that there is an infinite moral space now open for natural violence and domination' (1989: 69). The psychoanalyst Janine Chasseguet-Smirgel sees this infinite moral space as the pervert's accomplishment eliminating (at first Oedipal) opposition to desire and gaining objects without opposition. Hampshire argues that the violence inherent in the Nazi moral space has left 'a great vacancy . . . a moral void' (p. 69), which psychoanalysts such as Chasseguet-Smirgel, Khan, and Stoller, who study the perversions, would agree lies at the now empty heart of the pervert.

The moral void created by the simplifying violence of an ideology that brooks no true opposition is also an essential consequence of this stage in the evolution of the Fascist state of mind. For although the binding of signs and the power of certainty dull the subject into complacency, the moral void created by the destruction of opposition begins to make its presence felt. At this point the subject must find a victim to contain that void, and now a state of mind becomes an act of violence. On the verge of its own moral vacuum, the mind splits off this dead core self and projects it into a victim henceforth identified with the moral void. To accomplish this transfer, the Fascist mind transforms a human other into a disposable nonentity, a bizarre mirror transference of what has already occurred in the Fascist's self experience.

As contact with the moral void is lost through projective identification into a victim, and the victim now exterminated, the profoundly destructive processes involved are further denied by a form of delusional narcissism which is constructed out of the annihilation of negative hallucination, an idealization of self accomplished by the negation of any alternative (and thus enviable or persecutory) self or environment. As the negation of the qualities of the other are destroyed via the annihilation of the other, a delusional grandiosity forms in the Fascistically stated mind.

It is at this point that the process of annihilation is idealized in order to supply the Fascist mind with the qualities essential to delusional narcissism. Mental contents are now regarded as contaminates, and the Fascist mind idealizes the process of purging itself of what it has contained. The cleansing of the self suggests the possible birth of a new, forever empty self to be born with no contact with others, with no past (which is severed), and with a future entirely of its own creation.

The foregoing mental processes can be seen, in some respects, in Nietzsche's semi-autobiographical *Ecce Homo*. At a time when he suffered from continuous episodes of vomiting, traveling about Europe he became preoccupied with 'the question of nutriment,' by which he meant not only literally what one ate but also what sort of national culture one took into oneself. He proclaimed, for example, that 'the German spirit is an indigestion' while extolling the virtues of Italian culture and life (1908: 52).

Ecce Homo is, by any account, a deeply anguished text, full of contradictions, which, if they evoke our interest and compassion, are nonetheless remarkable actions of split consciousness. 'I am by nature warlike,' he proclaims (p. 47); yet elsewhere he claims: 'no trace of struggle can be discovered in my life . . . I look out upon my future as upon a smooth sea . . . ruffled by no desire' (p. 65). Perhaps this is a sea of vomit, accomplished through a continuous warlike spirit that leaves him feeling serene.

I refer to Nietzsche because at times he defines quite precisely the unconscious idealization of the self as an empty, and therefore pure, container. 'I possess a perfectly uncanny sensitivity of the instinct for cleanliness,' he writes, adding that this instinct has given him a sense of smell for the unclean 'innermost parts, the "entrails," of every soul' which are the cause of his 'disgust.' No doubt in such moments he would have to vomit up these noxious internal objects in order to maintain his sense of inner purity: 'As has always been customary with me an extreme cleanliness in relation to me is a presupposition of my existence, I perish under unclean conditions' (p. 48).

Such a state of mind extols the virtue of being pure, uncontaminated because nothing is taken into the self, the psyche living from its sense of antiseptic accomplishment by maintaining purity in its own right, achieved by the continuous oral evacuation of the noxious. We can find this phenomenon, however, in ordinary life, whether it be spoken by those who attempt to claim the position of pure Christianity, pure objectivity, pure science, or, dare I say, pure analysis!

The greater the annihilation of the opposition, the more delusionally narcissistic the Fascist mind must become, a psyche now empty of ideas other than those performing a pure sign function – to bind the state of mind – a mind that idealizes itself as a cleaning process. It is not difficult to see, then, why the Fascist did not share the Marxist's belief in a logical history, but supported a movement that idealized struggle (or riddance) in its own right. As Mussolini wrote:

> War alone brings up to their highest tension all human energies and puts the stamp of nobility upon the peoples who have the courage to meet it. Fascism carries this anti-pacifist struggle into the lives of individuals. It is education for combat . . . war is to man what maternity is to the woman. I do not believe in perpetual peace; not only do I not believe in it but I find it depressing and a negation of all the fundamental virtues of man.
>
> (1983: 185)

But this so-called struggle is, in fact, no combat at all. How far we are indeed from that 'noble' warfare found in the chivalric code of the *Song of Roland* when the virtue of one's opponents ennobled the act of physical battle. What is this male maternity to which Mussolini refers? Is it not the death camps, where the living are brought to a container, stripped of their culture, their loved ones, their adult characters, and turned into bizarre fetuses eventually to be killed in this deadly womb?

Some who opposed Fascism, such as Giovanni Zibordi, were able to diagnose the Fascist need to be at war. In 1922, in 'Towards a Definition of Fascism,' he wrote that after the First World War 'the officers sympathize with Fascism because it represents a prolongation of the state of war internally, and of a possibility of war externally' (1983: 89). Psychoanalytically considered, this permanent war is actually against struggle, against the conflicts brought on by continued engagement with opposition views. The idealization of war and of the warrior is a call to a state of mind that rids itself of opposition by permanent violence.

Cotta suggests that there is a 'circuit of de-personalization' conducted by the person who submits to domination by passing on to another victim his own circumstance. 'Violence has its origins and triumphs within the circuit of depersonalization thus actuated, which ultimately leads to a dispossession of oneself' (1985: 63).

This loss of self seems to me to be that loss of humanity to which Brenman referred, and which leaves in its place an idolized skeleton, a figure (leader, ideology, or state) revered for its militant capacity, in the end an idealization of the capacity to murder the self.

Thus the concentration camp, a metaphor of the psychic process of Fascism, is the place where, as the humane parts of the self are dehumanized and then exterminated, the death work is idealized in the death workers who cleanse the body politic of the undesirables. As Susan Sontag argues (1976), when illness is used as a metaphor for the opposition, then the act of elimination is viewed only as a necessary surgical intervention. Reference to the opposition as a disease or cancer that must be removed from society (and mind) is a frequent feature of the Fascist mental state, leading eventually to an idealization of the anti-human. Writing of the mobile killing units of the SS, Leo Kuper muses that 'the "ideal" seems to have been that of the dispassionate, efficient killer, engaged in systematic slaughter, in the service of a higher cause' (1981: 122). 'Higher' here is a metaphor of that grandiosity that achieves nobility by rising above the human: Kuper quotes from an address by the chief of the SS to his top commanders in October 1943:

> Most of you know what it means when 100 corpses lie there, or when 500 corpses lie there, or when 1,000 corpses lie there. To have gone through this and – apart from a few exceptions caused by human weakness – to have remained decent, that has made us great.
>
> (1981: 122)

Intellectual genocide

'Genocide' is a word coined by the jurist Raphael Lemkin in 1944, from the Greek *genos* (tribal race) and the Latin *cide* (killing). Lemkin found a word that linked up with 'tyrannicide' and 'homicide' and thus inscribed itself in the symbolic order, enabling us finally to think about this crime.

The process that leads to a Fascist state (of mind, group, or nation) is unremarkable, and evidence of its emergence is easy to detect. I intend to list the features of what I shall term *intellectual genocide*, to name the mental processes precursor to, and eventually part of, the genocidal act. I do so, as will be clear toward the end of the chapter, not only out of interest in this problem but because I think identification of ordinary genocide (the genocide of everyday life) may lead us toward self scrutiny and confrontation of others when we see that an individual or a group has taken on this form of representation of the other. Because it is so ordinary, it is easily identifiable but, equally, because of its unremarkable status, it is also capable of emergence into mass murder.

I start by differentiating between committive genocide, identifying its visible traits, and omittive genocide, which is an act of omission.

Committive genocide

Distortion. In the early stages of a possible move to a Fascist state of mind, the subject subtly distorts the view of the opponent, rendering it less intelligent or credible than hitherto. This is an ordinary part of debate, but in the extreme manifests itself as slander.

Decontextualization. A point of view held by the opposition is taken out of its proper context, which recontextualized would make the content more credible. This is an ordinary part of debate and the victim of decontextualization will naturally struggle to fill the gaps created by this rhetorical violence. The extreme of this act is the removal of a victim from his tribe, home (i.e., context), isolated for purposes of persecution.

Denigration. The belittling of an opponent's view combines distortion and decontextualization, rendering the opponent's views ridiculous. This is a door through which affects (of scorn and belittlement) move and displace ideation as the machinery of conflict with the opposition.

Caricature. This is the move from the denigration of the opponent's views to cartooning of the individual who presumably holds the views. Again, it is part of ordinary rhetoric to caricature the opposition's view and yet it is a transfer from the view held to the holder of the view. It therefore represents a significant step in the identification of a person or group with ascribed undesirable qualities.

Character assassination. This refers to the attempt to eliminate the opposition by discrediting the personal character of the holder of a view. An unacceptable form of debate, it is an ordinary part of discourse, usually referred to as 'gossip.' This perfectly harmless act of character assassination ('Oh, I do love gossip! Tell me all about it!') which discredits an opponent by conveying fictions or facts in a nonjudicial place – notably where the victim cannot speak for himself – can eliminate a person from the scene of consideration.

Change of name. Again, this is sometimes an acceptable part of debate but with obviously more disturbing manifestations ('kikes' for Jews, 'gooks' for Vietnamese) that form part of the act of elimination of the proper name, precursor to the elimination of the person himself (from the scene of consideration or from life itself). It is ordinary ('You know, what's his name. Thingy'), sometimes acceptable, if tiresome (when a person's name is consciously distorted for humorous purposes), and may be an unconscious parapraxis when the name is unknowingly altered.

Categorization as aggregation. These terms, used by Kuper, are useful to define the moment when the individual is transferred to a mass in which he loses his identity. It may be ordinary: 'Oh, but of course she is Freudian.' It may be permissible, if dicey: 'Well, of course she is ill' or 'Well, he is a psychopath.' Or it may be an extreme act of lumping together: 'He's a Jew.'

Omittive genocide

Absence of reference. This is an act of omission, when the life, work, or culture of an individual or group is intentionally not referred to. Again, this is an ordinary feature of life: one group may get rid of the contributions of another group by never referring to them, or a writer such as Solzhenitsyn may be removed from bookshelves, or in the extreme there are no references to crimes against humanity.

When a person or a group addresses the opposition in the terms outlined above, alarms should ring in the witnesses to such action, who may respond by not engaging in vicious gossip or by directly confronting an individual who distorts, decontextualizes, denigrates, or caricatures the holder of different views. Such confrontation aims to arrest, at the very least, intellectual genocide. It is ordinary. Yet even in its purely rhetorical expression it can be extremely destructive. If an individual or group, previously participant in discourse, is a ceaseless object of intellectual genocide, then the recipients will show the effects. Some will simply leave the scene, no longer partaking in the group – a kind of voluntary exile in the face of persecution. Some may be pushed to express extreme views, victims of a violent innocence who appear to have gone over the edge. Others may somatize the conflict: a heart attack, we know, is often the outcome of extreme duress in one's place of work. Others may attempt to form alliances with the persecutor in an effort to gain some form of protection against their own potential destruction.

My point here is to raise intellectual genocide within our consciousness as a crime against humanity. Since it is ordinary, we can do something about it in the simple Freudian way of talking about it in the here and now and therefore partly divesting the act of its potential by addressing it.

The vicious circle

We could say that until Lemkin created a word for mass murder, 'genocide' managed to elude the signifier and thus escaped its representation in a symbolic order. To this list of obstacles I wish to add a few more.

One of the most perplexing features of the success of intellectual genocide is that its most gifted practitioners not only seem to achieve places of prominence by viciously attacking others; indeed they also seem to become objects of endearment to those who otherwise – one would have thought – would be horrified by such behavior. I recall a right-wing political figure in my hometown in Southern California, a person who vilified the opposition, spread vicious gossip, and damaged many, many people. Yet he was almost loved as a kind of cute monster. I also recall, only a few miles down the road, another person known for his viciousness who was finding himself the object of endearment: Richard Nixon.

And though we knew of Stalin's monstrosity we still turned him into good old Uncle Joe.

The puzzle is why we 'love' these monstrous monsters rather than oppose them. Why are they allowed to climb so far up the ladder of success, sometimes to a place of leadership where they continue to eliminate the opposition in vicious ways? Perhaps they represent us. Perhaps we fear to challenge such an individual. There must be some truth to that, but I also think we observe an interpersonal sleight of hand in which the monster person is 'the impossible loved object' because love here exonerates the subject from responsible opposition: 'I wish I could stand up to Mary, but you know she's just impossible and I'm afraid I love the old monster.' Presumably confrontation of the monster must be reserved for those who don't love the monster, and yet almost everyone gives the same shrug of the shoulder: 'How can Mary be challenged? She is Mary and her very monstrous qualities, darn it, are what we kind of love about her.' In some ways this seems to me to be the interpersonal equivalent of creating a type of joke. Aggression – the anger or outrage evoked by such a person's behavior – is turned into humor: Mary becomes the basis of our laughter about the atrocious. But such an obstacle to confronting viciousness in a person, and in some cases the practice of intellectual genocide, is no laughing matter and deserves our continuing study. I consider this further through a personal vignette.

I attended high school in Orange County, California, during the 1950s, and for a limited period of time it became compulsory for the students to attend Christian anti-Communist crusades in – of all appropriate places – Disneyland, and usually with a visiting speaker, who now and then was Ronald Reagan. I particularly admired one of my history teachers, who struck me as an intelligent and very decent man. Yet in the weeks approaching such events and most intensively at the crusade itself, he became rabid in his hate of the liberal conspiracy that was plotting to overthrow the U.S. government.

I had not known his politics until then and I recall being shocked at the utter transformation in his character whenever contemporary politics entered his mind. I think most of us were bewildered by him and by what I would now term a local psychotic state. But what we did is of interest: we turned this aspect of his behavior into a joke. He became our loved madman, and occasionally one or another of the group would 'push his button' and send him across the boundary from the sane to the insane part of his personality.

Discussing the vicious behavior of a person, people will often say, 'But you know, she really is quite a lovely and kind person' or 'Well, you know, removed from her pulpit she is really quite a different person.' And this is true. But it is not the point. In fact, this opposes the point: humanity (the good parts of the self) is now used to excuse the destructive side of the self. The joke, as always, now borders on the perverse. The humane now authorizes the inhumane as Mary's viciousness is loved, in the economical exchange between the Fascistic and the non-Fascistic parts of her personality.

Even if we accept that compliance with a Mary is in the interests of vicarious support of one's own viciousness, which will always be partly true, the act of dissociative acceptance (the 'how Mary is really privately a nice person' story) colludes with the function of genocide. In this case, however, it is the witness who, by tacitly accepting Mary's viciousness, accepts the eradication of the humane as a joke: the world will then be full of monstrous Mary stories, tales of her beastliness.

When we excuse the destructive behavior of anyone by citing their humanity, we commit a crime against the function of humanity. When we distance ourselves from collusive responsibility for the destructive effects of the vicious person by turning them into a joke of sorts, we pervert the truth. It is this corruption in the citing of humanity that perverts truth and that constitutes essential contextual support for any vicious person's successful establishment of the Fascistic parts of themselves in the successful movement of the social group to its own Fascism.

The noncollusive witness to that personality change that occurs when the person crosses over from the sane to the insane parts of the self, is initially shocked by this transference. We all know how stunning it is, when discussing an issue with someone, to witness the person's vicious espousal of a doctrine that derives part of its energy from the intellectual annihilation of the other. We may be speechless. Such a rupture also occasions a sense of dissociation: we feel immediately separated out from the conversant's insanity. And following this dissociation, part of us will feel deadened by the eruption, as now it is clear to us that the other is subject to an internal Fascistic process. In a way our response is our victimage. It is in feeling shocked, dissociated, and deadened that we share elements in common with those who are more severely traumatized by socially operant Fascism.

We may also share responsive qualities in common with a collusive witness, whereby we may try to recover from this trauma by reminding ourselves how, in so many other ways, this person is not only sane but likable. In this respect we use our humanity and its link to the humane parts of the other to recuperate from the trauma, but, as suggested, the irony of this is that it ultimately excuses, and finally supports, the destruction of humanity. Often we feel a certain dread as we sense our responsibility to those who are the objects of this person's intellectual genocide. We must say something that at the very least marks our opposition to the Fascistic state of mind.

When we exonerate a vicious person's actions by citing elements of their humanity, I think we create a perversion in logic itself – in thinking – that is part of what we may consider the vicious circle. It is of interest that from the seventeenth century the word 'vicious' was used to describe a fault in logic, when a conclusion was realized by false means of reasoning. Webster's third definition of the vicious circle cites this fault in logic: 'an argument which is invalid because its conclusion rests upon a premise which itself depends on the conclusion.' The argument that Mary is really a good human being, in spite of her nefarious actions, because she is at the same time a human being, is a circular argument, a flawed logic that perverts the truth because it comes round full circle. Indeed, I use the word 'vicious' to describe the person in a Fascist state of mind not only because this word signifies one who is 'full of faults,' which seems an apt description of one carrying moral voids determined by massive evacuations, but because we may also speak of a particular process – the vicious circle – which is definitionally affiliated with the vicious person, that suits my analysis of such a person as involved in a particular mental process.

A vicious circle is also defined as 'a situation in which the solution of one problem gives rise to another, but the solution of this, or of other problems rising out of it, brings back the first, often with greater involvement.' Another definition states: 'a situation in which one disease or disorder results in another which in turn aggravates the first.' It is exactly this type of process which, in my view, takes place in the Fascist state of mind: whatever the anxiety or need that sponsors the drive to certainty, which becomes the dynamic in the Fascist construction, the outcome is to empty the mind of all opposition (on the actual stage of world politics, to kill the opposition), a process that ironically undermines the vicious person. It does this by creating a moral void which further increases the under-lying uncertainty which set the mind on its pathological track to certainty in the first place.

It is a procedure which Nietzsche regards as a virtue: 'the doctrine of "eternal recurrence," that is to say of the unconditional and endlessly repeated *circular course* [italics mine] of all things' (1908: 81). The cycle of purification through violent expulsion leaves a void which Nietzsche tries to fill with a notion of tran-quillity derived from the liquefaction of opposition: 'I swim and bathe and splash continually as it were in water, in any kind of perfectly transparent and glittering element' (48), which is possible until he meets up with any human element which fills him with a sense of disgust (48). To the extent to which Nietzsche portrays early on the process of thought subsequently peculiar to the Nazi movement, we can see how the Fascist sea of inner tranquillity is mirrored by those horrid seas of internment camps that contain the Fascist's vomit: the place that purifies them because it contains the indigestible opposition.

For a person incarcerated in the concentration camp, it is hard to find any vestige of the humane that could possibly offer resistance to the Fascist state. In *The Informed Heart* (1960), Bruno Bettelheim tells us that humane gestures expressed by one detainee to another were punished by death. One eventually could not help the other. Nor indeed could the subject express any of his feelings about the treatment meted out to the other and to oneself. Expression of feeling led to further torture and sometimes to extinction. Thus those qualities we value so highly as expressions of humanity – helping others in need and expressing our feelings and views – were eliminated. In that situation, incarcerated in Buchenwald, Bettelheim knew that to lose one's humanity was to risk personal madness. How could he remain sane? He discovered that it was through an ironic act sponsored by his extreme state: he would observe the SS, study them, consider at an intel-lectual remove what was taking place. 'If I should try to sum up in one sentence what my main problem was during the whole time I spent in the camps,' he writes, 'it would be: to protect my inner self in such a way that if, by any good fortune, I should regain liberty, I would be approximately the same person I was when deprived of liberty' (p. 126). He had to accept, therefore, a split in his personality between the private world of his own thoughts – which ultimately were unreachable by the SS – and 'the rest of the personality that would have to submit and adjust for survival' (p. 127). This is an extreme state of victimage in which the subject can only retain his humanity by preserving his sanity, which he accomplishes by accepting a split of sorts in his personality. It is interesting that thought and memory, the capacity to perceive reality, to think it, and remember it, become the core of potential recovery to a humane future.

We can see, then, why any person or group which has suffered a genocide must reach a point in the process of recuperation when remembering what actually happened is crucial. It is not only an action aimed at objectifying the crimes committed against the self, but, as Bettelheim hints, to recuperate from one's own destruction of the humane parts of the self in the interests of survival. As the victim seeks his own safety and deserts his fellow man, there will be an enormous loss of self respect. Only through further self analysis and self expression can the victim recuperate that love of himself that is an ordinary part of the generative narcissistic structure of human relations. I suggest, therefore, that the ultimate human response to genocide is self preservation: following physical liberation from the terms of aggression, this curiously inhuman side of the preservation of one's humanity (the will to survive) will move toward its abandoned humanities first by memory, then by speech, and finally by true grief. There is a triumph, here, of the seemingly inhuman (our Darwinian move) that is curiously more humane than the collusive acts of humanizing the monstrous parts of the self.

If a person, group, institution, or country truly wishes to recover from the traumas of intellectual or physical genocide, then it will have to remember the crimes it has committed. The act of remembering is the antecedent to forgiveness (of self and others) and instrumental to the reparative rehumanization of the group. This painful process is often bypassed by denials ('it is water under the bridge') aimed to thwart recollection, and by transfers to the next generation, which is somehow meant to naturalistically displace the crimes of the older generation and absolve that generation from its collective responsibility. And as we know, a new generation, though seemingly possessed of its own displacing vision of the future, is highly liable to inherit the sins of the fathers.

Chapter 7

Why Oedipus?

When Freud designated *Oedipus the King* as a theatrical metaphor of the crucial psychic conflict of the individual, linking the worlds of politics, literature, and psychology in one fell swoop, like Sophocles he dramatized the many factors that constitute human complexity, as he was astutely aware of the mythic, civic, psychic, and cultural elements that contribute to the living of a life.

There is a vast, intelligent, and compelling critical literature on the play and on Freud's view of the Oedipal scene in the life of the individual, which I shall not review here. Instead I shall consider the Oedipal dilemma as a complex that is independent, if that is possible, of any of its singular participants, including, of course, the child Oedipus who kills his father and sleeps with his mother. This is not to diminish the solitary significance of the Oedipal horror or its psychic place in the life of every child whose desire threatens him with terrors and whose father is essential to the survival of such fears, but I think Sophocles explores a more tragic fate than the frame of mind constituted by the Oedipal dilemma.

The planes of reference

Hesiod's *Theogeny* was the fundamental oral version of the Greek myths passed from one generation to the next. Curious forms of condensation, myths often derive from specific historical events, and when they do they bear some link to reality; but the persons who form the tableau of a myth exist at different times with represented events from diverse unrelated cultures yoked into one false unity, occasionally populated by fabulous creatures and fantastical events. Versions of a myth are also subject to change, in what Robert Graves terms 'iconotropy': the moment when a mythographer deliberately misinterprets the visual representations of a sacred picture (the pictorial place of myth as a visual condensation) by weaving a verbal picture that changes it (1977: 21).

The legend of Oedipus was well known to Athenians. The audience knew the outcome of the hero's future, and even though differing playwrights and story-tellers changed the inner details of the legend, Oedipus always slew his father and slept with his mother. As Knox points out, Sophocles used this fact to place the audience in the position of the gods who could see the full course of events and yet, by identification with Oedipus, be drawn into the inner texture of his specific dilemma: a mirroring of that oscillation we all endure in life between our complex reflective self states and the location of the simple experiencing self.

What are some of the elements that Sophocles weaves into what I term the psychic context of his play?

In the Greek middle ages, to which some of the play refers, kingship was the universal form of government. With the collapse of trade, kings could no longer afford their retinues and gradually their power was usurped by a regent, then a council, then a group of judges, to form the nine Archons of Athens which formed the structure of Greek democracy. The kings were not abolished, however; they served a ceremonial function closely allied to the temple and the patron god of the city, an ironic affiliation as the temple took the place of the palace.

The Greeks also had in mind – in some part of their mind – the transition from the world of the warrior-king (the Achilles figures of Homer) to the world of the figure of discourse – a Pericles – who could participate in democracy. This evolution is not total or absolute. In Sparta, only a hundred miles from Athens, was another society that continued to revere the patriarchal. Shall we speak, then, of Athenians knowing of two structures: one monarchial (or dictatorial) and the other democratic?

At the same time they would have had in mind the legendary transition from a matriarchal world order to a patriarchal one. It is unclear whether there ever was a matriarchal society in Crete before the invasion by the Greeks, but even if there was, it is hard to believe that such a culture was, in fact, known by the Athenians, as surely it would have spawned a rich mythological elaboration. But the Athenians certainly did have a powerful myth of a matriarchal line, as in their mythology Gaia was the founding god of all the gods and mankind. She was a kind of primordial element who gave birth to Uranus without coupling with a male, and then coupled with Uranus to propagate the gods. Greek mythology is in large part the saga of conflict between men and women. So, if there was in fact no matrilineal culture, there was certainly a powerful myth of an originating maternal power out of which men emerged and eventually took power. This evolution, if one can put it that way, was very much in their mind, and certainly Sophocles played upon its ontological resonance in the life of each child who was born from the mother and who became subject to the father's law.

If we believe Robert Graves, however (whose work on myths is open to serious question), there *was* a matriarchal society in Crete which was dominated by a queen who annually appointed a king. In prehistoric Greek culture this king was allegedly appointed annually (a probable representation of the seasons and of fertility), while the queen ruled until her death, passing on her power to her eldest daughter. Occasionally the king substituted for the queen and wore false breasts. At the end of his annual reign the king was 'sacrificed' and there were many and varied symbolizations of his death. Commonly, he endured a symbolic execution, yielding his kingship for one day to a boy-king who 'died' at the end of the day, although sometimes he remained as alternative to the king. Note how he might be killed:

His ritual death varied greatly in circumstance; he might be torn in pieces by wild women, transfixed by a sting-ray spear, felled with an axe, pricked in the heel with a poisoned arrow, flung over a cliff . . . or killed in a prearranged chariot crash.

(Graves, 1977: 18)

Perhaps audiences attending *Oedipus Rex* identified Laius's death by chariot and Oedipus's immediate reign as partly symbolic of a legendary annual ritual, practiced within a matriarchy, a mythic trace of an alleged prior social structure considered now within a democratic society which was still bearing traces of its more recent patriarchal power structure. Thus the mother, the father, and the group are part of the psychic texture of this play, layered into the action at different points of symbolic reference.

The audience also knew of a legend that Tiresias had once seen two snakes coupling and had intervened to kill the female. He was immediately turned into a woman and could only regain his masculinity some seven years later when he returned to kill the male serpent. Indeed, he was responsible for a small war between Hera and Zeus, who were quarreling over which sex gained the greater pleasure in intercourse. They called for Tiresias to settle the matter, as he had been both a man and a woman. He infuriated Hera by claiming that the woman had the greater pleasure, but that is another matter. What is of immediate interest to us is Sophocles's placement of Tiresias in this play as such a crucial figure, insofar as he represents not only bisexuality but bisexuality based upon the murder of the female element (snake) which can only be undone by another murder (of the male snake). The psychic density of the Tiresias myth only adds to the play's extraordinary complexity.

From the above mythical elements one could add many other features which become part of the psychic context.

1   That the return-of-the-exile story was a well-known pretext (or subsequently revisionist act) for invasion by a foreigner.
2   That children were sometimes abandoned and left to die, having been spiked in the foot, to stop the ghost of the child from coming back to haunt the parents.
3   That outside the cities were people in settlements not taking part in city life, people who were exiled for one reason or another – for example, younger sons who could not be included in the city space and so were abandoned to the fringes.

We could dwell on these different factors and deconstruct the play in a particular way following the logic of each element's contribution to Sophocles's argument. My aim, however, is only to establish that Sophocles's play operates on many planes of reference, and I shall now consider how this tells us something about the nature of the complex Freud associated with Oedipus.

The evocation of dense psychic texture

Sophocles constructs a drama that will evoke within the audience a dense texture of inner associations so subtle and complex that as they play upon the mind they invite the acute work of the ego to process them. But the ego will inevitably fail to grasp in consciousness the full meaning of the events – not simply as this is a cognitive impossibility but because the unconscious issues presented are so disturbing that the subject represses or splits off what is knowable. The drama invites the subject's psychic response to displace conscious frames of mind, which is partly achieved by subversive presentation of a myth which all presume to know in advance, thereby lulling the witnesses into a false and premature sense of the play's meaning.

Although the myth of Oedipus's life is not a complex tale, Sophocles dramatizes the story from so many interlaced dimensions (from Oedipus's view, from the leader's perspective, from Creon's place, from Jocasta's view) that its mythic integrity is subverted by multiple points of identification with its characters, challenging what we think we know.

For example, we know Oedipus discovers that he has in fact killed his real father; or rather, we know this will be true. But when, along with him, we hear that there were several men at the crossroads, like Oedipus, we have some momentary doubt. How could it have been he if there were several attackers? Indeed when the story of the murder is first put to Oedipus, his powerful conviction to root out the truth marries with Jocasta's later admonition to stop thinking and to forget. Creon's martial actions and Tiresias's befuddling riddles also bear the sense of powerful conviction and certainty that pervades the play. But this sense is continually undermined, as we know, by the course of events, which reveal more truth to challenge that sense.

If we were to review Oedipus's first response to Creon's story of Laius's murder, we would, like some in the audience, note how Oedipus inserts psychic truth into the discourse. Speaking of the attendant who survived the murder of Laius, Creon says:

> He said thieves attacked them – a whole band, not single-handed, cut King Laius down.
>
> (135–40)

to which Oedipus replies:

> A thief, so daring, so wild, he'd kill a king? Impossible, unless conspirators paid him off in Thebes.
>
> (140–45)

Oedipus changes the story to murder by a single thief, and no one corrects his error. He repeats this error in conversation with the leader.

LEADER: Laius was killed, they say, by certain travelers.
OEDIPUS: I know, but no one can find the murderer. (330–35)

Note now how the leader responds:

LEADER: If the man has a trace of fear in him he won't stay silent long, not with
your curses ringing in his ears. (335–40)

Oedipus has transferred one truth into the prior taken, or objective version, so that
now his truth usurps the former narrative account without any apparent conscious
recognition of this.

How many people in the audience caught this? How many in Freud's Vienna
recognized this, or how many today pick it up? We shall never know. But surely
some will miss it. Perhaps they are feeling the sense of impending trauma as
Oedipus echoes his own initial dispossession. He does not know that he is Theban
and that he was abandoned by the king to die upon a mountain. We know this.
And as he calls for the exile of the murderer and sets his people on a course of
action, we know that he will re-create the original trauma to himself, now lived
out in his mature years.

When he subsequently rails against Creon, who has in innocence gone to fetch
Tiresias, who in the audience is not overcome with a sense – from the emotional
unconscious – that Oedipus is correct to be suspicious and enraged? And if we are
not, note how deftly Sophocles nudges us to recall something:

CREON: . . . But this injury you say I've done you, what is it? ·
OEDIPUS: Did you induce me, yes, or no, to send for that sanctimonious prophet?
CREON: I did. And I'd do the same again.
OEDIPUS: All right then, tell me, how long is it now since Laius . . .
CREON: Laius – what did *he* do?
OEDIPUS: Vanished, swept from sight, murdered in his tracks. (620–25)

Have we noticed that Creon breaks in on Oedipus to demand what Laius did,
thereby calling attention to Laius's crimes? As Creon speaks, he unwittingly
represents Laius in the heat of a moment, so when Oedipus expresses his sense
that a deep injustice has been committed against him, we are reminded of his
victimage. Do we recognize the expression of unconscious truth? Laius's crime?
He 'vanished'!

But perhaps this moment is lost upon the audience, some of whom are caught
by Oedipus's suspicions that Tiresias is a 'sanctimonious prophet.' Caught up in
thinking about something else, they do not hear Creon's question, thus failing to
note its unconscious point.

The experience of being caught up in one's own particular train of thought is a
feature of all human mental life, but one that especially fascinated Sophocles as
he played upon the unconscious capacities of his audience by bringing them into

the web of the play's complexity, displacing coherence with the fecund violence of emotional turbulence and wild associations.

We – or, I suggest, Sophocles – could argue that at any one moment in time the truth lies right before us. Certainly more than one critic has commented on Oedipus's extraordinary failure to see the truth before he set himself to suffer it. Why didn't he realize that, having killed the wealthy man at this crossroads, he had in fact killed a king? Why didn't he ask questions upon his arrival? Many more points along this track could be raised, but we know that human denial and the power of the wish are sufficient to blind.

And if Sophocles intends to set us an example of the extremes of mental process by putting Oedipus before our eyes, as certainly he does – when we learn that we should allow time to pass before moving to action and that we should listen to others – he does so only to signify a feature of our own personality: that we are a human complex.

Indeed, Sophocles lets us know – if we see it (and many have not) – the true riddle posed by the Sphinx, or perhaps I should say, the other riddle. We all know the manifest riddle and Oedipus solves it, to apparently rid the world of a scourge. But the Sphinx poses a hidden riddle, which Sophocles puts before his audience. In the streets of Athens, after the play was over, did one Athenian turn to his companion and ask, 'Yes, but what was the true riddle?' I rather suspect so. Even as I think that, not having the text before them, they may have quarreled over what exactly was said.

What was the true riddle? Oedipus asks Creon why, after Laius was killed, the people of Thebes failed to investigate the crime and pursue the culprit. Creon replies:

> The singing, riddling Sphinx. She . . . persuaded us to let the mystery go and concentrate on what lay at our feet.[1]
>
> (145–50)

Familiar? It should be. How like Jocasta, who urges Oedipus to forget: 'From this day on, I wouldn't look right or left' (950). So the Sphinx who holds the city in its frightful female clutches is echoed by the near-wicked queen who urges denial. Look not to the left or right. But what if Oedipus looked below him, for example, at his feet, which name him? What if he did what the Sphinx said and concentrated on his feet? Perhaps by thinking of his affliction he would have connected it to the nature of child abandonment, as such children frequently had their feet punctured to prevent their ghosts from haunting the murderers. But what if Creon and his consort had in fact listened to this comment, which appears to evade the truth but which becomes the new riddle, that if recognized and solved would have

---

1 Fagle's translation is a literal rendering of the Greek text, thus remaining faithful to Sophocles's play on 'feet,' which renders the Sphinx's statement a new riddle.

prevented the horrors to come? For upon hearing of the stranger's name – Oedipus (swollen foot) – a particularly thoughtful Greek might have said, 'Ah! This is the foot that lies at our feet: the swollen foot of your name.' Focusing on Oedipus, then, as the clue to Laius's murder would have resulted in his arrest and prevented his marriage to Jocasta.

But perhaps this secret riddle has gone unnoticed by some. Certainly on my first readings of the play I 'missed it,' and, as with Oedipus, it is arguable that, having missed it, I was unaware of Creon's and Jocasta's complicity – among others, including Tiresias – in failing (refusing?) to stop the course of actions. Is this true? Am I right to see things this way? Or is it misguided? Is there something about my interpretation which is incorrect? Am I at the mercy of my own limitations, whatever they may be?

Yet is that not part of the true riddle posed by the Sphinx? When Oedipus killed Laius, the people aimed to deliver themselves from this beast by answering her 'old riddle,' but now new events had usurped it and she added to it with a new one which no one saw (except perhaps Tiresias). The underlying realities that cause anguish change. They change, as Freud saw, because of the dynamic nature of internal mental life, where wishes, needs, defenses, and reparations change our feelings about ourself, others, and events. To have answered the secret riddle was not a matter of figuring it out. Had the Sphinx said, 'I have a new riddle: the murderer of Laius will lie at your feet,' some clever Greek would have thought, 'Oedipus! Swollen foot,' and the murderer would have been found. But the point I believe that Sophocles makes, and the reason Freud is drawn to this text, is that solving particular mental contents (i.e., riddles) requires an understanding of the psychic reality generating the changes of mental content, as any mind is always reformulating its contents, and to prevent the plague of rash action one must not become too set in one's ways.

So to heed this Sophoclean admonition I shall now set my chapter on a new, somewhat different course, which I shall weave into the question 'Why Oedipus?' In what respects, then, does my argument bear on the Oedipal child's dilemma?

The child's discovery

Just as Athenian culture 'knew' it had once, at least in legend, derived from a maternal deity, so too does each child. The infant lives within the complex laws and unconscious principles of being and relating that are primarily conveyed by the mother, even when she communicates the father's views, her culture, the social order, and above all her language: the symbolic.

The dawn of the Freudian Oedipal era in the child's life is between the ages of four and six, a time when contributions from many previously latent sources now impinge upon the child who must consider them. Prior to this, he or she was being protected and held by maternal provision of care so that disturbing mental contents were always seemingly processed by the mother's many acts of containment as she often functioned as an auxiliary to the infant's self.

During the infant phase of the subject's life, in what we might term the matri-linear order, psychic structure is being laid down as the infant builds inner models of the world – of himself and his objects – that find reliable statuses as continuous points of inner view. By virtue of early infantile defenses, different psychic struc-tures can be established around various types of object set up around differing experiences of the mother, father, and parental couple.

In the good enough Oedipus Complex – so to speak – the infant has already slept with the mother and enjoyed the fruits of this triumph. This good position emerges from the intimacy of mother and infant who have killed the father, by temporarily holding off the outside world that he represents, and this killing off is a permissible pleasure, which the father supports as the not good enough mother. Then the father enters the scene as a new figure in his own right, but through the infant's, or now, I should say, child's body. It is the genital drive which puts the father and the child in a new place. A new psychic structure is being laid on, generated by libidinal development. It is at this stage in the boy's life that the mother is imaginatively specified as a different object of desire and the father is now seen as a different rival to the child's claim.

Anxiety about castration testifies to the specificity of this eros, as the zone determining the excitement is localized as a threat. But is it the fear of castration that drives the boy toward the increased identification with the father which even-tually resolves his Oedipal dilemma? If this were so, if an anxiety became the source of an aim for identification, such an identification would itself be a psycho-pathy. One need only compare this to Klein's depressive position theory, for example, when the infant's realization of its harming the object of love inaugu-rates a new perspective in object relations. Fear of castration as the motive of identification would be a seriously retrograde act.

It is my view that the child resolves the Oedipal dilemma by a discovery that emerges out of his anxieties and desires. He or she has a claim upon the mother: no child is in any doubt about that. Smell of the mother is still inside the Oedipal child. But each child also realizes in quite a profound way that the father preceded the child's relation to the mother, and it is recognition of such precedents – on the part of both girl and boy – that is an identification: a correct identification of one's place, of one's position in time, that informs the child of the mother's prior desire.

The child may oppose this recognition and murderous fantasies may increase as he strives to deny the fact of lineage, something we know that Oedipus did by sleeping with his mother, to give symbolic birth to himself as well as to make his sons and daughters into brothers and sisters.

The child in the Oedipal dilemma discovers the patrilineal line along with the Name of the Father that breaks the illusions emerging from the infant's place in the matrilineal order. But it is the child's emergent genital primacy that drives him to this discovery, that in an odd paradoxical sense breaks the matrilineal mold as the erotic mother – now his or her object – displaces the infant from the child's place. So it is not the father whose frightful presence displaces the child in the first place, but the child's own erotic desire for the mother which creates in him a new object and a new self, as a new psychic structure arises out of this libidinal position.

It is at this age that the child philosopher emerges, asking about ontology, the origin of the universe, and the reason for death's existence. The child poses these questions because he is developing a sense of perspective that naturally derives from his continuous oscillation between being two children: the new child who sees the mother as erotic and the old child who is her infant. However, during this transitional period, in the course of 'answering' questions about the origins of their body's genital urges, they discover with what sex they are identified, there-fore with what parent they are identified, and they realize their lineage. As they are in conflict with themselves between the two child states, the father will be defined largely according to the child's inner state of private conflict. In the course of discovering his desire the child recognizes the desires of the mother and the father and becomes fascinated by the father's specificity – his difference.

My aim now is to come to the core of this chapter: I wish to discuss why and how the Oedipal dilemma (Freud favored this phrase) is displaced by the Oedipus Complex, or how the child's anguish in the triangle is resolved to the point of a form of liberation from it – a liberation from dilemma into complexity.

Psychic complexity

As the child endures the Oedipal dilemma he recurrently splits in two: as child back to infant, returning to child. In the course of these movements he creates, destroys, and recreates new sets of internal objects: the parents of infancy, the new parents of genital representation. We could say that the child is discovering the nature of internal representations, that fathers and mothers change within one according to internal self states. This is not so much a fully conscious recognition, except insofar as the child becomes interested in the nature of episte-mology, which indicates preconscious recognition of the problems linked to knowing.

As Oedipus tells the Leader at Colonus that he is 'born of the royal blood of Thebes,' the Leader cries in horror: 'You, you're *that* man – ?' (235–40). All in Colonus know that man, who lives as a vividly disturbing internal object. But Oedipus stands before them as the actual other from whom all internal objects derive: 'Your name, old stranger, echoes through the world' (330–35).

When Oedipus meets Theseus at his second crossroads ('And now, seeing you at this crossroads, beyond all doubt I know you in the flesh'), he meets a new father who recognizes the difference between an internal object and its actual otherness (620–25). Theseus promises to give Oedipus time to speak, telling him 'I want to know,' and this father who can delay his impulses, give himself time, and think about reality is the new father of the Oedipal child who though driven by desires is not so rash, so harsh, or so omnipotent: not, that is, so infantile (645–50). '. . . once a man regains his self-control, all threats are gone . . . Rest assured, no matter if I'm away, I know my name will shield you well' (750–55).

If there is a father the absolute opposite of a Laius, it is present now in the person of Theseus.

Theseus is, however, simply a different paternal object. If Sophoclean tragedy tells us only one thing, it is that relations always change, nothing can be taken for granted; in other words, we are to be complex, indeed to live within the complex. The dream, for example, exemplifies to the child just how his objects change, leaving him bewildered by the shifting prophecies contained in these seemingly oracular moments. If the Western theatergoer finds it difficult to tolerate the Sophoclean hero's dispensation to the differing oracles, one perhaps only needs reminding that each night we dream we see and hear a strange other view of our life and our destiny.

This is a sobering discovery for the child as his infantile omnipotence would have all other minds and behaviors accord with his wishes, but now he begins to reflect on human difference and the inability to reach the other through omnipotence, a paradoxical occasion, as knowing now how unique the other is, he comes to realize the odd fact of his own peculiarity. In addition, he quietly recognizes that the place he has been living – formerly assumed to exist in order to further his needs – bears the name 'family.' He is in one. And there are other families which have altogether different characters, created by interacting subjectivities that transcend the individual contribution. The family is a group which dissolves the singularly powerful prior authorities of the mother and father.

The child whose Oedipal dilemma remains the organizing conflict of his life often sustains this personality conflict, in my view, because he cannot accept the labile and chaotic authority of the group. He remains attached to the father, or in combat with the authority of the parental couple, because such parental organizations are more comforting than the identity-defying features of the group where participants will find themselves continually displaced by ideas, feelings, and processes well beyond the influence of the individual.

Sophocles plays with that loss of definition that transpires through participation in the group as he alternately makes each of the figures in the play seem reasonable, empathic, searchingly wise, blind, vicious, stupid, and murderous. Who is Creon? Jocasta? Tiresias? . . . Oedipus? There seems a different figure for each shifting place in the group dynamic.

Furthermore, Sophocles was writing for a Greek audience that was somewhere between an oligarchy and a democracy. How was it to live in a democracy where one was a member of a group free to speak one's mind? What was the group that composed the democracy? We continue to pose this question today, not simply because governments are usually somewhere between democracies and dictatorships, but because these two states echo an inner problematic in man and woman: whether to stay inside a monarchical government or dictatorship, or whether to kill the king, revolt, and establish a group government.

There are anxieties in both directions. A monarchy can devolve into absolute rule. A leader can rule oppressively and compel the people to silence. This form of government seems a political analogue to the neurotic process, based as it is on the dominance of the ego, and its power to repress an unwanted view, when the only freedom of representation is by subtle derivative. In oppressed times allegory thrives as people read a hidden meaning beneath the manifest text presented to them.

A democracy can lead to a chaos in expression. Ideas are impossible to suppress, as no one has authority sufficient for such an action; but they can be split off and made bizarre in a deeply mad world that characterizes the psychotic process. In *Oedipus the King* the flux of mind of the chorus echoes the fickle movement of thought and feeling in the democratic process which permits any expression and invites cacophony.

Families live in what we term the household, and whether the 'headship' tends toward the matriarchal or the patriarchal, above all else it is a group, an interpersonal place, arrived at from the many contributions of its members who can establish an atmosphere of place, even if their private representations of the persons there are inevitably idiomatic.

As I have suggested, this new object – the family group – echoes the divergent and coterminus internal contributions to the child's sense of his own complexity. This 'spirit of . . . place' (75) that Oedipus finds at Colonus is a space sanctified by the founding father whose sense of fairness lives on in the hearts of the people. It is also a place combined with the maternal, as this sacred ground is the dwelling place of the Eumenides, who live under the mother earth.

At the point in the child's life when she or he can see the patrilineal and matrilineal lines, each becomes aware of who the father's parents are – particularly the father's father – and who the mother's mother is. This inauguration of a generational sense of personal place constitutes the emergence of a capacity to think about the links between grandparents (and their personalities) and parents (and their personalities). It is a line connected by a particularly mythic narrative as actual events, screen memories, embellishments, unconscious misreadings, and so on condense the grandparents' past – and what little history they know of their family – into the family's legend.

However much the father's name may constitute a law, which among other things prohibits incest, it is not the father who establishes justice in the group. 'Loose, ignorant talk started dark suspicions and a sense of injustice cut deeply too,' the chorus tells Jocasta (775), implicitly recognizing the power of the group to usurp any single authority. 'Strange response . . . unlawful,' muses Oedipus upon hearing Tiresias refusing to speak the truth (368). How can criminal acts come to justice? An issue which we know strikes at the very heart of *Antigone*. In a child's conflict with the mother, or the father, or a brother, where is a just settlement to be found? In the magisterial entrance of the father, who upholds the law true to his name? But his decisions may not be just; a grievance may well continue long past his adjudication, based on the child's psychic reality, especially when a true injustice is committed by a family member. It is certainly at this age of complexity that the child realizes that his psychic claims – for justice among other things – not only compete with the equally intense psychic claims of other members of the group, but his own area of judicial consideration, his internal world, is often torn between opposing positions and, finally, his internal world is well beyond the knowing of even the most insightful and patient father. Psychic life itself puts one substantially out of the reaches of intersubjective knowing, even if it simultaneously enhances it.

This is one of the child's discoveries at this age: that one is only a part of necessarily competing subjectivities, that one's omnipotence is radically altered by this, and invocations of the name of the mother or the father do not conjure justice. Sophocles knew this well, as did all Greeks. For the household was that space created by each family, sponsoring its only shared inner reality but also the axis of many conflicts and injustices. To some extent the *polis* evolved out of a need to resolve conflicts between households. 'You have to come to a city that practices justice,' Theseus tells the transgressor Creon (1040). Creon earlier tries to invoke the civic sense in claiming Oedipus: 'Years ago your city gave you birth' (860–65).

Beyond the psychic reality of the family in the civic place, men and women contribute to the body that supersedes and coordinates the authority of the household. For the child this new place will first be encountered at school, the place where I think child observers can clearly see whether or not the young have 'resolved' the Oedipal dilemma. Many will cling to an internal loving mother as they refuse intercourse with their peers, while others will reflect the conflict either by assuming the law of the father or by hiding in terror. Equally, though all children will show traces of both prior authorities, those who have achieved the Oedipus Complex have discovered perspective and know something of the nature of psychic life that makes no one a natural power. To live in the group one must be able to appreciate and live with this sense of life's complexity.

In the adolescent epoch there is a revival of the Oedipal child's discovery of the potential isolation suggested by the complexity of subjectivity. The adolescent feels the anguish of the shifting internal representations of self and other, just as he or she also lives inside a peer group that vividly announces the precarious nature of group dynamics. At a time of psychobiological growth, there is a re-emergence of transformed regressions, as the adolescent seeks deep first loves that provide sexual and emotional gratification, just as finding some way to be liked, to become one of the group, is an effort to overcome the anxiety generated by group life. By transforming the intrinsic nature of the group into a falsely organized peer culture, adolescent groups are like gangs congregated to fight the anxieties of groups themselves! As time passes, as anxieties diminish, as the fruits of complexity are appreciated – particularly the value of diverse perspectives – the need for group bonding wanes, as does the urge for intense symbiotic puppy loves.

'Time is the great healer, you will see,' Creon tells Oedipus, and for once we can agree with him (1664). It is at this point that time seems to possess something naturally curative. Resolution of the Oedipus Complex leads to this curative sense of time, enabling internal and interpersonal conflicts to heal as the subject finds that with time comes increased perspective: that which has been split off or denied – in the interests of one's narcissistic economy, for example – comes back into the picture, rendering one and one's relations more complex.

Resolution of the oedipal dilemma

In his theory of the primal horde, Freud imagines the earliest stage of society, one dominated by a powerful father who kept the women to himself and banished his sons. Eventually these sons form a group which operates under different laws from those of the primal father because they enjoy a kind of parity with one another, a shared deprivation that was organizing, and one eventful day the gang of brothers killed and devoured the father, which Freud saw as a form of identification. In the second stage of social evolution, according to Freud in *Totem and Taboo*, 'the patriarchal horde was replaced in the first instance by the fraternal clan,' but in a third era of progression the family became the unit that returned to the fathers what had been taken by the primal horde (1913: 146).

In his theory of the clan's displacement of the father, Freud seems very close indeed to grasping that the group automatically displaces the authority of the father. And one may wonder if the totem meal that he believes stands in for the cannibalized father, theoretically to prevent further parricides, isn't more a commemorative mourning of the true end of the father: his displacement in the child's mind by a colony of new cathexes, libidinal interests, and idiomatic investments. In *Group Psychology and the Analysis of the Ego* I think Freud suggested a different model for the dissolution of the child's 'father complex.' 'Each individual,' he writes, 'is a component part of numerous groups, he is bound by ties of identification in many directions, and he has built up his ego ideal upon the most various models' (1921: 129). It is the force of these 'identifications in many directions' that breaks up the father complex, resulting in a series of *progressive disidentifications* as the child seeks to select objects that give more precise expression to his idiom.

Thus the Oedipal child learns that it is his fate to be born into a very specific family, and more importantly, to be a subject who holds or contains in his own mind an object world, a group of percepts, introjects, and identifications that deepens his sense of his own complexity and radically problematizes the authority of his narrative voice. But if the child's discovery of the complexity of the human being radicalizes perspective and in itself usurps the patriarchal structure, it sends him to a new place, inaugurating a new order which derives from this decentering of psychic structure. What is the child's sense of himself and of life at this moment in his evolution? Knox views Sophocles's play as a model for modern drama because it presents us with 'our own terror of the unknown future which we fear we cannot control – our deep fear that every step we take forward on what we think is the road of progress may really be a step forward to a foreordained rendezvous with disaster' (p. 133). I think this partly captures something of the Oedipal child's inner emotional reality, for the child is coming to know something, something really quite like Oedipus's discovery, that in a sense is quite tragic and certainly disturbing.

Oedipus's demand to know the cause of suffering results in discovery of his own unwitting fulfillment of a prophecy, and Sophocles permeates this play and *Oedipus at Colonus* with another peripeteia: the king gradually comes to encounter the force of his own personality and how it has also caused his undoing. As I have said, it is this discovery, the recognition that one is a psychic entity, possessed of a mind divided between interacting logics of consciousness and unconsciousness, that I think characterizes the Oedipal child's epiphany. It is not the fear of the castrating father who bars the child's erotic access to the mother; it is, as I have argued, the mind itself which holds the child in place. It is not an anxiety that stops the child from acting; it is mental consideration of the entire wish, one that inevitably involves a fear of the father, but as Freud also indicated, one that equally brings up the love of a father, identification with the father, and also a sense in the child – his own moral sense – that there's something wrong with the idea.

For this is the age, is it not, when the child comes to understand something about the oddity of possessing one's own mind? A little Odysseus, each child ventures into the world of daydreams, carried off by the mind's capacity to generate theaters for heroic action. The daydream in some respects is the first truly heroic place, where the child can objectify the self engaged in ideal action that brings acclamation and recognition by an implicit other. Oh, if the mind were so simple! How easy life would be. But this very same place also brings with it uncomfortable thoughts, disturbing emotions, and persecutory daydreams. The mind and its spontaneous conjurings displace the heroic self's envisioning of life, compelling the child to struggle with evil ideas and feelings. What, then, does the child do with his mind?

Until the child becomes an Oedipus Complex I think mental contents have been rather more easily 'understood' as slightly external events, in which the child feels magically possessed by distressing mental contents, which may then be projected into the object world and, with luck, gracefully processed by loving parents. But with the breaking up of the patriarchal structure of the family by the social group and the patriarchal psychic structure by the group of competing internal objects, the child is invited by his own development to encounter the semi-independent 'itness' of his own mind. This may be most vividly studied in that painful but gradual recognition in the child that the dream he dreams is not an event external to the self that awakening or parental soothing can dispel, but an internal event, entirely sponsored by the child's mind. To my way of thinking, this is the Oedipal child's moment of truth, when he discovers that it is his own mind that creates the nightmare dramas that match poor Oedipus's fate, a discovery for each child that in some ways matches the search that Oedipus inaugurates when he aims to get to the origin of a curse that dooms his civilization. That curse is the bittersweet fate one suffers in having a mind, one that is only ever partly known and therefore forever getting one into trouble, and one that in the extreme can be rather lost (as in the losing of a mind) and one whose discovery by the child is a most arresting moment.

In this respect, then, we may rightly speak of the universality of child abuse, if by this we mean that each human subject is anguished by some of the products of his or her own mind: from the passing murderous idea that shocks the self to envy of a friend's good fortune; from the turbulent and essential pain of guilt generated by inconsiderate actions to the persecutory anxieties derived from acting out. Our own subjectivity will abuse us all! However important it is to recognize the traumas derived from environmentally occasioned harm, such as sexual abuse, physical punishment, or severe emotional harm, it is always important to keep in mind Freud's discovery that in addition to such traumas, the mind in its own right would often be the agent of self traumatization.

But as the mind is often enough an anguishing phenomenon, so that over time a child recognizes that his own subjectivity fates him to episodic suffering, he also realizes through useful thinking that the same mind is also capable of helping him to contain and process disturbed thoughts. The mind is a problem-solving agency even if it stages the representations of self traumatizing ideas and feelings. Likewise, the group can function as a container of disturbed processes, even if its structure often invites distress.

The view that the superego is formed out of the relation to the father, and intra-psychically stands in his place, is too narrow a reading of this important psychic development. The arrival of the superego announces the presence of perspective, which is the psychically objective outcome of the Oedipal Complex, when the child discovers the multiplicity of points of view. The superego does indeed derive from identification, but by no means simply with the father, either in figure or in name, as its structure testifies to the achievement of perspective: the child can now look at himself and his objects through the many points of perspective offered by identifications.

As the child comes into the presence of his own mind, he is launched, in my view, on a most disturbing journey. This is a place where all of us live, moment to moment, in an area that I think Winnicott specified in his notion of essential aloneness, and certainly implied in his concept of the isolate that each of us is. As we develop, this mind becomes more complex, ironically enough in ratio to its sophistication. Psycho-development, then, is in part *devolutionary*, not evolutionary: a dismantling of both pre-Oedipal and Oedipal early childhood structures. Fathers and mothers, early wishes and urges, primary needs and satisfactions, fade into a kind of mnemic opacity as we move more deeply into quite unknowable realms. Some people, and perhaps they are among our artists and philosophers, sense this psycho-devolution as a fact of human life and aim to stay with it, to see if it can be accounted for or narrated, perhaps celebrated: but the risks to such adventurers are high. Most people, in my view, find consciousness of this aspect of the human condition – the complexity born of having a mind to oneself – simply too hard to bear.

Given the ordinary unbearableness of this complexity, I think that the human individual partly regresses in order to survive, but this retreat has been so essential to human life that it has become an unanalyzed convention, part of the religion of everyday life. We call this regression 'marriage' or 'partnership,' in which the person becomes part of a mutually interdependent couple that evokes and sustains the bodies of the mother and the father, the warmth of the pre-Oedipal vision of life, before the solitary recognition of subjectivity grips the child. Ego development is thus a transformative regression: back to being in the family, this time through the vicarious rememberings generated through raising a family, absorbing oneself in cultivating a garden, and putting out of one's mind as best as one can quite what one has seen when leaving the garden in the first place. To go forward in life, we go back, back to the places of the mother and the father, where we can evoke these figures as inevitably comforting and practically as defensive alternatives to a madness always latent in groups: to the groups of social life, and more so to the group that is mental life.

As the child experiences the group's dissolution of the father complex, and as he strives to adapt to and become part of a social group, he gradually arrives at the exceptionally disquieting recognition that this cannot be done. How can one adapt to something that refuses to identify itself? Where is the core identity of the group to which one is called upon to adapt? Although the child is raised with a fictional entity in mind created out of parental and educational visions of the civic-minded collective to which the young child should affiliate, psychoanalytic studies of the group process have taught us what we already knew as children: not only that groups are not fair but that they often operate according to psychotic principles. It can be a form of madness to live in a group. Or the group as a reliable presence is a delusion, believed in because its labile reality would be a hard lesson to preach to the young even if they know it unconsciously and suffer the anguish of its reality.

But children do learn how to live in groups. Common tasks concentrate human collectivities and simplify matters wonderfully. There are festivals, manic moments, times of true accomplishment, inspiration, hope, and development; these are the occasions when it is wonderful to be in a group. But most children know that it is by transformative regression back to dyadic existence that the distresses of group life can be averted, so the finding of a close friend is a very particular aim of most children, although obviously some who will be loners find in their novels, or science projects, a reliable structure that serves the need to retreat from the madness that ego psychology terms reality. In the end, we all develop a false self (hopefully) that can assist our endurance of the madness of groups and we find passionate and narrowed interests (such as the form of work we choose or avocational interests) and most of all, we seek partners and a few close friends to be with us.

The Oedipal dilemma is replete with paradoxes and doubtless I have not helped matters by suggesting several others: in particular that the child's relatively simple psychic structures built around the dyadic and triadic relational situations are superseded by recognition of the mind's complexity. All along, of course, this mind has been developing and objects have been created as split-off fragments of the self, and from the dyadic and triadic structures; but the Sophoclean moment, if I may put it that way, is the self's recognition that a human life outlives the known relational structures. We are amidst two quite profound unconscious orders – our own mind and that of the group – which break the symbiotic and Oedipal cohesions. In time, a false self is evolved and engages the group, and false illusions of the self's unity are generated to assuage our anxieties about our personal complexity; these illusions and illusional engagements are absolutely essential to our life, and unsuitably named false if by that we mean not true of us – they are most certainly true of us all. And yet we do retreat, from my point of view, from the anguish of having a mind and living within a social order that outstrips our early childhood structures and wears thin our illusions of unity. We retreat very subtly back to transformed dyadic affiliations, back into triangular structures when we generate our own family, forward into passionate beliefs in the veracity of a single vision of reality (whether a psychoanalytic view, a political opinion, or a theological perspective), all unconsciously soothing – even when the occasions of mental pain themselves – because the mentally objectifiable dilemma is always preferable to the complex that is beyond its mental processing.

But if mental complexity ultimately defies the passing omnipotences of false organizations of content, and if the large groups of the human race – the groups we call nations, cities, institutions, and households – prove beyond the individual's successful organizational intentions, the diversity of such complexity allows each subject, as Winnicott said, to play with reality. One's unconscious use of objects, aimed to conjugate idiom into being, allows the subject to be disseminated through the complex events that constitute lived experience. We go with the flow. It is unconscious, not coherent, yet pleasurable. Though we cannot adapt to reality, as in some respects it does not exist, we play with it, bringing our subjectivity to the thingness of the object world and there – in an intermediate space – give reality to our life.

Why Oedipus then? Because when he picked this play to address the key problematic in human development, Freud selected a drama that represented that tension between our cohesions, whether relational (as in marital, family, or group) affiliations, or delusional (as in Oedipus's delusion of an organized persecution by Creon), and the psychic textures well beyond the possibility of mental organization, a dense complexity so intrinsic to the group process that it can only hold itself together through denials of its nature. Although Sophocles, like many Athenians, believed that it was the civic sense that could think through the madness of group life, I think he also constructed a play that defied anyone's psychic organization: a play that evoked a density of unconscious work in the audience that must have provoked an anxiety about the limits of comprehension. It is this tension between the limits of consciousness and the wayward destiny of unconsciousness, between the helpful internal objects of psychic life and the persecutory presences – which Klein brilliantly conceptualized as a constant tension between two positions, paranoid/schizoid and depressive – between the need for group life and the madness of such processes, that Sophocles brought to this play. Although *Oedipus at Colonus* would seem to celebrate the virtues of a well-governed *polis*, endowed with a spirit of place that is based on the integration of the matrilineal and the patrilineal lines, it is my view that our primary adult relations in life – marital, familial, ideological, political – are necessary regressions from the logic of human development, in which transformed simplified structures are found to comfort us against the harrowing complexity of life: be it the life of the mind or life in the strange mind of a social group. Complexity displaces the pre-Oedipal and Oedipal structures: the child discovers his own mind and the solitude of subjectivity. Knowing this, life becomes an effort to find inner sanctuary from the logic of psycho-development, and when this generative asylum is established it allows the subject to play with the samples of reality that pass by him during his lifetime.

Chapter 8

The functions of history

The psychoanalytical insistence on the priority of the imagined – juxtaposed, if necessary, to the happened – is understandable, if regrettable. Each person's inclination to describe his present state of mind as determined by external events is countered by the psychoanalytical perspective, which insists that such an account must be regarded in terms of the person's potential wishes or object-relational aims, even if it coincides with events which have, so to speak, happened.

Do we have to choose between the imagined and the happened? Are they opposed? The happened will always become part of the subject's imagined life – since perception of events is processed by the person's particular way of thinking and as time passes will become more subjective – but even if we take this into account, does this mean that the integrity of the actual loses status? To use Lacan's deposition from Kant: because we cannot truly grasp the real, does this mean that events in reality are left to our imagination? Lacan, however, ascribes powerful influence to the real. It is there. It may evade representation but the fact is, reality happens to one, and there is a kind of categorical memory of its nature. So, according to Lacan, we do not remember the actual event that happened to us, because our perception of reality is disqualified by our own subjectivity – guided as it is by its imaginative capacity and the latent rules of the symbolic order – but we do recall the categorical moment, if one can put it that way. We recall that something happened from the real (not the imaginary or the symbolic) that profoundly affected us.

Let us begin by thinking about some of the facts of life. A patient tells us that when he was two years old a brother was born. This is a fact. When he was four his family moved from a small country town to a large city. That is a fact. When he was six his grandfather died. That is a fact.

Fact (from the Latin *facere*, to do; *fact-um*, 'thing done') first of all means 'a thing done or performed,' in the neutral sense of action, deed, or course of conduct. But the Oxford English Dictionary, interestingly, lists four more usages of this first meaning of 'fact,' all now obsolete, in which we can see a virtual history of the word: 'a noble or brave deed, an exploit,' 'an evil deed, a crime,' 'actual guilt (as opposed to suspicions),' and 'an action cognizable or having an effect in law.' So in the first place it is essential to establish that certain events in a life are not just imagined, that 'thing' is 'done.' Notice how difficult it is to get it right. 'Thing done' is more accurate. It does not say that someone has committed the action. Throwing a spear at an antelope is a thing done, and a rock falling from a cliff or a tree blocking a path is also a thing done. Perhaps in the beginning of human consciousness it was more important to establish that certain things got done, and it was less important whether they were caused by man or not. What mattered was that they were done.

A thing 'performed,' however, certainly suggests human authorship. We could say that the sea performs high waves or that the weather's performance is dramatic (and perhaps thousands of years ago we were willing to accord dramaturgy to the elements), but 'a noble or brave deed' suggests human action, and epic narrative is constructed around brave deeds done by people. But the exploits are often attributed to mythic figures, and in the cases of actual persons (Jesus, for example) the deeds done are fantastical. It seems that the moment we enter the human arena, we lose our grip on the factual. A more modern understanding would be fact as evil deed or crime: 'Do you promise to tell the whole truth and nothing but the truth?' Gradually it has become important to establish the facts of a matter, particularly when a crime has been committed and someone is guilty. It was, of course, the tradition from which Freud emerged; his hysterical patients suffered symptoms that upon elaboration suggested stories, and by transforming the symptom into its narrative, he confronted a problem: had these young women suffered some sexual abuse or were these fictions that expressed their frustrated desires? Freud never resolved this dilemma: the abuse could have happened, but equally, it might be invention. One of his discoveries, however, was that unconscious wishes could lead to the invention of a history, and he turned his attention to the motivations of self-deception, recognizing that one has to attend to the lie before one can ever reach the truth.

Freud's conception of the psychoanalyst, as a detective sifting through the clues that lie on the surface, privileges the fact, which, certainly by the end of the nineteenth century, was becoming more important in jurisprudence, too. In a way, the analyst was detective, counsel for the defense, public prosecutor, and jury all in one: areas of his mind were delegated to these various parts, while the different parts of the patient's self presented conflicting evidence.

We find ourselves now, at the end of the twentieth century, with a strange and disturbing revival of the question: what is fact and what is fantasy? Since the mid-1960s, when the Kempes' important work on child molestation in Colorado startled the American people, state legislatures and government regulatory agencies have passed laws and guidelines that in some cases mandate clinicians to report any allegation of child abuse (whether made by the child, by a friend, or by a neighbor). With such mandatory reporting, the patient's relation to a therapist is displaced by the patient's relation to the police. The details must be reported to the authorities, and a reported event becomes a potential fact; an investigative process is initiated, and the presence of the real overwhelms and displaces the possible valorizations of the imaginary or symbolic. The psychoanalyst is no more, at least as far as this patient is concerned, and the psychoanalysis cannot continue. We can see how the suggestion of a fact carries enormous power.

Matters are more complex, particularly in American culture, where the notion of abuse by the mother or father of a child has been widened from sexual abuse only to include physical abuse, emotional abuse, and abuses deriving from parental habits such as alcoholism. Victim support groups have formed around the objectified facts of such histories; and ascertaining what really happened to the person, sharing the 'facts' of each member's life with the group, is now at the very heart of therapeutic recovery.

It might be viewed as comically ironic that psychoanalysis simultaneously is turning away from the value of history, removing itself from adjudicatory actions in relation to past facts, but the stakes are too high: more and more analysts are losing their right to consider their patients' internal worlds precisely because of a disinclination to take the factual past seriously, ultimately handing over this function to actual detectives! Indeed, with the emphasis on the concept of the here-and-now transference observation, a new and limited kind of fact-finding is being proposed: it is being suggested that we can pass judgment only on the clinical fact. And what is that? These are facts of performative action. How the patient treats the analyst as both an internal object and an actual other is observable over time and can be interpreted. The analysand is free to dispute these observations, although over the course of the analysis he may accept them. But the analyst will shy away from commenting on deeds done in the patient's life. It is claimed that this does not matter, since the facts that are truly pertinent to a psychoanalysis are those transpiring in the transference, and if things done to the patient in his or her childhood are true, they will be revealed in the transference which expresses the analysand's psychic life.

At the other extreme is an alarming Delphic therapy, occurring especially in the United States. Here is a typical example. A young woman who suffers anxiety is referred to a 'therapist' for consultation. She is asked if she would mind going into a regression under hypnosis. She agrees to this, and upon recovering from her trance, the therapist solemnly tells her that she has been abused by someone in her early childhood, when she was about six. Who could it be? An uncle? A family friend? The therapist and the now deeply alarmed patient investigate figures from the patient's past. The patient is profoundly moved. Obviously an important truth has been uncovered, and it feels right – it must be right: but who was it? Sessions continue. Further regression therapies. And then a vague feeling, an awful and uncomfortable thought, banished in previous discussions with the therapist, can no longer be suppressed. The patient remembers that her father had a peculiar way of touching her. She cannot recall just what it was, only a memory of sensations, received from the hand of the father. The therapist deepens her voice. Pauses now seem minutes, before the verdict is read. The facts are beginning to assert themselves. The truth cannot be denied. Tears overwhelming her, the patient is led to the inescapable conclusion that she was sexually abused by her father. That she cannot recall the moment of abuse or any subsequent references the father might have made in relation to it does not matter. This, it is argued, is consistent with the nature of being abused. An event such as this erases memory. There are no memories. Absence of memory is the indictment. Any patient who has suffered a serious borderline disorganization of personality is now, finally, coming into an integration. For the first time in her life she not only feels she knows what is true and what is false but also feels she is coming together as a person. Now, as she develops intense and focused hate of the father and all that he stood for, as she tells her sisters, as she joins a victim support group, her life is given a definition it had never had. The proof is in the recovery. Therapy does not lie. With this oracular therapy, facts are declared. The thing done is found. The perpetrator of the deed is identified. A judicial process is enacted in the clinical situation. The criminal is tried in a family court and his reputation is destroyed. He is a new kind of vermin.

Psychoanalysis, some have argued, has deserved the fate it has received in some legislative quarters: neglecting the facts of a patient's life in favor of the more elite and arcane world of psychic events, it is no longer in a position to speak to the actual events of a patient's life. When it comes to matters of abusive deeds done, this is for the police, oracular therapies, and victim support groups. Even a cursory walk through a bookstore will indicate scores of self-help psychology books relating to recovery from abuse. Little will be found in the section on psychoanalysis.

But in psychoanalysis, is there a place for a new emphasis on deeds done in a patient's life? Certainly the analyst can allude to the significant facts of a patient's life even if he does not know their psychic rendering. So if a patient tells his analyst that his mother is a Puerto Rican Catholic and his father an Iranian Muslim, this may be of significance and now and then needs mention. It does not need interpretation – unless the clinician has some idea of its meaning – but it requires occasional utterance and allusive reference. If, as an adolescent, the patient moved from a large city school to a small village one, this fact too will need mention, even if the analyst has no personal investment in its significance. But why refer to these events if the analyst thinks that doing so dilutes the intensity of the transference?

This brings us to what we might think of as the power of the deed: the evocative presence of reference to the real in a psychoanalysis. By referring to deeds done the analyst touches the plane of reality even if he does not know what he reaches. By referring to the actual he brings it into the imaginary on its own terms. It enters the analysis not as an elaboration – although that may subsequently happen – but initially as a dumb thing: a fact. 'Them's the facts.' Dumb. 'The simple fact is . . .' And herein lies one of the truths about facts. A deed done – a move, a death in the family, a car crash, the birth of a sibling, a bankruptcy – seizes the self. The imaginary and the symbolic are suspended – for a few days, for weeks, for months, sometimes for a lifetime – at least in the circle of potential elaborations that surround the fact.

What is the value of bringing simple facts into something as intelligent as a psychoanalysis? Because certain facts of a person's life are almost always intrinsically traumatic: many things done create momentary caesurae (blanks) within the self. By naming such facts the analyst brings the caesurae to the consulting room – these blanks are evoked, their emptiness is felt, and trauma enters the analytical space. Neither analyst nor patient will necessarily believe that these facts are in the least relevant, but in some respects that is the point. From the point of view of projective identification, we can say that the analyst's disinclination to discuss such events is his unconscious reception of the intrinsic nature of the dumb show: he feels the insignificance of trauma, feels emptied by the fact. It is not that it means nothing; it bears nothingness in it and feeling it to be insignificant *is* the outcome of trauma.

Is this surprising? Think of the historian's task. He is confronted by a series of facts. In 1594, Elizabeth is Queen of England. This is a fact. That same year Henry IV, newly crowned King of France, enters Paris. Fact. That year the Edict of St.-Germain-en-Laye grants the Huguenots freedom of worship. Fact. On the Austro-Hungarian border the Turks conquer the city of Raab. Fact. In May of that year, the theaters open again in London; Marlowe's *Edward II* is performed. Fact. Thomas Nashe's *The Unfortunate Traveller*, a picaresque novel, is published. Fact. Shakespeare's *The Two Gentlemen of Verona, Love's Labour's Lost*, and *Romeo and Juliet* are completed. Giordano Bruno is seized by the Vatican and imprisoned. Richard Hooker publishes Volumes 1–4 of his *Of the Laws of Ecclesiastical Polity*, Caravaggio paints *The Musical Party*, and Tintoretto dies. The first opera is written: *Dafne*, by Jacopo Peri. Galileo prints his Golden Rule. These are all facts. Set one against the other, they are rather dumb objects, aren't they? To be sure, the historian of the sixteenth century has numerous associations to each thing done because he has worked on these facts for a long time. Furthermore, we know now that these facts have proved to be noteworthy. They are worth remembering. With more difficulty I could have listed other facts of that time which would be less evocative: more dumb still!

These facts do not in themselves give the person who is only vaguely familiar with sixteenth-century history much to think about – at least not on first mention. But if each of these things done was discussed and talked about repeatedly over a long period of time and other facts were listed, then they would begin to take on a certain meaning. For the moment, however, I wish us to enjoy them as the creators of momentary blankness. Perhaps precisely because they are the deeds done, we are suddenly aware of their seriousness. Ironically, nothing much comes to mind. Are we to conclude, therefore, that in addition to the caesura created in an individual's life by a done deed there is a second gap (perhaps an echo of the first) in which we do not know what to do with the narrated fact, even when it has nothing to do with us? Again we are rather struck dumb.

Why?

As I imagine it, when the real is presented – as a thing done to us, or as a narrated thing done – we do not as yet know how to think it. There is something unthinkable about such facts of life. Winnicott would argue that this moment's loss of thought is in fact necessary. He noticed that in his clinical work with infants they needed time to recover from a thing done: he would present the infant with a spatula, the infant would have a look at it – a new object and therefore a new fact of life – and then look away; if he tried to force this new fact upon the infant the child would become distressed and cry, but if the spatula was allowed to stay there, exist in all its initial dumbness, then the infant could return to it with interest and investigate. Winnicott's highly suggestive observation can be applied to many situations prevailing in a psychoanalysis, but I would like to focus on the analyst's relation to the patient's presentation of the facts of his or her life. When a patient informs me of the death of a parent, or of a trauma, I do not know what to think; rarely does anything come immediately to my mind: I need time and I suppose I need to look away for a moment. As I am suggesting, the presentation of the factual, the outcome of a deed done to oneself, is always somewhat traumatic.

Does trauma create its own potential space? In a way, yes. Shocked by the effect of a thing done, the subject may not know what to do with *it*. Such a caesura becomes the potential matrix of psychic elaboration, if the individual can return to the scene of the fact done and imagine it, perhaps again and again. Indeed, it may be that such facts nucleate into unconscious complexes, collecting other facts from life which increasingly gravitate into a particular mentality that derives from the *hit* of the fact. There are fact addicts: persons who seem to feel that only the facts of their lives, particularly those which have been disturbing, have essential qualities. Ironically, however, if the 'fact addict' freely associates to the facts, rather than treasuring them as things in themselves, then their status as dumb and unremovable objects is cracked by the disseminative effect of thought itself. And the analyst's interpretation of the patient's psychic reality, one derived from these associations, is intrinsically detraumatizing, for it creates meaning where nothingness existed.

In my view, psychoanalysis errs if it turns away permanently from the presentation of the real, taking refuge either in a theory of narrative or in a misplaced empiricism, where the only facts recognized are those enacted in the transference. The analyst must return to the patient's presentation of his or her facts of life not because they bear some meta-truth in themselves that will displace the patient's projective constructions of an internal world, but because the patient is *entering the intrinsically traumatic in the process of analysis, unconsciously asking that the trauma of things done be addressed*. This can happen only if the analyst recurrently mentions those events in the patient's life that seem to restrict imaginative freedom. The psychic inertness of dumb facts is disproportionately heavy in relation to their conventional significance: an odd and compelling truth in its own right. When a patient tells me in the first consultation that his mother died when he was under three, I do not know what to make of it, and what disqualifies it from my ready imaginative response is its very significance. I am arrested by it. I do not want to give it meaning; that will have to come from the patient. This is the effect of the presentation of facts in analysis. Often the more profound the fact, the less significance it yields. Profound facts are wrapped in their own traumatic space, and the analyst cannot think about it yet, so the analyst's recurrent noting of them becomes a stage in *his* recovery from the trauma of fact presentation and, in turn, assists the analysand in his own imaginative elaboration of the fact. But facts must be returned to: facts bear the nature of the real, and as such seem to be forever elusive, saturated with the irony that they are less open to our validation of their significance than the purely invented.

The blank nothing created by trauma interrupts the fecund exploration of unconscious processes; it momentarily stops the cycle of condensation and dissemination that is intrinsic to an individual's unconscious elaboration of personal idiom. Indeed it provides an altogether different separate sense, the sense of one's development inside a structure imposed on the self rather than derived from it. The sense one develops from trauma is derived from the very precise facts of one's life – one's fateful moments – while the sense deriving from one's unconscious disseminations is part of one's destiny drive: the urge to elaborate and articulate the intelligence of form that constitutes any person's unique sensibility. Each of us has the possibility of evolving a separate sense derived from unconscious development of our idiom – akin to a skill that further enhances work of this kind – just as each of us may have this capability foreclosed by the repetitive intrusion of fateful events, which educate us in a different form of intuitive knowing: an unconscious talent for putting the self into traumatizing environments in which the self seems to operate with unusual skill.

––––––

Each person has a past, even if it is unclear quite what that 'past' is. In the simplest possible sense, it is all that has preceded the present; hence it is by no means limited to a chronological sequence of happenings, but includes all mental happenings. Dream and actual event coexist in each person's past.

One of the more intriguing aspects of a psychoanalysis is that patients inevitably find themselves talking about their past, although the talk is not subjected to a rigorous ordering of sequential events, and more is excluded than included; it is always a selective recollection. In going over one's past, even when returning to the same epoch in one's life, new events or prior mental states are recollected, and the past becomes a kind of layering of narratives, each ordering the revival of the past in differing ways with different intentions.

We may ask how a person can contemplate his past: what variations might there be in such a consideration and what problems arise from such a reflective activity? All of this quite naturally relates when the analysand talks about his past in a psychoanalysis.

No one can talk fully about his past, any more than a historian can succinctly answer the question 'What was the seventeenth century in England?' If the historian tries to answer the question in the abstract – that it was a transitional period from monarchical power to parliamentary democracy – this by no means does justice to all the facts of that time. No more, say, than if I were to state that from the age of nine to the age of twelve I was in transition from Pasadena to the coastal town of Laguna Beach. But in a way this is how we talk about the past when asked to objectify it thematically.

I have suggested that the past as a mental phenomenon is a sequela, in part, of dumb moments when the self was arrested by facts of life. Momentous events, markers in each person's life, are self-defining statements even though, as I maintain, not only do we not know what they mean but they also signify the power of nothingness. Equally, we live not only within the parochial world of our own unique family evolution, and the character of our own mental events (our dreams, erotic fantasies, daydreams, ideational preoccupations, and so forth), but also in a social world which naturally becomes part of our past. In 1967 I was in my final undergraduate year at the University of California at Berkeley. I worked as bibliographer for the history department during the day, and in the evening I managed a bookstore in Ghirardelli Square in San Francisco. I dated several women but continued to fancy one in particular. I was also having psychotherapy with a psychoanalyst at the student health service, gaining my first true experience of what psychoanalysis is. I can recall the flat where I lived, the car I drove, and later that year, the East Bay Activity Center, where I worked with autistic children. Pushed, I can recollect two or three of my favorite restaurants, recalling the Szechwan Chinese restaurants that became suddenly quite popular. I also played a lot of volleyball. And my antiwar activities continued. But 'my past' that year must also include data beyond my own local interests.

In 1967 the United States and North Vietnam began peace talks in Paris. There were riots in America's black communities. Thurgood Marshall was the first black to be appointed to the Supreme Court. The Greek-Turkish war on Cyprus broke out. Norman Mailer published *Why Are We in Vietnam?*. The Beatles released *Sgt. Pepper's Lonely Hearts Club Band*, and Jean-Luc Godard's *Weekend* hit the cinemas. Christiaan Barnard performed the first heart transplant operation, the Boston Strangler was sentenced to life imprisonment, the astronauts Grissom, White, and Chaffee were killed in their space capsule, and Expo 67 opened in Montreal. These are a very few of the memorable events of 1967. They too are part of my past.

But is my concept of my past actually informed by these events? I am not at all sure. Of course, once I begin to think of specific things I was doing and what was going on in the world in 1967, I can begin to recall something of my being then. I could describe some of these details and also reflect on the world events and what they meant to me. But I do not think this is how we think when we consider the past.

The OED helps get me closer to what I think this word means. 'Gone by in time,' 'lapsed,' 'done with,' 'over': first-order definitions bringing to mind the phrase 'It's over with, in the past: forget about it!' So does the past signify a forgetting? When we think about the past, are we, in fact, directing our reluctant attention to something which is meant to be forgotten? Does this in part explain why it is so difficult to remember our past? Not because we cannot recollect it – we know very well that if we break it down into years, we can remember quite a few things – but perhaps because we are not meant to 'delve into the past,' to 'awaken the past.'

Does nostalgia, that curious pining about one's past, refer to a different kind of loss, the loss created from forgetting? Is mourning an act of riddance, which expels memory and displaces it with a here-and-now consciousness? If this is so, what does it mean?

The abuse movement, now giving birth to thousands of born-again victims, may hold a clue to the annihilation of discrete memories evoked in the word 'past.' As an oracular therapist listens to a patient's description of his past, a powerful organizing message is cohered. Something happened in the past, and that past event casts an entirely new light upon the present and simultaneously organizes the past into a narrative order that will explain everything (or nearly everything) to the subject. The vague sense that the past is a mystery is now gone. The feeling that something awful happened is proved correct.

Yet what if the past itself is the vague something that is awful? What if there is something intrinsically destructive of self about it? Would this not make all of us victims of some sort – direct victims of the past? 'It is water under the bridge.' 'Let bygones be bygones.' 'It's history, man. Forget it!' A past that signifies forgetting, one that is very different from the Freudian theory of repression. The repressed, as opposed to the past, signifies the preserved: hidden away in the organized tensions of the unconscious, wishes and their memories are ceaselessly struggling to find some way into gratification in the present – desire refuses annihilation. But lived experience is shredded.

How can we conceptualize the past within psychoanalytic metapsychology? For what I am talking about is equivalent not to repression or denial, but to that amnesia which Freud writes about – the oblivion of *self* destruction, the eradication of all those fine and discrete details of a lived life that make each of us unique and unrepeatable, which sponsors a pining for what has been, a form of mourning deriving from a continuous intrapsychic process of self destruction.

Some might argue that it is simply impossible to remember one's past. There is so much detail – too much, in fact. We must forget in order to exist in the present. And in a way psychoanalysis supports this notion. Each session must begin with a blank screen. The prior session must not bias the analyst's open listening as he hears from his patient as if for the first time. Bion suggested that each analyst must dispense with memory and desire. In order to live in the present, we must, as it were, destroy the past. This makes some sense. Certainly we cannot 'hold on to the past,' or so we are told.

Much of psychoanalytic theory is concerned with loss – and loss of the object in particular. From Freud through Klein to Mahler, and throughout the literature, loss of the object is stressed again and again. We seem to have a thousand ways to lose it. Have we forgotten the loss of the self, its continuous destruction through consignment to oblivion? The ubiquity of nostalgia alerts us to the narcissistic issues relating to losses of one's past, losses that alter the self's history: the loss of one's youth, the loss of loved ones, the loss of 'futures.' When we speak of the past we conjure a signifier which identifies a self state that is almost appallingly obvious: we eradicate our lived experiences by forgetting them, turning discrete experiences laden with love and hate, turmoil and serene beauty, into a globular notion – the past. The term signifies the ultimate decay of finite lived experience.

Simply put, the *passing* of time is intrinsically traumatic.

––––––

I should like now to discuss a psychoanalytic patient whose relation to the facts of his past changed the course of his analysis.

Felix is an architect in his early thirties who emigrated from Hungary with his parents when he was three years old. His parents moved to Scotland, where they set up an agricultural business that did fairly well. They retired in 1979. Felix's father died in 1982 of a heart attack, and his mother died of cancer in 1987. Felix was their only child, but at the time of his mother's death his marriage of three years had produced two children, and when he began analysis he had three children.

In the first few weeks of his analysis he described his family's history in painstaking detail. When he was two and a half weeks old his mother developed an abscess on her breast and he was put onto a bottle. When Felix was a year and a half old his mother had acute appendicitis and was rushed to the hospital in the middle of the night. He told me this was his first memory. He could only recall being awakened, people bustling around the house, and an overall commotion that seemed very frightening. He is sure he remembers this, but cannot recall if the 'memories' of asking for his mother and being told she wasn't there, or of other sorts of 'askings' and 'sayings,' were revisionist. He vividly recalls the move at three, and he recalls that at four his father was crushed by agricultural equipment and had to be taken to the hospital. The mother's family moved to Scotland when his family did, and he remembers his age and what he felt like when each of them subsequently died. And of course there were other 'facts' in his life.

My psychoanalytical bias informed me that some of these facts were likely to be quite important: the loss of the breast at two and a half weeks, the mother's hospitalization, the move, the father's accident. Felix's first years of analysis, however, were taken up with matters of the present. He was estranged from his wife, Alice, and although they lived together they were not on good terms: he found her clingy and dependent. He told me that he found 'relationships' revolting, the very mention of the word causing his stomach to turn over. Unbeknownst to Alice, Felix had a sequence of lovers, from a week's 'stand' to several months of intense fucking. He loved the 'newness' of each sexual occasion, and found the very specific uniqueness of each woman's erotic requirement compelling. But whenever the woman began to depend on him or make demands on him, he could not bear this, and would very directly and often brutally break off the relationship and go to another lover.

When we discussed these affairs from several different analytical perspectives he refused them any potential meaning. They were simply good fucks, he valued erotic life very highly, and when *it* went, then unfortunately but necessarily his lover was jettisoned.

Among many considerations of these affairs I shall mention only two here. He would tell me in considerable detail what it was in the woman's way of lovemaking that he liked so much. It varied from one lover to the next. With X, for example, he found the way she sucked his lip and then nipped it at the end very exciting. She would also gently hold his testicles and then release them. She would climb onto his back and breathe into his ear from behind. He found instinctively that she liked to be licked under the arms, that when he put her hands on her pubic hair and pressed, while he kissed her ear, she had an orgasm. He learned that she liked to be lifted a few inches from the bed just before penetration. In time, as he increased his erotic knowledge he would look into her eyes, and she would look into his eyes, and this mutual gaze that recognized reciprocal erotic knowledge added enormously to his excitement, and made such encounters so blissful.

At a certain point I said that these love sessions were like breast feeds; his insistence that such erotic quests were essential seemed rather like an infant claiming a ruthless right to the breast irrespective of the mother's personal requirements. When his lover became dependent upon him, she changed from an object for ruthless use into a person who demanded something of him and thus spoiled what they had created.

For years I put this interpretation to Felix, but he always denied its significance and refused any and all interpretations of his relationships. For example, when his women became dependent and then desperate – because he was rejecting them – I said that I thought he could not bear to come into contact with his own dependent feelings and could deal with that aspect of himself only by expressing contempt for such emotions. When I added, as I often did, that he could not allow his need for me to come into consciousness, and that he dealt with his affectionate and loving feelings for me with scathing dismissals, he would reply, 'Well, you're a typical bourgeois moron who has lost his mind by having a family. You obviously think you're happy, but you don't know what true pleasure is.'

Now and then he would ponder his past. His parents' Hungarian origin and his extended family were of interest to him, and he could look into the past, even while he was intolerant of events in the present. I learned that his parents had been compelled to marry because his mother was pregnant. He told me that his father often described the tension in their home in Buda, when the mother's father argued with him and treated him like shit. The mother was anxious and depressed, lapsing into tears and begging for her father's mercy.

On the basis of these 'facts' I said that it seemed likely that his mother had been too anxious and distraught to breast-feed him, and that his conviction that relations were a disaster might have much to do with feeling that it was disastrous to be truly dependent on the mother, not only because she took her living presence from him but because she brought anxiety and despair to the feeding relation. 'I know this will sound farfetched to you, but I want to say it in any event, as I think your present view that relations are disastrous occasions of osmotic contamination by the other's malignant need is a conviction based on experience.'

One day Alice found out about one of Felix's affairs, then discovered a few more; he left her, and the marriage ended within a week. Alice was devastated and wanted to talk it over with him, but he was adamant: he would not tolerate her accusations, nor did he intend to bear her pain. Furthermore, she was to blame: she had misled herself all along in thinking that a marital relationship could be permanent and he had never promised this. As she became more distraught and in her desperation acted out socially, he became more and more contemptuous of her, adducing her behavior as proof that he was right all along to consider relationships a disaster. 'She is trying to make me feel guilty – as are you – and you can all go fuck yourselves with your own guilt, because *I do not* feel guilty. She is a sick woman and you are a bourgeois analyst with pathetic moral values of your own. While you just sit in your chair never moving all day, I am out and about, fucking some of the most beautiful women in London and enjoying myself. So don't you dare try to lay a guilt trip on me: I won't have it!'

In fact he was visibly shaken and vulnerable during such tempests. I would wait until he had calmed down (usually within the hour) and would then say that I thought his guilt was unbearable, too painful, and he was desperate that it be in his wife, or in me, but not in him. Sometimes I would say that he had to denigrate me, to insist that his way of thinking was the only way to think, lest he be swamped by powerful emotions which he was certain would overwhelm him. On rare occasions I would refer to his mother's withdrawal of her breast, saying something like 'I think you are afraid that if you allow your feelings to emerge, your feelings will be overwhelmed with your mother's feelings of grief and anxiety, that you will lose yourself unless you say *none* of this matters.' Referring to Alice – or one of his abandoned lovers – I would say that he evoked a hunger in them akin to his own desperate need as an infant, which had been ruptured by his mother, and that his confusion was between the power of his own emotions and the presence of his own mother's anguish. I was careful to pick the correct moment to make these comments. I had no expectation that they would prove mutative in that moment. I constructed a history for him, by linking past facts to present events only very rarely, but I did so in order to give him the frame for a potential act of eventual significance. Otherwise I stuck to the here and now of his feelings, his transference relation to me and the material he brought to the sessions.

A few years passed during which he became increasingly available for insight into himself. He could now talk about guilt and when he experienced it; he did not projectively identify it into others. He was able to bear transference interpretations and to discuss his feelings about me, including homosexual anxieties and primitive states of need and anxiety.

Then Felix met a woman named Angela, and they were soon involved in a passionate erotic relationship, only this time, after some months, Angela tired of Felix and dumped him. This had happened to him once before but not to such devastating effect. A friend of Angela's – Fran – took Felix into her arms to give him solace. For a while he was comforted by this, but then the relationship became quite eroticized, and soon they were enamored of each other. Fran's true boyfriend returned from a year's sabbatical (trying to 'find himself' in an Asian country) and after relatively little angst, Fran gave Felix his walking papers. It took months for him to recover, and while still in the midst of his grief he met Juliet at a convention of architects.

He had seen Juliet before, but only now did he find her exciting. To make a very long affair shorter, they fell into a mad kind of erotically mesmerizing love affair. The fact that Felix lived in London and Juliet in Scotland did not seem to matter: absence made more than the heart grow fonder. He would fly to Glasgow, she to London, and in airport lounges they would embrace with such passion that on one occasion airport security asked them to leave. Juliet adored him. She admired his work, which had brought him international acclaim. Now and then she would attend his 'site visits' and be truly astonished by his capability; indeed, she learned from him, and he was quite pleased when eventually she won a major project for herself in Wales.

They usually spent weekends together, and between projects would live in his London flat. They made love several times a day. Sometimes they stayed in bed for virtually the entire day, making love and falling asleep, then making love again and having a bite to eat, then falling asleep, then having a bath together and giving one another a massage, then making love again, and then falling asleep. By this time in his analysis he knew there was something particular and meaningful about these particular love relationships. Whereas before, he would tell me about his sexual life in a contemptuous and exhibitionistic manner (with unconsciously homosexual libido operating in the transference), now he reported what was taking place because he knew there was something rather odd about it.

He had been shaken by Angela's and Fran's desertions. He came into contact with that part of him which he realized I had always been talking about – his dependent and vulnerable self – and fear of desertion was now in the forefront of his mind.

Juliet's success in Wales was nothing short of sensational. She was featured in one of the major international architectural journals, voted the outstanding architect of the year in another, and offered one job after the other. She enlarged her office, hired staff, and began to collect frequent-flier miles from her trips to other countries. At first Felix joined in the celebrations, but gradually he felt that Juliet held him in contempt: he was now less well known than she was. Clearly there had been a redistribution of power in the relationship. More disturbing, he discovered purely by chance that she had had an affair with another man. He was devastated, but after long conversations with Juliet and what appeared to be genuine remorse on her part he decided it was in his best interests to trust her.

In the sessions he would still talk about their love life and its particularities, but from an increased distance, in that now he knew what I meant by 'erotic knowledge': he felt he knew her in a way he had never known anyone before and she knew him in a way that he had never been known. It was beyond words. Instinctive. Blissful. He tolerated my increasing use of the 'breast' as a metaphor: yes, he agreed, it was possible that he was now, as I put it, at the breast, feeling that Juliet-mother had an instinctive knowledge of him and that he had an instinctive knowledge of her.

Months passed. Juliet would come and go. On two occasions I had an uncomfortable feeling. She told him first that she was going to meet a client in Singapore but then that plans had changed and they met in Tokyo instead. I did not give it much thought, but I felt uneasy. Felix was distressed by its being harder and harder to keep up with where she was going. Then she was to attend an awards ceremony in Stockholm, and he asked her to get a room for both of them, as he would join her. She said that would be fine, but a week or two later mentioned that it now looked like a purely working convention, and asked whether he was sure he wanted to come. As it happened, his plans had changed and he accepted the fact that he would not come. I felt a kind of force, as if she were pushing him away. I also sensed that she was lying.

Then catastrophe struck. Summoned to Rome to consult on a colleague's project, Juliet left Felix after a weekend's bliss in London. Felix's phone rang. With astonishing parapraxal skill, Juliet blurted out, 'Gerald, where the hell are you!' Dumbstruck, Felix lapsed into immediate and intense silence. He knew it was Juliet, he knew she was phoning someone called Gerald; he knew she was in the midst of a mis-calling. 'For God's sake, I'm sitting here in this stinking Roman hotel, waiting for you, you aren't here, you are there, I can hear you, and I'm fucking fed up with this,' whereupon she hung up.

Felix's soul left his body. He walked around the flat not knowing what to do. He lay on the floor and did deep-breathing exercises. A botanist in his undergraduate life, he now watered his plants and talked to them in an empty voice. Finally he picked up the phone some thirty minutes later and rang Juliet in Rome. She was abrupt when answering the phone and he asked why. She said she was just overworked and a bit tired. How was he? Fine, he said. In fact, he said (lying a bit), he had booked a flight on the afternoon plane to Rome and would be with her that evening. When? she asked. Around eight, he said. Oh why, love, she implored, it's not necessary, I'll be back in London on Monday. No, he replied, he wanted to see her: he was coming.

That evening Felix was with her in her hotel when flowers from Gerald – a dozen red roses – arrived with a note attached saying his flight had been canceled, please forgive him, he would see her in a fortnight. For hours on end Juliet denied there was anything other than the purely innocent in all of this, but the more she talked, the more Felix could see chinks in her story. They talked through the night, and they made love several times. The next day, as they walked together along the Tiber, Felix managed to piece together certain *facts* she told him, enough finally to show that she had after all been lying. Put into that corner, she admitted it. She then laughed, said, 'Poor love,' slapped him across the face, and disappeared in the crowd. Dumbstruck, Felix sat on a bench for several hours. When he returned to the hotel she had gone. He dashed to the airport hoping to meet her, knowing in his guts that the relationship was all over but nonetheless hoping they could at the very least end the affair in some decent manner. But she was not there.

Odd as it may sound but perhaps understandably, given their intense erotic investment in one another, they had no mutual friends. There was no one he could turn to to ask about her. She had vanished. Phone calls to her office were met with icy responses. Married to his absolute desolation was the extraordinary fact of her complete and irremediable absence.

Felix had a breakdown. He could not eat. He was unable to sleep for more than a few hours at a time. He would wake up in the night, sit bolt upright, and 'see her.' He could not stop thinking about her. Every thought brought with it the pain of a feeling. An image would come to mind and with it whatever feeling it carried in its belly. He saw a hotel in Cornwall. It was where they had spent a lovely weekend, going for a walk along the sea cliffs, when she told him about her father's early death, and he was deeply moved. All the feelings of that moment returned in full force . . . and then, the awful pain that always followed: her absence. An image of the hotel in Rome came to mind and he was suffused with pain and anguish, and then the fact of her absence demolished that moment's emotion.

During this deeply anguished time in his life, Felix turned to the catastrophe in his recent past and painstakingly reconstructed the events leading up to the weekend in Rome, an hour-by-hour deconstruction of what took place in Rome, and as he did so, every few days he would 'recover' a lost fact. He had forgotten. When she picked him up at the airport she did not give him the yellow rose which she always handed him. The hotel manager had said upon his arrival: 'Ah, signore, glad to see you!' How did he know to expect him?

Session after session after session was taken up with his recollection of a single fact, or two or three. He remembered that two months before the catastrophe, while cleaning out the car, he had found a hotel bill that had slipped from her pocket and thought it unusually high. He recalled that six weeks before, he was on the phone to Juliet's secretary when he believed her to be in Wales, and heard the secretary call out Juliet's name ('Juliet, can you sign this for me?'); he had not asked about what he had heard. He recalled phoning Wales sometime later and talking to the project manager of one of her enterprises. He said she was staying at the Red Lion Hotel, whereas she had told Felix she was staying at the Boar's Head Inn.

And Gerald. Who was Gerald? He did not know. But not a session went by without his trying to figure out who Gerald was. One theory yielded another. His sense of humor delivered the necessary transference interpretations: 'I know, *you* are Gerald. What were you doing with Juliet!' The true significance of this link fell into a certain kind of place but did not displace the pain or the yearning.

The recovery of facts seemed a kind of lifeline. Each fact pieced him together as he tried to recover from his trauma.

Interpretative work at this level – of patient breakdown – is crucial. Felix was available for comprehension of himself as never before. For years he had rightly said that something was missing in his analysis, some essential truth. I felt we were amidst that truth, and I told him so. I said that I thought that he had unconsciously picked Juliet – as he had Angela and Fran – because there was a destructive element in her. With Juliet it seemed clear that she seduced him in order to conquer: once she achieved fame, he became the object of her contempt. His eventual dependence on her was his disaster. I said he had created this disaster with his female lovers prior to this, leaving them in his wake, but now here he was, with that wonderful breast that knew him and that he knew, and it suddenly vanished, taking his soul with it.

As he gradually put together evidence of Juliet's 'other' self, a troubling discovery ensued. She was an accomplished liar and had cheated on him and, he was to discover later, other men before; but his negative hallucination of this fact, I maintained, was akin to his saying that the bottle mother was the true mother: he had to deny what he saw in reality in order to maintain a delusion of continued maternal presence. This interpretation and its repetition released a flurry of redis-covered facts which illustrated his capacity for negative hallucination. For example, he finally realized who Gerald was, and he remembered a parcel in her Edinburgh office with a label saying 'From Gerald' with no return address. In fact, he had kidded her about it. 'Who is this Gerald?' he had asked. And she had laughed and said, 'Oh, one of my lovers, you idiot!' Then he recalled that the label was somewhere in his flat! They had traveled from Scotland in his car that day; they had scooped up all the belongings, including the parcel, put them in his car, and brought all the stuff into his place; Juliet had taken the parcel but for some reason had left the label. So where was it? After hours of searching he found it.

What he did then was of interest. He would stare at it, in disbelief, saying to himself, 'I cannot believe this is true.' Then an hour later, he would get the feeling that indeed *it was not true* and he would feel that he had imagined the entire episode. So he would return to the label and reread the name. In his mad state of mind he did this hundreds of times over a number of weeks, although the invest-ment in the act gradually reduced over time until it became ordinary. He brought the label to show me, and he now talked openly about how he had been negating facts all his life: new memories from his early childhood returned.

For the first time he used my reconstruction of his relation to his mother in a meaningful way. He knew the truth that had been missing from his knowledge of himself: the fact of his dependence on her and his determination in life never to become dependent again meaning that the loving and needy part of him was relo-cated into others. But the awful ache, the terrible psychic pain of losing Juliet, this registered a terrible loss of a different kind. He created an *elisionary moment*, saying, 'I have lost . . . I have lost . . .' and I said 'everything,' and in that moment he felt deeply known. We also knew that what he had unconsciously created with Juliet – although it started more actively with the other two women – was the scene of his own internal catastrophe. I said that I thought that however awful this experience was, it had constituted an enactment from the analysis; he had gone in search of a certain truth missing from the analysis and now he had found it.

For weeks he complained with great confusion about his state of mind. Repeatedly I said that for him it was a catastrophe *to feel*, and that having spent a lifetime being out of touch and not feeling, he regarded the arrival of his feelings as a disaster. It was, I suggested, his psychological birth, from the nonhuman to the human. This made sense to him, although it did not alleviate his pain. But the intention of psychoanalysis, as I told him, was not to alleviate this pain, as it could not, but only to indicate how it was ordinary, however awful, and to be expected. Working with him during this time, I felt as if I were working with an infant who could talk, and who spoke with enormous surprise and protest about his feelings. For a while he resented Juliet's supposed freedom. He wished he could be like her and walk away and I said that he no doubt did miss the 'smooth' parts of himself – those aspects that never felt anything for anyone – but now he was well and truly born, and there was no escape from his own psychic development.

Felix's relation to facts is of interest to our understanding of the individual's relation to his past and to our subsequent understanding of the function of history. A significant factor in his breakdown and recovery was his extraordinary devotion to finding out facts, yet each discovery bore with it the blank effects of deeds done. He was recovering trauma through the recollection of each and every fact of Juliet's abandonment. Since he had not been psychically present during his past (he had lived through instinctual ruthlessness and negative hallucination) not only were the facts of his life lost upon him, but their traumatic dimension was almost always passed to the other – usually the women he cast aside – who bore the dumb effect of events within themselves. Recovering these things done was his way of bringing trauma into the consulting room and working it through. His past would not, then, become an agglomerative signifier of profound personal injury.

Felix's preoccupation with fact illustrates one function of fact-finding in psychoanalysis, although most analysands are quite distanced from the important past facts of their life, as he was not. Because Felix had unconsciously reconstructed his past through a traumatizing set of circumstances in his present life, these present-day events were of extreme interest to him. He relived much of the trauma of his early infancy in the relation to Juliet, and the facts of that relation – what actually happened, as opposed to what he imagined or denied had happened – became quite pertinent. The unearthing of any single fact was not so remarkable in itself, but the process was essential; some of the facts – or things done – had been repressed or denied in the first place, so when he recovered the history of deeds done he regained contact with parts of himself that had been lost in acts of negative hallucination: quite literally, fact-finding became self-finding, even before the self could feel integrated.

Some of the recovered facts had been lost through forgetting; others through repression. Felix's disposition to rid himself of any contact with trauma – whether that of the unwanted idea or simply the suffering of things done in the first place – meant that he made no generative psychic differentiation between the repudiated and the forgotten. As facts of all kinds emerged in a proliferation of recollectings, he came to understand certain events as objects of repression, others as objects of denial, and most as simple facts from lived experience that bore the self state of their moment.

When we refer to 'the past' we agglomerate the fine details of lived experience under a word that signifies the eradication of the self. The past is a cemeterial concept. Not only a burial ground of that which was enjoyed and cannot be recovered, of the many prior selves lived that are now lost to their former moments, but a term which eradicates the truth of the lived present.

Indeed, historical markers in a person's life – occasions that seem to be of self-defining significance – impose themselves upon the subject as his historical content. The characters, events, and choices of the past, when narrated, would seem to bear a heavy weight. But psychoanalysis and contemporary historiography suggest to me a rather different way of approaching the past and constructing a history.

Psychoanalysis pays careful attention to what it terms screen memories. These memories are usually not about highly significant events. Indeed they have a kind of Wordsworthian simplicity: the more discrete and detailed the memory, the more laden it is with significance. One thinks here of Proust's sense that the memory of a side panel at Combray contained within it more of his being in that moment, a discrete recollection of the people and the events at the time.

Freud said that a screen memory was unusually vivid and apparently insignificant. Readers may see the link between his concepts of the screen memory and my earlier arguments about experiences of psychic intensity. Screen memories are condensations of psychically intense experience in a simple object: the evocativeness of the commonplace. In *Forces of Destiny* (1989a) I suggested that each of us contains historical sets, which congregate memories of simple events during the various epochs of our childhood; these screen memories bear the history of self experience, and insofar as they are often made up of displaced desire and trauma, they inevitably contain the essence of the more profound moments of our lives.

But when a person talks about his past, are these the events he describes? Almost certainly not. If given ten minutes, or half an hour, or even two hours, to tell another about one's own 'case history,' then the person will usually start with where he was born and raised, who his parents were, what events occurred in his childhood and adolescence, where he was educated, what interested him, what hobbies or sports he engaged in, and so forth. Since life affords us hundreds if not thousands of possibilities to create such historical narratives, after a while the person will even become rather practiced in them. Psychiatry certainly places great value on the 'case history' narrative. A typical 'case presentation' begins with the analyst recounting the histories of the individual's grandparents, then proceeds painstakingly through the history of the patient's entire childhood, diligently reporting the history of his sexuality, the history of his personal relations, the history of his education, the history of his family, and many other subhistories. The presenting clinician may then eventually work his way to the present, giving a history of the analysis up to the present time, by which time more than a few of those present may have nodded off or long since departed into private mundane mental preoccupations: what to buy for dinner that night, where to go for the weekend. However, when the clinician gets to the presentation of clinical material in the form of a process recording of an actual session or two, the atmosphere changes strikingly, and all but the senile are alert and concentrated, to hear – at last – *from the patient.*

I have rarely heard a case presented in this manner when I have not been surprised at the difference between the patient as a narrated historical object and the patient as a narrated presence in the session. Years back I would listen to the sessional material linking the prior details with the present report. This is not difficult and one need not be a psychoanalyst to make such links. But if one remains true to the difference, then often the analyst is left wondering exactly what, *if anything*, that historical narrative has to do with the nature of this person's being.

We come then to a strange paradox. The analyst's and analysand's report of his or her history is so often rather deadening, even though it is informative and theoretically enriching to the listener, while a session, even the mundane report of the patient's seemingly far less interesting parochial interests, is more intriguing. This paradox captures an important truth, which requires considerable thought on our part: the act of case presentation contains the eradications of the self, not the life of the self. This eradication is nullifying, and the sense of destruction is contained in the act of case reporting. Only when the present process session is reported does the case truly come to life. How do we reconcile this judgment with our placing value on the subject's history, on believing it to be crucial in gaining those limited truths in any person's memory of his being?

In an interesting way a historian has *to forget* narratives of the past, particularly those written by other historians. Although they are of some interest, part of the history of history, they get in the way. Nor, indeed, can the historian content himself with the significant moments of history as things in themselves. The names, deeds, and deaths of great monarchs or historical figures may be common knowledge, and the historian will refer to such facts, but he looks elsewhere.

Migrating from one great library to another, or to small libraries that house particular archives, the historian reads the *minutiae*. Even an intellectual historian writing a work of considerable scope, sweeping across centuries, still buries himself again in the texts, going to a familiar psychic place he knows well, one of great solitude.

For historians who become psychoanalysts, the analyst's daily work and the life of the historian do not occupy the same psychic space, but there is a sense of similarity. Evenly hovering attentiveness and that scholarly attitude the reader takes while quietly perusing a text are not so different. With both, the ordinary work of gathering material and considering and reconsidering it over a long time yields true insights. In *Being a Character* (1992) I described the nature of unconscious work in which artists, scientists, and, one might add, historians organize data into constellations that nucleate into as yet unconscious new perceptions; these eventually break out into consciousness and become new ways of looking at phenomena.

The psychoanalyst who listens to his patient's history will often learn far more about the patient's past when, and if, the analysand simply recollects very small incidents. Here the 'recovering of lost memories,' the reemergence of the previously amnesial – not only the repressed but the forgotten – becomes rich material for history, as the patient describes one event after another in minute detail.

Proust had the right idea. As did Felix. To find one's history, the past, signifying the destruction of lived experience, must be displaced. The individual must be free to wander in and out of recovered memories, in particular those which are seemingly trivial. This exceptionally crucial act warrants emphasis, as many analysands are unsure whether such rememberings are 'appropriate' for analysis. Of course, this breaks the golden rule that each patient should narrate any thoughts, but some analysts are inclined to regard the reporting of such facts as deviations from the here-and-now transference. These rememberings may be regarded, instead, as forms of splitting, in which the emotional intensity of the transference is displaced and projected into the recollections, and some patients, knowing this or having heard of it, will be reluctant to waste the analyst's time with such detail.

Naturally there are also neurotic reasons for these inhibitions. For as Freud said of the screen memory, the small details of a scene bear the most powerful wishes and anxieties, and a patient may resist speaking of these rather 'secret' and sometimes 'embarrassing' details; they are embarrassing in part because of precise unconscious contents, and the *detailing* in itself seems to be embarrassing – something historians recognize only too well. Asked what he has been researching over the past few months, the historian may feel embarrassed to disclose that he has been reading the purchasing records of several houses, the church, and other institutions in a small village, studying how much corn was bought, firewood stored, salt beef laid down, and the like. Why this embarrassment?

Freud's theory seems correct. The historian knows – unconsciously – that work of this kind is devoted to gaining the most profound secrets of an age. The scopophilic guilt, the voyeuristic anxiety, all these are part of his embarrassment as he knows only too well exactly how to investigate the past. And so too with the analysand. Each patient knows that he is engaging in a kind of introspective scopophilia, the speaking of which becomes then an act of preconscious exhibitionism. And for the psychoanalyst, in the countertransference, there will have to be an internal working-through of a similar sense: that to hear the patient's secrets condensed into trivial memories is to pry into the unconscious life of the other.

The shyness of the historian or the odd feeling in the analyst who does not intervene when the analysand dwells, perhaps for a long time, on very small details from the past is understandable if we remember that this kind of work surreptitiously defeats trauma and revives the selves that had been consigned to oblivion. As Freud has taught us, nothing is lost on the unconscious. Recollection of small details is a kind of screen function within the self, as the small memory evokes the self state that prevailed at the time: remembering the small episodes of life revives selves from the past, even if the past as a totality remains chained to its dumb facts and reveals comparatively little.

The function of history in a psychoanalysis is most curious. Like the historian laboring away in his fields of examination, the psychoanalyst attends to fine details, because in them the self is recuperated through its screen memories. The momentous facts of life, or the dramatic things done, are the entrance of the real into the life of the subject – creating a momentary caesura, or blankness – and they stand in isolation, as markers of the subject's history, notations of trauma and subjective absence. They tell nothing, or tell of the presence of nothing. It is only in the displaced mentation of the subject, in his asides, his sotto voce mumblings – in the details of the seeming trivia of his life – that one can discover the true response to the deeds done.

History becomes, then, a life instinctual activity: it forges links with *le vécu* and mitigates the death work of certain facts. Many contemporary historians will deconstruct their conclusions or aim to do so. No historian, or historically minded psychoanalyst, can expurgate his desire: his wish *will be* to make certain conclusive statements. But such realizations do not testify to the function of history, which has already taken place, in the endless action of immersion in the material, there to be available for recognition of significance laid down in memory. These details, recovered from ordinary oblivion, gather a certain psychic force to them and provide psychic material for new insights.

The psychoanalyst who understands the function of history will recognize the enlivening and informative value of reporting small details: these displaced facts – some of which are constructed from the imaginary out of the traumatic effects of the real – are the intensities of a lifetime, and history is the recovery of such moments. It is as if the trauma of time passing is unconsciously managed by screen memories, which become underground wells in the deserts of time. Once tapped, these sources liberate private experiences and unconscious associations that prevailed in the past, and what was partially erased by the trauma of passing time is restored through free association to screen memory.

An extension of the concept of unconscious dissemination would therefore have to include the function of history making. By immersing himself in his texts the historian, like the analyst lost in the patient's production of material, is *temporarily deconstructed* by the multiplicity of his own findings and his unconscious elaborations of those materials. (I prefer to use the psychoanalytic word 'material' to designate that which might otherwise be called data or facts, in that material also includes the nonfactual truth or the telling lie.) Each time a historian approaches his material or the analyst listens to his patient, his prejudices are *destroyed* by the action of reading or listening. Each also taps the screen memories of the other; the clinician directs the patient to liberate himself from the bleakness of ordinary trauma – the deserts of time gone by – to gain access to unconscious meaning stored all the while in the secret subterranean source of the screen memory.

Of course, both historian and psychoanalyst will have powerful beliefs, essential when the material is transformed by interpretation; this labor of consciousness is not only necessary but essential, an oscillation between one's beliefs and their existential deconstruction. The work of the unconscious not only destroys the manifest texts but fragments and scatters the views of consciousness. When there are points of convergence – between unconscious trains of thought, or between preconscious alertness and unconscious movement – then consciousness once again forms its interpretation. Good historians and analysts must be prepared for their own *undoing* each time they return to the material. For however biased they are, and however pleasurable it is to discover that one's views are correct, they should have another kind of desire, based on a separate sense, in which they take pleasure in the deconstruction of subjectivity, as they are resituated by encounter with their objects. They may be initially reluctant to allow for the implications of this deconstruction, but if they value the work of the unconscious, then they will find pleasure in this dismantling of self.

The function of history, then, is twofold. The historian-psychoanalyst brings his convictions to the analytical scene, where he listens to his patient sorting the material into convicted places, and he can then think about the patient according to his own ideological stance. But the very pleasure of seeking to be confirmed is destroyed by the analytical process, which breaks up unities and decenters the listening experience. Historian and psychoanalyst are experienced in the discovery of things done in the past. They know how to find hidden details, but once they are brought into the light of day, these details, although of course subject to interpretation, are too polysemous to stay in any one subjectivity's perspective. The discoveries – when true ones – displace the finder.

Historical thinking is a psychic function. Reviewing the past, retrieving finite details from it and giving them new, indeed contemporary, meanings, detraumatizes the subject who suffers from the ailments of many a thing done. By making past events meaningful, the historian exercises an important psychic capacity, that of reflection: this does not confer retrospective truth on the past – indeed, almost the contrary – but creates a new meaning that did not exist before, one that could not exist were it not based on past events and did it not transform them into a tapestry holding them in a new place. That new place – in history proper the text of the historian, in a psychoanalysis the series of reconstructions – is a psychic act: the work of the imaginary and the symbolic *upon* the real, creating a space in the mind that gives special significance to the real, transformed yet distinctly held, a space that for some people will always offer a kind of itemization of events which they understand to be the past. This movement of the real upon the self has the effect of giving the self the feel of its own many deaths; but in a psychoanalysis this past, transformed into a history, gives the real a place that is open to the continuously transformative workings of the imaginary and symbolic, the very movement that Freud termed *Nachträglichkeit*, translated into English as 'deferred action' or into French as *après coup*. This 'revision' of the past, which suggests that the memories of the analysand are open to continuous revision subject to his contemporary perspectives, does not, as some would have it, invalidate the idea of reconstruction: it is simply the ordinary work of any historical activity. The past is inert. The dumb facts of an existence still lie in their chronological place, weighing heavily upon personal development. Doing history, however – reviewing this past and thereby transforming it – is a psychic function always alive to changed ways of seeing the world that will occur in the patient. Each person's past is open to continuous acts of historicizing, but again, this should not lead to skepticism about the worth of history making but, on the contrary, should inspire renewed recognition of the creative function of our psychological capacity to see the course of a life in continually new ways.

Alongside the dumb fact of a lifetime's 'significant' events – which give the self its sense of trauma – are thousands of screen memories which also contain the history of the subject. Recovering the screen memories, or converting the dumb facts into projective screens for imaginative reliving, the psychoanalyst sides with the unconscious in its disseminative deployment of the subject's idiom, which has oftentimes been stopped and held captive by trauma. By transforming the past into a history, the psychoanalyst creates a series of densely symbolic stories that will serve as ever-present dream material in the patient's life, generating constant and continuous associations.

Unlike the past, which as a signifier sits in the self as a kind of lead weight, history requires work, and when the work is done the history is sufficiently polysemous to energize many unconscious elaborations. The work of recollecting seemingly insignificant details from the past symbolically brings prior selves contained in these mnemic objects back to life – and in this way transforms debris into meaningful presence – and thus is the work of a life instinct, but ironically it also puts these past lives into a new place of destruction, for the unconscious work has a dismantling effect, as historical texts of reconstruction give birth to other ideas and contrary reflective theories, which destroy the placid aim of creating commemorative plaques to one's new discoveries. Historical construction collects in order to retrieve the self from its many meaningless deaths – the amnesial 'gone' – and then it generatively destroys these details and saturates them with new meaning created through the very act of retrieval, which has given them the imaginative and symbolic energy to make this past available for the self's future.

Chapter 9

Cracking up

In *Jokes and Their Relation to the Unconscious* Freud calls the processes that construct a joke the 'joke work.' The mechanisms in this process are familiar to readers of *The Interpretation of Dreams*: a joke uses displacement, condensation, and substitution to arrange those acute manifest misunderstandings which convey the kind of hidden truth that always subverts. *The Psychopathology of Everyday Life* became a virtual celebration of unconscious trickery.

Freud's chapter 'Bungled Actions' is a comedy of errors, a description of ordinary slips, such as dodging an oncoming pedestrian only to find that moving to the left or to the right will bring one into intimate face-to-face collision – 'behind . . . a mask of clumsiness [such bungling] pursues sexual aims'; or less common mistakes, such as the one reported by Freud's colleague Stekel: 'I entered a house and offered my right hand to the hostess. In a most curious way I contrived in doing so to undo the bow that held her loose morning-gown together' (176).

Freud reckoned that there would be intense resistance to any sustained tolerance of this practical joker inside, but fortunately evidence of the unconscious as subverter of intentional speech remains abundant. We will always have a Dan Quayle, who seems to reach parapraxal genius on public stages. 'Republicans,' he admonished, 'understand the importance of bondage between a mother and child.' Or his spirited response to a television interviewer on the departure of White House Chief of Staff John Sununu: 'This isn't a man who is leaving with his head between his legs.' Quayle did not stop with this revelation of his sexual fantasies. He said things that allowed us to see the great potential of the unconscious to lead a nation: 'We are not ready for any unforeseen event that may or may not occur,' he told a reporter from the *Cleveland Plain Dealer*. Perhaps he had in mind – in unconscious mind – an earlier prophecy he had made while campaigning for George Bush: 'We have been pushing the idea that George Bush is going to make matters much, much worse' (Petras and Petras, 1994, passim).

The parapraxal act places banana peels in the self's path, forever undermining the arrogance of consciousness.

Even when a self has plenty of time to work over a statement – as did Daryl F. Gates, former police chief of Los Angeles, when he wrote in his autobiography about the incident when police officers beat Rodney King – it is possible for unconscious irony to seep through a rationale: 'We are the best police department in the world, but we are not perfect. Rodney King should never have been hit fifty-six times, yet many of the blows which struck him were correctly placed so as not to cause serious injury, exactly as we teach in the Academy' (Petras and Petras, 1994: 13). Perhaps the expression 'the truth will out' refers as much to these violent intercessions of the unconscious in arresting the conscious self as it does to the notion of externally applied pressure to bring out the truth. Certainly Richard Nixon would concur: here is how he tried to deny White House involvement in the cover-up of the Watergate break-in: 'What really hurts in matters of this sort is not the fact that they occur, because overzealous people in campaigns do things that are wrong. What really hurts is if you try to cover it up' (Petras and Petras, 1993: 33). Or consider these statements given by three separate motorists to the police, on three different days in different parts of the United States, about running over a pedestrian: 'A pedestrian hit me and went under my car.' 'The guy was all over the road. I had to swerve a number of times before I hit him.' 'The pedestrian had no idea which direction to go, so I ran over him' (Jones et al., 1987: 51, 55).

The idea of the unconscious turning the self into a fool is an important part of Lacan's clinical reformulation of psychoanalysis. He ended his notoriously brief sessions with a wave of the hand when the patient's unconscious fooled him; dejected but he hoped privileged, the latter stumbled into the streets to wonder what in fact he had said to get the boot. Lacan's relish in his posture as a jester – a virtual embodiment of the unconscious as disruptive other – was well known to Parisians. One never knew quite what he would say. Nor did he. By the end of his life, for better and for worse, he had made a virtue of the ordinary folly of everyday man.

He possessed an exquisite sense of the absurd. Camus wrote, 'All great deeds and all great thoughts have a ridiculous beginning. Great works are often born on a street-corner or in a restaurant's revolving door. So it is with absurdity. The absurd world more than others derives its nobility from that abject birth' (1942: 18–19). Lacan is famous for his own 'revolving door,' as something like twenty analysands an hour passed through it, but perhaps it is a particularly French sense of humor that makes this possible, as such violent dismissals allow for the abject births.

Too much is made these days – certainly in Protestant England – of the essential sufferings of a psychoanalysis. But pain and suffering in this confrontation – between the destructive pleasures of enactment and the enhancing loss brought by interpretation – is not the only way to characterize the structure of a psychoanalysis. Throughout, the analysand's speech undermines his authority; the mere fact of free association deconstructs any tragic hero's destiny. Indeed, a patient well into analysis knows that each session has an ironic fate: one begins with a notion of what one is going to talk about, only to discover that speaking dismantles intentions and brings up unexpected material. The self that wants to master its narration is continuously slipping up in its intentions. This aspect of psychoanalysis is an entirely different world from the tragic world where blindness meets up with

a calendar with a California beach on it, out the window at the ice drops racing to the ground – I saw that this already pale youth seemed to have lost any remaining blood in his face. I said 'Yes?' and he replied, 'Ummm . . .' and stammered something. A few more moments passed, and I looked at him again. I asked, 'What brings you here?' He looked exceedingly worried. 'I am in a lot of pain,' he said; minutes later, his fear looked like panic. I said, 'What kind of pain are you suffering?' He could barely mumble the words, 'In my mouth.' 'Hard to speak about your pain?' I replied, wondering now if he were psychotic.

My line of thought took me to recent papers I had read about mad people. I had just been reading some of Harold Searles's work, and recalled his description of a patient who, when told that he could not have his cake and eat it too, replied with immediate outrage, 'Cake . . . I don't want any cake!' So when the patient told me a few minutes later that he had a pain in his tooth, I thought for sure I had what Searles called a concrete patient on my hands. The phone rang, however, and interrupted my private musings. My secretary said, 'Mr. Bollas, your patient is still waiting for you.' 'I am with the patient,' I replied. 'You are?' she responded, her chair shrieking across the floor. 'Well . . . I see him right here . . . in the waiting room . . . Who . . . who are you with?' 'Who am I with?' I said, irritated by her incompetence. Embarrassed, I turned to the patient and said, 'I am sorry, but could you tell me who you are?' This is a sinful request for a therapist to make to a patient who is clearly in the midst of an identity crisis. He gave me his name, I repeated it to the secretary, and she informed me that this was not the name of my patient but of someone else. For a brief moment – and I don't wish to overstate this – I thought to myself that this was now a very psychotic patient who had made no arrangement whatsoever to see a psychotherapist but simply walked into the waiting room under the bizarre presumption that he could enter therapy without arrangement. My confusion ended when this bashful, frightened young man asked, 'Are you a dentist?'

I told him how the error had occurred and apologized, but when I said I was a psychotherapist I confirmed every suspicion he had ever held about the lunacy of our profession.

Circumstantial amusement when the self is caught up in a reality that makes less and less sense is the basis of one of television's most popular programs: in the United States it is called *Candid Camera*, in England *Beadle's About*. The invariable form of the practical joke here is a prank played upon an unsuspecting person who finds that his assumption about reality is undermined by the turn of events; increasingly puzzled, he believes that surely *he* must be mistaken, and whatever might be amiss, if anything, will be corrected in time, or understanding will prevail – but no such luck. Instead, reality seems to go crazy.

If the unconscious subverts the intentional subject, so too at times does circumstance. 'At the heart of all beauty,' writes Camus, 'lies something inhuman, and these hills, the softness of the sky, the outline of these trees at this very minute [when 'strangeness creeps in' to the observer's consciousness and he perceives the 'density' of the world] lose the illusory meaning with which we had clothed them, henceforth more remote than a lost paradise.' He concludes, 'The primitive hostility of the world rises up to face us across millennia. For a second we cease to understand it because for centuries we have understood in it solely the images and designs that we had attributed to it beforehand' (20). Whatever we know or think we know about this world, it may – and does – sometimes act in ways beyond our comprehension. This is not news to children, who are forever finding that the real does not cooperate with what they believe they know of it or with how they imagine it. A blow from unimagined or unforeseen reality is a common fate for children. And the practical joke of *Candid Camera* trades off *this*.

Inspired comedy often mixes the subjective parapraxal and the circumstantial to create a demi-dream. In 'The Psychiatrist,' Basil Fawlty runs to the kitchen in alarm to warn his staff that there is a psychiatrist in the dining room. He has not heard the psychiatrist discuss with his pediatrician wife how the Fawltys find time to take a holiday. But psychiatrists read minds and believe people are always thinking about sex, and when Basil returns to the table, the psychiatrist asks, 'How often do you manage it?' The scene proceeds:

BASIL: *(taken aback)* Beg your pardon?
PSYCHIATRIST: How often do you and your wife manage it?
BASIL: *(stunned and speechless)*.
PSYCHIATRIST: You don't mind my asking.
BASIL: Not at all, not at all. *(nervously)* About average since you asked *(trying to recover)*.
WIFE OF PSYCHIATRIST: Average?
BASIL: Uh huh.
PSYCHIATRIST: What would *be* average?
BASIL: Well, you tell me!
WIFE OF PSYCHIATRIST: Well, ah . . . a couple of times a year?
BASIL: What?
PSYCHIATRIST: Once a year? . . . Well, we knew it must be difficult. In fact, I don't see how you can manage it at all.
BASIL: Well . . . as you've asked . . . two or three times a week!
PSYCHIATRIST: A week?!
BASIL: Yes, it's quite normal down here in Torquay, you know. *(Exiting in a huff.)*

Thus does a comedy of errors blend the impossible waywardness of the circumstantial and the subject's unconscious self. The parapraxal and the accidental seem almost made for one another. If there is no resolution to the absurd condition of man, as Camus would argue, is there possibly some form of pleasure to be found in the play of these two rogues? Is there something in what Winnicott called the third area, as the self slips between his subjectivity and world implacability, that constitutes *jouissance*? A child does not notice a toy falling in front of him; he bangs into it and almost falls down but doesn't, and anxiety turns into laughter.

Desire meets circumstance. Something in the meaningless encounter – or the encounter of meaninglessness – becomes enjoyable. Experience of the error borders on anxiety, indeed is often close to true danger, but the self escapes, and in the end it is a laughing matter.

Two people who happen to sit next to one another on the subway strike up a conversation. They discover they are traveling to the same stop, indeed learn they live on the same street, finally find they are man and wife. Here in the encounter between the bizarre creations of the unconscious and the thoughtless events of the real world – between the agility of absolute determinism and the resolute dumbness of pure accident – Ionesco finds joy.

Is this the *jouissance* of the absurd?

The comic mode, then, in which the world is turned upside down and then righted, is a brief marriage of the subjective and determinate to the consequential and indeterminate, out of which a separate sense – grasping and enjoying this play of opposites – evolves to become a sense of humor.

Some time ago, a colleague said to me that an intended action on my part would take courage. That night in a dream I observed a rather large assembly of medical personnel and family discussing my plight. As I listened, I thought I might still be alive: they seemed to be talking about potential medical interventions. The dream space opened up further, and now I saw myself, or what I knew to be myself, lying on an operating table – or was it an autopsy bench, I wondered – covered in a sheet from head to toe. That worried me. I thought it was best to lift the sheet to see how I was doing, and found that I was a chicken. I never thought, Oh, there's a chicken, for this was clearly me. In fact, I was a roast chicken, rather well done. As the dream faded, I thought to myself that I looked rather well, considering.

On waking, I realized that this unflattering dream was my response to my friend's call to courage. I was 'dead meat.' I had 'chickened out,' and the dream expressed my fear that I would not be up to the task. This dream was a comic event and I was the butt of my own unconscious.

Every time we move from wakeful reality into a dream and back out into wakeful life, we traverse a route from relatively conventional existence into the upside-down world of the comic universe. The ego that constructs the dream shares with comic intelligence the tasks of right timing and correct spacing. The chicken dream opened a new space at exactly the right time to bring me into a new and different view of myself, with an almost unerring delivery. All comedy and humor trade off the inner knowledge we have that any one of us is inevitably returned to the universe of dreams, which mercilessly deconstructs us.

The dreaming experience is rather like being a stupe: the dreamed self is an everyman. No one who enjoys dream life could ever be without a sense of humor.

Humor borrows the naïve fate of the dream subject caught up in a world he should know how to master by now. The Irish or Polish or Norwegian joke – What does it say at the top of a Polish ladder? Stop! – captures the stupidity of the self but at the same time identifies with the thoughtless movement of the world, incorporating the unthinking into the intentional. The dreaming subject is not the director of a dream but is manipulated like any other element in a theatrical production. He seems indeed to be without subjectivity, proximal to the dumb objects of the inanimate world. 'A step lower and strangeness creeps in: perceiving that the world is 'dense,' sensing to what degree a stone is foreign and irreducible to us,' writes Camus, 'with what intensity nature or a landscape can negate us' (1942: 20). This negation is expressed in jokes about very stupid people. When you tell such a joke, your listener may well comment on how dumb it is, and intriguingly this is the very point: it is not only a joke about being dumb but a joke that takes into itself the dumb elements of life and personifies them. Dreams regularly turn us into dummies, lorded over by intelligence that seemingly excludes the dumb from the inclusive possibilities of thought and yet affiliates us with the meaningless meanderings of circumstance.

Comics live very close to trauma. When a stand-up comic goes onstage, it is not at all certain whether he will be the least bit amusing. The audience may hope for this, but they do not know what his fate will be. If his jokes are not good, if his delivery is poor, he will die onstage and everyone knows it. The audience has no obligation to find him comic, and aficionados can be as ruthless in their rejections of comics as those at La Scala are of singers. So the stand-up comic bears almost all the anxiety of the moment within himself. We often see this in the densely fraught tangle of a comic figure's body – like the hunched-over Harlequin of the Middle Ages, or the fidgety spasmatic plasticism of Steve Martin, or the spooked-out-of-his-body demi-dissociate Richard Pryor. But comics can uncoil and threaten to spring on the audience. Molière brought the stage closer to the front rows. His characters fell about, almost falling into the audience or opening up buttons and threatening to pee. Flying spittle dispersed an essence of body over a cringing swath of the audience. Modern comics occasionally threaten to enter the audience; in fact, move among them. Then one can see an immediate transformation within the group; anxiety increases while the comic selects someone for special victimization and remorseless humiliation. Does the object of such humor find the occasion amusing? No. It is rather awful. But, nonetheless, the person will not only smile but often laugh hilariously, be forced by this comic intrusion into cracking up. We are witness then to enforced laughter, as the person is compelled into a false self response.

Whether we find a comic's act or a person's joke or a wit's irony amusing will depend on timing and spacing – on whether the humor occurred at the right time and in a suitable space. Humor relies, as we will see, upon an unconscious sense of time and space, operating on an intersubjective plane. And the humorous act always risks bad timing and improper placing, in this respect allowing the potential for disaster always to be glimpsed.

When we observe a comic moving from the straight self into the shambolic domain of his art form, we take notice of a very special transformation – from the conventional to the bizarre, from the ordinary to the extraordinary, from the manageable to the chaotic. We could see this any night of the week at a comedy club. Well, almost. We might not quite observe it, because we know in advance that the comic is transformed once he is onstage. We haven't had an opportunity to see his ordinary self, to be unsure of what he might do, to suffer the pains and pleasures of being objects in his transformation (if he so transforms). This is a mixed blessing: if he does nothing and is perfectly straight, we are disappointed; if he goes too far, we are terrified. We are, in a certain sense, in his hands.

Fools of the court had a very special function. They could say what they wished, and if they roused anxiety among the courtiers, so be it; at least the anxiety did not follow them outside, beyond the space where they functioned as fools. The fool was a confined being, and I should like to argue that comedy – in stand-up, revue, film, or theater – also has its generic place of representation. It is too dangerous a commodity to be allowed to move beyond its reservation.

Why is it so dangerous?

Could we not envision a world that operated according to comic principles? What if our most valued discourse was free-associative, with everybody at least by their adolescence gifted in saying whatever crossed their minds? What if the prank or practical joke was fair game? What if any response to any question could be construed as humorous? What sort of world would it be? Would it be fun, amusing, entertaining? Well. We don't know, do we? It might be awful – however artful, however privileged. Humor let free like that, rather than incarcerated in jokes, comic performance, the theater, can be dangerous. People would live in considerable anxiety. No one could be taken seriously. Straight speech would be mercilessly deconstructed by double and triple entendres. Since there would be no end to it – an important feature of all comedy – people might die laughing.

Could anyone endure a force loose with such license?

In part, we observe this danger when a performance artist or an active comedian enters the real world and conscripts a hapless audience member to be part of his act. We identify with the latter, with the feeling of being taken from a safe remove from the humorist's turbulent capacities to sudden helplessness in a fate determined by this quixotic other. And we know this is exactly where we often place ourselves, flirting, as it were, with danger. What are we doing when we do this?

I believe we are entering a primary area and encountering a primordial object.

The clown may be our very first other.

Look for yourself.

Watch the mother engage with the baby. If you look at her face, you will see someone who exaggerates human expression – wide-open eyes, a great big smile, lengthened – and goofy – vocalizations, upper body swaying back and forth, head thrown back at a tilt, song and dance.

The literature on mothers emphasizes her holding and containing functions, which soothe the infant, that is for sure. But mothers also transform themselves into figures with exaggerated human characteristics in order to stimulate their babies into smiling and even laughing. While it is frowned on to tickle a baby with a 'gitchy gitchy goo,' a mother will still stimulate a baby with incremental increases in hilarity, from the moment the baby wakes – 'Ah! Look who is awake now!' – gradually to playful pushings of the baby's feet and 'Well! Who does he think he is? Who does he think he is? Who does he think he is?' – bringing gurgles, chortles, and laughs.

But whether or not the infant finds Mother amusing will largely depend on her timing and spacing. If the timing is poor and if she comes too close to or too far from the infant, she will not develop his sense of humor. Next time you see a stand-up crisscrossing the stage, watch how he plays with the space, rushing to the edge of the stage as if he were going to propel himself into the front row, retreating back toward the curtain, receding from his manic creations, which seem to hover in mid-stage between himself and his audience. Like the mother timing and spacing her approach to her infant, a comic will uncannily portray one feature of his art more visibly than others, which are incorporated more in the poetics of delivery.

Does a comic approach come too close for comfort? Does it compel laughter, driving a false self into a predetermined response? Or is it just about right, allowing us to identify with it, eliciting our true self's spontaneity? Does the individual ego inherit the mother's sense of timing and spacing? Does any person's construction of a dream partly evolve from an earlier state of being within the other's theater, within the mother's world and then within one's own dream world? Is it a transfer from the unconscious aesthetic of the intersubjective to the poetics of intrapsychic existence?

Anyone doubting the amusement that mother and infant take in each other need only book a place in one of the many psychoanalytic cinemas in town. There you can see films by the Truffauts and Godards of psychoanalysis, feature films by the likes of Stern and Trevarthen and Murray, with mothers and infants by now as famous as Greta and Harpo. Certainly, Charcot's theater at the Salpetrière, closed now for quite some time, has been superseded by the 2001 space lab of an Arthur Clarke world featuring the great baby on the big screen. Some of them are so wired up in their little chairs, hooked into spanking-clean computers registering every one of their gestures, that they resemble the wise founding god that Keir Dullea portrayed, though in contrast to the hysteric's almost sickeningly melodramatic gestures – after a while it must have been just too Hollywood – the baby is a minimalist genius. You have to be on the edge of your seat to grasp his gestural scriptures, the ever so subtle signs of a divinity expressed before the dreary deformations of development close the show.

There is a quiet life-and-death struggle going on: no laughing matter. These psychoanalytic filmmakers are now certain, after making countless features, that all infants suffer from 'basic misery' (Bradley, 1989: 117). Babies spend on average up to 180 minutes a day crying or fussing during their first three months – almost half the time they are awake! Well might we ask why the baby smiles in the first place – at around two weeks of age – but we can rest assured that it seems to have nothing to do with pleasure and usually occurs first while dreaming. Whether they make it or not out of this misery depends, we gather, on just how hard Mom works to entertain them. Baby presumably finds this amazing entertainer funny. And although he is gassed up, crapped out, wet with his own urine, and immobilized, at least he has something really to laugh about – other than those dream images that cross his mind when he is fortunately taken out of the world into intrapsychic darkness.

However clever infant researchers are in finding an infant's skills, the euphoria surrounding this research is reminiscent of the dolphin mania of the 1960s. An entire generation thought that it was merely a matter of a decade at most before dolphins would speak, write autobiographies about life at sea, move from Sea World to Parliament. Baby worshipping – a kind of mangerophilia – would have us believe that infants are on the verge of a similar breakthrough, but in fact baby *is* rather stupid. He smiles because he does not *know* what a miserable situation he is in. And the great clown in the sky knows this; when she puts on 'showtime,' she is luring him away from his true predicament into the world of make-believe. She believes she's with a sucker who will laugh because he doesn't know better. He is the first true ingenue: too ignorant to know that he is being taken in. Stan Laurel brought such a baby into the adult world and linked him unforgettably to one kind of comic figure: the half-wit who needs a goofy adult (Oliver Hardy) to see him through reality.

Melanie Klein believes that babies don't know at the beginning that the mother who is full of good milk and humor is the same mother who has no more milk and seems wicked. This may be just as well. For the position these two are in is at the very heart of what is humorous, a heart as ancient as farce itself. Clowns, who usually act together, have at the center of their repertoire one figure who is constantly hungry and miserable and another who is bursting with goodies to eat and fulsomely content. 'Clowns, like minstrels and "comics," always deal with the same problem,' writes Dario Fo, 'be it hunger for food, for sex, or even for dignity, for identity, for power. The problem they invariably pose is – who's in command, who's the boss?' (1987: 172). Thus, in the beginning, does baby *know* that the great clown in the sky is the one with the booty? A breast just brimming with milk? Will she give it up, or is there going to be a food fight? Clowns love to throw food at each other. In fact, according to Brazelton and Cramer, food fights are a feature of conflict between mother and baby: their ' "tug of war" type of relationship is common; it appears around issues of feeding, toilet training, and discipline. The basic issue is: "Who is going to dominate whom?" ' (1990: 152).

Cracking up baby, then, is a useful way to neutralize a power conflict, but mothers break up baby during tranquil times as well.

The mother—infant relation, then, is something of a farce: one person—much the superior in power, treating the other as an equal, though, in fact, the superior one takes pleasure in the inferior one's frailties, which then become endearing. Theatrical comic scenes usually play off just such a difference between any two people: one who is smart and sees something, the other who is a dunce and does not see anything; or one with the goodies (breast) and the other without (open mouth). But as the good-enough mother turns inequality into a pleasure for both participants, she also shows how amusement at one's plight can generate a special sense: the sense of humor. Freud thought of humor as deriving from an intrapsychic position: the loving superior superego taking pleasure in the ego's meanderings. We might add that this intrapsychic inequality owes its structure to the early imbalance of power between infant and adult, between the stupe and the know-it-all. In its origins a sense of humor takes pleasure in inadequacy. A mother who is amused by baby and who can get baby to laugh at himself before he consciously knows what the joke is all about helps to develop a sense of amusement in the human predicament well before the self comprehends his condition. The sense of humor precedes the sense of self.

What other functions does this humoring serve?

If the great clown simply talked to her baby like an adult, what would be lost?

Psychoanalytic literature is full of references to the first other as a mirror. This idea figures prominently in Lacan's, Winnicott's, and Kohut's theories of the origin of the self. For Winnicott and Kohut, the good mother must mirror the infant, giving him back an image of himself that accurately derives from his inner experience: if he is distressed, she soothes him, and in doing so provides him through a changed inner experience with a self that matches her own tranquillity. The differences between self and other – which the infant can cognitively discern – are muddled, for the mirroring mother lures the infant into a kind of merging with her own being, creating within the baby a feeling that his resolution of existential difficulties derives from nascent creative abilities of his own. Thus the great mirror helps the infant, who would otherwise feel chaotic and fragmented, feel integrated and self-assured.

For Lacan, the other-as-mirror gives the infant a false image of himself that creates an illusion of unity; the infant is really in bits and pieces but sees a whole self in the glass and says, 'That's me.' The mirror, then, is the basis of a split in self-identity which lasts a lifetime.

But what if Lacan's mirror were a funny mirror? One which gave back fragmented images? Cubist images? Distorted images? And what about the mother who mirrors as a clown, who forces the infant out of tranquillity into jocularity, who breaks up baby? What sort of mirroring is this?

We may be able to make sense of this if we keep in mind that the mother metamorphoses from her ordinary facial self into a clown; she breaks herself up in order to break up baby. They crack up together. Has she an uncanny sense, then, not only of mirroring alternate states of quiescence and disturbance but of transforming this potential for psychic disaster into pleasure? Does she take into herself, right before the baby's eyes, that internal madness which shakes up baby – as it were, absorbing and transforming the element of shock and disturbance? Does she do what comics and humorists have been doing all these centuries, taking up into their bodies and souls these disturbing aspects of life?

If so, then the provocative and disturbing mother who cracks up baby is a vivid and moving expression of the marriage of unconscious and circumstantial material. Her surprising, unpredictable attacks of jocularity seem accidental; but if her timing and spacing are good enough, she senses when the clowning is all right for baby, joining subject and existence in an exciting way. Some mothers apparently cannot do this, or the infant lacks humor and cannot sense the spirit of the event, does not catch the clues.

By finding pleasure in the infant's frailty – this is expressed in countless lullabies, like 'Rock-a-bye, baby, on the tree top, when the wind blows, the cradle will rock, when the bough breaks, the cradle will fall, and down will come baby, cradle and all' – and by provoking baby to do the same, the mother both relieves herself of ordinary hate and transforms violent feelings into mutual aggression: baby spits up food, urinates, shits, and laughs back; Mommy sings songs of murder and talks of loving the little bundle so much she could gobble it all up. It verges on a Punch and Judy show. Strings attached.

Mom the clown regularly deflates the baby's grandiosity by taking the piss out of him, and baby's laughter disarms the frustrated mom. In all this, the mother is building into the infant's psychic structure that pleasure which is intrinsic to the self's follies, that relief we all need from the tedious demands of a grandiose frame of mind. She transforms potential trauma – reality's rude impingement upon one's imagined life – by turning it into pleasure, and deconstructs the violences of the real into the aggressions of the intersubjective.

In thus developing hers and her infant's sense of humor, a mother brings under temporary human control something that is in fact beyond human influence. Beyond the infant–mother couple, outside the comedy club, is a world of the real that is deeply thoughtless. By clowning, the mother re-presents this world and allows vestiges of trauma to show in the human face, turning plight into pleasure.

Perhaps a sense of humor is essential to human survival. Amusement in the self and in the other may be a vital constituent part of a comprehensive perspective on life. The mother who develops her baby's sense of humor is assisting him to detach from dire mere existence, from simply being in the rather shitty world of infancy, for example. Such a child can, as an adult, ultimately find humor in the most awful circumstances, benefiting from the origins of the comic sense.

Of course, sadly, this is not always the case. Puppet and clown are not always a transitional Punch and Judy show leading to sensuality, aggression, and the symbolic: they may never be more than two disengaged stiffs.

———

Charlie Chaplin constantly hinted, in his art, at puppetry, using a tradition in which the comic borrows the schizoid postures of the wooden soul. 'It has been pointed out that much of the mime and many of the gestures of the Commedia [dell Arte] characters are closely related to the distinctive movement of puppets,' writes Dario Fo. 'I have been aware of it myself when executing one specific style of walk with swift about-turns where the sudden twist of the leg in the opposite direction is a classical imitation of the puppet twirl. The same could be said for the attempt to give an almost wooden quality to certain gestures, like falling and rising while maintaining a jerky movement of the head and shoulders' (1987: 24).

A sense of humor – which takes pleasure in the contradictory movements of two objects (two people, or a person and the environment, or a word and its other meanings) – incorporates the plastic and the wooden, the fluid and the fixed, it captures a strange balance we may have in ourselves between the languid pleasures of being and the stiffening frights of life, between the mother as succulent sensualizing other and the mother as mind-blowing fury, between the father as World Cup coach and the father as Cronus the castrator. A comic position is built into the very structure of our soul, occupying as we do a transitional and a transfixing state, energized as we are by desire and jerked about by fright, both plastic and wooden.

This radical contradiction in our being could become a fateful collision – as with Oedipus, whose spontaneous intuitions were pitted against his appalling stupidity – or the occasion for self-amusement. We may choose, then, between our comic and our tragic potential.

It is interesting that many of the great comic figures of this century – Chaplin, Keaton, Laurel and Hardy, Tati, Allen, Cleese – create characters who are accident-prone, who don't have a clue: that is, people for whom the unconscious is married to circumstances in disastrous ways. They are out of touch with their surroundings, however determined they may be to master their fate. They mirror an initial experience with the great clown in the sky that went wrong, one that married their generative unconscious abilities not with the object world but with wrong-mindedness. They are amusing to us because we can't imagine forever getting into such difficulties ourselves, however often we slip up. We all have friends or colleagues who seem to live precariously close to this kind of existence, who seem woefully canny in matching their unconscious destructiveness or anxieties with their circumstances in such a way as to court disaster. Down the road a piece – farther toward Thebes – stands the tragic figure who is so blind that his connection with the real is murderous and will end his life, the ultimately clueless man.

'Mirrors should reflect a little before throwing back images,' wrote Cocteau. But often we do not have time for reflection, things are happening too fast, and what we show in response to the other – 'Hey, why are you looking at me like that?' – is taken as bad mirroring. Poor black Americans, who may live with the possibility of violent encounter every day of their lives, have cannily evolved a system of remirroring that displaces the bad moment onto others and, at the same time, expresses many of the presumed insults that evoked conflict in the first place. This art form is called 'snap.' Typically, two combatants spar with one another, but not surprisingly, the mother is the ultimate object of this warfare. 'Your mother is so fat, when I got on top of her my ears popped.' 'Your mother's so fat she has to use a satellite dish as a diaphragm.' 'Your mother is so fat, after making love to her I roll over twice and I'm still on her.' 'Your mother is so fat she stepped on the scale and it read, "Fuck it . . . They don't pay me enough for this." ' Snaps also aim missiles at other members of the family and at the image of the body – 'You were so ugly at birth your parents named you Shit Happens'; at unwanted children – 'You're so ugly, every time your mother looks at you she says to herself, "Damn, I should have just given head" '; at poverty – 'I went to your house, stepped on a cigarette, and your mother screamed, "Who turned off the heat?" ' If the combatants last it out, one of them invents a snap that breaks it up and the defeated simply walks away in disgust: 'Shit, man, you're pathetic.' The joke is meant to be so bad that even though it bears an insult it is beneath riposte; conflict thus is averted, for the other is not deemed worthy of losing one's life for or getting into shit for (Percelay et al., passim).

Snapping's versatile ability to voice jocular exchange in the midst of extreme danger is intriguing. Has the mother, in the subtle art of reflecting, been a mirror throwing back images very quickly, stimulating the baby into many dances? Not an individual mother as such, but a mother created by the community, a mother of the mother-fucking world, a mother who, when asked what she's looking at, responds by humorously attacking all the valuables in the other's life. But the other, the attacked family and body, is a community object – a fat mama, a stupid father, a body with a nose too big, a collage of all these that bind the community together. Stand-up comedy here is nose to nose between two adversaries, and in the moment of potentially killing each other they allude to a common family that binds them together.

When one snaps at the other, a boundary is crossed. Conventional discourse is usurped by another language, one that alters those who use it. In a less distinct way, the same occurs when a person tells a joke. He may begin with what appears to be a straightforward account, but at some point the listeners realize that this is now a joke. The joker and the audience enter another place. Even a wry comment slipped in an otherwise serious order will refer to another place that everyone knows about. The ironic comment brushes the shores of another country, a dreamscape where people do not think conventionally and where they live according to different forces.

The comic, the joker, the wit who evoke this force remind their listeners of another world with varying degrees of effectiveness, at different points along a spectrum. The practical joker alters the real world and creates a mad one that traps the unsuspecting soul, a clear victim of this transportation. A wit tampers with the tediums of convention, nudging the others toward quiet rememberings of the other world.

The movement of humor in a comic act disables expectations. This may be intended or unintended. Some people have a natural sense of comic function: they appear to have abandoned any concern with adapting to convention and let themselves loose on the world. People like Ken Kesey, who was always getting himself and others into trouble. Once, for example, he joined a small gathering sponsored by the French Department of Stanford University to celebrate a meeting between Jean Genet and members of the Black Panther Party. Before he arrived, matters were rather tense. The Panthers did not know who Genet was and were also irritated by certain black well-wishers, to the point that one of them – Elmer 'Geronimo' Pratt – spit in the face of a man whom he deemed to be an Uncle Tom. Genet's admiring comments – he found the Panthers 'authentic' – did not lessen their increasing unease. Kesey arrived like a character from *One Flew Over the Cuckoo's Nest*: a bit smacked on drugs, wearing a silly grin. He shook Genet's hand and flashed a broad grin, revealing a front tooth capped in an enamel American flag. Genet laughed. Kesey then pointed to his socks: 'I'm wearing green socks.' Genet looked nonplussed. 'Green socks. Can you dig it? Green socks. They are heavy, man, very heavy.' Genet's translator gave a literal rendering: 'Les chaussettes vertes, elles sont très, très lourdes.' Genet gathered up some sympathy for Kesey's presumed plight, but then Kesey blurted out, 'You know what? I feel like playing basketball. There's nothing better than playing basketball with Negroes. I could go for a little one-on-one with some of these Negroes right now.' The Panthers were momentarily struck dumb. One Panther moved toward him threateningly, but their leader, David Hilliard, stopped him: 'Stay cool, man. This motherfucker is crazy. This motherfucker is crazy and we're getting the fuck out of here.' As they left, Kesey wondered out loud, 'Don't they like basketball?' (Collier and Horowitz, 1989: 13). He quite literally broke up the group.

A satirist may intentionally crack up a group, perhaps none more controversially than Paul Krassner when he was editor of *The Realist*. Several years after the assassination of President Kennedy, Krassner published a savagely satiric account of the ride back from Dallas on Air Force One during which Lyndon Johnson was sworn in. He used as his pretext the recently published book by William Manchester, *Death of a President*, several controversial passages of which, it had been reported, had been deleted. What had they contained? Krassner announced that he was publishing the missing portions in *The Realist* and the following appeared: ' "I'm telling you this for the historical record [says Jackie Kennedy to Manchester] so that people a hundred years from now will know what I had to go through . . . That man was crouching over the corpse . . . breathing hard and moving his body rhythmically. At first I thought he must be performing some mysterious symbolic rite he'd learned from Mexicans or Indians as a boy. And then I realized – there is only one way to say this – he was literally fucking my husband in the throat. In the bullet wound in the front of his throat. He reached a climax and dismounted. I froze. The next thing I remember, he was being sworn in as the new President" ' (Krassner, 1957: 133).

Publication of this account offended an entire nation. Yet, intriguingly, many people either believed that it was correct – thus bringing into focus their fantasies about Mrs. Kennedy's dislike of Johnson – or could not determine if it was true or not.

Krassner's account was a sick joke, but unlike the traditional sick joke (What did the Angel Gabriel say to Nicole Simpson when she got to heaven? 'Your waiter will be right with you'), the *Realist*'s jest failed to warn the audience that a joke was on its way. The humorist tapped the unconscious life of a nation: he was the comic let loose upon the world. Ordinarily, sick jokes, which are quite common following disasters, turn horror into amusement, so that the humor immediately creates a different frame of mind. But to the extent that humor and its agents – comedy, jokes, wit – move us into another universe, they always border on the catastrophic. Any reference to the other side – or the far side – usurps the otherwise privileged place of convention. It takes a certain kind of person engaged in a certain kind of violation to move himself and us across the border to the far side. Comics are in a sense leaders. They lead a group of engagingly unsuspecting souls to another place where the body, life's manners, serious issues, and human characteristics are ruthlessly exposed.

Krassner attacked two Presidents, a former First Lady, and, in effect, the sensibilities of millions of people. The stand-up usually lampoons current public figures or unfortunate souls who are good for a laugh. Billy Connolly, in 'Billy Connolly Live 1994,' mocked the victims of man-eating viruses, Fred West, the Member of Parliament who accidentally killed himself in intended near-death sex, yoga, men's scrotums, Italian waiters, bomber pilots, smart bombs, Michael Jackson, the Scots, the Swiss, schizoid schoolboys, daytime television, experts of all kinds, restaurants, members of his family.

The 'send-up' joke is a kind of gift of the stand-up moment. In the United States, lawyer-bashing jokes are in. 'How are a lawyer and semen the same? Both have a chance to become human beings.' 'Did you know that psychological laboratories are now using lawyers for scientific experimentation, rather than rats? They found that the technicians got less attached to lawyers. And they found there are certain things that rats won't do.'

Connolly, Krassner, the send-up comics stage a world mockery, inversions of convention. *Mundus inversus* is an ancient feature of the comic saboteur, practiced since classical times. Donaldson argues that there are three types of comic inversion.

> There are, first, those which show strange cosmic upsets: a sun and moon shining together in one sky, fish flying across land, men hunting on horseback across the sea. Then there are those that show reversals in the normal relationships between animals and men: an ox cuts up a butcher who hangs from a hook, fish angle for men, horses groom their masters and ride about on their backs . . . The third category . . . shows reversals in the normal relationships between people: here we see a man holding a baby or a distaff while his wife marches up and down with a stick and gun, a pipe stuck between her teeth; two girls beneath a balcony serenading a bashful man; a wife beating her husband; a daughter breast-feeding her mother; a son teaching his father to read; a client defending his lawyer; a servant putting his master to work.
>
> (1970: 22–3)

Or a patient charging his psychoanalyst, one might add.

When Eldridge Cleaver ran for President, he called Ronald Reagan 'Mickey Mouse.' The very sight of a black militant campaigning for this august position and nominating his opponents with Disney names seemed to middle-class Americans as if their world was turning over. Cleaver brilliantly captured the logic of humor: he could not be taken seriously and in this lay his strength. No one quite knew what he was up to, as, indeed, no one quite knows what Ross Perot would turn into – does he know that he is Popeye? – or what world he would create if elected to Pennsylvania Avenue. Oliver North, convicted of perjury, grins his way through an election campaign in Virginia, a twin of another cartoon figure, Alfred E. Neuman of the 'What Me Worry?' world of *Mad* magazine. Little wonder that the great American humorists – Twain, Mencken, Will Rogers – found American politics the most sidesplitting show in town. One need only mention Ross or Ollie to feel a joke coming on. Try it. Just say, 'Now, about Ross Perot . . .' or, 'Want to hear the latest about Ollie North?' and all but the fanatic supporter knows he is inside your humor whether he wishes to be or not. You can feel the anticipation develop.

Laughter often derives from this tension of anticipation, as the listener realizes that the comic is crossing the line, that for a moment he is getting hold of a force from the other side. Stand-up comics actually seem to have gripped the beckoning hilarity. If they manage to hold on to it and speak, then they will deliver *it* in a good way. Or they may be killed by it. Either way, they are interlocutors between a force on the far side and the social milieu. Conductors.

The recipient of a humorous remark has an initial response – 'Oh, a joke: ah . . . I know this happening' – but at this point the self unconsciously recognizes someone: 'I know this timing and spacing from somewhere . . . I know its effects . . . ah . . . I know you. Clown!'

When two people snap at each other, or when a comic goes onstage before an audience, a question in everyone's mind is whether or not a boundary can be crossed, a force got hold of, its energy used to crack up the other. Energy transferred is always there. Freud gave it the name of instinct, and psychoanalysis for a long time conceptualized it as free-moving energy. So we may say that the force that a humorist grasps when he crosses the boundary is the constant unconscious movement of instinctuality, which is associated with known urges: hunger and the urge to eat or drink, defecation and the urge to eliminate, genital excitement and the urge to fornicate. And so it goes.

These instincts usually determine themselves. They exist whatever the context. But a sense of humor may tap their energy, borrow not only their force but their sources and its aims. The comic moment may be a descent into the underworld, where it dips into the force of instincts and returns with enough energy to split sides.

Is it death-defying? Is this journey to the far side and back a minor triumph of the self, a self that goes to the dark world where humanity is shredded by ruthless humiliations, to the forbidden which gives life but also takes it? Are the court jester's jibe at the king, the stand-up's spitting image of a president, Cleese's mockery of the petty bourgeoisie – are these metonyms of flipping the bird at – we might have to say at God, inasmuch as he fits the image of the one who gives us life and then gives us death.

For a brief moment, then, the funny man defies the forces of life and death. He does deliberately what most of us do by chance. A joke comes to us, or we laugh at something we say, contented recipients of good luck. But the humorist intentionally goes to the world from which humor comes and walks a different path toward the same goal to which the psychoanalyst aspires, toward the world of instinct, into the ribald world of the unconscious, which decimates human intentions, and comes back with something.

They both crack us up.

Lacan clowned it up and embodied in his small theater something true to psychoanalysis – something that seems partly to have come from a powerful otherwhere that disturbs tranquillity. Beadle moves about tricking an unsuspecting population as he deftly manipulates reality to the disadvantage of hapless souls. These actions are rather in the image of our God, aren't they, especially if we see the Bible as a work of comic fiction.

We know, for example, that He was in the beginning a very great gardener. It is not difficult to imagine Him planning and tending Eden, and then inventing man. Nor is it difficult to see how His wonderful place was unfortunately mucked up by human error. We need only imagine a Woody Allen as Adam and a Diane Keaton as Eve – and perhaps Danny DeVito as the Snake – to help us along. We can certainly see the irony of His narcissism as He 'created man in the image of himself' only to see what fuck-ups men were.

He seems at times rather woefully out of it. 'Who told you you were naked?' He asks of Adam, who hides from Him. 'Have you been eating of the tree I forbade you to eat?' He seems to be less omnipotent than His otherwise impressive omniscience makes Him out to be.

When He punishes Eve by giving her pain in childbirth, He reminds one of Ubu – in Jarrès's world: 'I will multiply your pains in childbearing, you shall give birth to your children in pain.' One can almost hear Him say, 'So there!' before stomping off to some less troublesome – inhuman – part of His universe.

When he returns, He seems increasingly bizarre in His retaliations. Irked at the sexual habits of mankind, He decides, 'I will rid the earth's face of man, my own creation,' and so He announces to Noah that 'the end has come of all things of flesh' and from that moment all things are effaced from the earth. After wiping out the earth's populations, however, He smells the fragrance of Noah's burnt offering and changes His mind: 'Never again will I curse the earth because of man, because his heart contrives evil from his infancy. Never again will I strike down every living thing as I have done.' Whew! Well, thank God for that, eh!

But He does seem to relish tricking his poor creations. Irked now that men speak a common language and indeed are dedicated to building a tower to honor their unity, He apparently thinks to himself, Come, let us go down and confuse their language on the spot so they can no longer understand one another. Whereupon He scatters everyone around the earth with different languages so no one can understand one another. Terrific trick. Imagine if Beadle had the power to cast a spell on a family so that they wake one morning to discover to their horror that they no longer speak the same language; indeed, are founders of a new language and had best create a new world lest they suffer the horrid misfortune of a daily reminder of their essential alienation.

It must have been a mixed blessing indeed for His chosen people to follow Him. Think of the brilliant covenant He hatched – certainly the equivalent of breaking up the language: to command each of the men of His chosen people to cut off part of his penis. 'You shall circumcise your foreskin,' He tells Abraham. I would have thought that Abraham rather felt the demand acutely and surely suppressed a clarification – 'Are you sure about this one?' After all, he had asked for clarifications of previous commands.

Well, we all know the rest of the story, how God went on to do other great deeds, smashing up Sodom, acting as marital counselor to Abraham in his distress with Sarah, ordering Abraham to kill his son.

A God who comes from otherwhere, who has harnessed a power that shakes us, who comes too close for comfort, who plays upon our own incapacity, who presents us a face that presumably exaggerates our own, a clown face, seems a jester who not only puts us into existence but puts us on. If this figure is partly based on the function of the mother – a figure who comes from otherwhere, barely visible, yet audible, who provokes us with her clowning around and shakes us into life – then we may see a line running from God the father, who greets mankind; the mother, who is there to meet us on our arrival; our unconscious, mischievous imp of the soul, which guides us through life; and the comic, who carries on in our midst: infantile, omnipotent, vulnerable, enraging, disturbing, consoling, a figure at once godly and ungodly, maternal and infantile, aware and witless.

Thus does a sense of humor trade on our origins. It dips into a prior age. Something from the back of beyond, the above and below, the 'far out,' it plays with our reality. All along, humor grasps the absurdity born of human life, launched into existence knowing that 'in the beginning is our end.' That should be no laughing matter, except perhaps for the gods, who see it coming before we do, and except for our comics, who die our deaths for us so that we may live on, a little bit longer, all the merrier for the sacrifice.

Chapter 10

The structure of evil

In other works, for example, 'A Separate Sense' (Bollas, 1995), I have studied the ways in which the unconscious contributes to a separate sense – operating according to certain processes best illustrated in Freud's concept of the dream work – which can be considered the essential of creativity in living.

Although I have suggested that mental illness is a freezing of the unconscious (enabling us, paradoxically enough, to study it the more), I have deferred the question of what kind of inner sense an ill person has, or a person whose illness overpowers the cycle of condensation and dissemination that marks healthy unconscious living? Would it be a different inner sense, and if so what would this be like?

As we shall see, the person whose life is taken over by an illness, as it were, has a sense of living within something that determines him, and he may have an uncanny sense of the nature of that something which is his fate. Psychoanalysts write of pathologic structures, and we could say that the ill person has a sense of living within the logic of a pathology which, although beyond consciousness, is deeply familiar. Thus he has a separate sense, unconsciously determined and deriving not from the creative work of the unconscious but from the repetition of a pathology.

I shall consider the pathologic development of a separate sense by turning to a study of evil and of a person who lives inside an unconscious structure that both gives him a sense of his own evil and alarms us, who rightfully fear this pathology. A person who has a sense of his own evil derives it from a pathology which has unconsciously determined him, and from which he develops a logic and turns it into an extreme statement.

Indeed, the history of Western culture shows a clear and continuous effort to think about a process to which the word 'evil' is assigned, an effort obscured by the evocative power of the designation of any and all horrid events or malicious people as evil. As we shall see, there is a clear structure to evil, not only a series of stages in its deployment but a psychic logic that raises profound anxieties no doubt hindering the task of *thinking* about it. Each of the manifold representations of evil in Western literature expresses only a part of the process, leaving us only partly aware of what we are trying to objectify; we remain content to use the signifier in a sloppy and indiscriminate way, allowing moral fervor to cloud our understanding.

A theory of evil nestles close to the heart of the Judeo-Christian theory of human origins. The serpent tempts Eve to eat from the only tree in the Garden of Eden which has been expressly forbidden to her: a gifted deceiver, he lures her to a fateful judgment. In *Paradise Lost* (1674), Milton's serpent stalks Eve 'In Bow'r and Field ... By Fountain or by shady Rivulet,' waiting 'when to his wish, / Beyond his hope, *Eve* separate he spies.' The exemplar of innocence, Milton's Eve marries angelic heavenly form and femininity, and when the serpent finds her alone at last he is struck dumb by her goodness:

> Her graceful Innocence, her every Air
> Of gesture or least action overaw'd
> His Malice, and with rapine sweet bereav'd
> His fierceness of the fierce intent it brought:
> That space the Evil one abstracted stood
> From his own evil, and for the time remain'd
> Stupidly good, of enmity disarm'd.
>
> (Book IX)

Recollecting his hates, the serpent recovers and resumes his position as the 'Enemy of Mankind.' Sexy, eloquent, a 'guileful Tempter,' it casts a kind of spell upon Eve, who, throwing caution to the wind, succumbs to her hunger. The story of the serpent and Eve is a tale of seduction and temptation, in which the 'Evil one' presents himself as good and earns the other's trust. Empty-mindedness is present both when the serpent is momentarily struck dumb by Eve's goodness and when Eve succumbs to the charm of the seducer and the power of her own greed.

The link between the power of a tempter and the weakness of the subject's resolve was a familiar theme in medieval psychocosmology, and the Devil was expected to appear in disguise as an initially good figure. Kramer and Sprenger (1971), authors of *Malleus Maleficarum*, warn the flock that the Devil tempts those suffering from 'weariness,' 'young girls ... given to bodily lusts and pleasures,' and abandoned women who suffer from 'sadness and poverty.' One had to be constantly on the alert for the Devil, who popped up whenever there was a human need, rather like an ill-intentioned precursor of social services. No doubt this belief rationalized Western culture's wariness of succumbing to first impressions that might be ill-conceived, but the power of the charmer was seen as proportionate to the recipient's need. Being tempted by an offer (of succor, wealth, or sexual gratification) involved a person in a struggle not just with the Devil but with those parts of his personality elicited by temptation: evil triumphed when the victim failed to battle successfully with the self.

The deceiver's representing the self as good to an other whose frame of mind was less than discerning, artfully burlesquing virtue, was an important part of the movement of the evil gesture. The 'revenge tragedy' of the sixteenth and seventeenth centuries featured an evil plotter who befriends an unfortunate person, gains power over him, and utilizes the other's helplessness to his own end. Shakespeare skillfully represents this satire in *Othello*, as he shows how Iago appears to be good to Othello, using friendship to an evil end. Iago's success in seducing Othello illustrates how a powerful emotion, in this case jealousy, can destroy the mind, creating a murderous emptiness that has Othello throttling his love object. Iago gains Othello's trust by plying the Moor with doubts about his wife, creating a new kind of dependency, and Othello, entrapped in the structure of a spiraling psychic destiny, is preyed upon by Iago's uncanny deployment of the handkerchief, which was Othello's mother's gift to him before her death and which he has given to Desdemona. It bears in a corner a woven strawberry, the sign of nurture, and Iago's attack on the function and place of this object drives the Moor to murderous madness.

To return to *Paradise Lost:* Milton contemplates the structure of evil in the figure of Satan, emphasizing the unconscious grief that saturates him, having experienced not simply a loss of a paradisal place but a catastrophic annihilation of his position. Ruptured from the folds of nurturance, the Satanic subject bears a deep wound and good is presented now as an enviously delivered offering. In no other Western text is Satan characterized in such effectively sympathetic terms. Illuminating how loss of love and catastrophic displacement can foster an envious hatred of life mutating into an identification with the anti-life, Milton reaches the nature and effect of trauma. The prince of darkness is a traumatized soul who feels condemned to work his trauma upon the human race, trying to bring others to an equivalent fall. It is impossible to exclude from our considerations of Milton's Satan the overwhelming power and structural malevolence of God's authority, which seems grotesquely harmonized with the lust for power to which Satan succumbs.

One could point to many moments in Western literary history when writers explored the structure of evil: from the obstructive work of the Devil in the New Testament to his dank and cold presence in the atmosphere of place in Dante's *Divine Comedy*, from Defoe's *The Political History of the Devil* to Goethe's *Faust*, from the evil structures of seduction in the sentimental novels of Richardson to Hawthorne's *The Scarlet Letter*, from the complex novels of Dostoyevsky to Bram Stoker's portrait of 'spiritual pathology' in *Dracula*, and from Kafka's novels to Golding's *Lord of the Flies*. I cite these examples to indicate how a civilization such as ours thinks about a complicated feature of human life over a very long time.

Psychoanalysis brings us a step further down this road, and I should like to examine this structure of evil from a psychoanalytical perspective, borrowing a new figure in the Satanic lineage to help me in my considerations. To understand the ordinary side of evil, we should look at pathology, and, as Freud did at the end of the nineteenth century, this means looking at extreme disturbances in order to understand more ordinary aspects of the human mind. It may well be that the sight of the hysteric's limpid collapse was an icon of the late nineteenth century – an individual exemplifying how repressed conflicts afflict the body – a scene played out subsequently in the collective bodies of those dying in the trenches of the Great

War. One hundred years later the image of a serial killer's violent sculptures haunts the late-twentieth-century mind, objectifying a disturbing presence of thoughtless – empty, moving – violence. In the intervening century, the world witnessed two wars that annihilated all presumptions held about mankind, leaving fin de siècle man a kind of serial self, wandering through a life of increasing anonymity, the target of his thinkings, his despairings, or, in the extreme, his murders.

Genocide is the quintessential crime of the twentieth century, and genocide is exemplified by the serial killer, a genocidal being who swiftly dispatches his victims and converts the human into the inhuman, creating meaningless deaths that sully the concepts of living and dying. Even though these killers may be but dimly aware of their participation in an unconscious structure, and bearing in mind that the precise causes that launch each of them into his perverse existence will always be unique to the person and his lived experiences, there is much to be learned about the unconscious object relation being enacted. In the contemporary mind the serial killer is the statement of evil, and by studying what we imagine he does, we may come to understand what has always been part of our culture, our society, and the varying fates of some of our selves.

Bundy put his arm in a plaster cast now and then, presenting himself as a person in some need, reversing the usual pattern of a seducer offering his victim help of some sort. Lucas stopped his car to pick up a young hitchhiker. Dahmer promised money, a good drink, and company, in return for the right to photograph his guest. Nilsen offered a place to stay for the night. But in each case the aim of the seduction was to kill. As Nilsen wrote:

> There is honour in killing the enemy,
> There is glory in a fighting, bloody end.
> But violent extirpation
> On a sacred trust,
> To squeeze the very life from a friend?
> (Masters, 1985: 145)

This 'sacred trust' of which Nilsen writes is a trust at the very foundation of human relations, the belief invested in anyone who offers sanctuary, assistance, or nurture. Erikson called it 'basic trust,' so elemental that it precedes reflective consideration, almost a thoughtless assumption, derived from parental care of a child. We know, don't we, that this is the infant's and child's trust in the mother and father who look after the child, who certainly withhold any violent or murderous response, and who bear the child's greed, omnipotence, empty-headedness, and jealousies. Offering assistance to the other in need, the serial killer trades on the basic trust that derives from the child's relation to the providing world. But as we shall see, this offering that turns into the fist of death reaches the very heart of human vulnerability, and casts a sickly anxiety that spreads across society.

Before he began to murder, Nilsen would lie naked before a mirror and look at his body for hours on end. 'As my mirror fantasy developed I would whiten my face, have blue lips and staring eyes in the mirror and I would enact these things alone using my own corpse (myself) as the object of my attention' (Masters, 1985: 132). After he killed his victims, he would bathe them, put them in his bed, talk to them, dress them up, bury them under the floorboards, resurrect them, bathe them again, then dismember them, boil them, bury them, and so on. Occasionally he would sodomize the corpse, fascinated by its physicality but also 'fascinated by the mystery of death. I whispered to him because I believed he was still really in there' (Masters, 1985: 125), he wrote about one victim.

In his biography of Nilsen, Brian Masters traces this horrifying fascination with corpses to the death of Nilsen's grandfather: 'He took the real me with him under the ground and I now rest with him out there under the salt spray and the wind in Inverallochy Cemetery. Nature makes no provision for emotional death' (Masters, 1985: 47). From that day on Nilsen regarded himself as a dead man, a view that he was able to bring into consciousness according to his diaries, although obviously he lived much of his life as if this were not so.

Readers of the literature will note that many of the men who become serial killers of anonymous people have suffered the kind of emotional death that Nilsen describes. What happens when a child experiences the death of the self? Indeed, what is this sort of death?

It would seem to be the outcome of a trauma of some kind. For example, an apparently manic-depressive patient felt at the start of his analysis that the death of his mother when he was nineteen months old was of no significance to him. However, his sense of helplessness, his lack of belief in life, his incessant yet inef- fective imperatives pointed to a devastation in his early childhood. And even though his father never discussed this event and, furthermore, chided him for his various collapsings throughout his life, his father loved him, looked after him, and he was able to get on – although only just. There is no question that with the death of his mother, something within him had died, although he had been partly brought back to life by love and paternal care. He did not have that generative capacity which allows an individual to soothe the self; instead, he dealt with his uncon- scious grief by using his mind as an object that, through an endless supply of harsh imperatives and injunctions, was meant to boot-camp him into activity: 'Come on! Stop feeling sorry for yourself and get to work!'

Henry Lee Lucas, however, was repeatedly beaten by his mother throughout his childhood. She was a prostitute and copulated with many men in front of the children. His father was a double amputee and lived, if that's the word for it, on a slat of wood, rolling himself around the village. At an early age, an angry Lucas killed animals, cut up their bodies, and played with their blood. Before going on his killing spree, he murdered his mother. I think it is fair to postulate that he experienced the recurrent killing of the self throughout his childhood as the destruction of his own personally determined self state; it had been canceled by an irreducible act that annihilated the otherwise prescient authority of his inner life.

It is a *killing*, not merely death, of the self because the latter, however tragic, suggests a meaningful termination, and even though Nilsen believed his grandfather's death was the beginning of his demise, it is more likely that this identifiable loss was memorable *because* it was meaningful; it is more difficult to gather into memory the registration of meaningless killing.

The serial killer – a *killed* self – seems to go on 'living' by transforming other selves into similarly killed ones, establishing a companionship of the dead, as Masters concluded in his biography of Nilsen. In place of a once-live self, a new being emerges, identified with the killing of what is good, the destruction of trust, love, and reparation.

It may be fruitless to differentiate among types of hate, but I should like to focus on this passionless act of killing rather than the passionate act of murder driven by rage. The evil person horrifies his victim and those who study him precisely because he lacks a logical emotional link to and is removed from his victim, even if transformed in fury. Stuart Hampshire has said that the Nazi killers worked in what he called a 'moral vacuum'; the genocidal person identifies not with the passionate act of murder, but with the moral vacuum in which killing occurs, a meaningless, horrifyingly wasteful act. Carrying within himself this sense of horrifying waste, the killer finds a victim who will die his death, someone who will receive senseless blows.

Many acts of 'ordinary' murder are unannounced. A schizoid individual can kill without any prior aggressive states that might at least theoretically warn a victim of imminent danger. But the serial killer has become an especially powerful emblem of harm that may strike unexpectedly, with no warning. Popular literature and journalism portray him as quite the opposite of alarming: a friendly, if quiet, neighbor whom one might ask to water one's plants when one is away on vacation. The image of the logically trustworthy acquaintance springs to mind because of the absence of any alarming characteristics; perhaps he has *evolved* and taken on the very characteristics that allowed him to fit into the environment so that one couldn't see him!

Characteristically the victim does not know the serial killer. In psychoanalytic terms the killer would seem to be part of the environment of trust, providing no sign of danger to the victim, not alerting mental processes in the victim that might trigger lifesaving activity. The Yorkshire Ripper arises from the foggy fabric of the real that is always beyond perception yet is the basis of our imaginative re-creation of reality. Even though we know that the world is in part dangerous, and even though we are aware of our own destructive ideas and feelings, we seem able to delude ourselves that the world and the self are basically benign. This is one reason why the serial killer so alarms us: we cannot see where he is coming from and cannot comprehend his motivations, and whatever we know about him does not help us find him before he appears out of the blue and strikes again.

There is a place called *nowhere*, a country where the killer lives and from which he strikes. We know this place. Even if it is beyond our perception, we know it exists. It is the place of the split-off unknown, where actions with unanticipated consequences originate, where sudden destructiveness against or from the self arises, a zone of darkness that weaves in and out of selves, preserving darkness and nowhere in the midst of vibrant mental life and human relations. This is where the killer lives, finding in an actual, real habitat – a bleak apartment, an empty highway, a red-light district – the objective correlative of the nowhere land that has made him its citizen. This is a land from which one never sees movement of thought or action resulting in an action that defines the self, whether the blows come from an other who lives there or from some part of the mind now colonized by it.

The shocking harm erupting in the midst of a benign texture of the real (as opposed to our imaginary transformation of reality into something alarming) is deeply disturbing, and it preys upon a certain kind of fear we have that is so great we cannot even experience it as fear: a dread that reality will cease to support us in safety and will do us harm. Some people who were victims of a childhood trauma that occupied their subjectivity – in effect displacing the imaginary with a kind of theater of the real, capable of infinite repetitions but no creative variations – realize that even more shocking than the content of what happened to them is the trauma that the real in the first place actually did something profoundly consequential. The death of a parent is not in reality *meant* to happen, and a move that takes one from one's home and friends seems only an imaginary possibility: it is not meant to occur. A child whose parent repeatedly beats him will as an adult feel not that the physical pain of the beating was so painful, or even that it was the parent's hate that was so terrible, but that something happened which never should have happened; something displaced the true self and left in its place an irreversible identification with the act committed against the child's self.

––––––

When the serial killer offers help to the victim as part of his lure, he unconsciously reconstructs that potential space which the self is offered at the beginning of life; dependence, hope, and belief are elicited by this gesture. When the potential recipient of this seduction is hooked, the serial killer then usually 'creates' a sudden catastrophic disillusion which is precursive to the victim's psychic and physical death, a moment of total and absolute disbelief.

> Gerald had a roll of gray duct tape in his left hand which he passed to Charlene with a curt order: 'Tape their mouths shut first. Then do the same with their wrists and ankles. And do it right, got it?' Just as Charlene was about to clamp tape over the short victim's mouth, the girl looked soberly into her eyes for an instant and said, 'This is really real, isn't it?'
>
> (Hoffman, 1992: 43–4)

Little has been written of the serial killer's shocking occupation of the real, that terrifying moment when the grandmother turns into a hungry wolf, when the benign texture of reality mutates into something unimaginable.

Is the deadly blow of a killer who strikes sight unseen or who strangles a guest in his sleep the movement of the traumatic that cannot be seen, that gives no warning, that was never organized by an ego into a person? Pure trauma. On the other hand, is the killer who offers assistance and then, fully visible as executioner, betrays the trust, a witness that his life was terminated by a deadly other? Does he differ from the invisible killer, whose victim does not have a human executioner? When killers transport their victims through the terms of their own childhood, ritualizing their extinction by sacrificing them to a killing trauma, are the victims stand-ins for the killer-become-malignant-transcendent?

———

Georges Bataille argues that the sacrificial killing of an animal or human being gives to the witnesses of the act a sense of transcendence over death itself. They watch while a full-bodied, living being is killed. It loses its life, but the witnesses go on living. Given that all human beings are in fact 'discontinuous beings,' sacrifice partly serves the unconscious need to survive one's own death.

The person who has been 'killed' in his childhood is in unwilling identification with his own premature mortality, and by finding a victim whom he puts through the structure of evil, he transcends his own killing, psychically overcoming his own endless deaths by sacrificing to the malignant gods that overlooked his childhood. A strange brotherhood exists between the executioner and his sacrificial victim. In some cultures the victim's blood is consumed or witnesses cover their bodies with the corpse's blood. What had been alive only moments before still feels warm; it is as if the witnesses were privy to that vital transitional moment between life and death in which neither is entirely free of the other and life is still present. The executioner is covered with the victim's blood, and the formerly alive other seems to live on, with its warm substantial presence. Dahmer occasionally cut open the body of a victim and had intercourse with the intestines, sometimes 'placing his penis literally *within* the body and ejaculating among its organs' (Masters, 1985: 125). Does the serial killer who revels in the victim's blood and body seek kinship with that unconscious intermediate space – here, between life and death – because it is vital to them, the place where they once lived but where they were turned into ghosts of their former selves? Many serial killers seem puzzled by the simplicity of killing; one moment the other is alive, the next he or she is dead. What was the last moment of life? Where did life go? When did death come? Nilsen: 'I was fascinated by the mystery of death. I whispered to him because I believed he was still really in there' (Masters, 1985: 125). Nilsen himself was still there after his own psychic death.

———

Adolfo Constanze practiced black magic, depositing the ground-up remains of his victim's brain in a vessel called a *nganga*, derived from Congo culture and passed on in the West Indies. Edward Humes, a journalist who studied Constanze, writes:

> The true power of Congo magic . . . lay in a miniature, magical, universe of rot, decay, and death created inside a black cauldron – a feared and secret receptacle called the *nganga*. Inside this cauldron, the spirit of a dead man could be imprisoned and enslaved . . . the single most important ingredient is

a human skull and brain, preferably freshly dead, the source of the dead spirit to be entrapped.

(Humes, 1991: 58–9)

To imagine this object's psychic correlate is to identify an area of the self that stores and crushes the remains of a now decomposing victim.

Some serial killers seem bizarrely intimate with the rotting bodies of their victims, and they store the remains of the dead. For the killer, the rotting and decomposing others are living on after death within the incarcerated world of the killer's false self – a world designed to be perpetuated in the greater world around it. It is unlikely that he would ever consciously know this to be true (Nilsen and Dahmer may be exceptions), as he is obviously profoundly out of touch with himself, acting out parts of himself in the horrifying partitioning that constitutes the act of murder.

We should ask whether the structure of evil in this case, as a latent container, is a kind of internal *nganga*, constructed out of the remainders of the killed selves, waiting to receive the blood of a fresh victim. The serial killer identifies with an evil self that emerges from the moral vacuum created by the murder of the true self, and he also identifies with that former true self, projectively identifying it with the victim, now rotting or decaying in some roadside byway or under a floorboard or in a pot brewing on the stove. The horror over the act – the deep shock and eventual grief – is 'left' to the police, medical personnel, families, and worried parties to feel.

––––

There is a necrophilic aspect to sacrifice as the witnesses watch death copulate with life. Something of this can be discerned in some serial killers' eroticism: not only do they commit a posthumous sexual act but the act of murder itself is orgasmic. This death sex has its climax in an intercourse that kills – bearing the history of a childhood in which intercourse with the environment resulted in the repeated killings of the self. The primal scene's violent dimension is hypercathected, and bad fucks good to death.

It is disturbing to see 'positive' sides to the act of murder, when the killer unconsciously seeks to enter the live body of the other by cutting it up in an act of 'examination,' a bizarrely concrete form of empathy, coming to know the other only by cutting it into pieces to look inside it. And the taboo against cannibalism – after all, eating the victim's flesh offends anyone's sense of decency – may have much to do with its unconscious attractiveness for one who has been psychically killed, because it allows him a violent alternative to the generative intercourse he has not had. Death sex is partly an effort to merge with the living, to kill in order to be released into momentary identification with life as it exits a self. It brings to mind the idea of the soul's departing the body, which may be an unconscious objectification of those moments in which the life of a self is killed and departs the body, when one feels emptied, the body a container holding only the memory of a life now putrefying. Death sex, orgasm in the act of murder, curiously transforms that moment of horror when the child's self is so shocked that it vacates the body forever, an eros stamped by the excitement of extinction. The sexually driven killer, compelled to find a new victim, may at the moment of the murder be on the verge of a horrifying panic, when the killing of his self feels close at hand; with his victim he seeks an object into whom he can project the experience (by reversal) and who will also serve as the object of a transformation of the aim, from anxiety to excitement, and finally through murder to denudation of excitation.

Dr. George Palermo, who interviewed Jeffrey Dahmer, said in court, 'He killed those men because he wanted to kill the source of his homosexual attraction.' The terrible pain occasioned by instinctual life can create objects of desire, and places the self in such a relation to the world that not only is disappointment a possibility but one's instincts – sponsoring urges and gestures as they do – bring one into direct harm with significant others. In this case, the instinct can feel like an endangering force. The killer's eroticism is a strange condensation of the instinct and the killing of the instinct; the urge to fuck is negated by the killing of the fuck, which results in a fuck that is also a kill. Some serial killers have reported the urge to kill like some horrid force that takes them over, but we may wonder if this isn't testimony to their vain effort to separate themselves from instinctual life itself, which is now mixed with its own anticathexes, forming a matrix of instinctuality and its killing, a pathologic combination of the life and death instincts. Confusing the object of desire with the source of the instinct, the killer destroys the object in order to be returned to a state of nonexcitation.

———

The victim's innocence is certainly part of the economics of this primal scene, and it would be ludicrous to suggest that a serial killer's victim is somehow a willing partner in the act's intentionality. But it is nonetheless true that serial killers usually prey upon the victim's need, and that need may be so considerable that it renders the victim rather empty-headed. When Henry Lucas picked up his victims along the main highways of America, each person who accepted a lift from him pushed aside the knowledge that they were putting themselves at risk. And he could certainly be charming. Disarming. And they got in his car. No doubt many were poor and could not afford the bus fare, or their own cars had broken down; they were tired and chanced it. But it is certainly part of the serial killer's intersubjectivity to put on the charm, turning an otherwise intelligent human being into an 'airhead.'

I would like to suggest that the 'empty-headed other' is an important part of the structure of evil, for the killer finds this erotically exciting. The victim's seeming gullibility, stupidity, and lack of foresight are attractive. So far as the killer is concerned he deserves what he has coming to him. And as I have argued, when the killer announces his intent to kill the victim, his speech empties the other's head, creating a vacuum from mute incomprehension. But this airhead is also a sculpted manifestation of the killer's childlike, formerly alive self, now its victim; a form of unconscious transference occurs in which the killer's child-self lives through the victim, and the force of killing renders the self mute and empty.

Inasmuch as these killings are often acts of identification in which the victim is placed where the killer once lived, its erotic component becomes an onanistic sexuality; the killer gets off on his own annihilation. Psychic death becomes exciting. After describing in great detail how he made himself look like a corpse in front of his mirror, Nilsen concludes: 'I must be in love with my own dead body' (Masters, 1985: 106). The pathologic narcissism is clear: the killer is never with an other; all others being merely walking innocents, corpses of his former self, long before the Fall.

It is interesting and pertinent that we refer to one adult's abduction of another as a '*kid*napping.' When an adult is whisked away, perhaps to be killed, there is recognition of the effect of the act, which is to subject the victim to a radical and catastrophic infantilization. Very often the victim is bound and thus made immobile. Perhaps he or she literally cannot walk. Victims are often blindfolded, so do not even have an infant's visual capacity. They may be ordered not to speak, will often have to urinate or shit on themselves, and be fed by hand. 'No speak – no move' (Waite, 1993: 36), ordered Terry Waite's captors. A young woman recently kidnapped in England said upon her release, 'It was like learning to walk all over again,' and we know that hostages and kidnap victims need time to reacquire certain adult identifications.

Brian Keenan has described his radical infantilization when he was incarcerated in Lebanon, held hostage for nearly five years. After days and weeks of isolation he would drift off into dream and daydream, the distinction between dream and reality blurred. Bodily functions resumed a profound organizing centrality. 'I am reduced to sleeping in the smell of my own filth. Excrement, sweat, the perspiration of a body and a mind passing through waves of desperation. All of everything is in this room. I am breaking out of myself, urges, ideas, emotions in a turmoil are wrenched up and out from me.' He daydreamed a pleasant landscape: 'I feel the soft pleasure of it, as a child must feel when its mother or father gently cradles it and rubs its tummy' (Keenan, 1992: 67). The mind soothed him, and in such states, he wrote, 'I am in a cocoon which enfolds me like a mother cradling a child' (p. 68). Sleep became a kind of mother. 'Sleep, dream, escape into the arms of those whom you love. Let them shelter you, hold you, comfort you. Sleep – the great mother' (Waite, 1993: 36).

The hostage is violently reduced to the infantile, forced into an encapsulated state in order to survive an impossible reality. Surely the killer who puts his victim through a similar collapse of the adult into the damaged child – a form of condensed infanticide, matricide, and patricide, in which all kill each other – expresses unconscious rage toward his own infantile experience? The victim is now to experience a seemingly endless, terrorizing infancy, recreating this child's sense of *malignant* time, when mental pain and suffering decomposed the sense of time-as-development, putting in its place a no-exit time, the temporality of life in hell. Here, contained in the victim's experience, in what psychoanalysts term the countertransference, is something of that infantile hell the subject had borne, which he now transfers into the other's self experience.

Alongside the collective fear of the serial killer in our day and age is another anxiety, sometimes bordering on a kind of mass panic: people wonder just how many children are the victims of parental sexual or aggressive abuse. That such abuse is not uncommon only fuels the alarm, and because it is impossible to determine just how common it is, the doors seem to be opening to a new kind of horror.

The structure of evil exploits our primitive belief in the goodness of the other. However much a child's projective processes may invest the parent with nasty qualities, he ultimately knows the difference between his imagined constitution of the parent as a monster (e.g., in dreams, daydreams, willfully vindictive sulking) and the moment when a parent does something that is *truly* monstrous. When the entrusted good object suddenly changes its nature and betrays its investment, the child is stupefied, and his own ordinary vulnerability turns against itself. Malignantly dependent upon the violating parent, and often with no one to turn to, the child's dependence may deepen; even if the abused child seems manifestly distant from the violating parent, he feels secretly bonded to the parent, brought closer to the very object which has betrayed him.

Generative innocence is essential to the life of every developing person. It is important that one carry within oneself a belief in 'a golden era,' a time when all was well; this idealization of the past often takes the form of retrospectively bequeathing upon childhood a simplicity and goodness that do not hold up on closer scrutiny. But this innocence forms the basis for an illusion of absolute safety that is essential to life, even if we know it is a psychically artistic device. For this generative innocence creates a continuously renewed 'blank screen' upon which one can project one's *desire*. The child, for example, needs to split off the bad parts of his or her own personality in order to disseminate desire without premature closure brought on by persecutory anxieties or guilt. Even if the mother or father has been a 'monster of the moment,' both child's and parent's reparation needs to reconstitute a new parent, acquitted of previous charges. The innocent walk free.

The child who has been abused cannot create that generative innocence which allows the self to have blank screens upon which desire can be continuously projected and reprojected. Nor indeed can the child use that screen to visualize projective identifications of the monstrous parts of his own personality (more often than not conveniently sited in the parents). For the abusive parent has muddied the screen and it will never be blank again. There can be no intimate relation to an actual other or to the internal objects of everyday projective life that are not tarnished by the hand of the real, which has invaded the imaginary and scarred it.

The violated child has lost his or her generative innocence forever. It is a profound tragedy. People who participate in the contemporary festival of victimology trivialize the tragic effect of abuse when they insist on the absolute and irretrievable evidence of human innocence rather than the generative innocence of origins; they cannot bear to own responsibility for their own destructiveness, and can only project it into the mother or the father, unconsciously and hysterically trading on a truth. Malignant innocents, who may insist upon absolute innocence of the self throughout life and who designate certain objects (mothers, fathers, 'men,' homosexuals, or whatever) as perpetual villains, trade off the sympathy and need that all of us have to believe in the necessity of innocence.

———

It is a commonplace question to ask why a woman who is battered by her partner should continuously return to be victimized yet again. There are doubtless many different reasons why people do return to such a scene: some from unconscious guilt, others to engage in a scene of masochistic pleasure, some who have become parasitically dependent on the partner, others who have children and extended family connections with the violent man and who cannot make the break that is necessary to their long-term survival. And of course, many are simply terrified that if they really try to make a final break they will be pursued to an even more violent conclusion. Refuge from this dilemma is the privilege of upper-middle-class or upper-class women; few others can afford to disappear successfully from the homes they share with violent men, unless they have the institutional protection of a women's refuge.

Marjorie entered analysis with a storehouse of symptoms, many of which suggested her dread of a loss of self-control that might put her in an endangered situation vis-à-vis the parenting environment: she did not travel by Underground because she feared she would faint on the train; she did not go into a butcher shop because she feared that if she saw the sight of blood she would fall down and crack her head and no one would be quick enough to catch her. She was living with a gifted and colorful man who had had an exceedingly deprived childhood. He was given to occasional and horrific fits of violence during which he would beat Marjorie: she often came to sessions with a bruised face and once with a broken joint.

In part her analysis had made her partner intensely jealous, and Marjorie, for reasons of her own, had stirred him up, inviting him to imagine me as an ideal man and certainly drawing his attention to his inadequacy. Yet under no circumstances would she leave him. Her attraction to him, therefore, became an object within the analysis: initially to his phallic prowess (which was partly true), then to his ability to be atrocious and get away with behavior she would have enjoyed doing but daren't, but finally to something more insidious. There were times when she really did try to separate from him, most often after he had beaten her. Then he would apologize in a grief-stricken rather than abject way, telling her he loved her, vowing that he would never hit her again. He would remind her of their past together and tell her of what a promising future they could have, forging a potential space from the debris of the previous days. In time, she would melt. She loved him. They stayed together. She lived inside a newfound trust. Then one day, after drinking too much, he lost his temper and, in a shocking change of behavior, pummeled her especially hard. Battered, weakened, disoriented, Marjorie came to analysis having gone through a process that was now increasingly familiar to both of us.

At this point we had successfully analyzed her symptomatic expressions. Her fear of fainting expressed a wish to be held and cuddled by people, though her experience was that this did not happen. This was partly based on her mother's strident insistence on self-determinism and the rivalry she had with her mother, whom she would try to outdo by being even more self reliant than her mother insisted she be. But her experience of me in the transference liberated a different set of feelings and self and object representations, and we eventually got to the underlying wishes.

Fortunately Marjorie could see that her participation in her partner's batterings enacted her infantile wish to be in the wonderful care of the other. Her vulnerability to his re-seduction of her expressed both her wish to be reconnected with infantile pleasures – after a terroristic rupture – and her memory of her mother's ongoing availability to her in certain sorts of ways. She could increasingly objectify the process she was inside, and in turn report it to her husband, who, though partly infuriated by this insight, nonetheless acknowledged that it now meant something. He accepted psychotherapy after a long struggle and eventually they were able to live in a violence-free, albeit turbulent, relationship.

What does this have to do with the structure of evil? It will be remembered that I am stressing the *process* of evil – involving seduction, the promise of a false potential space, the development of a stupefying dependence that empties the mind, and feelings of shock, betrayal, and the like. The victim of battering may be involved in an unconscious object relation, constituting her memory of her earliest object relations, in which she tries to accept the curative sides of the man's seductions in order to live for a while in a nurturing universe. The sequence of events, I suggest, tells us not about a sadomasochistic contract but about a need that is destroyed by the object of a sacred trust.

And the batterer? Like the serial killer, although obviously less so, he lives through his own experience of having been battered as a child, when the charm of the mother's or father's false self was used by the parent to help the child recuperate from recurrent abuse. In this respect, his evil seduction can sometimes be an unconscious act of disavowal. Marjorie's partner constructed a false self, a charming and devious self, to deal with the destructive potential of his mother and other relatives he lived with. As he charmed Marjorie back into a system created by false reparations (his mother's) with which he identifies (becoming a false charmer, aiming at all costs to avoid his wife's fury), he fashioned a shallow world of meaningless alliances that gutted the self of its passions. In the act of 'unmasking' himself – when he thundered about the house throwing objects, and battering Marjorie – one can see his effort to break through the false self, which obviously released true-self states in a primitive and inexperienced form.

Marjorie and her partner both benefited from psychoanalytic treatment, and his batterings stopped. But other women return to the object who traumatizes them because in so doing they revisit the terms of their own relational origin. Something from nowhere, something purely out of sight, something without warning emerges with a violent rupture from the otherwise comforting presence of the mother or the father. The parent hits the small child violently, but when the parental storm is concluded the child and the parent return to a family situation that betrays no memory of the event. Indeed it is *as if* it had not taken place. Women who return to battering men, then, sometimes do so because of its *uncanny* re-creation of *that* violent abruption which emerges in a seemingly safe – that is, good – relation.

———

The psychoanalytic recognition that perverse sadomasochistic relations are a means of transforming the potentially traumatic effects of instinctual life, emotional experience, and interpersonal intimacies into mastered events where no catastrophe occurs is well known, and there is a vast literature on the topic. I shall not review that literature, but we should not exclude this clinical phenomenon from the present topic.

For it is patently obvious that a perverse sadomasochistic couple also enacts the structure of evil. In many such rituals, there is an orchestrated 'innocent moment.' Jacob, a patient in his mid-twenties, told me that he would invite a woman to his flat when he had the rather uncanny sense that she *might* be 'into' what he was 'into.' He was never really quite sure, so he always began the evening's adventure as a very gentle and considerate host. He loved to cook and usually prepared a nice meal. He was a comedic sort of man and enjoyed being amusing, and telling the occasional joke, which brought forth 'girlish' or 'feminine' squeals of delight from the lady diner.

I don't think his guests actually got drunk, but they feigned a sort of intoxication, and established an ambience of vulnerability, which Jacob found exciting. At a certain point in the evening, usually after dinner, while sitting on the couch or looking at a book together, he would say quite abruptly and without any preparation, 'I would like to tie you up. Do you mind?' This direct approach never failed to be shocking. The guest would be startled and, head thrown back, look at him, usually very closely.

He rarely told me of the misalliances. I am sure they occurred, and can only assume that some women readily rebuffed him, ending the evening on very clear terms. He *never* touched his female guest at any point prior to his announcement, nor did he ever try to force himself physically on her. As Smirnoff has written of masochistic activity, Jacob just 'announced the contractual possibilities.' It surprised me for some time just how many women agreed. Indeed, after the initial shock, they would have little or no hesitation about proceeding immediately to the act. Jacob would take the woman to his bedroom and 'instruct' her. As is common in such partnerships, his personality would change from that of a humorous and animated host to a seemingly menacing presence, the threat contained by the apparent expertise of his instructional knowledge. 'Here is what you are to do. You are to bend over the bed with your back to me. Good. Now turn around. Fine. Now sit down and take off your clothes: shoes first. Fine. Now underclothing.' And the ritual of the undressing would occur according to his dictates; he in turn would undress, go to his chest of drawers and get his leather straps, which he used to bind his guest to the bed, lying on her back.

When the woman was in this position he would say, 'Now you are completely in my power,' and he would ask, 'Aren't you worried?' Whereupon the guest would usually, I gather, say either 'No, I trust you' or 'Well, what are you going to do? It depends.' So far as Jacob was concerned, once the woman indicated that she trusted him and he could now do what he wanted to her, the act was over. Sometimes he would burst into tears; other times just sit by her side – after he had untied her – and talk for several hours. He rarely proceeded to make love on that first meeting, and when he did, he never felt there was a relation between the two acts, except, of course, that tying the woman up had been very exciting to him, and had everything to do with establishing trust, which then made the sexual situation much more satisfying for him.

He was somewhat puzzled by the need for all this, although eventually he could see that he entertained unconscious fantasies about the harmful potential of intercourse, an occasion when one could be at the mercy of the other. His anxieties about the primal scene became an important feature in his treatment. He had idealized his father and seen his mother as a very castrating and frightening woman. He claimed to have lived in terror of her throughout his childhood. When she entered the room he swore that he could feel his penis shrivel up, and he described this feeling as one of his earliest memories of her effect upon him. He could never find his 'proper' voice when he talked to her: it would go up an octave. Further, it was clear to him that she found his response to her presence irritating, asking him, 'For God's sake, what is the matter with you?' as he perspired and sometimes trembled in her presence. But he could never answer this question. He did not know the answer. His mother was a very attractive, colorful, intelligent woman, well liked by just about everyone, including his siblings, and all he could ever conclude was that there really must have been something the matter with him.

Unfortunately for this mother–child partnership there really was a series of shocking events between them when he was less than a year old. The mother had been the victim of serious trauma herself during that first year of his life; in effect, she recurrently 'dropped' him and then resurrected him through guilt and great personal courage as she tried to overcome her own trauma in order to look after him. She knew, as she was to say to him years later, that her state of mind had damaged him during that first year, and I found their negotiation of a form of settlement quite moving. But try as they did to feel really relaxed in one another's presence, it was just not possible.

One of the most interesting aspects to this analysis, however, was the patient's statement that his mother would often give him 'the evil eye,' which sent a shudder down his spine. These early traumas had constituted a breach of the child's imaginary and illusional construction of a shared reality, and had broken the infant's peace of mind beyond his sight and imagining. This, in my view, was the basis of his reconstruction of that kind of event in the sadomasochistic acts he performed with his female guests. The terms of evil were present: the offering of the self as good; the creation of a kind of dependence and vulnerability; the sudden shock which takes the victim by surprise; a kind of infantilization. But then a recovery. The people who enact the sadomasochistic event ritualize each other's brush with a near-death experience. They enact the terms of the killing of the self, but they are survivors. However physically brusque or punitive toward one another's bodies they may be, each partner in this exchange triumphs over a much more dire event: the killing of the self.

But the sadomasochists are still trapped by their need continuously to remaster an early trauma, and although they have converted the anxiety of annihilation into the excitement of its representation, it bears the weariness of the compulsory. Jacob was fairly exhausted by his acts. Although he could not stop himself from inviting a woman to his flat, he was always filled with a kind of dread about all that *it* would require from him. This 'it' which came from some other place. This 'it' which compelled him to ritualize his life with women. This 'it' that was so real but so inexplicable. But the act expiates the self of the secret it carries. Jacob felt that his wishes were horrific (we might say evil) but when a woman agreed to 'share the experience' he felt a reprieve from a malevolent form of desire.

These sadomasochistic alliances that enact the near-death of the self, in which the child self avoids its killing but forever feels the near-hit as a kind of narrow escape, offer thrillingly close encounters with annihilation. The sadomasochist will find a companion who has endured a similar psychic event and together they bring one another to the dramatic place where such near-collisions with mortifying events are pleasurably enacted to their hearts' content. That the self did indeed once nearly meet its end, that there *was* something awful in the environment that caused such mental intensities, is an unexamined feature of the sadomasochist's life; indeed, the function of the excitement is to dull any introspective action.

We know that one of the functions of perversion is to transform an infantile trauma into a form of excitement. The trauma is represented in transformed disguise, and it is continually enacted in dramatic space with the other as accomplice, but the enactments militate against a deeper knowing of the self and its other. This is a world of makeup and artifice, of false selves celebrating the virtue of disguise and dissemblance. No one is fooled, as all know they are fooling. Innocence is represented but not believed. As Genet so brilliantly illustrates in *The Thief's Journal*, the perverse subject can live a serial life, transforming the structure of evil into a burlesque. Certain homosexual cruisers, in the best of moments 'artists of the real,' offer the other total care, absolute dependence, and infinite embrace – all condensed into a few seconds in a park or public toilet. Death seems to be right behind them, but always left in the wake of the swift movements and orgasmic deliveries; the cruiser's joy in cheating death is an important part of his sexual accomplishment.

———

'Evil' is a signifier that we may rightly assign to any intention or action which expresses a specific structure that, wittingly or not, is undertaken by at least two people. I have outlined the distinctive steps to the process:

Presentation of good to the other. The evil one searches for someone who is in need and presents himself as good. Even though the victim may have doubts about taking up this contract (cf. Faust), he believes that on balance he will benefit from the exchange.

Creation of a false potential space. The arrival of the apparently good one creates a potential space for the recipient. Whether because the evil one seems to possess something the recipient had always thought was forbidden, or whether because the recipient's true need now appears on the verge of being met, the subject, by presenting apparent goodness, evokes hope (or greed, or the urge for power), and the recipient views him as a potential resolution to circumstance.

Malignant dependence. When the victim takes up the offer of assistance, he becomes dependent on the provider; we may regard this form of dependence as malignant since the nurturer feeds in order to destroy, since the initiator of the structure will turn this need into a dire fate.

Shocking betrayal. Although sometimes the victim is killed while asleep or totally unaware, the perpetrator often first presents the good appearance and then suddenly and violently changes his presentation, and the victim is catastrophically shocked by this reversal of fortune – at the deepest level not simply by the individual who commits the act of harm but by the change in reality itself, which he had assumed to be relatively benign.

Radical infantilization. With the total collapse of trust and the madness expressed by a sudden dementia of the real, the victim experiences an annihilation of adult personality structures and is time-warped into a certain kind of infantile position, possibly depending now for existence itself on the whim of incarnated madness.

Psychic death. The victim experiences the murder of being. The self that was in need, that trusted the world, that felt the arrival of a potential space, that became dependent, and that believed in a good fate, is suddenly killed.

This structure is part of the unconscious knowledge of Western man. It need not be fully deployed for the structure to be perceived; a single allusive gesture evokes its entire presence. When Saddam Hussein 'entertained guests' in a widely disseminated scene that was broadcast on television, he made one fatal error that personified him as evil in the eyes of those who watched; he beckoned to a child and, resting his hand on the child's head, assumed an affectionate pose. He meant to look good. Instead, the gesture instantaneously evoked in the mind of the viewing public the structure of evil, and everyone now *knew* that here indeed was a man capable of the hideous crimes of which he had been accused.

––––

Did Saddam Hussein also represent a political regime that operates within the logical structure of evil? Are governments or groups capable of deploying this structure of evil, and if so what form does it take?

Hussein's Baathist regime, like Pinochet's Chile or the Generals' Argentina, is notorious for being a police state in which ordinary citizens are subjected to a very particular kind of terror. Samir Al-Khalil's book on Hussein begins: 'Salim was about to sit down to dinner when the knock came' (1989: 3) – a phrase that could relate to moments lived under a disturbing number of other regimes and that immediately captures a terror that lives in the imagination of all men and women. The individual is plucked without warning from the warmth of domestic life and taken to another place by some violent representative of the real. To account for what?

Salim was not a political opponent of Saddam, and he was incarcerated without reason. He was well treated by the police but was too disoriented to comprehend what they claimed he had done. Where had he been on a particular day some time before? He could not recall. 'Dates and numbers were now being combined into single questions, and Salim was becoming so frightened he could not retain the different parts of each question, much less put them together into a coherent answer' (Al-Khalil, 1989: 4); a loss of intellect obviously arising from a collapsing of the adult self. Soon he was speaking 'nonsense.'

The police are understandably one of the most important arms of the state and the way they behave is instrumental in the population's interpretation of its government. A benign state, one not governed by leaders who intend the people serious harm, will trade off the citizens' unconscious presumption that it wishes them well. This will happen even when police, government officials, or political leaders make mistakes, as inevitably they do, for they know that citizens understand that corruption is part of life and will forgive the structure of their state.

Terrorist states also trade off the unconscious belief in one's safety, but they do so in order to divide and rule the subjects, who may be desperate to maintain the illusion of a benign reality even when they clearly see the dangers. However appalling the serial murder is, his singularity is almost a relief: he is an isolate, one of a kind, and he can be caught and incarcerated. But what of the state that operates according to such a mentality? What do we do with the Saddam Husseins?

We try to forget about them, not simply because they pose military or terrorist threats but because it is too disturbing to contemplate their presence. We can think of military powers that concerned people but that did not evoke quite the same blanking of the mind. A Saddam Hussein is unthinkable because his regime operates a structure so evil that he undermines our most profound assumptions about human safety, a need to believe that our guardians wish us no harm.

The politics of evil trades off this need. A Baathist party will terrorize its citizens, using this need to believe in a benign parent even as (indeed especially as) it pursues its malevolent ends. Each state is a derivative of the parenting world that exists in the mind of its citizens, and a terrorist regime will exploit the unconscious relationship to obtain a denial of its terrors among the citizens, who will support the denial. The state is unconsciously attacking the earliest and most profound of human relations and assumptions: the relation to the parent.[1]

---

1 To examine the psychology of torture is beyond the scope of this chapter, but the torturer illustrates a perversely brilliant exploitation of the structure of evil, as he alternates between being the good parent and being the bad parent. He oscillates from being a malevolent demon who inflicts appalling harm on his victim to being a benevolent listener who truly has his victim's best interests in mind, if only the victim would talk. This is part of the psychology of torture: the alteration in presentation of the real, designed to bring about a kind of infantile regression in the victim, who comes to need the torturer to define relational structures.

There are regimes which inflict appalling cruelty on their citizens but which are not evil. Only those regimes that knock on the door in the night, trading off the population's unconscious need to have a good parent, operate according to the logic of evil, and with these evil regimes that logic malignantly transcends its constituent features and becomes the voice of political terror. Caught in the structure, the population collapses. Inevitably it has to rely upon people outside the structure who, it hopes, will be able to act against the process to liberate them.

———

Political evil, which has power, is an extreme in human behavior, but all of us know of more ordinary kinds of evil. Every child will now and then be shocked by the failure of parental love. This is perfectly ordinary and common among even the most blue-ribbon parents. Mothers and fathers become irritated with their children, get angry with them, and maybe tell them to 'go away.' But when a parent is unexpectedly angry with the child – not in response to something the child has done – the child's shock may result in what seems like a temporary migration of his soul from his body. This is not a willed action. It feels to the child like a consequent fate, as if the parent has blown the child's soul right out of his body.

Each of us has received such an apprenticeship experience in the art of dying. We know what it is like for the soul to depart the body even though we have as yet no knowledge of actual death. We could say this is what psychoanalysts mean by the experience of 'annihilation,' but this experience and the anxieties attendant upon it have, in my view, been too bound to catastrophe. It is true, of course, that infants who suffer severe trauma will have an annihilation anxiety; in some cases a person's hatred of the world will be so intense he will have a talion fear of being fatally poisoned by his own venom. But each of us has a less severe dose of the experience of extinction, one which is also linked up to a concept of return. We return to our bodies. Peace reigns on heaven and on earth. We are back again. Each adult who has had 'good enough parenting' will have a psychic sense of a kind of migration of the soul, sometimes shocked out of the body, but always returning.

This cycle of shocking exit, emptiness, and return gives us our confidence, so that even when we are deeply disturbed by traumatic events – the death of a friend or a parent – we feel that somehow 'it will turn out all right in the end.' People can maintain this belief right up to the point of imminent death. Even knowing they are about to die they can nonetheless believe they are going to be all right.

The concept of heaven gives the Christian this kind of 'turning out all right in the end' place, and other religions also provide destinations for the soul and death rites that ensure a fortunate conclusion. These are as ancient as mankind itself, for even the most primitive and ancient cultures buried the dead in special – not just dispensary – ways, putting food or offerings along with the body in the burial site, as nourishment for the journey to the other world. In the Catholic religion, a priest will be called to give the last rites to a person close to death, ensuring that the person is blessed prior to the soul's departure from the body, safeguarding it against the demons that await near the bedside. The priest hears confession and forgives the Christian for his sins.

It is this peace of mind that Othello denies to Desdemona:

OTHELLO: 'Have you pray'd to-night, Desdemona?'
DESDEMONA: Ay, my lord.
OTHELLO: If you bethink yourself of any crime
    Unreconcil'd as yet to heaven and grace,
    Solicit for it straight.

When Desdemona realizes that Othello intends to kill her, she cries out, 'Then heaven have mercy on me!' But as we know, she does not understand *why* she is to be killed. Thus, although she has prayed and has called upon heaven to have mercy on her, she does not have the psychic integrity essential to the act of confession that precedes one's death. That is why she pleads for more time.

OTHELLO: Out, strumpet! Weep'st thou for him to my face?
DES: O, banish me, my lord, but kill me not!
OTHELLO: Down, strumpet!
DES: Kill me to-morrow, let me live to-night!
OTHELLO: Nay, if you strive, –
DES: But half an hour!
OTHELLO: Being done, there is no pause.
DES: But while I say one prayer!
OTHELLO: It is too late.

(Act v, scene ii)

Desdemona pleads for time, not only hoping that her husband will calm down in the morning but also so that she can compose herself before death, achieve a psychic integrity that will heal her disintegrated state of mind. When Othello says, 'Being done, there is no pause,' he recognizes that he has in a sense already killed her: her soul destroyed, her psychic integrity denied, her smothering is the last act of an execution that has already begun.

Few moments in dramatic literature are as horrible as this killing: Shakespeare reaches a trauma known to all who watch or read this play. The trauma is the experience of feeling deeply shocked and confused by the other's anger or rage, when for a moment one's soul leaves one's body, one loses contact with oneself, and one wonders if there will ever be a return to psychosomatic integrity again. In the evil moment, the self experiences psychic disintegration while remaining alive. Fortunately for most of us, we do return safely to our body selves after such shocks. But we know the experience, and it is to this unconscious knowledge that Shakespeare directs his evocative insight.

The serial killer has, at the very least, unconscious knowledge of a dire extinction of his own true self, but the murder he carries within him is not simply a memory of a catastrophic betrayal inscribed in his character: something has changed him, and it is this something that leads those not so destined to stand back in horror and isolate these killers as *different*.

———

When we are inclined to see the killer as the personification of evil, this transfers him to an allegorical plane as the representative of the hideous. Allegories thrive in authoritarian societies, when those in opposition try to represent forbidden ideas in personified form.

An allegorical character usually represents only one quality – virtue, sloth, seduction, faith, for example. Concentrating one quality in a single character gives a greater *force* to that quality, but it lacks the complexity of an ordinary character who might contain all these elements. And the structure of allegory, its rigidity and lack of emotional play, bears the terms of its origin.

Although allegory is an ancient narrative device, not usually regarded as a criterion of human behavior, I believe the serial killer is someone who has been allegorized: he is squeezed into an identification with one quality, evil, that obliterates other psychic qualities. As his soul departs, leaving him emptied, he identifies with the killed self, which he then distills and represents as the essence of his being. He identifies with the force of trauma and out of this fate develops a separate sense of the work of trauma, which, like Lucifer, he turns into his profession: squeezing others into his frame of reference.

Allegories involve the compartmentalization and splitting of human qualities; and an allegorical struggle involves characters reacting on each other in an externalized conflict. The serial killer sets off a chain reaction in a community and, ironically, his allegorical condition is transferred to a broader allegorical structure; community representatives are interviewed to obtain a distilled comment on this kind of evil: church leaders speak of the theological meaning of serial killing, psychologists talk about the malevolent psychosocial factors that breed him; educators discuss the failure of schools. The gruesome feature of this transference is that the killer catches the population in his pathology; everyone is allegorized and plays a part in a very precise kind of theater. Where there had been separate universes of divergent and complex unconscious evolutions of individual selves, there is now a community of the anxious, bound in the narrowing confines of danger.

Whether consciously or not, the serial killer indeed has become an individual obsessed by his compulsion to kill. The obsession obliterates the effective functioning of other parts of his personality, and he comes to identify with *the force* of his passion. The displacement of the complex checks and balances in an operant internal life by the force of an urge – this is not only the hallmark of such a person's character but the reason why the serial killer is fittingly allegorized by people, who understand that the allegory objectifies the destruction of complexity by the force of prevailing ideas.

Evil, considered as a structure, points to a complex reorganization of trauma, in which the subject recollects the loss of love and the birth of hate by putting subsequent others through the unconscious terms of a malevolent extinction of the self.

The structure of evil, then, is personally knowable to each person not only because we all have experienced shocking betrayals in an otherwise trustworthy parental environment, but also because we all have transformations to the allegorical plane when we identify with the force of a feeling – in the case of evil, the force of the emptiness sponsored in our selves by the shock *and* its unconscious marriage with the destructive sides of our personalities. All of us have experienced this trauma, and we all know its structure. Each of us will in some respects subsequently identify with it, mesh it with the mental valorizations of our own sadisms, and entertain its future in fantasy – when we are cruel to each other, or in the so-called practical joke, when we play to unfortunate (but usually not disastrous) effect on the other. (One of the most popular television programs across cultures was *Candid Camera*, a program that converted the structure of evil into comedy.) But some people come to suffer deeply by the process I have discussed, and in the extreme, these genocidal people occupy our thoughts to an unusual degree, haunting our minds as the Grim Reaper did in the Middle Ages. We fear him because he stands for execution without mercy, without meaning, without an intact soul. He is the perfect executioner for a population that has come to feel increasingly serial and meaningless.

Chapter 11

Mental interference

I think, therefore I am.

(Descartes)

Something is thinking me. Where am I?

(Helmut)

Helmut lies in bed. It is eight-thirty in the morning and although he has slept at times throughout the night, his mind has been racing. It is hard to remember what exactly he had been thinking about. He could recall pondering a conversation with his brother who had told him with earnest affection that he should start up in business as an ice cream vendor. He had replayed this conversation many times. He had imagined applying for a licence, looking for a van, reading up on the production which should be so simple, but well . . . he just did not know. He could see his elder brother's love and exasperation, a face that haunted him. But where would he go to find a van? Where do they make them? What would his friends think of him sitting in the van? Perhaps he should hire somebody to do that side of the business. He could try to set it all up and then hire a person. But if he did that, then how would he learn the true end of the business? No one would be successful in a new venture, he knew, if they tried to run it from the top. One needed bottom up experience. He found himself thinking of the colours of the van. White with a blue line around it? Blue with a white line? Did that fit in with the customer's association with ice cream? Maybe it should be red with white lettering. What would it say? What would he call the ice cream company? Helmut's Ices? The Flavour Van? The Ice Cream Van?

What would people think? He imagined countless types of people all responding differently to the name. Increasingly exhausted by these considerations, he thought to himself that maybe the ice cream business was not for him. What did he know about it? Nothing. Nothing at all. And he had read that it was controlled by the Mafia who used it to launder money. What would they do to him if he tried to enter their turf? Scene after scene of his ice cream truck being attacked occurred to him. They came after him in his home. They tried to kill him. They attacked and threatened his family.

The night wore on.

He thought of other forms of work. Should he go into retail sports, concentrating on winter recreation? He had friends who lived in the mountains of France, Switzerland and Italy. Long ago he had liked to ski. He could open a shop in London and one in each of the above countries. Friends would join the venture. How much would it take to invest in the setting up of such a business? Probably about £75,000, and he thought about how much each friend would or could put into it. He recalled separate experiences with his friends, going over their recent times together. There had been problems. Some disputes. Ill considerations. He had gone out with one friend's ex-girlfriend and he had said it would be all right, but of course that did not turn out to be so. The ex-girlfriend returned to her former boyfriend – the now considered potential partner – and he wandered off thinking about their recent contacts and all the ins and outs. He tossed and turned in bed with each painful thought. The business brought him back to centre, and he went back to thinking about sports shops. But he thought, one had to be a sporting type and this he definitely was not. He did not really like people. Or he thought he didn't. How do you talk to strangers who drop into your shop? Anyway, what did he know about sports equipment? Where could he go to find out? He supposed he could spend a few weeks in the Alps and travel from one shop to another. That was a good idea. He could see what they stocked and what he thought was missing. But how would he know what was missing? And what would they come to think of him if later he set up shop in competition with them and recollected that he spent time hanging around their shops not buying anything? Thus he would have to purchase something in each shop. That means he would have to rent a large car, a four-wheel drive van, but what would he then do with all the stuff he purchased?

As the clock ticked through the wee hours he became even more exhausted by his thoughts. He moved from one job to another. From the travel business to the local recreational business. From the life of the drop-out, just painting or doing ceramics, to a middle-man bringing people together who could do business. This night was no different from all other nights. He dreaded going off to sleep and stayed up till one or two. He knew that although he would drop off for ten or twenty minutes he would wake up again and then he would be launched on this endless journey of rumination. Yes he would, he thought, usually fall asleep sometime around six in the morning and get a few hours sleep, but then he would awake again, and another struggle would ensue as he would try to find some way to get back to sleep, trying one strategy after another – thinking of a woman, thinking of a vacation spot, thinking of a recent pleasant experience, squinting his eyes to force stars and trying to disappear into sleep through them – but nothing ever worked.

He would lie in bed between nine and noon just thinking. It was always the same and went something like this.

Oh God, I'm awake for sure. I can't go off to sleep again.
Well, get up then.

Why?

You have to get to work.

I don't want to go to work.

That's not a good attitude.

But there is no point. We aren't doing any business.

That's because you don't try.

Okay. I don't try. Maybe I should get up . . .

Yes. Get moving. Come on. Up and at 'em!

I don't know.

Come on. You can do it!

I suppose I could.

There you go. That's the spirit.

But.

But what? There you go. Getting down in the mouth again.

But what is the point? I will just get to the office. The car business stinks. My brother will only be embarrassed.

Business isn't great, but someone out there is selling cars. Why shouldn't it be you?

I can't work. I just sit and stare out the window. I don't answer the phone. I stay away from people. I feel a sick feeling in my stomach.

You are pathetic. Absolutely fucking pathetic. You are just lying here in bed, feeling sorry for yourself, doing fuck all, when you should get out there and work.

I am pathetic. It's true. What's the point in living.

Oh! Oh! So it's suicide time is it?

Why not?

So if you can't get out of bed, and you feel like not working, it's time to just kill yourself?

I would be doing everyone a favour.

Oh sure. Your dad, your brothers, your friends. They would be all delighted.

No. But they would get over it.

That's considerate.

I should do it.

Well fuck you anyway. You haven't even got the balls to kill yourself. So how would you do it?

Well, I could jump off a bridge. But I suppose if I did that . . . well, I might still be alive when I hit the water and funnily enough I don't like the idea of floating in cold water, half alive. Um . . .

You're not going to kill yourself.

Or I could take pills. I could take a lot of them and do it . . . well, not in my flat, because I would not want my brother to be shocked. I could go to a hotel, although then the cleaning lady would find out . . . I could try it in my car.

(This script goes on and on)

Okay, so I'm not going to kill myself. Oh God, I suppose I should go to work.
Well you've pissed away half the morning. Damn right you should go to
   work. Get up and shower.
I should do that.
Get moving then.
I'll count to ten and then do it. 1, 2, 3, 4, 5, 6, 7, 8, 9, 10.
Well?
I just can't do it.
Can't do what?
I just can't *force myself* to get out of bed. Maybe my brother will telephone
   me and then I will have to get out of bed. That's it, I'll wait for him to call.
What a pathetic creature you are. And you want to start a business. You can't
   even get the fuck out of bed. You aren't even worth a shitload of thought.
   Go on, lie in your own lazy excrement.
But what am I supposed to do?
Get up!
I'm too depressed!
You are depressed because you don't do anything!
No. I don't do anything because I am too depressed.

Eventually he gets up, although it is never clear to him what sponsors the gesture.
He is exceedingly exhausted and first thing when up he stares at himself in the
mirror, and for a few minutes engages in another conversation about how badly he
looks. Worse than yesterday? Better? Signs of deterioration? So bad he should
stay home? Off-putting? And so it goes. In the course of showering, without
exception, he weeps. He calls out 'Father, please save me', and in so doing he
comes apart. But after this cleansing, he towels off, makes some coffee, and then
has a bite to eat.
   Then there is another battle which can last from fifteen minutes to two hours
about what he should do. Should he call his father and brother (who own and
operate the used car lot where he works) and tell them that he is ill and cannot
come to work, or should he bite the bullet and go to work? A long conversation
can then ensue about his worth on the job. If he shows up to work – often after
midday – he will retreat to his office, and spend the entire day wondering about
his worth and whether he will ever sell a car.
   I haven't described him.
   He is thirty-five. Tall, blonde, lazy green eyes, rather handsome. Catholic, but
not practising. He has been hospitalised three times since mid-adolescence. At
sixteen he began singing in a shopping mall and was arrested. It was unclear
whether he was just high on drugs (which he took throughout his teens and into
his twenties) or whether he was also crazy. He was released from hospital after
three months. In his early twenties he had another breakdown, this time unaccompanied by euphoric dissonances, but clearly a depression of some kind. His last
hospitalisation, some two years before he came to see me, was more preventive.

His GP, his father, his two brothers, and his family's priest all thought that he was on the verge again and mainly out of a wish to protect him, they put him into a private hospital for a week, after which they thought he seemed a bit better.

The family had met again a few weeks before I saw him. His father had a sort of sixth sense about him. He was pretty sure he could tell when Helmut was losing it, and he met with the GP in Helmut's presence. They had a calm, even congenial, conversation about how to handle Helmut this time, and hospital seemed perhaps a good idea. But the GP, who was quite experienced and thoughtful, was less than content with this notion and after considerable bargaining with the father, it was agreed to give Helmut a shot at psychotherapy. The GP had never put the patient on medication. Not because he was averse to doing so. But for some reason, he thought that Helmut was the sort of man who once on medication would stay drugged for life, and anyway he wasn't sure this would help him. There had been only modest outcomes from the medication he received in hospital. The GP made the referral, saying that he was quite sure Helmut was unanalysable and he was not sending him along for analysis. But he hoped that Helmut might gain some minimal insight into himself so that re-hospitalisation could be avoided, and perhaps he could even begin to find his way in life, with some sort of jump-start or nudge.

When Helmut arrived for the first session I found a man who looked more of a vulnerable kid than an adult. He smiled repeatedly throughout the session in a kind of forced way, trying to put on a good expression. But he was also clearly anxious and almost stuporously depressed, and as I told him so, he seemed even more confused by my – as he admitted – accurate identification of his feelings. I asked him how he felt about attending the session and he said that as all else failed he was willing to try anything, but when I went silent he asked me if I could please ask him questions: he found it easier. He asked me how one spells psychoanalysis and what it was. I explained how I worked and lapsed into silence, whereupon Helmut said that he might just as well tell me about himself.

He described his problems sleeping and the way he thought throughout the day, which I have tried to capture in the descriptions above. He occasionally showed up at the used car lot, but usually stayed at home. He described the several part-time ventures he had tried in the last few years, selling small sailing craft, self-defence alarms for women, and a credit card security system, but each attempt had been less than half-hearted and all that he accomplished was the loss of £60,000.

I saw him in twice-weekly psychotherapy for seven months. The sessions were strikingly similar. He would report at length on his paralysis at work or in the home. As he described his inability to work he spoke of himself in critical and denigratory terms. I said that I could see why he found it so hard to work, as such a critical voice would make it hard to accomplish anything. He admonished me and told me that it had nothing to do with his inner voice, which if anything was helpful, but it did have to do with a defect in his personality: he was unable to respond to perfectly reasonable urges from within himself. He said that he was disappointed in psychotherapy because he expected me to tell him what to do and to side with the part of him that did the same. But I didn't do this and this worried him. I was silent too much of the time, and this was a waste of his time, as what he needed was tough questioning and my expertise. 'I don't know why Dr X sent me to see you, but you are meant to be an expert, so I have come along, but I don't understand any of this.'

He was puzzled by my affirmation of his feelings. I said that at least he seemed convinced of one thing, and that was that he felt uncomfortable in my presence, and did not think psychotherapy would help him. I pointed out that this seemed to be the one thing he managed to have unequivocal feelings about. He caught the humour in this and said that he could see, then, how psychotherapy was helpful, as it allowed him to have a firm belief in something. For some weeks he then proceeded to talk to me *outside* of the psychotherapy structure, in that he would try to talk to me about his life, assuming now that psychotherapy had failed, but that we should now talk about what he could do next. He continued to see me because he had promised the GP that he would stick it out for six months, so he would, as I said to him, fulfil his 'sentence'.

In the first sessions he told me that his mother had died when he was a baby – he didn't know how old he'd been, but he thought it was before he was two. He also told me he was sure it had not mattered and of course he could not recall her, nor for that matter any of the details of his childhood. Memory seemed to begin with adolescence.

As the months passed, however, and the trial period concluded, Helmut decided to stay on for a while longer. There were several reasons for this. Listening to his long and deadening accounts of his internal mental life, I had repeatedly told him that with a mind that was always ordering him about I could see why he felt defeated. One session, when he told me that were it not for his constant mental approbations he would just do nothing, I said 'Really? You mean, if you did not tell yourself that you should do something, you really would do nothing? You would just sit there?' Yes, he was sure he would, for quite a long time, for a very long time. How long, I wondered. Two hours, ten hours, a day, two days, a week, a month? He was puzzled by the question. I said that he seemed to be living with a powerful idea, that unless he constantly prodded himself, he would just be an inert heap, but personally I thought this an impossibility. I bet him that if he let himself alone he would surprise himself by doing something. What, he wanted to know. How would I know, I said. It hasn't been thought yet, has it? It would just happen. However, for this bet I required two conditions. I said that so far as I was concerned, if I were to be given a fair chance, I would need two very simple things from him. (As he was full of hundreds of demands, two simple requests struck him as almost amazingly reasonable.) I said that he had to come to psychotherapy regularly, whether he liked it or not, and that he had to show up at work, whether he wanted to or not. That was all.

What time should he show up at work, he wondered? I said it didn't matter to me. Any time. But he had to show up every day of the week. (He had been staying at home and not working, perhaps putting in one appearance a week, sometimes missing two to three weeks.) Why go to work if he didn't do anything? I said that this, of course, was the bet. I reckoned that he would do something, whether he liked it or not, but to do it he would have to be at work. The same was true of psychotherapy. He had begun to skip sessions, missing one entire week, and I told him that he had to come. What was the point, he queried, if it wasn't working. I said it couldn't work if he wasn't there. In any event, he agreed to this bargain.

Weeks passed. Quite to his surprise he discovered that indeed I was to win the bet. He found that if he simply arrived at work and sat at his desk, although an entire day would go by without his doing anything – not answering the phone, not opening letters, just looking out the window – that two such days did not occur in succession and he would just do something. He would walk out onto the car lot and suddenly go up to a customer and talk about cars. Or he would go to an auction and watch the bidding. He would not bid as it was too anxiety-provoking, but he learned a bit each time, he would see how people valued things.

As the weeks passed into months, he found a particular set of consistent interpretations on my part useful. Each time he would launch into one of his self-instructional diatribes I would say to him that with that kind of intimidation – I would often call it the 'sergeant-major' self – it was no wonder he collapsed in a heap of desultory inertness. 'Listen', I said once, 'if I had a mind like yours I wouldn't do anything either!' To his immediate, but eventually diminishing, ripostes of 'But what will I do?' I would reply 'nothing'. Nothing, that is, in response to such internal molestings which, I argued, paralysed him and para-doxically – because they were meant to inspire him to action – sent him to certain inactivity. So just see what you do, I suggested. And that pretty much is what he did for several months. And now and then he would report in a session that he had done something and on occasion it would result in something, such as the sale of a car, or the discovery of a new source of automobiles.

We can see, in this respect, how Helmut's mind, full of militant instructions, was at odds with his self. If we apply the concepts of transference and counter-transference to the intrapsychic sphere, we could say that the mind acted upon him like some unempathic, thoughtless, and demanding other, which left the rest of him feeling inert, vulnerable, close to tears, and completely misunderstood. His response to the mind's split-off activities was to collapse in its presence. However, we were beginning to see that in fact he fought back by refusing to do what his mind ordered him to do; but because such passive resistance was quite uncon-scious, only over time did he realise that a part of him was saying a quiet 'fuck you' to the sergeant major. I said once, 'You know, I appreciate why you lie in bed; it's a kind of defiant vegetable saying to that mind of yours "Fuck you, what can these commands of yours do about this kind of absolute uselessness?"'.

Work in this area was assisted, I think, by my attending to his differences with me. After an interpretation or comment, about which I could see he had doubts, I would say that I thought he disagreed; more to the heart of the matter, I would often say 'ah, so you think, more analytical rubbish, eh!' and he would concur, eventually taking over this more generative critical response. In fact, his disagreements were often accurate and surprisingly informative, and led to a more constructive dialectic between the critical factor and its object. We managed to enjoy these moments and the pleasure of difference was gradually, very gradually, internalised into his intrapsychic life, so the battles that took place between the self and the mind became more evenly matched, even pleasurable at times.

Eventually I thought he could use analysis, even though I sustained doubts about how insightful he might become. The reason was fairly simple. Toward the end of the first year I could see another very important dimension to his depressive illness. His helpless states were sustained conditions of need and in my view he was unconsciously calling for a maternal figure to come and rescue him and look after him. That figure had been the father, who indeed did often come to his rescue, by giving him money, by telling him he did not need to come to work if he did not want to, and by worrying about him. I told Helmut that in my view his collapsed self was like an infant or small child in need of mothering rescue, which he had found in part from the father; he was therefore armed against his mind, because this mind demanded independence and motivation on his part, when what he desired was care and attentiveness.

Helmut listened to my comments with respectful silence, clearly relieved however, when I said he must be wondering what to do with these 'psychoanalytical remarks'. That I was recommending more psychoanalysis, not less, was initially received by him with a kind of amused disbelief, but certain details deriving from our work supported my advocacy of psychoanalysis.

For months I had been puzzling over his mother's death, something which he clearly regarded as completely irrelevant and analytical nonsense. But no one in the family knew how she had died, nor did anyone talk about it. Out of grudging respect for what he regarded as my intelligence he had asked an aunt about his mother's death and she had replied that he should ask someone else in the family. He took this in two ways: it confirmed his view that it was unimportant, not even significant enough to discuss, but he also agreed that it was a bit odd if she did not want to tell him because there was something she did not want to say about it. Bearing in mind that Helmut was not an insightful person, and furthermore that he tended to simply recount his daytime events with little interest in what anything meant, I had assumed the function of occasionally producing an interesting idea, one that rather caught his slight interest, even if he regarded such ideas as really quite far-fetched. In the beginning, simply to be curious about something and believe one had the right to look into matters was itself somewhat new to him.

He eventually agreed to begin analysis after a particularly difficult summer break. He had spent time with his family on the west coast of Ireland, and had fallen ill with some kind of flu. His father and brothers had not only not attended to him, but gone off climbing for two weeks, during which time he had a high fever and was hospitalised. In hospital he felt he had 'seen the truth' which he took to be the 'fact' that no one had ever cared for him and he had always been deeply alone. This revelation occurred during a significant mood elevation. Out of hospital, his deep insight galvanising him, he rented an astonishingly expensive car, travelled round Europe, hit the casinos in Monte Carlo, and spent £25,000. By mid-October he somatised the manic state into a non-specific illness that was to last four months. He was flattened into a kind of depression, but still haunted by his discoveries of the summer.

My comments about his need for analysis had occurred before the summer break, but he was not initially agreeable. However, the events of the summer and his depression in the autumn convinced him that perhaps he needed to be seen more intensely. It so happened that apparently coincidentally he began to ask questions about his mother and her death. The father had managed to divert him by saying that she had died of an asthma attack, but when I recommended psycho-analysis, and Helmut told his father, it was as if in the father's mind this meant that now the truth had to be told. Visiting his father, ostensibly to discuss the arrangements for the analysis, Helmut's father greeted his son by saying he supported his entering analysis, but there was something he wanted to talk to him about. He disappeared into his study and returned with an envelope. As he told Helmut to read the letter he broke down in tears and Helmut spent the next twenty minutes reading and re-reading his mother's suicide note. His father told him that she had been a very vulnerable woman, that she had had several breakdowns, and that he had not known what to do about it. He knows looking back that he left her alone too much, that he should have sought treatment for her, and that the week of her suicide she had returned from hospital, and he had just decided to look the other way, going off to work. She killed herself when Helmut was nineteen months old. Helmut's oldest brother was nine. Neither he, nor the other brother (five at the time) ever discussed the mother's death, which whenever mentioned had been understood to be the result of an acute asthma attack.

Some months before I had told Helmut that the family's reluctance to talk about the mother suggested to me that this might not have been a natural death. On one occasion I said to him that indeed (though of course I did not know) it could have been a suicide. When he discovered from his father that this was so, it added to his growing conviction that my oddball ideas had some measure of truth to them. I said that given the uselessness of his own mentational advice to himself, I could well understand that he was not particularly keen on any mind's ideas, including my own. How had I come to my idea, he wondered? I said that it was *a feeling*, derived from the fact that no one talked about it in the family, and also one I thought he conveyed by his absolute negation of her significance. I was careful to point out how feelings derived from certain facts of life, but also that a feeling without a validating context – such as the one he provided through his own inves-tigations – was potentially misguided. From this moment he had a greater respect for my mind because it had been of use on several occasions, and he could see that although I relied upon feelings, I also needed more than a hunch to validate an idea. It felt safer to rely upon a mind that worked like that.

Beginning analysis was not easy. In psychotherapy, by looking at me, he felt that he could sense my interests and my disinterests, and now, on the couch, he did not know what I thought or how I felt. Analysis felt like being cut adrift. In the first week he was close to panic and conveyed it. It was not that I considered him on the verge of a decompensation, but that he seemed to have no personal assistance to help him through the loss of the visual object. I said that his response to the visual loss of me brought to my mind the loss of his mother, and that at this moment he was seemingly without anyone. He agreed that he felt that he was without anyone, but added that he did not see how any of this had to do with his mother. She was dead and that was that. This simply had to do with the fact that I was out of sight and he found it uncomfortable. By the second week his mind was racing. He had a hundred things to talk to me about, to fill up the hour. I said that it was interesting how he used his mind to help him fill the void created by my absence. He agreed. I responded 'Of course I know you will find this typical of me, but again, my association is to your using your mind as companion when your mother disappears. I think we are seeing that right here and right now'. This made a certain sense to him in that although he still claimed that his mother's death simply was too long ago to have affected him now, he could see the sense in what I was saying. This was different. He had found a way to find sense in these interpretations, even if he disagreed, while before he had only found them to be off-the-wall actions of the analyst.

Our senses of humour helped us through this period of work. When I would make links like the above he would complain that I was being psychoanalytical again, and I would reply 'of course', and 'I would not want to disappoint you'. Sometimes he would predict my interpretations and I would congratulate him and tell him that I agreed: he was right. Insight was now a kind of amusement, but not one which was gratuitous: it was truly something which he expected of me, and which he looked forward to, even if he was certain to keep his side of the equation present by knocking down the comments each time. He would bring in material with a clear sense of expectation – 'well . . .?' – and was delighted to see how I thought. He was, looking back, finding the pleasures of mind.

For some time, however, he had complained that his father, whom he loved very much, usually showed only a cursory interest in him. He did not doubt his father's love: it was feelable. But his father only seemed to ask after him in a way that was like taking his temperature. 'Are you okay?', he would ask, obviously wondering about his mental state. When Helmut replied in the affirmative the father would sign off abruptly. The father did not want to know more about him. This allowed me to make a particularly useful transference interpretation, as Helmut was characteristically abrupt when I would make a comment that was aimed at a deeper understanding of him. For example, I once asked if he had dreamt that night and in a clipped tone of voice he said, 'Nope, nothing I know of.' Moments later while describing his father's way of cutting him off he said 'You have no idea how frustrating that is' and I told him how he did to it me, with the father's voice. He was genuinely quite stunned by this interpretation. He had no difficulty in seeing the parallel and although he was less than enthusiastic about extending it to a family principle of not wanting to know about inner feelings and thoughts, he accepted that this was in fact the case.

For months he felt his plight more deeply. He did not think about his mother, nor his life history, but the discoveries had shaken him. He was increasingly aware that his brothers, like his father, had removed themselves from any insight whatsoever. Indeed, a pattern of paternal alarm occasioned by the slightest sign of depression in him, followed by immediate detachment upon reassurance, invited a speculation on my part: it seemed to me that his father unconsciously linked him with his suicidal mother. I said once, 'You know I think your father is overly worried about you because unconsciously he associates you with your mother'. This helped us to understand the unusual concern of the father, the GP, and other members of the family about Helmut's safety: everyone had linked him to the death of his mother. It also enabled us to analyse his own dissociated idea that he might kill himself, a view which he had held since adolescence, which he had conveyed on numerous occasions to his father, his GP, and attending psychiatrists, but a view that had no conviction. He did not really want to kill himself, he told me; nor indeed did he have any proper suicidal thoughts, but with engaging naiveté he said: but it could happen, couldn't it? It took time to work this through so that he could see that he was living out his father's memory of his wife's suicide, one that the father associated with her infant, and with which Helmut had identified as he grew older.

Interpretations such as the above were helpful and the first indications, for Helmut, that thinking – the work of the mind – could assist him. For years his own mind had been occupied with militant injunctions and merciless adjudications, and he had unconsciously turned against it, becoming a listless recipient of the endless stream of berations, but defying it by embracing an increasingly vegetative existence. In turn, he became more dependent upon myself and the analysis. In the first year he had frequently complained about the journey to sessions and when he began four-times-weekly analysis, he found it unbearable and unhelpful.

He had, for example, complained incessantly about the silence. What good was it to lie in silence for four hours a week, he would ask, what were we accomplishing? Sometimes I would say that I did not know what would come from the silence: perhaps nothing at all. Nothing at all, he would yelp, how could we justify silences that produced nothing at all? I told him this did not worry me as I knew that in time something would eventually occur to him spontaneously, and he would tell me. He protested with more worry than anger, genuinely feeling that this was really the beginning of some kind of end, and soon I noticed that each session he played with a rubber eraser which he pressed and distorted between two fingers of his right hand. I said nothing about this, but he mentioned that he always did it (it had only emerged however in the analysis) and had done since childhood. I said it seemed to soothe him and he agreed; he would lie in silence for quite some time playing with his eraser, now and then complaining that the silence was useless and that we were wasting time. I have to say that I found his preoccupation absorbing and I felt quite sorry for him. Now and then I would ask after his thoughts and he would report ruminative goings-on, but as time passed I remember hearing for the first time the birdsong outside my window, and I noticed that I was now sitting in my chair in a restful posture, relaxed and reflective. I also noticed that he seemed much less fretful. And he began to talk about matters that occurred to him spontaneously: a dinner he was to attend that night and the thoughts he had about it, a woman he had met at a party the previous week, reflections on his father's way of treating him at work. As he spoke up, I would occasionally ask for elaborations, or associations. Sometimes I would add associations of my own, and now and then I would make an interpretation. The point is that by the end of the second year of work Helmut was able to use silence, to speak up spontaneously when he had a thought that carried weight to it – rather than the impinging weightless obsessions of his split-off mind – and he listened to interpretation and used it.

We could say that through a subtle form of regression within the transference he was giving up some of his inner self states to the other who used mind to help sort out the feelings and to reflect usefully upon lived experience. To my way of thinking this was the analysand's symbolic[1] return to the mother who had not been there for him in the earliest months of life.

This period of the analysis gave us the working relationship that was necessary to understand the next stage of difficult work. As his dependence upon myself increased there were occasions of sudden and virulent outbreaks of mental interference, in which he would panic and then assault himself with hundreds of recommended courses of action. As he did so he was even more helpless, saying in one session that he was certain now that he would accomplish nothing and be a failure forever. I said that I thought there was an infant in him that in a way did not want to have to think or work and wanted looking after, something he was now experiencing with me, and that this alarmed his mind which as we know had to do the looking after for him as a child. (Early in our work I had emphasised the positive side of the mind's effort to pull him up out of infancy and childhood by the bootstraps.) But there was indeed a part of him that did not want to have to do anything, and this inert vegetative self, I suggested, seemed to me the infant who was demanding that the mother return and look after him. He vigorously protested this interpretation in the beginning, but by now I knew that he had to deny all links to the mother. So I would let him fully and completely express his protest and then gently say, 'There is to be no memory of mother, no link to her, is there?' and this very particular comment unfailingly allowed him to reconsider whatever interpretation I had made. In effect a certain kind of resistance had to be worked through each time, before he could make use of analytical interpretation, but arguably such comments – the work of intellection – only felt safe to him if it took into account his aggressions, his needs, his desires, and was adaptive to his self state. Then he could use mind: mine and his.

---

1 The ego can symbolise a need by using an object as if it were another object, in this case using me in a sense as if I were the mother. Ego symbolisations such as this take place frequently in any person's life and express the symbolic through use of the object rather than substitution of the object. A thing does not stand in the place of another thing: the use of the thing changes the meaning of the thing.

The final part of our work that I shall report was his growing realisation that his 'failures' in life – and he had been out of work for long periods of time – expressed his demand that he be mothered. As such these failures were understandable and psychologically sensible. They were no longer simply to be the object of attack. As understandable as it was, in retrospect, that his childish mind would chastise and berate him for being childish, he had used his mind as a kind of militant other that had goose-stepped him out of his infantile self. But with the coming of his adolescence he instantiated a rebellion against this 'mind object' (Corrigan and Gordon, 1995) and refused its companionship, moving relentlessly back into an infantile state, unaccompanied by a sentient other who understood where he was. That presence emerged with the analysis, and in turn, he was able to internalise through understanding a companionable part of his mind that took his infantile states into account, that did not berate him and indeed helped him. Characteristically, then, he would tell me of moments when he had felt helpless or simply rather inert and he would say 'Well I just told myself that this was not going to last forever, and that eventually I would come out of it', or 'I was on the verge of having a go at myself, but I just told that part of my mind to fuck off, and sure enough, after a while I did know what to do'. Finally these reports of his inner contests faded away completely as the process was being accomplished within the unconscious and needed far less active use of the analysis than before.

As he realised that his helplessness was in fact a destructive protest I brought to his attention that years of day and night reversal – when he would stay up until the early hours – had been his way of protesting the absence of maternal structures in his life by in effect refusing any structure to his existence. It was only with this insight that he agreed to a more reasonable schedule of his life. Prior to this he had partied many times during the week, sometimes staying up all night, and had taken vacations on impulse. The result had been to weaken his ego even more and although I had always pointed to his lack of a structured routine as self-defeating he had refused to take this on board. At this point in our work, however, he saw the sense in my comments and gradually developed a routine that ultimately he was to find very comforting and useful.

Helmut helps us to see how patients suffering from depressive illness experience the mind as a split-off other that is remorselessly attacking them. When the depressed person collapses into an infantile state, he projectively identifies into his mind all the adult parts of the personality, but because of the severity of the collapse, these otherwise potentially helpful parts of the self become so split-off that they are virtually yelling at the infantile self to hurry up and join with the mind lest there be a catastrophic structural split. In ordinary depressions such a catastrophe does not occur. The individual may sink into helplessness and inertness for a while – a few hours or maybe one day or two at the most – and although the more mature parts of the personality may have been projectively identified into the mind, which berates the self, or into an other who is now the object of envy, eventually the person comes out of the slump, rejoins mind as a helpful processor of lived experience, and all is reasonably well. But the severely depressed person experiences a catastrophic loss of mind which increases in its hostility to the self as it incrementally receives projectively identified healthy parts of the personality. If, as was the case with Helmut, the child part of the personality hates the mind because it is identified with a growing up that is a growing away from an essential truth about one's being, then the person can sustain trench warfare between the self and the mind.

Psychoanalytical language is inexact and highly metaphorical. Were we not to have a clinical context for the distinction between self and mind, then readers of the literature would quite rightly wonder what exactly is meant by a split between them, as such terms in the very first place are by no means clear. But as always, psychoanalysts are obliged to justify their language by indicating how patients can only be properly imagined and considered through such terms. And in the case of the depressive, it is striking how this person makes the theoretical statement that the self is at war with the mind. This is not the analyst's invention, but one of the most common statements made by the depressed patient, and as such deserves even more attention. It is a startlingly precise statement of affairs. In the patient's subjective sense of self, in their own core being, they feel assaulted by their mind which pushes them further and further into a corner. They see the mind as something harmful and awful. They prefer to be asleep rather than awake, to avoid the hammer blows of the mind. They may consider suicide in order to stop the mind from attacking the self. They will engage in long, exhausting, and futile conversations between their self and their mind, experiencing in this polarisation the distinction between their private subjective state of being and the mind that opposes that being.

Of course, they know that their mind is part of them. They can even, now and then, try to identify with it, and from the lofty superego heights of mental reproach, they can even joyfully cast aspersions on the inert self, declared finally to be a thing of the past. But such moments are short-lived, although naturally they become the basis of the manic development which can last for months. Eventually, however, the person is back to square one with the mind attacking the self with renewed vigour and distaste. But because this mind is part of the self, indeed known to possess some of the most important and essential parts of the self, it can become an object of envy[2] and the person can bizarrely enough come to hate what is in fact theirs. This may give rise to that masochistic glee of the depressive who takes pleasure in turning the mind's attacks into a form of pleasure, engaging in an intrapsychic war between helplessness and intelligence, between cynicism and megalomania. Less obviously but no less importantly, the depressive person is always mourning the loss of contact with the generative companionship of the mind. The mind in health is a useful and essential companion to the self. Those

---

2 See Clifford Scott, 'Self-envy and envy of dreams and dreaming', *The International Review of Psycho-Analysis* 2 (3): 333–7, 1975.

particular forms of destructive views that emerge from the idiom of the self, occasioned often by the precise lived situation, or the moods of a moment, are processed by the mind: one which may on the one hand projectively identify such contents, but one which eventually is part of the reconsidering process. As a self, the individual will feel helped by the thoughtful capacity of his mind: its storage of memories of better moments with the object, its capacity to objectify guilt and consider means of reparation, its time sense which allows it to soothe the self with the notion of a curative factor in life that will assuage the self's more immediate interests.

It is interesting in light of these considerations to rethink the confusional states of the depressive individual. As we know such a person can seem quite lost. Forgetful. Inattentive. Easily distracted. Loose in thinking. Perpetually muddled. If the mind is hated then such self states become means of attacking the presence of the mind, even if, as we have seen, they invite its attack. But more than that, confusion is often an attempt to defy the mind's intellectual acumen. Confusion becomes a screen that aims to deflect the mind's attack and depressive individuals may embrace confusion in order to minimise the precision of mental reproach. Of course the self will be the victim of a mental standing order (e.g., 'you are always in such a total muddle'), but the self habituates to such crude reproaches and hides its mental contents from more precise and devastating attacks by maintaining the confusional state. Psychoanalysts have no doubt observed the difficulty in getting the confused depressed patient to free associate. This is often due to the patient's deep fear that he is now on the verge of giving the mind the material it is seeking as the object of its fierce attack. It is better, reckons the depressive, to be a silent wreck than to be an articulate conveyer of mental contents that will only render the self more vulnerable to attack. The analyst's impartial consideration of the free associations, including his analysis of the patient's moral interferences, allows free thinking to occur and in time helps the patient to see that their mind's reproaches are often very wide of the mark, as the free associations refer to feelings and ideas that are beyond the penetrating glares of consciousness. Unconsciousness then becomes a kind of new-found freedom in being, adding to the patient's sense that they may, after all, be in ordinary defiance of the moral reproach, as unconscious life is too complex for single judgements and moral injunctions. Here is creative muddle: out of the con-fusions of unconscious processes, new visions and creative reflections emerge (see Milner, 1969).

In the manic state the individual identifies with the mind as an omnipotent and grandiose synthesiser of all selves everywhere, and a separate essay could be written on this side of the equation: mind as object. For in the manic state the mind becomes the treasured and adored vehicle of a triumphant trajectory over the woes of mankind. But my emphasis has been on the depressive state and on depressive illness, in which the mind is experienced as an alien object that attacks the self, driving the person into a profoundly vicious state of victimage. Psychoanalysis affords a unique and special treatment for the depressive individual as the analyst will have to encounter the patient's defiant hatred of mental processes in themselves, and the analyst's mind will be attacked and nullified. Eventually, however, the analyst can present mind as an interesting and sentient companion, one able to bear and indeed invite the subject's fury and demand. When this happens the patient begins to present increased mental contents to the analyst's mind for their processing, gaining relief, and eventually coming to believe that the mind – the analyst's and his own – can become an essential companion to the self.

Chapter 12

Creativity and psychoanalysis

In 'What is Surrealism?', André Breton recalled how he 'practised occasionally on the sick' during the war using Freud's 'methods of investigation', as he experimented in written monologue by throwing out ideas on paper, followed by critical examination. He invited Philippe Soupault to do this with him and soon they were writing automatically and comparing results. Although of course their contents varied, Breton noted that

> there were similar faults of construction, the same hesitant manner, and also, in both cases, an illusion of extraordinary verve, much emotion, a considerable assortment of images of a quality such as we should never have been able to obtain in the normal way of writing, a very special sense of the picturesque, and, here and there, a few pieces of out-and-out buffoonery.
>
> (1934: 412)

The writings proved 'strange', invested with a 'very high degree of *immediate absurdity.*' It was out of this experiment with Freud's method that Breton founded surrealism and when he asked himself to define it he wrote that it was 'pure psychic automatism', which through the spoken or written word, or some other means of expression, would reveal 'the real process of thought'. The associations created by the surrealist act created a 'superior reality' – more purely because they came from the unconscious – otherwise known in the forms of the dream and 'the disinterested play of thought'.

Breton's manifesto was a passionate attack on a trend in civilisation. Bullied by 'absolute rationalism' mankind 'under collar of civilisation, under the pretext of progress, all that rightly or wrongly may be regarded as fantasy or superstition has been banished from the mind, all uncustomary searching after truth has been proscribed' (1934: 413). 'All credit for these discoveries must go to Freud', he wrote, concluding: 'the imagination is perhaps on the point of reclaiming its rights' (p. 414).

Freud's method of free association launched one of the more intense, if programmatic, periods in Western fine art, and Breton was not alone amongst those influenced by this way of imagining. In the novel, poetry and music, Freud's stance was liberating, suggestive and morphogenically concordant with a certain type of emergent representational freedom.

I doubt it was puzzling to artists that Freud shied away from their own particular transformations of his method. Even a casual reader would have noted his repeated effort to affiliate his discoveries with the scientific world and his odd habit of claiming that one day all his theories would be explained biologically. Readers of 'Civilisation and its Discontents' would also have noted that in his analysis of Western culture, he stressed the exchange of pleasure for civility, part of the psychical change brought about by development of the superego.

Whatever one thinks of the surrealist celebration of Freud, it is of interest that Breton and his colleagues brought to the foreground what Freud marginalised in his writings. If civilisation was a triumph of the conscience in a war with instincts and the pleasure principle, Freud subverted this reality – perhaps what Breton meant by 'absolute reality' – by inventing the free associative process.

To some extent, Freud took his method for granted, and as with many assumptions, it escaped further consideration and development. Like an astronomer who, having marvelled at the discovery of a telescope, subsequently gets lost in what he sees, he was naturally more interested in what he found through his method than in the method itself. We may see something of the same tension in much modern music, literature and painting – a conflict between examination of the method that is one's craft and concentration on what can be manifested through the process. We can paint a figure without having to scrutinise the type of thought that is painting. We can compose a melody without having to think about what a musical idea is. Or we can write a poem and not have to examine the poetic process.

Indeed this tension gives rise to certain intellectual wars, with some artists decrying the representation of the process of creativity and celebrating the figurative outcome of the creation, and others expressing clear irritation with the mimetic simplicity of a figure. Perhaps we all recognise the essentials of this debate: each side in this conflict loses meaning if its opposite is eradicated. Indeed, we know that writers, musicians or painters who profess impatience with the deconstructivists – those artists whose figures are breaking down or cracked to begin with – are also intensely interested in the process that generates their creativity.

It is not too difficult to understand at least one of the sources of this impatience. If one is too self conscious, or too self examining it may interfere with one's creativity. Perhaps the surrealist movement failed to realise its wish to employ the unconscious because an anxious self awareness in their undertaking resulted in an overly stylised art. Indeed this extreme in self observation – or representation of the character of the mind – led Dali to his celebrated 'paranoiac-critical method', which elaborated the irrational character of mental contents in order to further illuminate the structure of the irrational. Paranoia, he wrote, was the 'delirium of interpretation bearing a systematic structure' and he defined 'paranoiac-critical activity' as 'spontaneous method of 'irrational knowledge', based on the critical and systematic objectification of delirious associations and interpretations' (quoted in Breton, 1934: 416). The surrealists experimented with the primary process in earnest: Max Ernst used hypnagogic illusions to provide material for his collages, Miró went hungry to inspire hallucinations, coming from what he thought of as the form of the object. But they did so in a curious combat of absolute unconsciousness and absolute consciousness, rather like a meeting of absolutes negating one another.

Perhaps abstract expressionism became the vital compromise. For in the works of de Kooning, to take just one example, one can see how a technique, once sufficiently divorced from the figurative, allows for a certain type of unconscious influence that can be observed but not readily comprehended. Even as the process of painting becomes to some the aim of the painting, heralding what could become a disturbingly intrusive self observation, the result is mysterious. Even as the patterns typify and identify the works as the product of one artist, they nonetheless open the project as a question. What is this? What is one looking at? From which perspective?

De Kooning knew paints. He knew how to keep the paint on the canvas alive until the last possible moment, ready for its eradication and substitution with another colour, another shape. For every vision there was a revision. And revisions of the revisions. The cumulative visual effect is of time and space suspended in a moment, congealed into one representation. If this leads us to think of Freud's mystic writing-pad as a metaphor of the unconscious, realised in these paintings as layer upon layer of the many strokes of the brush, it also suggests Freud's metaphor of life itself, the self as the city of Rome in all its stages – Etruscan, Empire, Medieval, Renaissance – visible in the same gaze and superimposed on one another. Such is the story of any self. In the works of de Kooning one gazes upon an object that in its revisional intensity reflects the dense overdetermination of psychic life. We witness it, indeed for some we are bewilderingly moved by it, guided less by Western conventions of narrative and figuration, than by objectification of us, not as body or social being, but as unconscious movement or intelligent emotion.

'Art is a method of opening up areas of feeling rather than merely an illustration of an object', writes Francis Bacon (1953: 620). Our words – feelings, affects, moods – are not adequate signifiers, as Bacon means much more through 'feeling' than is conjured by this word. He adds, 'A picture should be a re-creation of an event rather than an illustration of an object; but there is no tension in the picture unless there is struggle with the object'. Emotion (from 'movere'), or moving experience is an inner event and may get us closer to what we try to signify by affect or feeling. We seem to be set in motion either by internal stimuli (such as a memory or a wish or a mysterious idea) or external stimuli (such as meeting someone, or reading a book).

Complex states of mind, emotions arise out of the vagaries of life, thick meetings between inner interests and circumstance. 'The way I work', said Bacon, 'is accidental . . . How can I re-create an accident? [Another accident] would never be quite the same' (quoted in Chipp, 1968: 622). So too with an emotional experience. Bacon continues: This is the thing that can only probably happen in oil paint, because it is so subtle that one tone, one piece of paint, that moves one thing into another completely changes the implications of the image'. Many would agree that no two emotional states are alike, that each emotion changes the contents on the internal canvas.

It is possible to see, therefore, how some painters – following the surrealists – managed to identify (consciously or not) with the project that was Freud's. Indeed, it is more than possible that abstract expressionism actually has succeeded where surrealism failed, extending our understanding of the creative process that was tapped by free association, presenting us with a different type of Rome: a history of the differing emotional experiences of the painter, congealed into one single image, one that materialises psychic life in the form world of painting.

Dream theory, which includes the dream day, the dream event, its breakdown into other scenes upon association, and the discovery and interpretation of tissues of thought, is a particular theory of creativity. Examining this may enable us to see how – if at all – what takes place in analysis shadows some of the more radical representational expressions in the worlds of poetry, painting and music.

Freud however was stubbornly opposed to consideration of the dream work as art-like. Wary of over-enthusiastic adoption by aestheticians, whom he feared would appropriate psychoanalysis, he openly ridiculed any vestige of the aesthetic in the dream. He worried that the transcendental aims of the aesthete would bypass the body's raw urges – the instincts – which held no aesthetic ambitions of their own, eviscerating the drive from the gestalt. Indeed, he thought that the aim of all instincts was to extinguish excitation, though he could find few examples to support this view. Stravinsky might have agreed with him. 'All music', he wrote, 'is nothing more than a succession of impulses that converge towards a definite point of repose' (1942: 35).

Perhaps if Freud had constructed his theory of the dream after Kandinsky, Pound, Stravinsky and Schoenberg, he would have thought differently, for their works have a lyrical raw passion, asserting the pleasure of the aesthetic that gives rise to new expressive forms. Perhaps he would have seen that the total dream process is very likely the cornerstone of the creative, a movement of the 'to be represented' towards the fulfilment of this desire.

Those psychic intensities that are the ordinary inspirational events of everyday life are largely accidental, so what is their psychic status before they are dreamed? They would be, I suggest, internal mental structures – the little Rome of the day being designed but not yet dreamed – energised over-determinations moving towards some form of elaboration. In *Being a Character* I used the term 'psychic genera' to identify an unconscious complex that uses its own gravity to draw to it previously unrelated mental phenomena. The gathering of these psychic gravities would be unconscious, but perhaps sensed as a mood arising out of a previous experience. The continuous presence of these psychic phenomena in the self often provides us with the feeling of being guided by a shaping spirit. What Wordsworth wrote in 'Tintern Abbey' – 'in the mind of man / a motion and a spirit that impels / All thinking things, all objects of all thought, / And rolls through all things' – is strikingly similar to the way artists describe the creative process.

Stravinsky believed emotion that passes as inspiration is a sign of the presence of something being worked upon by the artist in the moment. 'Is it not clear', he writes, 'that this emotion is merely a reaction on the part of the creator grappling with that unknown entity which is still only the object of his creating and which is to become a work of art?' (1942: 50). The inspired state of mind in the artist, he suggests, is a sign of an internal generative object emerging toward consciousness: 'This foretaste of the creative act accompanies the intuitive grasp of an unknown entity already possessed but not yet intelligible, an entity that will not take definite shape except by the action of a constantly vigilant technique' (1942: 51).

The dreamer-to-be carries around unthought known foretastes of their dream during the day, not only elaborating disseminations from past dreams but seeking objects that will move them further along the paths of dream life.

For the most part Freud ignored the daily role of unconscious observation – the collecting, scrutinising, and selecting of psychical objects – an imbalance that Anton Ehrenzweig (1967) redressed in his theory of 'unconscious scanning'. We might also say that each person will of course have a long and exceedingly complex history of dream experiences, which over time will establish a kind of inner unconscious network that scans the world, collecting, scrutinising and separating out those elements that are of interest. The dreamt looks for its dream objects in subsequent lived experience.

The dream is a puzzling illumination of one's unconscious interests, a manifestation of intangible interests seeking presentation. This transformation of the unthought known into consciousness becomes a kind of sphinx – a compound object – wrought from the intercourse of the self's psychic life and the aleatory movement of evocative objects. It is the moment when the collective impact of the day, bound into complexes of memory and desire, presents itself.

Freud's dictate that the dreamer should free associate to the dream, meant that whatever integrity the dream seemed to have as an event in its own right was illusory, as associations fragmented it into shards, eventually disclosing tissues of thought that could be knitted into an interpretation. The unconscious latent thought of a dream could be found after free association created enough material to reveal the connecting links.

Depending on one's point of view this is where Freud either limited or empowered psychoanalysis. For some, including many artists, Freud's reduction of this extraordinary process to a single latent idea, was anti-climactic. Just as he declined to credit the work of the unconscious ego in the assimilation of psychically significant moments during the day, now he played down the fecund power of free associations. Freud was not interested in the dream as a paradigm of the creative. His more restricted aim was to gain access to the unconscious meanings of the patient's symptoms through free association to dreams. He did, however, allude to the impossibility of fully interpreting any dream, even though the extraordinary range of his own dream associations seems a pleasure in itself, equal to the delight of interpretation. Furthermore, it seems likely he would have agreed that, once set in motion, free associations not only reveal hidden tissues of thought but become a network of thought that will continue into the next day, and, together with other surviving networks, will collect, sort, dream and disseminate future emotional moments.

It may be a measure of Freud's genius that this discovery, which would have been sufficient for many people, was only the first of many. For me, however, this is his greatest accomplishment. In a few years of work with his patients – affected by their rejections of his techniques – he settles on free association, and in that moment Western culture is changed forever. Many artists, like Joyce, were wary of affiliating themselves with Freud, yet grasped the psychoanalytic revolution, arguably more immediately and perhaps more extensively than did those in the psychoanalytical movement.

And what was so radical?

To find the truth determining one's peculiar, inevitably conflicted states of mind, one discards the energy to know how and why and instead simply reports what happens to be on one's mind in the presence of the analyst. Of course there would be resistances to this request – although paradoxically enough a resistance often pointed directly to the ideas that were being held back – but we would have to say that an entire civilisation would find itself in resistance to something so up-ending.

Yet it is alluring, even when it brings up unwanted ideas. It is speech as true self, the verbal equivalent of Winnicott's 'squiggle' or the moment when, according to Lacan, the subject discovers his own voice, revealed through slips of the tongue and curious wordings.

'It is through the unhampered play of its functions', writes Stravinsky, 'that a work is revealed and justified', and in the pure state he adds, 'music is free speculation' (1942: 49). Free association is also a speculation, a visionary moment in which the self derives from the prior day a hint of its future.

What does psychoanalysis bring to creativity? Freud unconsciously comprehended the process that was not simply at the heart of the creative, but was the creative process – a process involving two people where only one in privacy had been before. Narrating their day, their dream, their associations, analysands create themselves in the presence of the analyst. They may try to 'figure' themselves, but the associative eventually breaks down these figures, and from the broken lines, discordant harmonies, and *caesurae* the psychic creations assert themselves.

The dream materialises the day's psychic reality through a transformation of form. It takes psychic intensities, held inside and sensed, and puts them into the form of a dream. This may be partly why people are not simply puzzled by their dreams, but curiously rather proud of them. We are not only impressed by their content, but because they are transubstantiations – intangible psychic reality is briefly visualised – we are slightly in awe of the process. 'The basis of musical creation', writes Stravinsky, 'is a preliminary feeling out, a will moving first in an abstract realm with the object of giving shape to something concrete' (1942: 27). But the musical idea moving about in Stravinsky's mind will change upon moving into 'sound and time', the material of music.

This brings us to the oddity of creativity. When the painter paints, or the musician composes, or the writer writes, they transfer psychic reality to another realm. They transubstantiate that reality, the object no longer simply expressing self, but re-forming it. This might be considered a type of projection – a putting of the self into an object – but it is also a transubstantial change, where psychic reality leaves its home in the mind and moves into a different intelligence. Commenting on a recent work, Gerhard Richter said: 'that was an expression of my personal state of mind, and it hints at a method of translating my changed way of thinking into reality' (1995: 60).

The term 'transubstantial object' allows me to think of the intrinsic integrity of the form into which one moves one's sensibility in order to create: into musical thinking, prose thinking, painting thinking. These processes could be viewed in part as transformational objects in that each procedure will alter one's internal life according to the laws of its own form. But a transubstantial object also emphasises the 'body' of the transforming object that receives, alters, and represents the sensibility of the subject who enters its terms and now lives within it.

An artist does not go easily into this altered state of unconsciousness. They feel the boundary between ordinary psychic life and the artistic workspace, as one that is always difficult to cross and sometimes unbearably so. Even as they become accustomed to entering this other realm they are acutely aware of leaving themselves behind, thrown into a different form of life.

This challenge is not without precedent as at least once we have been presented with the challenge of language, whether to enter it and to be transformed by it, or to refuse speech. For Lacan, to enter language is to accept a deep change in the human sense of form, from the sensorial imagined order (of an apparently unified self) to wording the self in a new form of being. Art forms offer further challenges to the self and as with language, what emerges from one seems not to be of one's own making, but guided by the form of an other.

Writers, painters and composers often comment on the unknown yet felt inner structure gathering a specific work and its outcome.

'Often when I sit . . . and turn on my computer or my typewriter and write the first sentence, I don't know what I'm going to write about because it has not yet made the trip from the belly to the mind', writes Isabel Allende.

> It is somewhere hidden in a very sombre and secret place where I don't have any access yet. It is something that I've been feeling but which has no shape, no name, no tone, and no voice. So I write the first sentence – which usually is the first sentence of the book. . . . By the time I've finished the first draft I know what the book is about. But not before.
>
> (in Epel, 1994: 7–24)

Art not only embodies this shapeless something, it transforms it into a different realm altogether. A thing is brought forth which we didn't know we had in us', writes Milosz (in Gibbons, 1979: 3). Wallace Stevens writes:

While there is nothing automatic about [a] poem, nevertheless it has an automatic aspect in the sense that it is what I wanted it to be without knowing before it was written what I wanted it to be, even though I knew before it was written what I wanted to do.

(1979: 50–51)

'If each of us is a biological mechanism, each poet is a poetic mechanism', he continues, to which we might add that the mechanism of transformation from the unthought known object that is the poem to be to the poetic object is derived from the aesthetic process that goes under the name of poetry. In the same way, that order of thinking that is painting, or composing, is the structure of transformation that transubstantiates internal objects from the deep solitude of an internal world into altered external actuality. 'The poet at work is an expectation', writes Valéry (1952) in *A Poet's Notebook*. He is a transition within a man'.

This transition is not representational. It is presentational. What the poet writes or the painter paints or the composer composes has not existed before.

Something of this same transubstantiation occurs in an analysis. The patient has in mind a dream, or an event of the previous day, or a thought about the analyst, and as they speak their thoughts they experience its alteration through speech. Thinking something and speaking it are differing forms of representation. But speaking in a freely associative manner inaugurates a transubstantial shift, as the self senses a move from what has heretofore been the common ground of self experience – thinking and talking – to a new form for being. As with the paints splashing on the canvas, or the musical ideas forming notes on the page, the free associating analysand not only creates himself in another place, but instantiates himself in the logic of an aesthetic that differs from purely internal experience or conversation.

Is it possible that this ending of a person's idiom as a self, and new beginning as a different form, is part of the pleasure of creativity? Of course the leap into a different skin may be in order to evacuate the self into the object rather than elaborate inner life. Often enough the new form articulates psychic reality in ways not possible through customary modes of expression.

This raises a further question. What do the differing artistic realms offer as transubstantial objects? If I paint my ideas rather than put them to musical sound I not only select a different form, I also find a different unconscious aesthetic. My ideas will materialise, transformed according to the characteristics of the representational form's unconscious structure. Perhaps we are all evolving towards some day in the far future when each of us will have developed sufficient skills as a poet, artist, musician and mathematician – amongst others – to live in different forms, each of which must of necessity process us very differently, and of course reflect us in aesthetically distinguished manners. Creativity, then, could be viewed as a development in civilisation, not necessarily in terms of the evolution of art or poetry, for example, but as multiple expressions of psychic reality, which in time would be more intelligently served by crafting it in music, paint, poetry.

Works of artistic imagination are form objects, samples of individual idiom made available to the other. Each form object demonstrates the compositional intelligence of its creator and its aesthetic structure suggests to its subsequent appreciators a peculiarly evocative integrity. Although the reader, listener, or viewer will always receive a form object according to the idiom of the self's receptive intelligence, each form object evokes a formal response.

This helps me understand the reassurance I experience on seeing the works of an artist whom I admire. If I travel to a new museum and find a de Kooning I feel delight and reassurance. These are works I feel I know. But what do I know? The transubstantial object certainly allows for the possibility that my aesthetic grasp of the other is linked with the aesthetic category of the object. That is, these works evoke the experiencing me that exists in and through the medium of paint. It brings something out in me, or to put it in the vernacular: it 'speaks to me'. I could not, however, put what it 'says' or what I 'hear' into words. Some individuals are irked by the critical examination of their work, not only because they may be distressed with the judgement, but also, it seems to me, because they have entered a different realm which is not the written word, even if their realm is prose fiction or poetry which uses the word as its medium.

In a psychically literal sense we are moved by the work of art, processed by its form. And even if we only glance at one painting, hear a few bars of music, or read a few lines of a poem, we shall have been gathered by the aesthetic of the other, remarkably preserved in the after-effects of their life, forms of their idiom left behind.

'If I alter any reader's consciousness, it will be because I have constructed a consciousness of which others may wish to become aware, or even, for a short time, share', writes William Gass (1996: 47). But as Gass knows only too well the consciousness constructed by the novel is not the same as ordinary consciousness, although each writer uses that medium to express aspects of his own idiom.

Is it accurate to say that the artistic object only reflects the self, even if we qualify this by assuming that the artist also expresses contemporary culture and artistic tradition? As the transubstantial object differs in form from the self, it bears the self yet becomes a new body for that being. 'The music of prose', writes Gass, 'elementary as it is, limited as it is in its effects, is nonetheless far from frivolous decoration; it embodies Being; consequently, it is essential that the body be in eloquent shape' (1996: 326). The 'object' through which we create – painting, prose, music – has its own processional integrity, its own laws, and when we enter it to express our idea within its terms, we shall be altered by the object. 'For the last two years I have been making a series of paintings with 'je t'aime' written across them', writes Robert Motherwell. I never thought much about it, but I am sure in part it is some kind of emphasis or *existing in* what is thought' (in Caws, 1996: 18). Existing in a thrown thought, projected into a different aesthetic realm, and objectified in a different and challenging way. Transubstantial projective objectification.

The same principle operates when the analysand enters analysis. There are familiar elements – a vestige of social life, ordinary talk, a unit of time etc. – but the free associative medium, although borrowing its integrity from inner speech and inner association, becomes a new medium for self expression. Entering analysis a person will never be the same again. He will have found a new object for self transformation and there is nothing like it, just as there is nothing like painting, nothing like poetry and nothing like music.

'Art belongs to the *unconscious*!' wrote Kandinsky to Schoenberg.

> One must express *oneself!* Express oneself *directly!* Not one's taste, or one's upbringing, or one's intelligence, knowledge or skill. Not all these *acquired* characteristics, but that which is *inborn, instinctive.* And all form-making, all *conscious* form-making, is connected with some kind of mathematics, or geometry. . . . But only unconscious form-making, which sets up the equation 'form = outward shape', really creates forms.
>
> (Schoenberg and Kandinsky, 1984: 23)

Perhaps that inner object that is the work to be finds its most direct expression in the geometry or mathematics – i.e., the specific intelligence – of the medium of the creativity rather than in the object. The work that Allende says is 'in her belly' only emerges through writing, and one of the features of any person's creativity is the selection of the particular form through which to express the creative idea.

'In one way only can form be discussed in an objective sense', writes Ernst Bloch in *Essays on the Philosophy of Music.* 'This is where the formal, construc-tional, objectifying element is not a medium but itself an objective component', he adds, 'as is especially the case with stage effects, with rhythm and especially with the different types of counterpoint that determine the shaping subjects as categories of their innate being' (1985: 87). This determination of the shaping subject – the logic of form – is an expression of the innate being of the subject, now moved from inner experience to the property of musical expression. He continues: 'here the shaping subject has truly entered into a 'form' as its deeper aggregate condition, a 'form' accordingly representing the lower, quasi-epistemological, metaphysically skeletonic part of the object arrangement itself (pp. 87–8). Musical form, we may add, is not simply a medium, it is an objectifi-cation of that intelligence that is shaping its idea, and the structure of inspiration reveals itself in the object arrangement, that is, in musical form.

Creative life usually involves a drawing in of the self perhaps because all the self's inner resources are devoted to the creative act. Freud also recognised this need in the formation of psychoanalysis, as patient and analyst retreat from stimuli of the world. A withdrawal in order to crystallise the work harks back to the age before social responsiveness, predating even the primary mediating presence of language. Each of us has been part of this drawing in of being, first when we are inside the mother's body and then held by her concentration for many weeks after our birth, what Winnicott termed primary maternal preoccupation. In psycho-analysis the recumbent position, the absence of visual socialisation, the presence of an auditory intimate, and the absence of an agenda recreate the mood of the earliest states of consciousness. Free associative thinking may begin as a type of chat, just as the artist's sketch is a way of beginning, but eventually analysand and artist respond to what is being called for. For the patient it means a deepening of the associations, in the artist/analyst as well, a generative loosing of self into the work.

In our beginnings, held inside the mother's body, then immersed in her psychic and somatic textures, we are enfolded beings. Wilfred Bion believed that analysis allowed for an alteration in the analyst's being, as he dreamt the patient's material, transforming the patient's communications into his dream objects. This craft certainly derives from a maternal process and gives birth to inspired ideas and interpretations. In the composer, writer, or creative artist, a similar reverie is established although after years of practising this retreat, creative people enter it alone, manage it by themselves, and take the object-to-be as a type of other.

Retreat into this realm taps and develops the skill of unconscious creativity, driven by the core of one's being. Psychoanalysis transforms unconscious complexes – symptomatic, pathologic, transferential – into consciousness, but it also enhances the self's unconscious capability. Bion reckoned that psychoanalytic training was an education in intuition.

The kind of thinking required in psychoanalytic work evokes those objects of conflict that are a part of our existence. No one represented conflicts with early objects as well as Melanie Klein. In her mind, each self is engaged in a ceaseless remembering of the earliest encounter with the object, enacting them in all subsequent relations. The type of thinking evoked by psychoanalysis or the concentration of the creative artist calls forth the passions of love and hate, the objects of each, and the self's violent evasions of the consequence of being. Thus free association may intend to be objective and dispassionate, but as the associations move deeper into the self, they will convey the self's experience of its objects, a burden that saturates the freely associated thought with meaning. For these ideas not only bear their symbolic structure as Lacan emphasised, they are also like independent characters in a developing opera of sorts. The classical way of listening allows the logic that is sequence to arise out of the material, taking into account those ruptures or shallows that indicate resistance, those emphases created by parapraxal moments, and those disseminations occasioned by polysemous words. The object-relational way of listening to the same material transforms the sequence of ideas into characters – treated as parts of the self or parts of the object – who constitute the theatre of transference. Each way of listening finds a different type of conflict operating in a different realm. In literature, it may be the difference between the conflict revealed in the idiom of the writing and the conflict demonstrated in the enactments between characters. In painting it may be the difference between the logic of the developing ideas – thought constituting itself in the intelligence of the step-by-step move of the brush – and the theatre of established figures of the painter's world once again engaging themselves on the canvas.

In 'The Use of an Object' (1969a), Winnicott argued that spontaneity could only develop out of a principle of ruthlessness. In order to use an object, the self must be free to destroy it. It is the mother who sanctions this in the first place; indeed, she is to be the initial object of such destruction. After a period of relating in which the infant's love and hate are mingled through a sense of concern for her, the infant gradually feels more secure in his or her ability to use the mother, not confusing such wear and tear with damage.

Perhaps something of the same principle underlies Freud's injunction to the dreamer to break up the body of the dream through free association. The feelings and self states brought into the dream as an experience are stored as is; breaking them up through free association will not erase memory of the dream experience. Indeed, the security of the dream as a thing in itself allows for its destruction, and use as an object of inspiration.

Whether one considers the dream or the mother as object, both the Freudian principle and Winnicott's idea amount to a breaking-up of the figure. Freud breaks up the figures of the dream and Winnicott breaks up the mother, and from each emerges a dynamically fragmented universe of potential meanings. These psychological theories were developing over a period of sixty years when something of the very same principle was being celebrated in fine art, music and prose. Following the impressionist breaking of representational figuration, we find in cubism, surrealism, abstract expressionism a moment in the artist's development when the figure breaks up. It may shatter into the cubist, futurist, surrealist, or abstract. Furthermore, this dissemination of the object was often signified by the figure of a woman, painted again and again, who begins to break up.

Many critics, looking at Picasso's or de Kooning's paintings of a woman, argue that she is being destroyed in a misogynist attack on the female. These criticisms miss the context of this breaking-up. It usually occurs just before the fragmentation of the sublime other into a bizarre refiguration or a shattered object, often abstracted into a thick movement of colour and shape. I suggest that what we see here mirrors what Freud and Winnicott wrote about the breaking-up of the figurative. Breaking the woman becomes the breaking of the mother's body, momentarily losing the need for figuration but employing her as a project for the realisation of self. She is now the process of painting, an immanent presence, de-objectified and reformed as the guardian intelligence of the form of painting.

Certain abstract works of art, like certain modern novels (of Joyce, Faulkner) disfigure customary representation in order to present the work of creativity within the form itself, playing with the elements of form, implicitly recognising the desire in the recipient to see something of the magic of form at work.

Psychoanalysis can show a similar lack of respect for the sanctity of the figurative. In the struggle to engage the invisible, the analyst (like the artist) breaks the figure: not to find out what is inside but to realise the immaterial intelligence of form that is authorised in the name of the mother. If the infant is to come into true self relating, says Winnicott, then he or she must be free to invent the mother and self. For patients to use analysis, they must be free to invent many an analyst in the transference and to destroy the integrity of the person of the analyst in order to express themselves. The analyst up to a point accepts this use.

Painters, composers and writers who take liberty in destroying the figures of our life, nonetheless rely upon the integrity of the figure even as they destroy it. Like psychoanalysts, they recognise the paradox of this freedom. It could not occur without a sense of privilege deriving from the figure – the mother who gives birth – but who shall be 'destroyed' as she is used. Taking liberties, as it were, is not sublime. As a self creates many an other out of the primary figure, what is gained in freedom of expression is lost in terms of personal security. In time the waves of representation suggest too many possible figures and eventually the primary mother is beyond reach. Abstract expressionists may well have pined for the simplicity of the figure, just as the self, beset by creation of so many multiple representations of the primary object, grieves the mother lost to us all.

A Picasso or de Kooning may well return in mind to the woman, armed with the ambivalence that comes from the freedom to destroy. How, it might be posed, can the mother allow us to destroy her? Refinding her, even in altered form, then, may be a relief in the midst of what will be renewed efforts of destruction.

We are separated from the mother, the father, the family, and arguably from our culture, by the fecund complexity of psychic life. No figure shall survive intact. Our thoughts – in visions and revisions – will revise all figures so frequently that only the principle of figure shall remain. Free association releases this complexity in a bound space further narrowed by the reluctance of the patient to fully embrace it, and by the analyst who seeks his interpretations. Creative work in dance, poetry, drama, prose fiction, music, painting, sculpture, also involves tacit devolutions of the figure as revisioning creates multiple figures, overlying one another.

If we cannot have singular objects to embrace for consolation's sake, we do have the body of separate forms, into which and through which we alter and articulate our being. This is the great promise of any art form. It is often enough the reality of the psychoanalytical method.

Chapter 13

Architecture and the unconscious

In interesting ways the world of architecture – broadly defined here as the deliberate consideration of the constructed human environment – and the world of psychoanalysis – broadly stated, the place for the study of unconscious mental life – intersect. A building derives from the human imagination, in some dialectic that is widely influenced by many contributing factors: its stated function, its relation to its neighbourhood, its functional possibilities, its artistic or design statement, its client's wishes, the anticipated public response, and many other factors that constitute its psychic structure. Even if the building springs from the known idiom of its architect and is clearly a Le Corbusier or a Mies van der Rohe, it will still have passed through many imaginings, influenced by many factors, the totality of which will be part of the architect's unconscious direction of the project.

We know that there is an unconscious life to each self. Is there an architectural unconscious, that is, a type of thinking which directs the projection of a building, influenced by many demands, yet finding its own vision out of the constituent elements?

Interestingly, Freud attempted to use the image of a city as a metaphor of the unconscious. In *Civilisation and its Discontents*, maintaining that 'in mental life nothing which has once been formed can perish', he reckoned that if we wished to imagine the unconscious we could do so by visualising Rome in such a way as to see all its periods – the *Roma Quadrata*, the *Septimontium*, the Servian Wall period, and the many Romes of the emperors to follow – at the same time. 'Where the Coliseum now stands,' he wrote, 'we could at the same time admire Nero's vanished Golden House' (Freud, 1929: 70).

Freud abandoned his metaphor because, as buildings are demolished and replaced in the course of time, a city is not a suitable example for the timeless preservations of the unconscious. Perhaps if Freud had sustained the metaphor a bit longer its dialectic would have worked. For obliterations are indeed part of one's unconscious life – so much so that depending on how one wished to look at the Rome of one's unconscious life, one could see both the preserved and the destroyed.

Certainly for architects and the cities or clients who employ them, destruction and creation bear an intimate proximity to one another. In the inner city most new builds are developed after the demolition of the former structure, one body standing where once another stood. For those who live through these moments there will always be two buildings in mind: the obliterated and the existent.

Ghost towns

I grew up in the small coastal town of Laguna Beach, some 45 miles south of Los Angeles. Even though it has had a surprisingly coherent and vigilant building code, which makes it difficult to build new structures, over time, of course, buildings have come and gone. At some point in the late 1950s an entire row of timber-framed buildings, fronting the main beach in the centre of town, was torn down – now revealing the sand and the sea to motorists passing along Highway 101. Whenever I think about it I can easily visualise these rather quaint seaside shanties, which housed such noteworthy occupants as a photographer's studio, a café, a chemist, a typical beachwear store, an orange juice stand, and the like. I visit the town several times a year and when my friends and I meet, in the course of giving directions to one another, we often refer to places that no longer exist.

Each city has its ghost towns.

Although the ghosts will be the inhabitants whom one recalls (and here I think of our town's first educated book dealer, Jim Dilley, and his glorious bookshop, now long since gone), the presence of the ghosts is, of course, entirely a matter of one's own unconscious life. I know of these places because I visited them. I loved the hamburgers in Bensons; I recall the stools at the counter where one sat, and the handsome machinery lining the wall, like the malt makers. So the energy of the ghost is of course my own: the ghost as the occupant who has suffered a trauma and is not yet prepared to leave this world is of course me. I have suffered the shock of losing this favoured place, and until I die it shall always be somewhere in mind.

To lesser and greater extent, this is true of all of us, especially when we move house. To leave a home, even when the contents go with us, is to lose the nooks and crannies of parts of ourselves, nesting places for our imagination. Our belief in ghosts will always be at least unconsciously authorised by the fact that we shall always linger on in our former houses, just as we assume that upon moving into a new dwelling, its former inhabitants will also still be there.

Architects mess with this psychic reality. Usually the ruthlessness of demolition is allowed its curiously stark nobility. A bulldozer (or its equivalent) arrives, we watch the structure dispatched in a surprisingly short period of time, and the earth – at least for a moment – receives sunlight once again. Sometimes architects will honour the demolished, as Evans and Shalev did in the Tate Gallery at St Ives in Cornwall. The new gallery was built on a site occupied by a gas tower; even though it was rather unsightly during its day, it was still the former occupant, and is now remembered in the rounded shape of the museum which mirrors it.

The wreckers

Who drives the wreckers?

Like the dreaded visits of the grim reaper in the literary imagination, the wreckers seem to be death on our doorsteps. Their actions are irreversible. Once they take out a building, it is gone for ever. So when notice is given to a community that a sector will be destroyed and something new will be built, even if the project is promising, there is always a certain dread of witnessing the efficiency of these wreckers. Of course, it is also exciting: like watching a fire or a flood wipe out an object, the sight of the wreckers brings out something of the child in us who builds sand-castles and delights in destroying them. On this side of the psychic equation is liberation from our attachments, and just as the child takes pleasure in destroying his or her creations – part of signifying the growing pleasure of leaving the secure architecture of the world created by mother and father to strike out alone – the adult watching demolition has his or her attachments wrested away.

Demolition is sacrificial. Before too long we shall be eradicated from this earth of ours, removed gracelessly from our spaces, our place to be taken by the other. Until that day, removals will seem like sacrificial offerings: at least I do not go with the obliterated. Well, not entirely. A part of me goes, a part I can apparently live without. Destruction of a building I like is emotionally painful, but I carry with me certain memories of the structure.

The work of the architect, then, involves important symbolic issues of life and death. Demolishing the existent structure to make way for a new one plays upon our own sense of limited existence and foretells our ending. Given this psychic issue, buildings seem to opt for one of two possible alternatives.

In one option they may either blend fully into their surroundings, as if to deny that a new build is anything new at all, or differ slightly from their fellow structures, as the seemingly logical extension of a seamless progression in architectural time.

Signs of the future

The second option is a radical departure from past and present: to declare themselves in the human future. If taking the latter solution – we may think of Richard Rogers' and Renzo Piano's Beaubourg, or Frank Gehry's Bilbao – these structures may seem more than simply buildings, rather material testimonies to our vision of the future. As such, we might identify with them. As they shall outlive us, they shall nonetheless signify us in the future, giving us a place in historical time and the existential reality of future generations who, upon gazing at these objects, may think of our era.

However, to identify with a building as a testimony of our intelligence cast into the future, it must be both beyond our immediate vision and yet not so far into the future as to alienate the imaginative idiom of our generation. If a building goes too far into the future – as the Eiffel Tower may have done in its day – the people feel a reverse effect: the future has invaded the present and cast scorn on that present's sensibilities.

Building is a form of prayer. Through our structures we pray that our minds and hearts have been well guided and that time will prove those structures to be true. Yet the very mass of a building – going back to the ziggurats of the Sumerians, the pyramids of Egypt, the temples of Greece – incorporates the tension of the living and their death. Such noble structures are, one way or the other, intended to honour the gods who live in eternity, and are offerings of our own limited being to the limitless. Buildings are, therefore, always verging on the profane: how dare we build anything for the gods?

Dead labour

The monumental structure – the mountain built by men – is one of the great paradoxes of architectural accomplishment. The monument is meant to outlive generations of men; yet in its construction many lives will be lost. Some, like Gaudí, who work their entire lives on the monument, will never see its completion.

All monuments, whether functionally intended so or not, are tombs. They not only shadow the deaths of the workers, and outlive their creators; they seem in their mass to be forms of death amongst the living.

Is architecture invested, then, with the grave task of bringing death into human life? Are these monuments houses of death? Does the immense implacability of the mass signify the destruction of the organic in the hands of the inorganic?

If so, then monumental structures are highly ambiguous objects. Out of the materials of the earth, we create a symbol of our death, sometimes as a tomb proper – as with the pyramids – but most often as a functional object presumed for the living, such as a great temple, cathedral or office building. If meant for the living, the monument is a kind of play-space within a death zone, as the living animate the cold marble or mass of cement, day after day during their lifetimes, before dying as new generations walk in the same space. Monuments allow us to move into and out of death space, the human being travelling in the world of great stone mass.

Like the sepulchre, however, we aim to put some sign of our lives on the monument, either in the form of ornament – aimed to be a sign of life inscribed into the death object – or, as in Greek nomenclature, by giving the parts of the building human names, such as the head of a column, or the throat of a chimney. As an embodiment of the real – understood here as the material expression of death that eludes our ultimate knowing – does the monument allow our signatures? Does it express human frivolity? Does the architect's imagination slightly mock its towering mass, such as Philip Johnson's AT&T (Sony) Building in New York? Or, as with Stalin's proposed Palace of the Soviets and Mussolini's architecture, does it show no sign of irony, no human dimension revealed in its massiveness?

Monuments and vivid built structures are evocative objects. 'A distinctive and legible environment not only offers security but also heightens the potential depth and intensity of human experience,' writes Kevin Lynch (Lynch, 1960: 5). Objects possess degrees of 'imageability', he maintains, and certain cities have a higher degree of imageability than others. If monuments are forms of death in life, then they play both sides of the struggle between life and death, as they are also perceived as places of safety. During differing eras of the Egyptian dynasties the people took refuge in the walled-in temple cities and may well have joined those merchants and persons of standing who occupied dwellings next to the sacred place. Perhaps, like a chap called Panemerit, they built their house 'in the first temple courtyard up against the pylon, so that his statues should derive virtue from the sacred rites' (Montet, 1958: 18).

Panemerit may have believed he was holier because he lived close to a sacred place; perhaps he hoped that the journey after his death would be a favourable one. Whatever this meant to him, it was inescapably an emotional experience, perhaps layered by many different intersecting meanings. Those who live near La Scala, the Empire State Building or the Golden Gate Bridge experience what Minkowski called the 'reverberation' of the object. As particular objects are constructed and we dwell upon them, 'we ask ourselves how that form comes alive and fills with life . . . we discover a new dynamic and vital category, a new property of the universe: reverberation' (Bachelard, 1958: xvi). La Scala might be the spirit of great operatic music, the Empire State of corporate virility, the Golden Gate of bridging the waters.

Some anthropologists believe that the ziggurats were either memories of mountains, left behind by the Sumerians who migrated from a more mountainous northern region to the Tigris–Euphrates delta, or simply devotions to the mountain as a noble object of nature (Crawford, 1991). Hersey believes that Greek temples may well derive from sacred trees. He points out how many differing human and environmental objects are given place in Greek buildings, through inclusion by name (Hersey, 1988). Lynch argues that vivid landscapes are 'the skeleton upon which many primitive races erect their socially important myths' (Lynch, 1960: 5). Incorporating the striking objects of the environment into their cultural visions. Bachelard muses that through reverberation 'we feel a poetic power rising naively within us. After the original reverberation, we are able to experience resonances, sentimental repercussions, reminders of our past' (Bachelard, 1958: xxiii).

Our worlds

Great mountains, large rivers, the sea, the prairie, the jungle and remarkable edifices are etched in our mind like psychic structures; each seems to possess its own small universe of emotion and meaning. Every Venetian school-child learns to draw a map of how to get from home to school, as Venice is a city where one can easily become lost. These children's maps show how striking buildings are important markers for one's basic sense of orientation. St Mark's Square, for some, would be a lifelong sign of the orienting function of the object world that is essential to human survival, not unlike the sight of the beacon from the lighthouse during a fog, or the enduring presence of the national parliament during a time of war, and so on.

In his remarkable work *The Poetics of Space*, Gaston Bachelard calls for a 'topoanalysis' which would be 'the systematic psychological study of the sites of our intimate lives' (1958: 8). There is, for example, a 'transsubjectivity of the image' so that those of us situated next to prominent sites share the image – even though, of course, each of us renders it differently. Lynch has found in his comparative analysis of Boston, Jersey City and Los Angeles how important it is to the citizens to have legible objects with high imageability. People in Boston, for example, contrasted buildings based on their age difference, while people in Los Angeles were of the impression that 'the fluidity of the environment and the absence of physical elements which anchor the past are exciting and disturbing' (Lynch, 1960: 45). Inhabitants of Jersey City, a colourless industrial city close to New York, suffered from 'the evident low imageability of this environment' as they found it difficult to describe differing parts of their city, felt a general dissatisfaction living there, and were poorly oriented (Lynch, 1960: 42). Living in a city, then, is to occupy a mentality. To be in Los Angeles is quite different from being in Boston.

How would a topoanalysis deconstruct the mentality of a city? We could hardly argue that a city reflects a singular unified vision. We know that there are many competing interests and diverse perspectives that generate differing structures. What would drive such a mentality? What would sustain it?

Winnicott argued that each mother provides her infant with an environment. In the beginning it is a 'holding environment', as one is literally embraced and moved about by the mother's self and her deputised objects (a walker, a toy car or a cot, for example). This holding environment sustains something of our earliest senses of being held, as we spend our first nine months as occupants of the womb. In his essay 'Berlin Walls', Winnicott considers the wider concept of environmental provision and its effect upon the development of people: 'The inherited maturational processes in the individual are potential and need for their realisation a facilitating environment of a certain kind and degree' (Winnicott, 1969b). Boston, Los Angeles and Jersey City are facilitating environments as they direct their occupants in differing ways. One of the mother's tasks, argued Winnicott, was to present objects to her infant. This was something of an art, for if she forced a new object upon the infant, the child would inevitably turn away; but if she allowed for 'a period of hesitation' during which the infant would turn away, presumably from lack of interest, the infant would soon enough return with heightened interest and desire towards the new object. In this respect, cities continually present their inhabitants with new objects – and the planning stage, when proposals are floated in the press, may constitute an important psychic element in the population's relation to the new.

Numerous plans for celebrating the turn of the millennium were floated in the UK, evoking almost universal opposition. In part it was because any supposed public spending on what seemed a frivolous adventure was objectionable. The eventual choice of site – an unpleasant post-industrial area of Greenwich Peninsula – was like foregrounding the Jersey City of London in the mind's eye of Londoners. Time needed to pass before the very idea itself could become acceptable. It is more than interesting that the gigantic object which the British selected for the centrepiece of the Millennium Dome was, initially, to be the body of a woman next to her child, so that queues of visitors would experience a showcase of Britain by climbing into a woman. It was finally decided to create two anodyne figures, a desexualisation of the bodies which still indicated one was entering two human forms: one big, the other small.

Unlike the Statue of Liberty, into whom one could climb (until its closure following September 11, at least) in order to see if one could get to the top – a rather phallic object, suggesting an equally phallic conclusion to inner exploration – the Dome woman was to have reclined, hands extended behind her, while the population entered just about where the womb would be, to gaze at exhibits of the internal organs of the body.

The living city

The Millennium Dome structure, again a Richard Rogers project, was however simply another expression of the British mentality, realised through the work of architecture. Taking Winnicott's view that a holding environment is an act of psychic intelligence, then a city is a living form that holds its population. Mentality is the idiom of holding, reflecting the very particular culture of place. No vision of it becomes its totality; in those epochs when men have attempted to impose a totalitarian vision of a city, it has denuded its population. Part of the error of such thinking, it seems to me, is the view that consciousness alone can form a city. Cities are rather unconscious processes. There are so many competing functions, aesthetics, local interests and economics, with each element influencing the other, that a city is more like the seeming chaos of the unconscious mind. Indeed it bears rather striking similarity to any ordinary self which has biological, sexual, historical, spiritual, vocational, familial and economic interests, all of which find themselves interlaced in some kind of moving form that gives rise to a type of organising vision, or mentality. Psychoanalysts working with a person long enough enter into a very particular culture, not unlike moving into a city and coming to know its oddities: its aesthetic preferences, its dislikes, its overcome obstacles, its wastelands, its partitioning of interests and its long-standing conflicts.

When evocative structures are built they will give rise to intense associations in the population. For example, when the Getty Museum in Los Angeles opened it was the object of widespread critical response. Driving north on Interstate 405 towards West Los Angeles, one sees on the hillside an evocative cultural object, 'speaking' to us through our associations. Before its opening the Getty was just a new rather impressive building; but now it is part of what it means to be Los Angeles. These elaborations, however, will eventually subside, and like the Metropolitan Museum of Art in New York or any other imposing museum, such disruptive impacts on the inhabitants of its time will be lost on future generations, who will subject it to their own sensibilities. Indeed, as we walk or drive through our cities, we know relatively little – if anything at all – about the great majority of structures. Once evocative, at least to the locals affected by their arrival, they are now like silent obelisks which would require considerable historical work and decoding to resurrect their voices.

So we are back to death yet again. Our cities contain hundreds and thousands of buildings which, once alive as evocative objects and part of the culture of place, are now cemeterial. In our consideration of the unconscious life of a city, then, we must reckon with a certain mute presence, a silenced voice, that perhaps is evidence in the everyday of the dying of the voice of the built. We know, don't we, that even simple buildings have stories to them. These tombs of the unknown citizens are nonetheless a part of our life and of living in the quotidian. The silence of the buildings is a premonitory presence of our own ending, inevitably part of our life. We could, if we so wished, put placards on each building, giving the date of completion, the name of the architect, a list of the workers, and perhaps selected local response from newspapers or oral notations. For the most part, however, we choose not to do this. Even the architects who build great structures are usually forgotten, unless, like Eiffel, their name – for better or worse – is identified with the object.

Remembering a name is a curiously conflicted event. Most people like wandering in a wood or gazing at wildflowers, but how many people can identify more than ten trees? We eat a fair amount of fish, but how many know what a cod, a turbot or a monkfish look like? Freud's theory of repression suggests that if we know the name of an object it generates a greater network of personal meaning, as names distinguish objects and interact rather intelligently with other names, in the moving psychic experiences of everyday life. The word 'oak', for example, designates a unique tree, but it also contains the phoneme 'oh' within it, and it could suggest 'yoke' and its meanings. If we knew all the names of the different trees in the forest, then as we saw a birch, a laurel, a dogwood, a maple, or the endless other trees, we would also be in a symphony of phonemes that would be playing along with the visual order. If we knew the names of our buildings, the years in which they were completed, and the names of their architects, we would also create a wider and denser universe of personal meaning.

Why don't we do this?

Nameless forms

The problem cannot simply be intellectual or cognitive. We have much less difficulty learning a foreign language or the characters of novels than we do remembering the names of trees, plants or fish – yet these objects are more immediately a part of our everyday life than Emma Bovary or the French for 'Please direct me to the nearest tourist office.'

At first glance it would seem as if we have a certain lack of interest in trees, plants, fish or our buildings. Are they of so little interest to us? It would seem this is hardly the case. So why are we mute when it comes to naming these visual objects? Perhaps the answer lies in the unconscious meaning of beholding a form which we treasure. Imagine for a moment that we do indeed like trees, that flowers and plants are very important, and that certain built structures, about which we know nothing, are truly important to us. They are part of our visual life. Perhaps they are intended to remain in that order of perception and imagination, fundamentally as silent visual objects.

I remember driving across the Plains states in North America, where to this day one may travel for hours without ever seeing another car. Countless American novelists and poets have likened the tall grass to a vast sea, as it moves in the breeze like ocean waves on a flat plane unmodified by hills. The sky and the prairie seem to meet in one continuous vast canvas. Now and then you will see a tree. As they can be miles apart, a single tree stands out in all its formal beauty as the essence of tree. A farmhouse, separated visually from any other farmhouses, can be seen for miles, and as you approach it, it seems to embody the essence of a house. A flash of lightning in the distance, a cloud passing across the sky, a flock of birds, a field of sunflowers, a tractor: all of these objects stand out in stark singularity against the silence of the background. Each object seems to be the spirit of its brothers, one tree standing for the existence of all trees, one house standing for the presence of all houses. It is as if one contemplates the purity of a form.

Perhaps we choose to ignore the naming of objects because we find ourselves more moved by their form. Until we know the precise name we know only its generic name, and this may be a compromise between the natural world and the built environment. Perhaps we choose to walk only amongst the trees, the plants or our streets, in order to commune with form itself. When we break down these forms and give them their names, whose names do we use? Do the names derive from the form itself? Of course not. The names derive from that patriarchal order which arbitrarily names objects. So to defy the knowing of the names may well be to decline the secularisation of objects which we believe carry great spiritual weight.

Buildings and structures that become nameless, that simply meld into the matrix of a city, may fulfil our need for nameless forms, rather like pure objects unsullied by knowledge. We choose to live in the visual, not the verbal, order. We choose, therefore, to live part of our life in the maternal order – that register of perception guided by the maternal imaginary – rather than in the paternal order, which names objects and possesses them in language. And part of our wandering in this visual world – that shall go nameless – is to meander, then, in the preverbal world: one organised around sights, sounds, smells and affinities. This is a world of ours that has in many respects gone by. One's life within one's mother and then

216 Architecture and the unconscious

alongside her, before one knows about obligations and speech, fades and fades with age. Like the silent buildings with no name, the maternal order is rather lost upon the workaday maturity of the languaged self.

If we need to know the names of streets, and the names and locations of many different public buildings – from the motor vehicle licensing office to the opera house, from the tax office to the post office, from the ticket office to the best bookshop – we may also need to walk among many buildings that shall be without name.

Our paths

'Every citizen has had long associations with some part of his city,' writes Lynch, 'and his image is soaked in memories and meanings' (1960:1). As we walk or travel about our city we select various routes, each of which has differing evocative effects. 'What a dynamic, handsome object is a path,' writes Bachelard (1958:11) – as those paths we choose are lined by objects that shall play upon our mind. Even though certain routes will be ordained by the mentality of the city (so that in taking the highway to the airport, or the only road to the ferry, we are guided by the intelligences of form of those who have planned and executed the routes), we elect our own paths throughout our life. During a year lived in New York City, I had a wide choice of routes from my home on West 94th Street to my office on East 65th Street. I had to cross Central Park, which offers innumerable paths. Although I walked different ways when I tired of my favoured route, I enjoyed one particular path. I walked along Central Park West as far as 81st Street, which gave me a long vista of the west side and the families spilling out of the elegant apartment blocks on to the streets. I entered the park and walked between the Great Lawn and Turtle Pond – the field the location of baseball pitches and the pond full of ducks and turtles. I then either walked through a tunnel and along the edge of the Metropolitan Museum of Art, or across a street to Cherry Hill, before winding my way from 72nd and Fifth until arriving at my destination.

Each segment of this journey is well known to me. Each unit has its own 'structural integrity', that is, its own particular character. But of course what they evoked in me will differ from what they evoke in another person. And although I enjoyed being lost in thought during this walk, I was certainly inspired by the sequential implications of each integral form. One is, as Blake's poem suggests, always a 'mental traveller' in this world, and the paths we choose to take in our lives – even as simple as the way I walked to work – are vital parts of the expression of our own personal idiom.

Each city, then, has its own structural integrity (the material realisation of imagined forms) through which we travel. Cities evolve their own interspatial relations as roads intersect, as parks are placed, as high streets are segregated from residential areas, as industrial parks are segregated from art centres, and so on. If spatialisation were the unconscious development of space according to the evolution of any city, then interspatial relations would define the psychology of spaces as they relate to one another, and as they invite the citizen to move across boundaries and into new 'nodes' that define areas. Moving in this unconscious organisation of sites and their functions is the individual, who will elect favoured paths and who will, quite idiosyncratically, find certain locations more evocative than others. Most obviously this occurs when one has been raised in a particular 'neck of the woods', so that the objects experienced during childhood will contain parts of the self's experience that will have been projected into the objects as mnemic containers of lived experience. But in time, any individual will find a new area more interesting in some respects and less interesting in others, as he or she gravitates towards certain objects that become points of personal reverie.

Walking and evocation

Walking between the Great Lawn and Turtle Pond, I am between two distinct structures (one a field of Kentucky Green Grass with baseball diamonds here and there, the other a large pond with a rock cliff on one side and a marsh-to-grass sector on the other) serving public visions (the field for human play, the pond for observation of natural life) but each structure evokes associations peculiar to my life.

To take the Great Lawn. As a structure in its own right, with its own integrity, there is a simple beauty about a baseball field. The diamond shape of the 'infield' is earth, while the 'outfield' is grass. In a well-groomed baseball field the contrast between the grass and the earth is beautiful. As a purely empty space – minimalist, as it excludes the players – it is like a familiar, though varied, rendition of a potential space. When the players occupy the field, usually in brilliantly different costumes, a baseball diamond is like a Paul Klee painting – especially if one considers the teams upon teams that shall occupy the space. Each team has nine participants who, though occupying set positions, will move out of place – creating lines of movement against the earth/green outline of the pitch – becoming a figurative form of abstract expressionism: the figures who move create the abstraction that gives the game its visual poetry.

The Great Lawn, considered not as an integral but as an evocative object – something that inspires idiosyncratic parts of myself which have been projected into that space during the course of my lifetime – holds that part of me which nearly went on to play professional baseball in my youth. Depending on my frame of mind, on any day the sight of the Great Lawn may inspire differing types of memory: actual recollection, a type of mood, a wish to play the game.

But on the other side of me is Turtle Pond, which, though of course an integral object – something with its own structural integrity not altered by human projection – is also an evocative object. It does not bring to mind myself in my youth, but in my early forties, when I lived for two years in the countryside of western Massachusetts. Although it does evoke the spirit of the pond – and certain recollections of the ponds of western Massachusetts – it also evokes memories of my place of work, of my family's interests, and quite personal issues deriving from that time of my life.

Without thinking about it much, when we traverse a city – or walk in our district – we are engaged in a type of dreaming. Each gaze that falls upon an object of interest may yield a moment's reverie – when we think of something else, inspired by the point of emotional contact – and during our day we will have scores of such reveries, which Freud termed psychic intensities, and which he believed were the stimuli for the dream that night. But as a type of dreaming in their own right, the reveries wrought by evocative objects constitute an important feature of our psychic lives.

People who dislike the area where they live are in a sad state of disrepair, for they are denied the vital need for personal reverie. Each person needs to feed on evocative objects, so-called 'food for thought', which stimulate the self's psychic interests and elaborate the self's desire through engagement with the world of objects. Indeed, although such movement is too dense to be interpreted, each person senses something of his or her own unique idiom of being as he or she moves freely through space. We will not know what that idiom is, but will sense that we are moving according to our own realised intelligence of form, shaping our lives through our selection of objects.

My walk through Central Park is not available to a simple psychoanalytic (or any other) interpretation, but the movement of inspired musings is uplifting and is part of the feeling that life is for the living, and not just for recumbent thinking or vocational productivity.

This prospect is not lost on architects, who certainly know of the evocative potential of any of their buildings, even if the precise idiom of reverie derived from the citizens would of course be largely unknowable. And although new towns may be said to have planned obvious places for reverie – parks and the like – the evocativeness of objects cannot be charted into a psychic journey, even if the layout of Disneyland in California (with no directions, just the next realm of fantasy life) attempts to prove the exception.

We know, however, that vivid structures find their way into our dreams at night, and it is here – in the dreamworld – that the visions of the architect and the dreams of the citizen find curious communion.

To the dream

Just as Athenians must certainly have had the Parthenon in their dreams, we too take vivid structures into our dreams; the unconscious that operates in the material realm of the built, and the unconscious that organises each self, meet. Visionary architects intend their structures to suggest dreams to their dwellers, but I shall maintain that all along we know that vivid structures will enter our dreams and affect our dream life. Indeed we might say that just as perspective in fine art was achieved through the architectural effects of Renaissance architecture (the extraordinary influence of Brunelleschi), our dream life is influenced by the perspectives accomplished in the architectural imagination. I had best give an example. I shall report a dream of mine:

> I am walking down a sloping street in Laguna Beach that leads to Victoria Beach. I am with my wife, my father and mother, my next youngest brother and my son, and we are all in a mood to hang out on the beach. I look to the right and, to my surprise, see the reflection of a wave breaking over a high cliff that is rimmed with tall trees. The wave is bright green and translucent so that it does not actually obliterate the sight of the cliff and the trees. Above the wave is a brilliant blue sky and the overall effect is visually astonishing. I point this out to my family and we are all amazed and delighted, and head toward the beach with even greater enthusiasm. Although the event is felt to be remarkable, it is not understood to be unusual. In the next scene we are bathing in the water, in really quite big waves. I see my father, with arms crossed, floating in the white water right up to the shore, being carried along and obviously enjoying himself. In the final scene I am leaving my family at our favourite outdoor restaurant near Main Beach (about two miles from Victoria Beach) in order to nip off to Dilley's Bookstore. The mood of the dream is one of well-being.

Certain facts shall help illuminate part of the dream, which I shall not subject to analytical association or interpretation, but shall instead use to illustrate a specific point. The dream took place approximately a year after my father's death; his ashes were scattered at sea off Laguna Beach. Victoria Beach was the place where we hung out as a family, until I was 14 years old. Up to about the age of ten, I was not permitted by my father to go out into the very large surf, but instead had to play in the white water, indeed, in much the way my father did in the dream.

In a former restaurant of the Surf and Sand Hotel (about halfway between Victoria Beach and Main Beach) there was a mirror on the ceiling. Sitting at a table with a view of the sea, you could also look up and see the waves moving across the ceiling, which was an unusual and pleasant visual effect. I think I incorporated this design innovation into my dream, in that I saw the reflected wave breaking on the hill. But the object and its design origin – a mirror – seems also to be a part of the dream, as my father mirrors the way I swam as a boy. Only now, however, he is gone – dispersed in the sea – and although I may be the titular head of the family (victorious in the Oedipal sense, as in the name of the beach) my son is also along for the trip to the sea, and so, in a way, my own ending too is in sight.

The restaurant in the dream no longer exists, and neither does Dilley's Bookstore, except in my dream, or in the world of literature. Going off to the bookstore that is no longer there may very well have been a premonition in the dream of the task of writing this essay, which, not incidentally, is now written down and part of a literature of sorts.

For some days after the dream I asked myself a question that had occurred following previous memorable dreams. What is the function of such vivid beauty? Why does the unconscious bother to construct such a setting?

Perhaps because truly profound dreams are meant to be memorable, to be commemorated for ever through a high degree of imageability. Perhaps we are meant to pass them along from one generation to the next. And perhaps the part of us that constructs the unforgettable dream – alongside those that are more pedestrian – comes from the same part of us that seeks to build unforgettable structures.

Is visionary architecture a dreaming?

Buildings: between life and death

Do we intend monumental structures to be dreamt upon and to extend themselves into our dreams and those of the generations to come? Yet if they signify death on earth, the immobile inert mass of silence, why should they be vivid? Would we not want death to be as marginal and as inconspicuous as possible, and for as long as possible? The uncanny compromise achieved by the monumental is that it is both a sign of life and a sign of death. As we sleep, we all go off into a darkness, perhaps never to return. To dream is to take a sample of lived experience with us, indeed to take our entire history with us into the darkness. If we survive to live another day, so much the better. But our dream objects, the furniture of life, may be the last articles we see before everything goes completely and irreversibly dark. A monument that bears death in its mass, supposed ironic triumph of the inorganic over the organic, of the creation over the creator, may transcend its terminability with evocative suggestiveness. It intends, in other words, to stimulate the imagination as we walk about in the shadows of death.

One city in particular seems to have grasped the strange ambiguity of the monumental as intercourse between life and death. When the sun sets and dark descends in the Nevada desert, the city of Las Vegas comes alive as an extraordinary illumination of human fancy, perhaps capitalising in all respects on the wishful nature of the dream event. By day the buildings of Las Vegas are simply rather dead and uninteresting, all the more reason for its visitors to sleep during the day (perhaps keeping the city of the night alive in the dream) waiting for the moment to wake up and re-enter the night vision. One lives in the midst of a type of managed dream in Las Vegas, which in the past two decades has broadened the scope of its dream furniture to include the cities of New York, Venice and Paris, and the Egyptian pyramids. Perhaps the world is dreaming itself through this architectural structure, as if the planners of Las Vegas, having astutely extended the evocative function of design to influence the dream life of citizens, have found a place where design and dream can meet in the middle of the night to the profit and loss of both participants.

Architects intermittently play with the idea of meeting the self's desire for the integral object's other function (that of evocation). On the slope of a hill leading from Hampstead Village to Golders Green in North London lies a well-known English progressive school. The buildings of the King Alfred School (KAS) surround a large and irregular, but slightly circular, somewhat uneven playing field. From the small single-storey structures to the immediate left as one enters the school, where the younger children reside, moving clockwise around the field, other structures house the children as they grow up. The Lower School has several new builds from the last few years which catch the eye of visiting prospective parents as signs of modernity and good funding. At 12 o'clock are wooden fortress-like structures for the more adventurous, at 1 o'clock tennis courts and the gymnasium, at 2 o'clock a rectangular building constructed in the 1980s, at 2.45 a kind of pagan space called Squirrel Hall, surrounding a gigantic chestnut tree where the older and more wizened adolescents hang out, and at 3 o'clock is the Blue Building (Field, 1995: 23). It is a new build which rises above an old temporary building on stilts, so that one day when the school can afford to remove the old building, the stilts will act as the new skin of what would then be a new structure.

Prospective parents and school members view the spirit of progressive education in this structure, in part, because it signifies cost-saving inventiveness and integrative adaptation while at the same time coming across as quite innovative in its own right. The rectangular structure, the pagan area and the Blue Building bear little architectural integrity (as in most architectural evolutions, no plan would have intended this) but collectively they do seem to work in an odd kind of way. If we bear in mind that two tethered goats have the run of the large field in the centre and that the school's children and staff are all on first-name terms – and that children at different stages in their lives there construct small villages on the field to learn about materials, planning, execution and cohabitation – then the evolution of design at the King Alfred School seems to have captured the overdetermined capability of buildings.

The buildings are meant to serve functions, but they may also serve the differing evocative implications of their location. In the interesting rendezvous of children, parents, educators and administrators, buildings are constructed which reassure all (they can sleep in peace) and which constitute a kind of embodied dream.

A progressive school like KAS, even if endowed with the funds to do so, would not want to raze its existent structure and build an entirely new school. Nor would it want the temporary buildings (many now well into their thirtieth year) to exemplify too much the spirit that each child (in the form of each building) must be allowed to go forward at his own pace in respect of his or her progressive capacity. KAS is a kind of fairytale world for the diverse requirements of its participants, dreaming its way into shared reality at a pace that is just about right.

Set against these design dreams – of a Las Vegas or a KAS – are objects which would seem to be clearly meant to offend. Both the Eiffel Tower in Paris and the Post Office (BT) Tower in London were regarded as 'shit' by large proportions of the population when first constructed. What we might think of as archi-excretions – that is, buildings that seem intended to offend the population – are nonetheless interesting features of the architectural unconscious. The offensive object, or 'eyesore', may be created by the architect, or allowed to go into existence by the planners, as an unconscious defiance of the population: popular as notorious, putting noses up in the air out of offence. If we set aside simple sadism as the function of such offending acts, why might archi-excrement be tolerated?

The value of a mistake

Architecture, to develop, must make mistakes. As new materials develop they may outpace the architect's grasp of their limitations and for a while ugly structures will certainly be produced. But one generation's excremental object may be another generation's gold, as is somewhat the case with the Eiffel Tower these days: at least, so far as the visitors are concerned, who rather admire it.

The offensive object, however, may be unconsciously welcomed – even as it is consciously vilified – because it raises an interesting psycho-spiritual question. Is this self of ours, which is deposited upon this earth, nothing more than shit? As our bodies decay, as we see early signs of our wasting away, knowing that one day we shall be wormed to a kind of stinking waste, will anything come of this excretion? Will we ever truly be resurrected? How could anything be made out of our waste?

The same question is raised when architects create shit. Surely, the people wonder, how can this excrement ever come to anything? What form of intervention in the minds of the generations to come could possibly transform this dross to gold? Disguised in this offended frame of mind may well be a deeply hidden wish that, quite possibly, some day this building will be loved by those who surround it. Perhaps waste will be transformed into live matter. Perhaps the rejected will be the resurrected. But if so, this will happen in the minds of man. The eyesore, then, awaits a future frame of mind, perhaps one more sophisticated than our own, perhaps one that will function in the world of futuristic medicine, perhaps even in a world where, through DNA replication of our blood samples, we can be resurrected after all. Perhaps then, these piles of waste are strange prayers to the future, very different from those admired monuments discussed earlier.

New buildings, especially visionary ones, elicit the sounds of awe. In the visual field of the Empire State Building must be the auditory inscriptions of many an 'Ahhhh', Ooooh' or 'Wooow'. The mouth opens to take in the sight, the self perhaps thrown back to the infant's opened mouth of surprise as yet another astonishing new object is presented before it. Certainly the scale of New York puts all of us back into the realms of the child amongst the giants, but the spectacle of the object, its spectacular value, trades off the history of any self born into a world of surprises.

Equally the 'Yuuuck!' and the averted gaze express the unpleasures of the unwelcomed objects of one's beginnings. Alternatively the unspectacular, surprising design – for example, a newly built small shop that fits into a previously derelict site rather nicely – might elicit an 'Ahhhh! I didn't know that was there.'

To build the evocative on whatever scale is to open the psyche–soma, seemingly expanding the mind and the body in one singular act of reception which links the new object to the pleasantly surprised subject. As discussed earlier, buildings trade on our unconscious awe of the stature of the physical world – the 'breathtaking' view of a mountain, the sea or the prairie – and to this extent they have an ontological potential: we may be returned to the origin of our being in its first perceptions of the object.

When this occurs the building occupies a certain spirit of place, its design establishing ontological value, as we are put back in the place of birth – as new objects open our mouths and our psyches to the continuing spirit of birth. If the body from whom we arrive, the mother, may be regarded as the god who delivers us into our being, then her subsequent presentation of objects may be seen as consecrations of the object world. Each object the infant puts into his or her mouth for the taste test is communion of the mother's breast.

In our unconscious, then, buildings sustain (or fail) this communion. This good breast, as Melanie Klein famously terms it, is disseminated in the object world, to be found for each person in those objects which either physically or psychically open the mouth and mind. New-found objects either pass or fail this taste test, and people will of course vary enormously in their idea of what is in good taste or in bad taste.

Is the sight divine or not?

Designers and architects, as we have seen, create a world of taste or for the taste, and inherit the task of the mother who delivers the self into a new place with new views and new objects. Cities will have well-known areas for the probably awe-inspiring; but the small material objects of life – a glass, cutlery, a lamp, etc. – are every bit as likely to carry this delight in them. Love of our objects, sometimes something of an embarrassment, is a passion that performs a communion.

Man-made

The man-made world contrasted with the natural world, however, raises a different duality, as built objects seem testimonies to the patriarchal order, while the natural world is likened to the maternal order. As discussed, however, there are countless forms of intercourse between the maternal and paternal orders. If we allow that the decision over insemination is a patriarchal action – take a Greek temple, for example – and its construction is named by man, then its birth to the newcomer (that is, the first moment of seeing it) always trades off maternal presentation of the surprising object. If the monument seems a hallmark of the monolithic triumph of the inorganic over our organic lives, then our giving its structure names from the parts of our bodies seeks inscription. These same temples also bear the names of parts of the animal and botanical world, just as cave paintings and Egyptian tombs bore representations or artefacts from the natural world.

We have been bringing together objects from the maternal order and the paternal order and from life forms and death forms since the beginning of time – a sequence of juxtapositions that is part of the unconscious obligation of architecture.

The park in the city, the garden at the back of the house, the potted plant in the room, the flowers in the vase: these are emblems of the natural world in the built world, just as a small chapel in the forest or a sculpture in the meadow are signs of the built order in the natural world.

Spirits of place

These forms of intercourse are spiritual moments if we understand by this that each embodiment carries with it the spirit of the signifier. A flower in a vase is the spirit of flowers; a church in the woods is the spirit of Christian faith. City planning is not simply functional and locally meaningful: it also involves a type of psycho-spirituality, that is, it is invested with the psychological task of bringing the spirits of life into certain place.

As time does not permit what we might think of as a spiritual deconstruction of Western society – we could examine a house in terms of the spirit of its plumbing, or the spirit of its heating, or the spirit of its living space – let us limit ourselves to the spiritual representation of certain social phenomena vital to human life. We farm the land and we fish the seas. Our survival depends upon these two very ancient functions. In the modern city the fruits of farming and of fishing will of course find their way into the large supermarkets, but we might ask if architecturally we are succeeding in representing the spirit of the fisherman and of fishing as well as the spirit of the farmer and of farming.

Most cities do have open markets containing fishmongers and farm produce, and the market square bears something of these spirits. Fisherman or farmers, for example, visiting the market square will feel that their lives – and the world of fish or of crops – are represented to some extent. Yet sometimes city planners and architects do more than this. In Bergen, for example, in the central harbour there are several large fish tanks, so that citizens and tourists may gaze at these remarkable creatures from the other world moving about in tanks of seawater, well before they go elsewhere on their journey. The same presentation of the sea, its contents (the fish), and the lives of those men and women who work in this world (fishermen) are given honoured place in Helsinki and in Gothenburg. But a similar architectural representation of the spirit of fish disappeared quite some time ago from the area near the Old Town in Stockholm. We could call this a loss of one element of the city's spirit.

At the time of the Conservative Party's ruthless destruction of the mining communities of Great Britain, during Margaret Thatcher's era, Covent Garden (the former fruit and vegetable market of central London) was transformed into boutiques and tourist shops, with New Covent Garden Market having been previously re-sited many miles away. One need not quarrel with the structural necessity of these decisions: perhaps it was necessary to restructure the mining industry, just as it may have been to relocate and enlarge the produce market. But if my argument is correct, that planning and building is not simply functional, rather the work of meaning – indeed, the work of spiritual communion – then the eradication of such sites from the centre of a city amounts to a form of spiritual elimination.

One need only visit Pike Place in Seattle to see how the sea and the land can be functionally and spiritually located. Planning could easily allocate the vast majority of its fish, meat and agricultural processing to the perimeters of a city, while at the same time comprehending the need both of those who work in these distant fields and the people who live within the city to have a spiritual relation to one another. (Recall that by 'spirit' I mean the precise idiom of evocative effect derived from the integrity of each of these differing realms.)

There is no reason, then, why a city like London, for example, could not have in its centre a monument to the underworld of coal mining and to the spirit of mining. The great mining towns of Yorkshire and Wales could find spiritual representation in their capital city, were half a city block designed to reveal it. The same could go for the shipping industry, the automobile industry and so forth.

Such totems, as it were, would invite the spiritual worlds of man and woman into places of representation. However interesting and deeply meaningful monotheism has been, were the monotheistic drive to eliminate the spiritual world embodied in differing lesser gods (i.e., the corn spirit, the rain spirit, and so on), it would be a senseless eradication of the spirit of life on earth. We do all derive from the mother, and in that sense our monotheism is apt, but what kind of mother would we be recalling if honouring her was to be accomplished by destroying the embodied spirits of the object world that she set us into enjoying?

The monotheistic might then be a totalitarian spirituality presided over by what André Green terms the 'dead mother', a figure whose psychic anguish, self-preoccupation and dementia have precluded her passing her relation to her child on to the child's relation to reality.

The architectural unconscious

Part of the task of the architectural unconscious, then, may be to survive monotheistic genocide of difference and, through the diversity of structures, to at least provide the form for many spirits even if – as yet – the true houses for the spirits of life have yet to be fully comprehended and attended to.

Fifty years before the construction of the Eiffel Tower, Roland Barthes reminds us, the nineteenth-century novel materialised in the literary imagination that point of perspective creating a panoramic view that would be achieved in the technology of the Tower. In a chapter of *The Hunchback of Notre Dame* which gives a bird's-eye view of the city, and in Jules Michelet's *Tableau chronologique* which does the same, one looks out upon Paris, something one could do later following the Tower's construction. Barthes argues that travel literature had described scenes of life, but the traveller was always thrust into the midst of the scene, describing the sensation of the new; while from these novels and from the Tower 'a new perception' was born, 'that of concrete abstraction; this, moreover, is the meaning which we can give today to the word *structure*: a corpus of intelligent forms' (Barthes, 1964: 3–22). Gazing down on Paris, one sees the structure of the city as a body of intelligent forms.

The multitude of co-terminus dialectics that drive the differing intelligences of a city – eradication and creation of new roads, new parks, schools, and so on – constitutes the body of a city's form. Like the unconscious life of any one self, the intelligence of a city's forming and transforming of itself derives from no single stimulus, but will always have been a dynamic matrix of many influences that none-theless seems, in time, to create its mentality. Although that mentality, or let us say, collected vision – a dreaming derived from the many constituents – may be destroyed, once alive and in place it constitutes a very particular system unconscious that will generate the complex meanings of a city and its inhabitants.

Bion argued that mental life couldn't be assumed. The only reason we develop a mind, he maintained, is because we have thoughts and eventually thoughts demand the arrival of a thinker to think them. We have many experiences in life, but if these experiences are not transformed into some form of material for thought, then from Bion's point of view these would therefore be 'undigested experiences'. He gives the arbitrary sign B, or Beta, to such elements. But if the self's mind is forming then the ontic factors of life may find ontological signifi-cance, and we may derive food for thought, to which he assigns the term A or Alpha.

We may be able to borrow some of Bion's thinking to consider the life of a village or a city. The mere existence of buildings and cities does not mean that they have a mentality. They may once have been 'a corpus of intelligent forms', but now they could be dead. Those living in the city might be hard pressed to derive from the city's Beta functioning – that is, purely functional operation – any food for thought: it would not give rise to legends, myths, memories, dreams, contemplations or new visions, like Jersey City in the Lynch study. But if the city transforms itself, generating new forms of life, then it would be creating Alpha – that is, the food for thought – and the city's mentality, its unconscious forming of itself and its inhabitants, would be alive and well.

The topography of southern Orange County in California shows how so-called developers have tried to bypass the struggle to move from Beta to Alpha, from the undigested to the digested, through the creation of ready-made towns, with themes like 'Spanish Village', or 'Cape Cod'. Although the schools, parks, shop-ping malls and graded housing districts were executed in one single swift act of development, and certainly intending to exude the spirit of place (i.e., Spain or Cape Cod in California), cloning a mentality is not equivalent to working through those stages of human strife out of which a community grows its own true spirit.

The anodyne new towns of southern Orange County are the city equivalents of the human false self, an invented identity meaning to stand in for authentic civic life. These environments themselves suggest that their inhabitants share in a kind of shallowing out of the self, meant to live in apparent immediate normality, as if the theme-park city has true integrity. Such places would then be empty forms, falsely presumed intelligences, aiming to produce a mentality by copying and pasting other sites and mentalities to the new site. At the end of the day, a Lynch studying these cities would find, I think, that its inhabitants were possessed of a curiously dislocating contentedness: they have everything, and yet it would appear to mean nothing.

The study of unconscious life is a project that we associate with Freud's announcement of the formation of psychoanalysis. Still very much in its early stages as an intellectual project, Freud's designation should not stop with the limits of the individual self. Winnicott wrote:

> A diagram of the human individual is something that can be made and the superimposition of a thousand million of these diagrams represent the sum total of the contribution of the individuals that compose the world and at the same time it is a sociological diagram of the world.
>
> (Winnicott, 1969b: 221–2)

It remains for us to follow the psychoanalytic project towards all its implications, not simply as has happened in the study of literature and culture, but elsewhere, as in the continued study of the unconscious dimensions of architecture, or what the French Situationist Guy Debord termed 'psycho-geography': 'the study and manipulation of environments to create new ambiences and new psychic possibilities'.[1]

---

1 This definition of the Situationists' concept of psycho-geography is provided by Harris, Steven and Berke, Deborah, 1997. *Architecture of the Everyday*. Princeton: Princeton Architectural Press, p. 20.

Chapter 14

What is theory?

When Freud wrote himself into a corner he would engage a literary trope. It would go something like 'if you believe what I have been arguing up till now you will have been following the wrong line of thought.' Then off he would go on his merry way leaving many a reader flummoxed over why so much time had been spent thinking incorrect ideas. Freud's writing simply demonstrated his view that we think free associatively. Typically, he followed not just one line of thought but scores of 'chains of ideas' – a term he often used, like 'trains of thought'. When these lines of thought were in outright contradiction with one another, Freud would engage the above trope or claim he was stuck and defer the issue until later.

I find a particular moment in *The Ego and the Id* (1923) touching. Writing about the repressed unconscious, Freud is about to finish up Chapter One when a thought pops into his mind. Not only are the repressed contents unconscious but so, too, is the agency that commits them to the unconscious. He pauses. He states that it would seem that he has several different theories of the unconscious. For a moment he turns to God to see if the issue can be resolved: 'A part of the ego too – and Heaven knows how important a part – may be Ucs., undoubtedly is Ucs' (*ibid.*, p. 9). Freud lapses into a very brief literary depression, implicitly wondering if he should scrap his entire theory of the unconscious – 'we must admit that the characteristics of being unconscious begins to lose significance' (*ibid.*) – but finishes the chapter with a nod to the future and the hope that somehow this problem can be resolved.

Freud was clear that there were two forms of unconscious: an unconscious *process* and unconscious *content*. Yet, looking back, as no doubt he was in some ways, his prior failure to keep this distinction in mind created a confusion about what he meant when he was referring to *the* unconscious. Was he referring to repressed contents or to the process of repression? But the problem does not stop there. Unconscious processes are not restricted to repressing unwanted ideas. As Freud repeatedly pointed out, there are non-repressed unconscious contents, and so, by implication, there are unconscious processes that do not operate to repress contents but to form contents for other reasons.

Unfortunately, psychoanalysts have tended to focus on the repressed unconscious to the exclusion of the non-repressed unconscious. For decades the non-repressed unconscious has been mischaracterized as simply the 'descriptive unconscious', which means that it is not dynamically organized and just rather inert. It could be argued that unconscious memories, for example, are simply part of this descriptive, non-repressed unconscious.

For classical psychoanalysts, the dynamic unconscious refers to the repression of sexual and aggressive drives that seek return to acceptable consciousness in some form or another. *This* unconscious is, by definition, drive-like; it is a pulsion seeking discharge any way it can and when it ropes in thinking it does so rather expeditiously.

Contrast this with Freud's dream work model.

Here the unconscious is an intelligence of form. Its proprioceptive capabilities receive endopsychic data from the storehouse of the unconscious; it also registers 'psychically valuable' experiences of the day, sorting them as the day goes on into a kind of pre-dream anteroom, and then it organizes thousands of thoughts, arriving through the intermediate space of lived experience, to be dreamed. The creation of the dream is not only a remarkable aesthetic accomplishment, it is the most sophisticated form of thinking we have. A dream can think hundreds of thoughts in a few seconds, its sheer efficiency breathtaking. It can think past, present, and imagined future in one single image and it can assemble the total range of implicit affects within the day experience, including all ramifying lines of thought that derive from these experiences. With the arrival of the Freudian Pair (see Bollas, 2002) the dream work at last has a companion in the analyst's receptive unconscious and we can see, in the remarkable chains of ideas released through the *process* of free association, infinite lines of meaning. The process of free association is an accomplishment of the ego's work.

It is astonishing, given Freud's emphasis on the dream work (followed by his book on jokes and his book on the psychopathology of everyday life), that he never constructed an explicit theory of unconscious perception. Nor did he spend time indicating how the ego was the vehicle of unconscious organization and communication with the other. I have speculated that Freud, ironically enough, repressed his theory of the unconscious ego. Perhaps he preferred to focus on the repressed unconscious because this seduced the name of the father, the authority *banishing* unwanted ideas. But the ego (the *process* of our mind) is partly formed during the self's relation to the mother within what I have termed the maternal order. The mother *welcomes* the infant into mental life. Banishment of the forbidden is a long way off. Indeed, *this unconscious process* is a long period of fulfilling needs and wishes. When Freud repressed knowledge of the maternal order he also rid himself of a theory of mind that was based not on banishment, but on seduction. He 'forgot' that part of our unconscious that creatively fulfils our desires all the time, in daydreams, conversations, relations, creative activities, and whatnot.

In his 1915 essay on the unconscious, however, Freud stuns the reader by stating that it is a remarkable thing that the unconscious of one person can react upon the unconscious of the other without going through consciousness. What is remarkable is that he should throw this observation into his metapsychological essay on the unconscious where there is no conceptual room for this thought. What an arresting return of the repressed!

Had Freud unequivocally stated that the ego was not only mostly unconscious but it also created the dream, the symptom, and all works of creativity, then he would have allowed subsequent generations of analysts to see matters differently. His concept of unconscious communication, de-repressed in the above comment about one person's unconscious reacting upon another, *alluded* to unconscious thinking as a highly sophisticated form of thought.

Instead of recognizing that sophistication, Freud 'dumbed down' his theory of the unconscious in the structural model. He tried to transpose his topographic model of the mind into the structural model. Thus, the unconscious of the topographic model morphed into the Id. The unconscious of the topographic model and the Id are *not* the same. What we have is a kind of model molestation as Freud tried to segue one theory of the unconscious into the other. It not only sustained a muddle, it contributed to it. More to the point, by morphing the non-repressed unconscious into the *Id* the unconscious was now an 'aboriginal' part of the mind that the ego was meant to somehow tame.

It is not difficult to understand what Freud was trying to work out. On the one hand, he knew that part of a person's unconscious life was primitive. It carried the history of the early species within it, it contained infantile sexual phantasies, and it was also the source of the drives. On the other hand, the work of the dream revealed a highly sophisticated form of thinking. How can one reconcile the primitive unconscious with the sophisticated unconscious? In fact, there is no contradiction if one simply understands that *in the beginning* both the form and the contents – that is the process and its productions – of the infant's unconscious were primitive. During the course of time, however, the self's ego becomes more sophisticated. This does not mean that primitive elements of the unconscious – the drives, infantile fantasies, envy, greed, etc. – cease to exist; it simply means that the unconscious processing of these contents becomes more and more sophisticated. Indeed, right from the beginning of life the self is dream working the primitive, transforming urges into images.

Classical analysts to this day think of free association as returning drive derivatives. They rightly point to Freud's writing to support this view. I do not disagree with this, and certainly it is confirmed in clinical practice. However, the *other* unconscious, the non-repressed unconscious, is of little use to classical analysts.

Contrary to the view that this receptive unconscious is the descriptive unconscious, as opposed to the dynamic, the way we organize what impresses us during the day (what is evoked, and what forms we choose to further think them: dreaming, talking, writing, painting, composing, etc.) is actually a highly dynamic process.

Here, I am condensing two points into one, as I would like them to converge for a while before going separate ways. First, we need to be aware of the continued dynamic implications of repression of this kind. Second, Freud's conundrum serves to highlight the hazards of theory formation and both the reach and the limits of theory.

Freud's topographic model is, for example, the best way for us to conceptualize repression. Even if many would throw out his concepts of cathexes and anticathexes as outdated, I would submit that we still do not have a better set of metaphors to conceptualize mental intensity. I do not care if Freud's metaphors are hydraulic or electric any more than I care that the Klein–Bion model of ingestion, digestion, and metabolization is alimentary. The point is, does one understand what the metaphor conveys? *This is the definition of metaphor. It is a mental transportation system.* So, does it tell us what it intends to convey or doesn't it?

The topographic model helps us to see how a repressed idea gathers other repressed ideas into mental clusters and how it returns that idea to consciousness. The structural model is less helpful when it comes to conceptualizing repression. But it 'sees' the psychodynamics of certain parts of the human mind. It helps us to imagine the play between our drives represented in the concept of the Id and the psychic organization of the rules of our society, allegorized in the theory of our Superego. The agency given the responsibility for sorting out this play, for negotiating, for making compromises, for allowing relief from the needs of the one or the other, is the Ego. This model, now somewhat out of fashion, is invaluable.

The structural model, however, does not advance the topographic model. Although it is historically further along in Freud's thinking and obviously was hugely popular with Freud's daughter and others, it does not address the same issues as the topographic model any more than the topographic model replaces the dream theory model of the unconscious.

Analysts think of newer models of the mind as 'advances' in the wrong sort of way. They do increase understanding of the mind but they do *not* replace prior models. This skewed modernist bias, that every intellectual development inevitably improves existent views, has unfortunately resulted in abandonment of important prior models of the mind.

In one psychoanalytical society where I spent a week lecturing and supervising, the analysts were topographical folks and hated the structural model. To put it in geo-political context, the structural model is associated with the Americans and the topographical model with the rest of the classical world. It can actually come down to a kind of culture war. In fact, the structural model and ego psychology were popular first with child analysts, because these models 'saw' psycho-development. It was not otherwise visible in the other models of the mind. Try imagining psycho-development according to the topographic model. I wish you luck. The French, in particular, saw the concept of ego development as spurious. They craftily pointed out that as the unconscious was timeless, the entire notion of psycho-development was based on a false psychic premise. Yes, we did obviously develop – there were outward and inward signs of this – but such development had nothing to do *per se* with unconscious life. Unconscious life does not make temporal distinctions of any kind; indeed, it lives in its own a-developmental temporal kingdom. The idea of a psycho-development was a quaint tale told by those who seemed to have a more commercial notion of the self as progressive product. American analysts were the soft target of this critique because not only were they ego psychologists, but also they were selling psycho-analysis to the medical establishment and insurance companies by removing the more radical features of analysis from their representations. No longer could one find in the major texts of the ego psychologists the passage in Freud stressing that the analyst was to catch the drift of the patient's unconscious with his own uncon-scious. Had they pointed this out to the people of Blue Cross or Blue Shield it would have been a jaw dropping moment.

II

Freud's topographic and structural models come complete with respective images. This helps one to see what they mean. An image, worth a thousand words, serves unconscious purposes. Like a condensed dream fragment it is rather ready-made for the unconscious. It can be more easily internalized and helps a clinician to think about a highly complex matter.

Lacan's Symbolic, Imaginary, and Real does not come as an image, but once we have this tripartite model of meaning in mind it is not difficult to *imagine* the act of listening as involving an interplay between these three orders. Klein's paranoid–schizoid and depressive position theory comes with a small image of arrows (ps-arrow and d-arrow) to signify movement between the two positions. Having internalized this image and the concepts, Kleinians often visualize the material from this perspective.

In addition, all psychoanalysts have unconceptualized theories embedded in the way they practise. Setting aside the inevitability that one's character is a complex set of idiomatic theories functioning on the operational level, clinicians each have individual ways of ordering what they hear and what they say.

It will come as no surprise that each of the differing theories of the psychoana-lytical experience constitutes a different perceptual category. If we listen to the material through the structural model, rather than the Kleinian, we will see things differently. Lacan's categories of the Symbolic, Imaginary, and Real gave me a new way of seeing my analysands. Before this I had not seen what I could now see.

This led me to appreciate the value of psychoanalytical theories as *forms* of perception. One theory sees something that other theories do not see. Freud's theory of the logic of sequence imbricated in the flow of any person's free talking allows one to perceive that logic. If we have not learned how to see things in this way then sequential logic will go unnoticed and one will miss an incredibly important field of unconscious material. Klein's ps and d allow one to see forms of splitting and integration that are not otherwise observable.

'A system of thought is something we live in', writes the British philosopher Simon Blackburn (1999) 'just as much as a house, and if our intellectual house is cramped and confined, we need to know what better structures are available' (p. 10). Blackburn terms such building 'conceptual engineering' *(ibid.*, p. 11) and I think this is a good way to describe the acquisition of psychoanalytical perspectives. As theories are forms of perception, if we settle with just one or two theories we live in a confined intellectual house.

How the psychoanalyst sees human life is obviously conveyed to the patient. The theory by which he thinks constitutes a psychic world-view. Upon entering psychoanalysis the analysand may be unaware of that view, akin to someone getting on an aeroplane headed to a country without knowing where they are going: just a country. There is a difference, however, between landing in Baghdad or Beijing. There is an astonishing difference in the world-views of analysts, just as there are different cities that breed radically different cultures.

Theory, therefore, is not simply a way of perceiving something. It influences the way analysts transform their analysands. Practice follows theory.

Take Freud's theory of free association. If the analyst listens in a state of evenly suspended attentiveness – without trying to concentrate on anything, remember anything, or anticipate anything – his unconscious will occasionally perceive the analysand's unconscious patterns in thought. A form of practice put into place by European analysts, this theory meant waiting, perhaps for long periods of time in sessions, until the analyst got the picture. They suddenly saw a line of thought, which might lead to a comment, or they might elect to remain quiet, meditative.

One person talking; the other listening.

Contrast this with the British School's view of the transference. *All* the people, places, or events in the analysand's narrative are indirect references to the psychoanalyst. If the analyst remains quiet, while the analysand projects a thought into a surrogate, such silence is understood by the analysand – so it is argued – as agreement with the projection. The analyst must therefore translate each and every reference to, or action upon, the self in order to mitigate such a process.

It would be hard to find two more strikingly different ways of perceiving the psychoanalytical experience or two more radically different ways of being with an analysand.

III

There is an ethics of perception. Theories are not simply forms of perception. When practised they *become* ethical decisions.

The Freudian view, just outlined, implicitly assumes the analysand's unconscious construction of meaning. By remaining silent and ostensibly out of the picture, the analyst attends not simply to a line of thought but many divergent lines.

At this moment a thought may arise. 'But what about the analyst as a participant? Isn't this a relationship? The idea that the analyst is neutral is a fallacy, as he is affecting his patient all the time.'

True, of course.

However, meditation *is* action. It is intended to affect the analysand. It creates the possibility for free speech. By creating the illusion of neutrality the analyst partly suspends the oversight of consciousness. Analysts who *practise* neutrality enable the patient's free associations to guide the sessions. They are more receptive to the analysand's free talking than analysts who believe that analysis is a highly interactive event. Inevitably, highly interactive analysts will interpersonalize a session. The illusion of neutrality is intended to function as much for the analyst as the analysand. The analyst believes he is just listening. This is not dissimilar to a reader who believes he or she is just reading, or a listener who is just listening to music.

Let us ask a different question. How might one's subjective response to the analysand be discoverable? Setting aside the reality that an analyst – like a reader or listener to music – should be so deeply lost in listening that he would not know how to answer this question, let's still proceed. Where *is* his subjective response to be found? *If* we really do believe in the unconscious, then this question has a most disconcerting answer. Neutrality recognizes a plain fact. Even though we have some conscious responses to what our analysands say and do, we rarely know our 'personal' unconscious response. Neutralized by our unconscious, we simply do not have access to the sort of information the question seeks. Frustrating as this fact of our life is, if we cheat – and try to manufacture news from our unconscious, if for no other reason than to come up with some kind of storyline – we deny ourselves and our patients *the fact* of living as an unconscious being.

IV

Theories vary in depth and range of view.

A psychoanalytical theory only becomes useful when it has entered the psychoanalyst's receptive unconscious. Joining other theories, it will operate according to the dictates of the analytical experience in a session. Sometimes a theory will pop into consciousness not before the clinician has come to its realization, but afterwards. It functions in much of the way 'genera' (Bollas, 1992) work, a concept I coined to identify the arrival of new unconscious realizations that lead to a different way of viewing life.

Some will see here what seems to be a reversal of one of Freud's paradigms: the movement of unconscious issues into consciousness. Freud was rightly concentrating on unconscious conflicts and believed that moving them into consciousness was therapeutically efficacious. That is certainly true some of the time, although I have argued that the greater part of psychic change occurs unconsciously and need not enter consciousness, either in the analyst or in the analysand. My reversal of Freud's paradigm accounts for the obvious and ordinary internalizations of informative models that people absorb all the time to become part of their unconscious structure. Were this not so we would neither learn nor benefit from lived experience.

The legitimacy of any one psychoanalytical theory resides in its function as a form of perception. To plumb the depths of this depth psychology a theory must have a *capacity for* unconscious perception. Some theories obviously have greater depth than others. Therein lies a challenge to all psychoanalysts, because the deeper a theory, the harder it is for a psychoanalyst to embrace it. Not only because it takes longer to acquire and structuralize, but because it inevitably involves the clinician in a more exacting personal experience.

Theories, then, have varying degrees of depth potential.

Freud's theory of the dream work gives meaning to the term depth psychology; indeed, he defined depth psychology as the interpretation of dreams. His understanding of how the dream works the previous day's experiences, guided by the self's psychic history, *is* depth psychology. The dream work theory embraces both the phylogentic and the ontological realms of human subjectivity. His use of free association allows us to see some of the work of that depth psychology, thus enabling us to follow chains of ideas that may occur just for a few seconds in a session, or trains of thought that may be elaborated over a life span.

Freud's dream work theory is a complex perceptual matrix that takes years to acquire. Like Lacan's theory of the Symbolic, Imaginary, and Real, or Klein's infantile mind theory, the analyst learning these models must be patient as the acquisition of a form of perception takes time

V

Most students seek 'super-vision' from a clinician steeped in one model of the mind who is gifted in conveying how one can see the material from his or her particular perspective.

An irony of psychoanalytical practice, however, is that for theory to be effective, once it is grasped it must then drop out of consciousness. For this to happen the supervisor must sense when the supervisee has understood the basic paradigms being taught. Once this has happened it is time to stop.

This does not always happen. While it is understandable that a supervisor or teacher will outline, discuss, and indicate how a theory can help the student comprehend certain clinical material it is not so common for the teacher to indicate to the student that after internalization it is in the best interests of the patient and the analyst for the analyst to be without conscious preconception. To this day it is all too widespread a public practice to hear analysts talking about finding the drive derivative in the material, or the ego position, or the here and now transference, or the true self, extending the idea that one can see these matters *continuously* in consciousness.

One of the most troubling features of psychoanalytical training is the degree to which some theories are meant to reside in the analyst's conscious mind all the time. That may be keeping an eye on the analysand's ego position, or projective identifications in the here and now transference, or the drive derivative, or the analyst's personal effect on the analysand. The retention of such theories in consciousness – not allowed to sift down into the unconscious to join other theories – not only leads to a hypertrophied consciousness, but amounts to an unwitting evisceration of the work with unconscious experience. It is unsurprising that a considerable number of analysts are now wondering if the unconscious exists. Little wonder, then, that there is an embarrassing soap opera romancing of consciousness theory in psychoanalysis.

VI

Schools of psychoanalysis are invaluable. It is an ethical obligation, in my view, for all psychoanalysts to immerse themselves in the theoretical orientation of the major schools of psychoanalysis: Freudian, Kleinian, Hartmanian, Kohutian, Bionian, Winnicottian, and Lacanian. To do so is to increase one's perceptual ability, to expand one's mind, to greet patients with a wisdom that can only be realized by passage through difference.

A school usually studies the text of one or two seminal thinkers. Students are taught by experts in that school, sometimes by the seminal thinker, and later by those who have carefully read and scrutinized the writing. Great teachers are invaluable because the way they teach sinks down into the unconscious life of a student and is effective for a lifetime.

A theory is a metasensual phenomenon. It allows one to see something not seen by other theories; to have as an unconscious possibility should clinical need for it arise. To declare oneself against other schools of thought is like someone stating that one is an eye person and does not like the ear or auditory sense data, or for someone to declare that they trust what they hear, but never trust what they smell. The metasensual equivalent, operating in psychoanalysis today – where one needs all the differing perspectives one can possibly structuralize in the course of time – is a form of auto-castration. To entirely oppose the Kleinian or Lacanian view of mental life is to wilfully reduce one's psychic capability as an analyst.

Psychoanalysts need to learn all the theories they can so that they may become unconscious perception-structures enabling practitioners to participate more deeply in the psychoanalytical experience. The analysand's unconscious will sense the range of perceptive receptiveness of the psychoanalyst. This will both deepen and broaden the analysand's skill in unconscious communication. While the work of rendering symptoms, character distortions, pathologic structures, and trauma into consciousness remains a crucial feature of a psychoanalysis, *the work of the unconscious* will increase the analysand's capacity for unconscious perception, creativity, and communication. We see this not so much in the removal of a symptom, pathologic structure, or character deformation (although those, too, will go or be modified) we see it in the way the analysand engages life in a more creative way.

If theory is perception, if it indicates an ethics of practice, it also serves as a sign of the limits of consciousness. However much a theory presumes to tell us something about a person, its actual function is less in what it discovers than in how it sees. Klein's theory of what takes place in the first year of life is less significant than the allegoric perceptual structure that permits us to imagine infancy. Lacan's theory of the subject's instantiation through the chain of signifiers is less a theory of found unconscious meanings than a portal to entering a world of linguistic relations.

Even though the psychoanalyst can only ever know unconscious expression through its effects (or derivatives), these complex articulations are the matrix of our being. As psychoanalytic theories are, among other things, forms of perception, each will inevitably be of some use in helping us to unconsciously perceive unconscious processes and their contents.

Chapter 15

Character and interformality

At the beginning of Soseki Natsume's 1916 novel *Light and Darkness*[1], Tsuda arrives home to meet O'Nobu, his new wife, who is staring intently in the opposite direction. 'Oh, you startled me! – but I'm glad you're back', she says. Tsuda asks what she was doing, and she replies that she was waiting for him. 'As she spoke', writes Natsume, 'she brought together all the brilliance her eyes possessed and cast the full force of it on him. Then she leaned forward somewhat and bowed slightly.'

O'Nobu's eyebrows seem stark set against her fair complexion. She 'also made a habit of twitching them'. Her eyes are 'too narrow' and her 'one-fold eyelids were rather uninteresting', but, Natsume quickly adds, 'the pupils flashing within them were the deepest black, and therefore she used them to very good advantage'. At times her look appeared 'despotic' and Tsuda would find himself 'captivated' by her eyes, although at other times 'for no reason at all, he was suddenly repelled by it'.

O'Nobu's gaze is compelling.

> When he casually raised his head and looked at her, he felt a kind of weird power dwelling momentarily in her eyes. It was a strange brilliance, utterly out of keeping with the tender words she had just been using. His mind, in attempting to frame an answer to her words, was somewhat confused by this glance. Then suddenly she smiled, showing her beautiful teeth. As she did so, the expression in her eyes disappeared without a trace.
>
> (Natsume, 1916: 6)

'His mind' is 'confused by this glance'. Mind cannot think the effect of human character. While it is possible to note which of O'Nobu's features struck him, Tsuda can no more read O'Nobu's actions than O'Nobu could explain them to herself. Natsume draws attention to a different category of communication, the realm in which we do not think our thoughts and then put them into words or

---

1 The original title was *Meian*. The book was not complete at the time of Natsume's death.

signs, but where thoughts arrive as actions. Whatever O'Nobu is doing cannot be grasped by consciousness.

Like the epic poets and novelists of the Western world, from Homer to Joyce, Natsume knows that character speaks through action. The domains of the various types of action are vast, from facial and bodily expression to physical movement through space and time; from the use of images as actions, and words as illocutionary acts, to the employment of any object in the universe of one's culture. (Character speaks through musical objects, through painting, through dance, and so forth.)

When we convey meaning through speech (the symbolic order), the forms through which content is conveyed – the human voice that delivers it; the syntactical form that constructs it; the diction, metre, rhythm, the poetics of form – operate in a different realm from the representational. They are in the domain of the real. They are not representational but *presentational*. (We shall return to this in a moment.)

In seventeenth-century Japan, Hakuin grasped this way of knowing. In a section on 'the way of perfection of action' from *The Four Ways of Knowing of an Awakened Person*, he wrote:

> Coughing, spitting, moving the arms, activity, stillness, all that is done in harmony with the nature of reality, is called knowing through doing things. This is the sphere of freedom of the transformation body (nirmanakaya).
>
> (in Low, 2006: 63)

To act is to realise.

If the internal world refers to the activities of the mind, then character refers to the activities of the self in the real. One may have a very difficult time describing a person's idiom, but the *fact* of idiom is perceivable. In their end-of-year exams, literature students are given previously unseen passages from novelists or poets whom they have studied and they are asked to identify the authors. Since the passages are too brief to be recognised from the thematic content, they can be identified only by the style in which they are written. Likewise, art history students are asked to identify the work of different painters from brief glimpses of details, and music students are played a few seconds of music by various composers in order to test their familiarity with their compositional styles.

In *Being a Character* (1992), I wrote that character is self as form. To know a person's character we have to experience it. In the deepest of relations (in families of origin, in marriages, in psychoanalysis) the self receives thousands of expressions from the other, destined to become the self's impressions of that person.

A character disorder is surely not the same thing as a self's character. Character disorder refers to a stylised (and predictable) forming of one's being, more akin to caricature than character. Repetition of action in the same manner over time freezes idiom into a type of visibility that is impossible when a self's character is free to articulate its idiom. This raises intriguing questions about the possible unconscious desire to retain a character disorder as it allows a holding on to some coherent evidence of the self's uniqueness. Dostoyevsky recognises this pride in *Notes from the Underground* as his protagonist celebrates his uniquely ill character.

Character refers to the pattern of being and relating generated by the idiom of each person's self. Even though the pattern is identifiable, as is, for example, the music of Beethoven, it is not predictable. What Winnicott called the true self, or 'the kernel'[2] of the self as he termed it in his early work, generates an infinite number of spontaneous variations from its core aesthetic intelligence. Character disorder, in this context, may be understood as an area of limitation within the realm of character. Although it might form part of the self's overall character, it would be a part that has been frozen, that repeats itself and is predictable, that is not free to be creatively elaborated.

The character of the analysand uses the analyst through countless micro-actions that in-form the analyst of that individual's idiom. The challenge of this fact of life is that we cannot translate it into words. I cannot tell you what it is like to have experienced my analysands, my wife, my children, or my parents. To be sure, this does not seem to stop us, as we often attempt to tell the other about these people. If the act of narrative is imbued with hopelessness, we tolerate the inevitability of this failure because there is a curious pleasure in the effort to describe the immanental. We cannot represent a person's spirit, but this does not stop the biographer from aiming to do so.

In the novel, play or film we find simulations of character and an awareness of how one person's idiom affects another. When Ibsen creates Hedda Gabler he lets loose on the stage a person whose character vividly impacts those around her. He creates the illusion that Hedda is alive before our eyes, and theatregoers will certainly leave impressed by her character, but his genius at the beginning of the play is that he shows the effect Hedda has had upon those who wait for her to arrive. Her character thus precedes her arrival on the stage. In understanding exactly where character is to be found – in the other as sets of impressions – Ibsen brings character to life perhaps more profoundly and radically than any playwright before him.

The novel, play and film are essential worlds in which we play in the realm of character. In this 'third area'[3] we share with our fellow human beings the otherwise solitary depths of character experience in everyday life. We come away thinking that we have perceived the same thing, that we can talk about the same thing, that we are all part of this together. This illusion is comforting in the face of the ineluctable aloneness of our experiencing of any other's character – and the knowledge that they experience us in the same vein of solitude.

2 'The centre of gravity of consciousness transfers from the kernel to the shell, from the individual to the care, the technique' (Winnicott, 1952: 99).
3 A concept developed by D. W. Winnicott.

My friends and I can talk about all kinds of things, but there is one profound issue that we can never put into words. I cannot tell my friends why they are so important to me, how I feel the shape of their being carrying itself through me, residually organised in an internal matrix of the mind assigned to their being; nor can I ask them 'who am I?' – much as I would be most curious to love to know who I am to my others.

Deep communication, communication from character to character, is encapsulated in *forms* of being and of relating. The relational assumptions that are part of the cultural unconscious – all those rules that elude words – are easily grasped by character, as it is guided first and foremost by processional axioms.

A processional axiom is an assumption about the conduct of being and relating conveyed to the infant and child by parental presences[4] and actions. It is an axiom established through *procedures*, communicated through the infinite lexicon of unconscious behaviours. Although language itself will serve as a means of expressing such axioms, they are not transmitted through verbal explanation. Many will derive from the wider cultural axioms indigenous to the society into which one is born, whilst other core axioms of living will be communicated by the mother's unconscious idiosyncratic interpretation of being. Furthermore, as an infant is not a tabula rasa, maternal communication will always be a formal response to the infant's inherited disposition, unique to each infant–mother couple.

What is the difference between self-representation and self-presentation?

Self-representation is the verbal act of describing the self and its world. It conveys a thought-content – our history, our personality, our tastes – and it is a form of self-disclosing communication especially popular in highly verbal cultures. Indeed, in the United States some schools of psychoanalytic thought place great emphasis on the analyst's self-disclosure. So, for example, an analyst might decide to tell the analysand of a personal experience in his life in order to share with her how he too has suffered from difficulties.

The conscious aim of such a self-representation might be to demonstrate that the analyst is an ordinary human. Yet a quite different message may reside within the *form* the disclosure takes. The unconscious self-presentation might be, for example, seductive or patronising. Self-presentation, from the linguistic point of view, conveys the self's being via the unconscious form of the narrative. It is the formal movement of one's self acting upon the object world.

In his novel, Natsume plays with a belief that it is possible to observe the shape of such self-presentation upon the other after the interaction has ended. He describes the moments after Tsuda has visited some 'friends', the Yoshikawas. O'Nobu greets him as he enters the house.

'It was the Yoshikawas, wasn't it?'

'You're right.'

---

4 A 'presence' would be an attitude about being conveyed through a specific way of being in the moment.

'I can usually tell by your manner.'

Tsuda protests that she must have figured this out from what he had said before the visit. But O'Nobu is not to be put off:

'Even if you hadn't said that, I'm sure I'd have known.'

Natsume is illustrating here the trace of character. O'Nobu knows that he has visited the Yoshikawas because she discerns the pattern of their effect upon him; she perceives that something of their personalities has entered Tsuda. Up to a point, the theory of projective identification helps us understand O'Nobu's perception. It gives us a way of conceptualising a recipient who finds himself with what are otherwise alien thoughts or feelings that have been projected into him by an other. However, this model does not take account of the movement of character.

As Tsuda gets to know O'Nobu, just as all partners get to know one another, knowledge is acquired unconsciously as each becomes the object of the other's use. Of course, projective identifications take place. Partners hold projected aspects of one another and, to refer to the work of Joseph Sandler, they share differing roles and role relationships. But the density of any person's being and their axioms of relating are too complex to be understood simply as discrete and discernable projections or role representations.

Another essay should certainly be devoted to the effects of this movement upon the recipient. We might consider the possibility that our encounter with another character, a deep level of self-employment, is in some ways intrinsically and universally traumatic. As the self in the moment, it is not possible to know what one is enduring, but an *après coup* occurs sometime after the encounter with the other's character, and this may be experienced in many different ways.

Character communication is the heart of human interrelating and so deeply affecting that it often needs to be spoken about afterwards. After a meeting, a social engagement or a chance encounter we may need to talk. Talking aims to transform the real into the symbolic, and even if this fails to represent the presentations of the experience it *adheres* to the experience and carries its after-effect in verbal form. Even if we do not turn to actual others we may have an internal dialogue about the recent encounter in which memory functions as a dynamic container for the after-effects of the real.

In this respect the 'talking cure' meets an ordinary human need to transform the impact of the other, and especially the traumatogenic effect of being a child, existing with the things called a mother and a father, within the entity called a family.

The internal effect of the other on the self may begin in advance of the encounter in the real. When I anticipate meeting up with a close friend the next day I may have a 'preview' of this meeting. The forms of the preview will vary – they might include memories of recent conversations, a shared event, a dream about my friend. I will almost always have a snapshot in my mind of what he looks like, and condensed into this picture will be a moving collage of his characteristic mannerisms and gestures. Upon meeting, in the lived experience of this moment, those anticipations are realised through the actuality of this other's presence. It has been looked forward to, it is a moment embraced in time, but it is also a stimulating formal event as my friend's force of character impresses itself on me.

How does the analyst analyse this aspect of character?

To analyse, in this area, is to engage in perceptive identification,[5] which is derived from the work of the receptive unconscious.

To receive another's character requires an unconscious decision on the recipient's part to allow this. This decision may be communicated as the intelligence of reception, the capacity to allow the self to be impressed by the other. The roots of this capacity are pleasurable; they reside in the mother's receptive relation to her infant, and we carry it forward as adults in the way we enjoy receiving other people and the object world.

To engage this receptiveness in the psychoanalytic space the analyst must empty his mind, to be in Bion's terms 'without memory or desire', so that unconscious character-perception is possible.

One can perceive character, in an analysis, only when one recognises the impossibility of organising such perception into themes. Character disorders can be organised in this way, but with character itself it is impossible.

The need to structure what we experience into something wordable is a feature of human omnipotence. To allow something to exist, to know of it, and yet to give up the effort to word it takes rigour and consistency, but also an understanding of phenomenological categories. To illustrate this with an analogy: whilst it is possible to recite the lyrics of a song, it is not possible to recreate verbally the sounds that constitute the complexity of the music within which the lyrics reside. So we can describe a character disorder rather as we can describe the lyrics of a song, but we can never put character into words in the same way.

While narrative free association informs the analyst of the *contents* of the mind, revealed through the chain of ideas, *character association* informs the analyst of the *idiom* of the analysand's being and relating through the sequence and idiom of actions.

To attend to this sequence the analyst might report his impressions of the analysand. Such comments are not interpretations and should be expressed in the form of observations. So let us imagine for a moment that O'Nobu is in analysis. Upon greeting her in the waiting room the analyst notes that she has her back turned and seems shocked by his arrival. He might then say 'you seem shocked'. In another moment on a different day when she is 'bringing together all the brilliance her eyes possessed' as if she is 'casting the full force of it' on the analyst, he might say 'what a powerful gaze . . .'.

Equally, however, the analyst's own formal response might communicate these observations, eliminating the need for verbal comment. When O'Nobu seems shocked to see him, the analyst might raise an eyebrow, thus registering his perception of this feature of her character. When she throws her gaze upon him,

5 See 'Perceptive Identification', in *The Freudian Moment* (Bollas, 2007a).

he might lean ever-so-slightly backwards. Such responses would ordinarily be unconscious but would express the analyst's formal registration of being impressed. It is important to keep in mind, however, that the *way* one analyst raises an eyebrow or leans back will differ formally from the way another analyst does the same thing. Even at the level of ordinary gesture we all appear or behave idiosyncratically.

As time passes, however, the analysand comes to understand and to accept that the psychoanalyst will on occasion comment on the analysand's idiom. Sometimes these observations may lead to interpretation, but for the most part they are reports of impressions. They have a very different feel to them from concept-driven interpretations. The very looseness of the impressionable gives the analyst a form of freedom that cannot accompany interpretation proper. It is as if the analyst places these impressions into an intermediate space between self and other where they gradually become part of a matrix, a shared sense of the analysand's being.

It is important that this function is noted. The analysand increasingly appreciates that her idiom is being received by the other, that the art-form of character is now recognised in this theatre specifically designed for its expression. Indescribable, yet at the heart of human communication, this fact needs verbal witnessing.[6]

The analyst working with the other's character does so form to form, in the way he shapes a sentence, lays stress on certain words and not others, decides when to allow silence to speak on his behalf following an important communication from the patient, allows for affections to articulate themselves like punctuation from the world of human sensibility. These decisions are also actions. They operate from and within the realm of character.

What is the analyst's frame of mind during the act of reception? Such work is, of course, overdetermined. The complexity of a psychoanalysis means that in any moment the analyst may be receiving many categories of communication from the analysand, including the logic of sequence in the narrative, the enigma of a symptom, or the puzzle of the character disorder. But when it comes to character reception the analyst's sensibility is akin to the frame of mind one is in when listening to poetry. It is a form of meditation, a type of concentration, when one suspends critical judgement and the search for meaning so that a part of one's unconscious may be shaped by the other.

Let us consider, for example, three of the elements that go into this form of meditative listening. As we listen to a poet we are affected by verbal style, by inflection and by illocution. Verbal style refers to a speaker's selection and arrangement of words. Inflection refers to a speaker's alteration of the form of a word to reflect its grammatical function, through pitch, tone and volume. Illocution – especially as formulated by J. L. Austin (1962) – refers to the intent of a speaker, as opposed to the literal meaning of the utterance. These three vectors, each a

---

6 The analyst's function as a witness to his patient's life is movingly described in W. S. Poland, 'The Analyst's Witnessing and Otherness' (2000).

category in which a speaker expresses her idiom through the act (action) of speaking, are some of the ingredients of character as form.

In *The Freudian Moment* (2007a) I proposed that we are unconsciously driven to find someone to whom we can tell our dream and with whom its wisdom can be explored. When Freud created the psychoanalytic space, the core axis of which is the analysand free associating to the dream whilst the analyst engages in deep free listening, he provided a conceptualisation of a phylogenetic need, or preconception. The realisation of this phylogenetic preconception was as radical a step forward in human relations as any that preceded it – akin to Shakespeare's reframing of the Western mind – but its revolutionary approach has been repressed by the psychoanalytic movement, which has, for complex reasons, found Freud's invention disconcerting.

To complement Freud's revolution in the development of thought through a new type of relationship, there has been a contrasting revolution in intersubjectivity which we can term the Winnicottian Moment.

The Winnicottian Moment realises the need for the true self to communicate being-to-being, with its primary other. From a phylogenetic perspective this would originally have taken the form of the self's wish to meet his God – and from an individual perspective it may still take this form. In Winnicott's psychoanalytic space, which simulated the infant's relation to the mother, the self's unconditional being was met by this primary other. Thus he realised a phylogenetic need: he placed the self before the God that gave him being. When Marion Milner, his analysand, colleague and friend, sought a title for her account of her work with a highly disturbed young woman, she chose *The Hands of the Living God* (1969).

Winnicott intuitively found a way for the self to re-experience its origins through the transferential illusion of infant with mother: the arrival of a desired *après coup*. The second coming of the non-verbal, a repeat of the remarkable constituents of the infant–mother relation recast in adult life, it is as if the adult can be in on the beginnings of the self: in touch with the other who receives the self's being-as-is, with a seeming unconditional love

As people journey through the life cycle they share their immanent being, expressed through the forms of engagement between self and other. Different societies have evolved differing forms for sharing the life cycle. In Japanese culture there resides the unique relational phenomenon of 'amae'[7] (the generative state of dependence upon the expected grace of the other) that begins with the infant's relation to the mother and ramifies throughout all subsequent intimate social relations. Japanese intimacy, predicated on the axioms of amae, therefore generates many non-verbal forms for the reciprocal move of one character into and through the other.

---

7 All students not only of Japanese culture but of human personality will forever be indebted to the genius of Takeo Doi's comprehension of how amae functions in Japan and in human relations (see Doi, 1971).

For this reciprocal movement of the idioms of two selves, I suggest the term *interformality*.

If intersubjectivity refers to the unconscious communication of unconscious ideas between two subjects, then interformality refers to the way in which we are affected by the way the other forms (or transforms) a communicated axiom into his or her own peculiar idiomatic delivery. The intersubjective (content) and the interformal (form) constitute the core vectors of what Winnicott termed 'interrelating'. These terms allow psychoanalysts to consider the play of ideas and the play of forms: two different but complementary categories of communication.

Unconscious axioms form part of the structure of the self's mentality and are available for expression as a feature of the self's sensibility. One such axiom might be, 'I must find and evoke the other's empathy to store for future use.' But there would be many forms in which that empathy could be elicited from the other. It could be by stumbling, or indicating some physical vulnerability; it could take the form of telling of some sad event in the self's recent life; it could be communicated through a subtle facial expression. All of this is unconscious, and it will affect the other; it is part of the interformality of human relations.

In 'The Capacity To Be Alone', Winnicott writes: 'Ego-relatedness refers to the relationship between two people, one of whom at any rate is alone; perhaps both are alone, yet the presence of each is important to the other' (1958: 31). He concludes that this relatedness has to do with 'liking' one another and is an ego activity, while 'loving' is more of an id relationship. In this way, Winnicott brings the capacity to be alone into the relational field. The two people feel the shape of individual solitude in each, they sense its interformal effect, and this imbues both with a sense of deep communicating that is profound but unworded. In a Winnicottian analysis it is viewed as an accomplishment for the analysand to develop the capacity to be alone whilst in relation to the analyst.

As we approach the conclusion of this essay we shall take these thoughts a step further, linking them to Freud's metapsychology and defining more clearly the role and function of character reception.

Freud argues that the primary repressed unconscious is formed early on (before secondary repression) through the self's encounter with 'things'. These things leave impressions on the ego that form into clusters based on early memories of these encounters. Freud included in this early thing-world the mother-as-thing, who impresses on the infant through thousands of everyday ministrations the thingness of her being.

In interformal relations the participants are affected by one another's character. As the analysand conveys himself in the real, through countless impressions upon the analyst, the analyst receives the analysand's form and will bear these impressions. Whilst in an analysis the structural axioms of character are negotiable up to a point – especially through transference interpretation in analysis – the formal presentations of character are irreducible. A French person is still himself when speaking Russian. Indeed, this irreducible character dimension, a baseline to each personality, sometimes brings about despair in analysts who would like to effect change in this domain. But in leaving it alone one does not leave the self in isolation. On the contrary, in the communication between two idioms a remarkable rendezvous of two irreducible natures is accomplished.

In a classically based psychoanalysis, both participants understand the rules of the game, so to speak: that the analyst lessens his character effect in order to give more room to the analysand's character so that it may be the more determinative of the two. Nonetheless, the analysand will experience aspects of the psychoanalyst's character, and that experience will be impressive and deep. It cannot be translated into another category (the imaginary or symbolic) any more than the analyst can translate the patient's character into representation.

So, what can we know from the experience of the other's character? How do we define this knowledge? Of what use is it?

This is a knowledge that *just is*. Such knowledge is part of the matrix of human intuition. We intuit one another; as the other's medium, we have been in-formed of the other's idiom of being. And we use this information to guide us in the countless unconscious decisions about what to say, when to say it, how to say it, and all the subtle cues that we pass back to the other as part of the movement of interformality.

Over the many years of a psychoanalysis the analysand comes to know how deeply he has informed his analyst. This is not a matter of what the analyst knows about the history, the sexual desires, the psychic states, or the emotional travails of the patient – although these are important dimensions – it is that the core of his being has been 'held' through formal reception. This unrepresentable fact of self-presentation constitutes one crucial aspect of the depth of this depth psychology.

The analysand is *always* a recipient of the analyst's formal effect. A psychoanalyst may be rejected early on by a patient, not because of what she says to the analysand but because of who she is. Neither participant may realise this consciously and both may seek some other reason, but the right of such rejection is a fundamental right of human personality.

A question arises.

If character is expressed as a movement of diverse forms, affecting those who encounter it, will it not be subject to the other's interpretation? Surely we must differ in the way we perceive an individual's character? And, furthermore, will we in turn not have some interformal effect upon this thing, such that in a true interaction what we perceive will be partly a return of our own form, projected back to us by the subject?

No matter how one is perceived by the other, the premise of this essay is that character is the DNA of individual being. One's self as idiom of form. We are certainly influenced by the other's form – it moves through us and leaves impressions – and we in turn will affect the other with our own idiom. We will also be engaged in constant interformal exchanges, and this is certainly a type of deep communicating. But our DNA remains as is.

People may be drawn to one another because of similarities in their personal tastes and formal approaches to life, or they may be attracted to differences, but either way in a thriving interformal relation the participants will be inviting greater, deeper and more extensive interformality. Two people who are intimately 'into one another' have found ways to engage one another's formal expressions. Actions may be few, words silent, but there will be a matrix of formal understandings. Form to form, one being to another being, is part of the unthought known. The unthought known may indeed be the basis of a *jouissance* of the interformal real, the bliss of *thoughtless* engagement between self and other.

The American poet, William Carlos Williams defined imagist poetry as 'no ideas but in things'.[8] The poetry critic Lewis Turco believes this is very similar to the ambition of Haiku. 'The Zen poet', he writes, 'is trying to put himself or herself into the place of the thing perceived, empathizing with the inanimate object . . . trying to become one with the object and thus all things.' He adds that 'the haiku has perhaps been best described as "a moment of intense perception" ' (2000: 230).

I shall quote two passages from Basho:[9]

> A bee
> Staggers out
>   of the peony.
>   . . .
>   Exciting at first,
> Then sad,
>   Watching the cormorant-fishing.

In recent years I have watched my peonies grow and blossom and I have seen the bees come staggering out of them. Every year I watch the cormorant, awkward-flying yet sleek, fishing in the water.

A few lines about a bee convey the exhilaration of life. A few lines about a cormorant evoke the pathos of our being.

Haiku finds a form of wording that mirrors the interformal real of the natural world. The style of this poetry is a thing-in-itself that moves words into juxtaposed positions, to evoke images of things that in turn reflect human emotion. It moves our being into the object world, it mingles us with the other things of life, and it brings this meeting (this interformality) back to us. This is no doubt one reason why many Occidental poets – Gary Snyder, Robert Hass and others – have found in Haiku the remarkable power of poetry to move us through the form of things.

Similarly, in a good psychoanalysis the interformality of character relations involves moments of intense perception in which patient and analyst speak to one another from within the thing-itself, from within the thing of being, from within the heart of human moments and personal encounters.

8 In Lewis Turco, *The Book of Forms* (2000).
9 Translated by Robert Hass, in *The Essential Haiku* (Hass, 1994).

Chapter 16

The wisdom of the dream

I

For millennia, throughout the ancient Middle East, people would travel to a sacred space to ask a question of a god or divine being.

For the most part the question had to be answered by a priest or specially designated person whose task it was to submit the question to the god and then translate the answer to the seeker.

The word 'oracle' is used to denote both the person who functions as the intermediary and the message. They are not separated. *The Free Dictionary*[1] (states that an oracle is 'a person, such as a priestess, through whom a deity is held to respond when consulted', but it also defines it as 'the response given through such a medium, often in the form of an enigmatic statement or allegory'.

We shall return later to this interesting fusion between object and other, between message and medium.

In ancient Greece the seeker would go to a sacred place and, after performing certain rituals, would receive a special dream. The rituals preceding the dream and the act of sleeping were considered to produce 'incubation' oracles. The seeker expected to receive a lucid dream, one that would provide an answer to a pressing question. When dreamt in the sacred space a dream thus became an oracle, a 'divine announcement', a message from a god.

The dream expressed wisdom. It constituted *a form* of guidance.

In psychoanalysis, the analysand becomes a seeker of dreams and the psychoanalytic frame becomes part of a ritual preparation for their incubation. The dream arrives. The analysand takes the dream to analysis and to the analyst – both to the process and to the other who is its official guardian.

The sleeping analysand is *in analysis*, mid-way between the dream day's evocative experiences and the following session's conversation with the psychoanalyst. The dream is therefore dreamt within the analysis. It is both created and

---

1 www.thefreedictionary.com

explored in a particular psychic space, one in which the dreamer knows that the dream will impart some wisdom about him/herself. In that respect, this combination of place and event constitutes the modern oracular.

The psychoanalyst is involved with the dream and its contents in certain ways that are similar to the roles of the ancient priests or shamans. The interpreter and the dream, the container and the contained, become almost indistinguishable from one another. Thus the psychoanalyst is regarded as a highly special person – almost like a religious figure, but also a potentially frightening one.

There are not as many psychoanalytic consulting rooms as there are churches or temples, but there are still many thousands of these sites around the world. Every day, analysands walk into these sacred spaces bearing their dreams. Usually places of privacy, people have taken recently to photographing these sites, with the results displayed at conferences or published in books. It seems that psychoanalysts themselves are just as fascinated by the sites of analysis.

However, if these sites offer a special form of *jouissance* for their participants, both analysand and psychoanalyst know the price they must pay for this secret bliss. They suffer the persecutory anxiety of being seen to participate in some form of soon-to-be banished forbidden activity. And in spite of all the efforts to sanitise the appearances of psychoanalysis through verbal dry cleanings – 'evidence-based practice' or 'competencies' – the psychoanalyst is still widely regarded as someone dripping in the unseemly. He is still the Freudian, hanging out with sexuality and aggression; still the figure who encourages discussion of that which culture insists should be forbidden.

Like the confusion surrounding the term oracle – is it the message or the other? – the psychoanalyst is confused with the dream. Like the dream, he is meant to stay in his place. A dream displaced can become a terrifying hallucination, and the psychoanalyst who appears outside his space is a disturbing spectre indeed. It is little wonder that when contributing to cultural or political debate he will tend to dress in some other outfit: as a psychiatrist, psychologist, philosopher or literary critic.

In the public or social domain, the psychoanalyst creates immediate anxieties about his ability to read the minds of those around him. This idea may be absurd, but it holds sway nonetheless, and it arises, perhaps, because the psychoanalyst is seen to embody the mystery of the dream. By encouraging the analysand to bring the dream into the light of day, he illuminates objects of the night. Dreams should remain in their place. And so should psychoanalysts.

But the analyst does something else to heighten this complicity: he asks the dreamer for associations. By doing this he transforms the dream into an oracle and gives it a uniquely powerful place, not simply within the analysis but in the ongoing life of the analysand forever. Long after the treatment is ended, the analysand will look upon his/her dreams in a very particular way.

By asking for associations the ordinary verbal descriptions of a life are shifted from gossip, reports of domestic events, indexical accounts of self states and so forth to dream derivatives. Even as the everyday spills out through the process of free association, and even if the dream seems displaced by the day residues and memories, these contents differ from simple accounts. Because they are dream associations, they are resignified. What might seem to be a simple, ordinary association becomes the vehicle of the dreamer and evidence of the unconscious at work during the day, picking through our experiences to weave tapestries of thought, some of which will arrive in the dream space.

Associations to the dream are, as Freud taught, indistinguishable from the dream itself. The dream ramifies through the associations, spreading its condensed contents throughout a widening field of objects that have an infinite reach. Fortunately, however, Freud had a specific task. He was there not simply as a witness to the dream process; he aimed to discover what the dream could tell him about what might be ailing the dreamer. Whilst acknowledging that a dream contained an infinite web of meanings, he set a limit to its logic within his own practice.

Had he not done so he might have suffered the fate of those academics who, steeped in psychoanalytic thinking, return to the same poem or text time after time to discover that, through a process of renewed free association, the text will yield endless new connections.

We may see, then, how important it is for the psychoanalyst to have a local interest in a dream. He must be after *the* meaning of a dream even as he knows that it has many meanings. Were he to ask the dreamer to re-present the same dream each day, to subject it to a new set of associations, then he and the analysand would discover that the single dream would endlessly render further meanings and open up new avenues of thought.

Psychoanalysts are bemused by the fact that when any group of analysts considers a reported session, each one emerges with a different reading of the material. This is a troubling reality. Despite a reluctant move towards pluralism occasioned by the politics of difference, the illusion remains that there must exist some 'correct' interpretation.

Any complex dream is a condensation of thousands of latent ideas. It is constructed from the day residue – a particular day event is nominated for dreaming because it is unconsciously perceived as already representing a condensation of meanings. Any dream reported day after day would always yield new associations because the events of a day are part of the dream fabric of life.

Perhaps it is just too disturbing to consider the implications of the myriad meanings of a single dream. The method of free association gains access to this infinity of meaning, to a world of thinking and of communicating that is entirely outside of consciousness. Indeed, consciousness simply cannot claim agency of thought. It can only ever be a momentary simulacrum of those unconscious processes that continue to scan our universe alongside, within, and long after the expository claim of consciousness.

So does the psychoanalyst protect the analysand from this secret?

Psychoanalysts vary in the frequency with which they interpret an analysand's material. Some are quite talkative, translating perceived unconscious ideas or motives into consciousness. Their sessions are rather like dialogues. Other analysts say little for weeks; the analysand is cut loose onto the seas of free associations, with any islands of lucidity experienced as almost hallucinatory moments, as new waves of association displace unities of thought.

These are two experiences at opposite ends of a spectrum.

But let us consider, for sake of discussion, a middle-ground analyst who says little for some sessions but who is not ideologically opposed to making interpretations and who could even be rather wordy from time to time. His analysand will have two kinds of experience of analysis. There will be long periods where the analysand is at sea with just a few islands of conscious sense. So the analytic journey will move in an unforeseeable path from island to island.

Note that I do not say that the *analysis* will be at sea.

It is striking that when people who have had long analyses are asked what it was like, they rarely describe the islands of sense. They are more likely to say that it was an impossible-to-describe experience. Their memory may be that they were at sea for most of the time.

If we are at sea in our own unconscious, where are we?

We are in a certain position or place, one that facilitates articulations of the unconscious through the process of free association. The self becomes the medium for other *forms* of thinking, those that exist outside consciousness.

Now and then these unconscious articulations bundle together into 'nodes' or groups of ideas that enter consciousness and can be thought about. Indeed this may happen regularly enough for us to evolve a certain conscious appreciation for our relation to our own unconscious. The analysand and the analyst are in a rather daring place. Both find themselves within a process with no limit other than that imposed by the task of analysing symptoms or pathologies or aspects of character. Otherwise, they experience together the strange character of unconscious thinking. And it may be possible for them to discuss this very special form of object relation.

When the dream becomes an oracle in psychoanalysis – when it is spoken – both participants are immediate and intimate partners in shared relation to a source of wisdom. By virtue of the dream's representation of knowledge through the figure of the dreamer, this other person becomes – so to speak – the self's Orpheus in the other world.

Imagine this other self to be like a double. Analyst and patient associate to the actions of the double and over time become familiar with the analysand's other self, who becomes an increasingly familiar figure in their considerations. Sometimes we have the experience of meeting our double in the dream space. Whether due to the content of the dream or a disruption in the night, we enter the dream experience as a conscious being, aware that a dream is taking place. As we watch our double going about the dream experiences, we remind ourselves that this is just a dream.

The lucid dream is a rendezvous of two parts of a self.

II

The ancients looked forward to dreaming; they believed they would be visited by a divine being that would speak to them through the dream. In other words, they consciously sought news from their own unconscious.

And of course it is here, in searching for a dream and in the awareness of the wisdom of the dream, that psychoanalysis and ancient oracular culture share qualities in common. The psychoanalyst and his analysand hope for a dream, a redolent dream that might prove to be illuminating. And these dreams produce pleasure, even awe, at the revelation. The analytic pair are in debt to the dreamer who has constructed this oracle that meets the desire for wisdom and that may solve pressing problems in the life of the analysand.

In *The Infinite Question* (2009b) I addressed the ways in which analysands are unconsciously at work, aiming to objectify their conflicts in the interests both of gaining unconscious insight and of relieving the self of pain by resolving problems.

In recent years I have noticed something that is perhaps widely noted but that I had not truly appreciated. In difficult or urgent times analysands often have dreams that seem to take up their problems in ways that are illuminating and helpful. These dreams are ordinarily not too complex and may be lucid. One analysand, for example, was uncertain of whether to move into the financial world, where he would make a lot of money, or to remain in a more artistic realm where he would make less income but where he thought he would have a more fulfilling life. During the week in which he was to be forced to make his decision, he had a sequence of dreams. On the Sunday night he dreamt that he was at the financial place of work being welcomed by new colleagues. They were all 'suits', and he had mixed feelings – he was pleased to find himself in such a prestigious environment but he also felt out of place. On Monday he dreamed again that he was in the same workplace, but on his lunch break he wandered down a hallway and entered a room where he found people making ceramics: the other profession he had hoped for but was giving up. He felt an intense sense of loss – the art space was where he should truly be – but he was overcome with a feeling that he should return quickly to the financial world. On Tuesday night he dreamed that he ran into an old friend from childhood outside a railway station. The old friend knew him better than anyone else. The friend said 'so where is your studio? I would love to see your work' but the analysand had to reply that he had given it up, to which his friend shook his head sadly and said 'that was nuts'.

During the weeks preceding the dreams the analysand had consciously considered all the options. It made economic sense to work for ten years with this financial firm because then he could put money aside to help with his children's college educations. On the other hand, he countered, he would see little of his children if he took this line of work. He had wondered whether the world of finance represented adult life and the artistic world childhood. Perhaps he should accept that finance was the equivalent of maturation and just decide to grow up.

These were intellectual reasons. But when his dreams arrived they did so with emotional force and vivid clarity. There was no doubt *within* the dreams that the dream logic favoured his remaining an artist, and his free associations followed lines of thought that confirmed this view. Although he countered with more conscious options, the force of the dream seemed truer. When the friend bemoaned his decision, he felt it was a revelation. Finally he came to a session and announced that he now believed he should not work for the company, and he resumed his career as an artist.

Piqued by this facet of his analysis, I began to note that this was a more common-place event than I had realised. Other analysands in difficulty produced a dream or series of dreams that seemed intent on objectifying the very problem that the individual was discussing in analysis, and often they seemed to supply an answer.

Of course, we could think of this as mere wish-fulfilment – and surely it must be that at the very least – and we might have to allow that these persons could be wrong in accepting the advice of the dreaming self. However, I want to focus on something else.

During such times, the wakeful self and the dreamer seemed to be closer to one another than at other times. Indeed, they seem to know about each other *in situ*. The dreamer seems to know the wakeful self is present; the wakeful self seems to be watching the theatre of the dream in anticipation of what will unfold.

The two aspects of the self are aware of one another. Indeed, I think it is proper for us to consider this a form of relationship. It is intrasubjective, constituted out of two subjective positions – the night self and the day self – that are continuously inter-dependent throughout the lifespan and that seem to recognise their relative positions.

Our night self seems more than willing to engage intensely with our existential dilemmas and to enlist our wakeful self in the effort to objectify the issues. Does the night self know of the occasional visit of the day self?

I believe I can answer this only in a limited and tentative way. When a person is in psychoanalysis, both analyst and analysand seek the dream – this search is a designated analytic task. We can observe how the sustained act of psychoanalysis cultivates an unconscious communication between the night self and its double. What I propose is that, due to the uniquely sustained interest on the part of analyst and patient in the patient's dream self, the night self begins *knowingly* to dream *for* the day self. This constitutes a new form of object relation and a type of reverse wish-fulfilment. The sleeping self discovers an other who is listening.

In *The Freudian Moment* (2007a) I considered the idea that psychoanalysis fulfils a phylogenetic need. My reading of ancient texts indicates that the dreamer has always been in search of the listener to the dream and, eventually, of the one who puts the dream in a special place where this part of us can be understood. And we certainly know from our study of infancy and ego formation that the maternal unconscious informs the infant of axioms that become part of the self's unthought known. This primary object relation conveys assumptions that become assimi-lated into the ego and thus become structures that govern part of mental and relational life. My argument here is that when the phylogenetic preconception (the search for dream understanding) meets with the psychoanalytic process, it comes to a structural realisation in which the dreaming self is now dreaming for its other: for consciousness.

We may see, therefore, in the formation of psychoanalysis, the fulfilment of an ancient wish for the self to come to an oracular place, a place in which to have a dream that will bear wisdom. The site of the ancient oracle can be seen as a fore-runner of the analytic consulting room, the priestly intermediary as the prede-cessor of the interpreting analyst.

The argument I propose now is that the relation of analyst and analysand *to* the patient's dream life *becomes structuralised* within the analysand. What begins in psychoanalysis as a relation of two minds to the dream life of one becomes part of the mental function of the analysand. The dreamer now assumes the continuous presence of an auditory interpreter who is continuously in touch with dreams.

Why is it structuralised?

We cannot assume that all object relations become part of the self's mental structure. Often an introject will do. When a patient says 'And then I heard your voice saying . . .' this indicates the presence of an introject but not yet the fulfil-ment of structuralisation. Likewise, a dreamer may simply represent the day self as an internal witness to the dream, but if the night self actually dreams *on behalf of* the day self, serving an overall wish of the self-as-a-whole, this shows that a relation has become part of mental structure.

The formation of this inner structure – the pairing of the doubles through whom we imagine ourselves – constitutes a step forward in the development of our minds. By bridging the worlds of night and day, psychoanalysis brings together two worlds of thinking, two intrapsychic positions that, once structuralised, can then work in partnership.

A good analysis indicates this accomplishment. The analysand does not so much report the dream as indicate through sentient narrative the collaboration of the two realms. Patients seem to 'lose' the distinction between the night self and the day self, but this loss signifies the development of a structural gain. Mental life now operates with the two domains in continuous creative relation to one another.

We have long understood that from the point (or position) of the conscious self the other is the unconscious. But now we may add that after structuralisation of the Freudian Pair,[2] consciousness also becomes the 'other' for the unconscious. As we dream, we are informed by the presence of the listening other, an other that is contributing thought to the process of dream life and was invested all along in interpreting the creative work of the dream.

Writers, composers and others know something of this structure. The novelist writes from the unconscious but scans the arriving fictions with the interpretive

2 The Freudian Pair is a term I use to identify the functions performed by the analysand (free association) and the psychoanalyst (free listening) which *together* constitute the uniquely Freudian
   relationship.

scalpel of consciousness. In time the two orders not only work together, they rely upon one another. An inner structure has been created. In this respect, psychoanalysis takes its place in the evolution of this acquisition of structure, the one we find in the creative arts.

III

If there are dreams that fulfil the analysand's wish for wisdom, there are also dreams that seem designed to frustrate the desire for understanding. Some appear to have a sort of theatrical integrity – the course of events in the dream seems more or less self-explanatory. Others are bizarre, enigmatic dreams that are representationally baffling. The ancients understood this and viewed the latter type as requiring interpretation.

Similarly nowadays, psychoanalysis has two fundamentally different ways of approaching dreams.

To express a complex topic in simple terms, those dreams that seem to present unconscious ideas as a theatrical story, relatively undisguised, tend to be interpreted at the manifest level according to the school of object relations. We might say that this type of dream fulfils the Freudian Pair's wish to be the recipients of the dreamer's wisdom. However, the dreams that are too enigmatic for such a quick understanding pose more of a riddle. Like the riddle of the Sphinx, they are let loose on the helpless – fateful, possibly deadly, bearing disturbing ideas. For these we require the Freudian technique of patiently examining the dream in its constituent parts, subjecting them to free associations, and reassembling the product into a newly formed and now coherent gestalt.

In other words, the form of the dream may vary – from the clear to the enigmatic – according to whether its function is to solve problems or to present new and troubling dilemmas for consideration.

The interpreter of dreams always has a choice – rather like that of any theatregoer. We can attend to the manifest *content* of the play – to the characters, their actions, relations and feelings, and to what they seem to be talking about. Or we can examine the underlying *form* of the work, with its specific language and idiomatic effects. The two are parallel elements of meaning. The theatrical presentation may overlap with the semantic one, but they represent different categories of articulation.

A dreamer in need of wisdom is likely to be disappointed if he finds himself presented with an enigmatic dream. Similarly, a dreamer who needs the representation of troubling material in order to engage with his unconscious problems may feel cheated if he produces a simple theatrical dream.

However, the ego's choice – simple dream or enigmatic dream – may reflect an unconscious wisdom.

I have referred to the difference between any particular dream and the process of dreaming. If we turn our attention to the self's experience of a dream, there is always an implicit *Nachträglichkeit* (deferred action, or *après coup*) in the analytic session in which the dream is recollected. The conscious self may receive deferred affect and meaning from even an apparently inconsequential dream.

Freud's simple term 'dream work' (an astonishing but wonderful understatement) denotes a way of thinking completely different both from the thought world of consciousness and from the shared reality of everyday life. As the participants in a psychoanalysis work every day with the structure of dreaming, they explore repeatedly a world that becomes increasingly familiar. In so doing, both engage in a form of unconscious communication, one that takes place between their joint intersubjective and interformal consciousness and the dream life.

However accurate or inaccurate the individual interpretation of a dream may be, the *process* of psychoanalysis is always increasing the self's unconscious understanding of the dream process.

But how is it possible to make a statement such as this? How can we say that we develop an increased unconscious communication with our own unconscious?

I think of it this way.

Everyone dreams. And people often think about their dreams. But psychoanalysis establishes a partnership (the Freudian Pair) that extends the dream and communicates with it. The ego now grasps that it has a partner, and we discover another pairing: the one between the ego that offers the matrix of its own creativity in the form of the dream and the analysand who transforms the material into a new form of unconsciously worked-upon meaning. Over time, the Freudian Pair becomes structuralised and sets up a new paradigm within the ego that proceeds to generate more sophisticated forms of unconscious work.

A painter *imagines* his object. His operational unconscious connects to the imagined and transforms it into a painting.

A composer hears the condensed matrix of a melody delivered from the unconscious. His musical intelligence transforms this into a composition.

Psychoanalyst and analysand receive the dream, but as they study the dream process (like the painter studies painting or the musician, music) they develop unconscious abilities to connect to the structure of the dream and to extend it. Over time the analysand structuralises this new relationship and continues, even after the analysis is over, to generate the Freudian Pair as an internal structure.

IV

The wisdom of the dream, then, lies in its projection of meaning to the dreamer who, if he or she works with the structure of the dream, can transform it into new forms of creative insight.

Dreams have always contained this wisdom. Psychoanalysis searches for the wisdom contained in each dream and, over time, transmutes this search for meaning into an internal structure. Wisdom is then 'found' in an ongoing mental structure that produces flashes of insight born of this encounter.

This accomplishment comes with that irony that informs the history of a self's search for wisdom. Across the millennia and in many cultures that irony has taken an aphoristic form: in order to find one's way, one must search without searching. To attain wisdom, one must accomplish a certain humility. It cannot be found through a clever premeditated path towards it. It will arrive only if one can put oneself in a certain position, a wakeful sleep, or meditation, or lost-in-thought, in which the search is forgotten.

Freud's methodology of simply talking what is on the mind without trying to search for the truth is an act of revolutionary genius that makes available to ordinary man the gift of wisdom.

Seen in this light, the structuralisation of the Freudian Pair creates a tension between the curiosity of consciousness and the creativity of the unconscious. It concerns not so much the psychopathology of everyday life as the *psychocreativity* of everyday life. The phrases that simply pop unbidden into the human mind are packaged statements with ramifying implications. In an analysis this work can result in epiphanic moments: sudden flashes of knowledge about the self, the other, or life.

How many dreams does the analysand report in an average analysis? Imagine it is a five-times-a-week treatment, that three dreams a week are explored, and that analysis lasts six years. That is 720 dreams. My argument is that the psychoanalytic relation to the dream grows an internal and structured operational intrapsychic correlate to the Freudian Pair. We may see that as this process takes hold, over years, it constitutes a new and different form of individuation and independence. Furthermore, we may see how the ingredients of termination are built into this new structuring. As the analytic pair gradually becomes divested of its traditional working relationship, both roles are eventually taken over by the analysand.

Indeed, I believe that this is another way of describing the self's creation of reverie. What we find, here, is a two-in-one mental structure; it is the inner relation in which we are both the active agent and the passive recipient of our thoughts that leads to a state of mind that we term reverie. When the analysand can reliably turn to the state of reverie to process his or her mental life, I think we observe the end stages of a psychoanalysis.

We have considered, then, how a psychoanalysis extends the work of the dream and develops the Freudian Pair into an internal structure that in turn produces transforming moments, redolent with insight. Such verbalisations reveal, through a transformation into language, another form of work that has prepared unconscious wisdom for consciousness. Just as everyday wit appears in the course of a social conversation to regenerate the *jouissance* of the encounter, wisdom arises in aphorisms that enliven our conversations with ourselves, and with those others who find the ongoing search for meaning one of the agonising pleasures of life.

Bibliography of works by Christopher Bollas

Nonfiction

The Shadow of the Object: Psychoanalysis of the Unthought Known (London, Free Association Books, 1987).
Forces of Destiny: Psychoanalysis and Human Idiom (London, Free Association Books, 1989).
Being a Character: Psychoanalysis and Self Experience (London, Routledge, 1992).
Perché Edipo? (Rome, Borla, 1993).
Cracking Up: The Work of Unconscious Experience (London, Routledge, 1995).
The New Informants (with David Sundelson) (London, Karnac, 1995).
The Mystery of Things (London, Routledge, 1999).
Hysteria (London, Routledge, 2000).
Free Association (London, Icon, 2002).
The Freudian Moment (London, Karnac, 2007).
The Evocative Object World (London, Routledge, 2009).
The Infinite Question (London, Karnac, 2009).
China on the Mind (London, Routledge, in press).

Fiction

Dark at the End of the Tunnel (London, Free Association Books, 2004).
I Have Heard the Mermaids Singing (London, Free Association Books, 2005).
Mayhem (London, Free Association Books, 2006).
Theraplay (London, Free Association Books, 2006).

Select essays (English)

'Melville's lost self: Bartleby.' *American Imago* 31 (1974): 401–11.
'Character: The language of self.' *International Journal of Psychoanalytic Psychotherapy* 3 (1974): 397–418.
'Sylvia Plath: Absence at the center' (with Murray Schwartz). *Criticism* 18 (1976): 147–72.
'Aspects of the erotic transference.' *Psychoanalytic Inquiry* 14 (1994): 572–90.

Select essays (French)

'Le langage secret de la mère et de l'enfant.' *Nouvelle Revue de Psychanalyse* 14 (Automne 1976) 'Du Secret'.
'Comment l'hysterique prend possession de l'analyste.' *Nouvelle Revue de Psychanalyse* 24 (Automne 1981) 'L'Emprise'.
'La révélation de l'ici et maintenant.' *Nouvelle Revue de Psychanalyse* 27 (Printemps 1983) 'Ideaux'.

Publications on the work of Christopher Bollas

Sergio Benvenuto and Anthony Molino (eds.). *In Freud's Tracks: Conversations from the Journal of European Psychoanalysis* (Lanham, MD, Aronson, 2009).

Georg Diez and Christopher Roth (eds.). 'Distance to destination', in *80*81 Travelogue* Vol. 5/6 (Zurich, Edition Patrick Frey), pp. 1–39.

Joseph Scalia (ed.). *The Vitality of Objects: Exploring the Work of Christopher Bollas* (Middletown, CT, Wesleyan University Press, 2002).

Anthony Molino (ed.). *Freely Associated: Encounters in Psychoanalysis* (London, Free Association Books, 1997).

References

Al-Khalil, Samir. (1989). *Republic of Fear*. London, Berkeley, 1991.

Arendt, Hannah. (1986). *The Origins of Totalitarianism*. London, Deutsch.

Austin, J. L. (1962). *How To Do Things With Words*. Oxford and New York, Oxford University Press, 1989.

Bachelard, Gaston. (1958). *The Poetics of Space*. Boston MA, Beacon Books, 1994.

Bacon, Francis. (1968). 'Statements, 1952–1955', in Chipp, p. 620.

Bakunin, Mikhail. (1869). *Revolutionary Catechism*. Ed. Sam Dolgoff. New York, Knopf, 1972.

Balint, Michael. (1968). *The Basic Fault*. London, Tavistock.

Barthes, Roland. (1964). 'The Eiffel Tower', in *The Eiffel Tower*. New York, California University Press, 1984, pp. 3–22.

Bataille, Georges. *Eroticism: Death & Sensuality*. (1957). San Francisco, City Lights, 1986.

Beetham, David. (1983). *Marxists in Face of Fascism*. Manchester, Manchester University Press.

Bergson, Henri. (1911). *Creative Evolution*. Lanham, MD, University Press of America, Inc.

Bettelheim, Bruno. (1960). *The Informed Heart*. London, Penguin, 1987.

Bion, Wilfred R. (1958). 'On hallucination', in Bion, 1967, pp. 65–85.

—— (1962). 'Learning from experience', in Bion, 1977, pp. 1–111.

—— (1967). *Second Thoughts*. New York, Aronson.

—— (1977). *Seven Servants*. New York, Aronson.

Blackburn, Simon. (1999). *Think: A Compelling Introduction to Philosophy*. Oxford, Oxford University Press.

Bloch, Ernst. (1974). *Essays on the Philosophy of Music*. London and New York, Cambridge University Press, 1985.

Bollas, Christopher. (1978). 'The transformational object', in Bollas, 1987a, pp. 13–29.

—— (1987a). *The Shadow of the Object: Psychoanalysis of the Unthought Known*. London, Free Association Books.

—— (1987b). 'Extractive introjection', in Bollas, 1987a, pp. 157–69.

—— (1987c). 'Normotic illness', in Bollas, 1987a, pp. 135–56.

—— (1989a). *Forces of Destiny: Psychoanalysis and Human Idiom*. London, Free Association Books.

—— (1989b). 'The destiny drive', in Bollas, 1989a.

—— (1992). *Being a Character: Psychoanalysis and Self Experience*. London, Routledge.

—— (1995). *Cracking Up: The Work of Unconscious Experience*. London, Routledge.

—— (1999). *The Mystery of Things*. London, Routledge.

—— (2000). *Hysteria*. London, Routledge.

—— (2002). *Free Association*. London, Icon.

—— (2004). *Dark at the End of the Tunnel*. London, Free Association Books.

—— (2005). *I Have Heard the Mermaids Singing*. London, Free Association Books.

—— (2006a). *Mayhem*. London, Free Association Books.

—— (2006b). *Theraplay*. London, Free Association Books.

—— (2007a). *The Freudian Moment*. London, Karnac.

—— (2007b). 'Perceptive identification', in Bollas, 2007a, pp. 65–69.

—— (2009a). *The Evocative Object World*. London, Routledge.

—— (2009b). *The Infinite Question*. London, Routledge.

—— and David Sundelson. (1995). *The New Informants*. London, Karnac.

Bradley, Ben S. (1989). *Visions of Infancy*. Cambridge, Polity.

Brazelton, Terry, and Bertrand Cramer. (1990). *The Earliest Relationship*. New York and London, Addison Wesley.

Brenman, Eric. (1988). 'Cruelty and narrow-mindedness', in Spillius, pp. 256–70.

Breton, André. (1934). 'What is Surrealism?', in Chipp, pp. 410–17.

Camus, Albert. (1942). *The Myth of Sisyphus*. New York and London, Penguin, 1975.

Caws, Mary Ann. (1996). *What Art Holds*. New York, Columbia University Press.

Chasseguet-Smirgel, Janine. (1985). *Creativity and Perversion*. London, Tavistock.

Chipp, Herschel B. (1968). *Theories of Modern Art*. Berkeley, CA, University of California Press.

Cleese, John, and Connie Booth. (1979). *Fawlty Towers: The Psychiatrist*. Video, London, BBC.

Collier, Peter, and David Horowitz. (1989). *Destructive Generation*. New York.

Corrigan, Edward, and Pearl-Ellen Gordon. (1995). *The Mind Object*. New York, Aronson.

Cotta, Sergio. (1985). *Why Violence?* Gainesville FL, University of Florida.

Crane, Hart. (1979). 'General aims and theories', in Gibbons, pp. 179–83.

Crawford, Harriet. (1991) *Sumer and the Sumerians*. Cambridge, Cambridge University Press.

Doi, Takeo. (1971). *The Anatomy of Dependence*. Tokyo, Kodansha, 2001.

Donaldson, Ian. (1970). *The World Turned Upside Down*. New York and London, Oxford University Press.

Donnet, Jean-Luc, and André Green. (1973). *L'Enfant de ça*. Paris, Les Editions de Minuit.

Duncan, Dennis. (1990). 'The feel of the session', *Psychoanalysis and Contemporary Thought*, 13: 3–22.

Ehrenzweig, Anton. (1967). *The Hidden Order of Art*. Berkeley, CA, California University Press, 1971.

Einstein, Albert. (1952). 'Letter to Jacques Hadamard', in Ghiselin, pp. 43–4.

Epel, Naomi (ed.). (1994). *Writers Dreaming*. New York, Vintage.

Field, M. (1995). 'Classroom on stilts puts new life into an old prefab', *The Architects Journal*, 3: 23.

Fo, Dario. (1987). *The Tricks of the Trade*. New York, Routledge, 1991.

Freud, Sigmund. (1900). *The Interpretation of Dreams. Standard Edition* 4 & 5.

—— (1901). *The Psychopathology of Everyday Life. Standard Edition* 6.

—— (1913). *Totem and Taboo. Standard Edition* 13, pp. 1–162.

—— (1915). 'The unconscious'. *Standard Edition* 14, pp. 159–215.

—— (1919). 'The uncanny'. *Standard Edition* 17, pp. 217–53.

—— (1920). 'Beyond the pleasure principle'. *Standard Edition* 18, pp. 3–64.

—— (1921). *Group Psychology and the Analysis of the Ego. Standard Edition* 18, pp. 67–143.

—— (1923). *The Ego and the Id. Standard Edition* 19.

—— (1927). *The Future of an Illusion. Standard Edition* 21, pp. 3–56.

—— (1929). *Civilisation and its Discontents. Standard Edition* 21.

Gass, William. (1996). *Finding A Form.* New York, Knopf.

Ghiselin, Brewster. (1952). *The Creative Process.* New York, Mentor.

Gibbons, Reginald. (1979). *The Poet's Work.* Chicago, University of Chicago.

Giovacchini, Peter L. (ed.). (1972). 'The blank self', in *Tactics and Techniques in Psychoanalytic Therapy.* London, Hogarth.

Graves, Robert. (1977). *The Greek Myths,* Vol. 1. London, Penguin.

Green, André. (1973). *The Fabric of Affect in the Psychoanalytic Discourse.* London, Routledge.

—— (1981). 'Projection', in Green, 1986, pp. 84–103.

—— (1986). *On Private Madness.* London, Hogarth.

Grinberg, Leon et al. (1975). *Introduction to the Work of Bion.* London, Maresfield Library.

Hampshire, Stuart. (1989). *Innocence and Experience.* London, Allen Lane.

Harris, Steven, and Deborah Berke. (1997). *Architecture of the Everyday.* Princeton, NJ, Princeton University Press, p. 20.

Hass, Robert. (1994). *The Essential Haiku: Versions of Basho, Buson and Issa.* New York, Ecco Press.

Heaney, Seamus. (1980). *Preoccupations.* London, Faber.

Hedges, Lawrence. (1983). *Listening Perspectives in Psychotherapy.* New York, Aronson.

Heimann, Paula. (1956). 'Dynamics of transference interpretations', *International Journal of Psychoanalysis,* 37: 303–10.

Hersey, George. (1988). *The Lost Meaning of Classical Architecture.* Cambridge, MA, MIT, 1995.

Hoffman, Eric von. (1992). *A Venom in the Blood.* New York, Pinnacle Books, 1999.

Humes, Edward. (1991). *Buried Secrets: A True Story of Serial Murder.* New York, Dutton.

Jacobson, Edith. (1965). *The Self and the Object World.* London, Hogarth.

James, Alice. (1979). 'The diary', in E. Murphy, *The Macmillan Treasury of Relevant Quotations.* New York, Macmillan, p. 212.

John-Steiner, Vera. (1985). *Notebooks of the Mind.* New York, Perennial.

Jones, Rodney, Charles Sevilla, and Gerald Velmen. (1987). *Disorderly Conduct.* New York, Norton.

Low, Albert (ed.). (2006). *Hakuin on Kensho: The Four Ways of Knowing.* Boston, MA, Shambhala.

Keenan, Brian. (1992). *An Evil Cradling: The Five Year Ordeal of a Hostage.* London and New York, Viking.

Khan, Masud. (1974). *The Privacy of the Self.* London, Hogarth.

—— (1979). *Alienation in Perversions.* London, Hogarth.

Kramer, Heinrich, and James Sprenger. (1486). *Malleus Maleficarum.* London and Magnolia, MA, 1971.

Krassner, Paul. (1957). *Confessions of a Raving Unconfined Nut.* London and New York, Simon & Schuster, 1993.

Kuper, Leo. (1981). *Genocide.* London, Penguin.

Lifton, Robert J. (1986). *The Nazi Doctors*. New York, Basic Books.

Lowell, Amy. 'The process of making poetry', in Ghiselin, pp. 109–112.

Lynch, Kevin. (1960). *The Image of the City*. Cambridge, MA, MIT, 1996.

Lyotard, Jean-Francois. (1989). 'The dream work does not think', in *The Lyotard Reader* ed. Andrew Benjamin. Oxford, Blackwell, pp. 19–55.

Masters, Brian. (1985). *Killing for Company: The Case of Dennis Nilsen*. London and New York, Arrow Books, 1986.

McDougall, Joyce. (1980). *Plea for a Measure of Abnormality*. New York, International Universities Press.

Melville, Hermann. (1851). *Moby Dick*. New York, Norton, 1967.

Milner, Marion. (1969). *The Hands of the Living God*. London, Hogarth.

Milosz, Czeslaw. (1979). 'Ars Poetica', in Gibbons, pp. 3–4.

Milton, John. (1674). 'Paradise Lost', in *Complete Poems and Major Prose*. London and New York, Prentice Hall, 1957.

Montet, Pierre. (1958). *Everyday Life in Egypt in the Days of Ramesses the Great*. Philadelphia PA, University of Pennsylvania, 1981.

Moore, Henry. (1952). 'Notes on sculpture', in Ghiselin, pp. 73–8.

Mussolini, Benito. (1983). 'Dottrina del fascismo', in *Encylopaedia Brittanica*, Vol. 7. Chicago, University of Chicago, pp. 182–8.

Natsume, Soseki. (1916). *Light and Darkness*. Tokyo, Charles Tuttle, 1981.

Nietzsche, Friedrich. (1908). *Ecce Homo*. London, Penguin, 1980.

O'Sullivan, Noel. (1983). *Fascism*. London, Dent.

Percelay, James, Ivey Monteria, and Stephan Dweck. (1994). *Snaps*. New York, Morrow.

Pessoa, Fernando. (1979). 'Toward explaining heteronymy', in Gibbons, pp. 5–15.

Petras, Ross, and Kathryn Petras. (1993). *The 776 Stupidest Things Ever Said*. New York, Doubleday.

Picasso, Pablo. (1952). 'Conversation with Picasso', in Ghiselin, pp. 55–60.

Poincaré, Henri. (1952). 'Mathematical creation', in Ghiselin, pp. 33–42.

Poland, Warren. (2000). 'The analyst's witnessing and otherness', *Journal of the American Psychoanalytic Association*, 48: 17–34.

Pontalis, Jean-Bertrand. (1974). 'Dream as object', *International Review of Psychoanalysis*, 1: 125–33.

—— (1981). *Frontiers in Psychoanalysis*. London, Hogarth.

Richter, Gerhard. (1995). *The Daily Practice of Painting*. Cambridge, MA, MIT.

Rosenfeld, Herbert. (1987). *Impasse and Interpretation*. London, Tavistock.

Schoenberg, Arnold, and Wassily Kandinsky. (1984). *Arnold Shoenberg, Wassily Kandinsky: Letters, Pictures, Documents*. London and Boston, MA, Faber.

Seldes, George. (1985). *The Great Thoughts*. New York, Ballantine.

Smith, Sidney. (1977). 'The golden fantasy: a regressive reaction to separation anxiety', *International Journal of Psychoanalysis*, 58: 311–24.

Snyder, Gary. (1979). 'The real works', in Gibbons, pp. 283–94.

Sontag, Susan. (1976). *Illness as Metaphor*. New York, Farrar Strauss.

Sophocles. (1984). *Oedipus The King*. In *The Three Theban Plays*. London, Penguin.

Spender, Stephen. (1952). 'The making of a poem', in Ghiselin, pp. 112–25.

Spillius, Elizabeth. (1988). *Melanie Klein Today*, Vol. 1. London, Routledge.

Stern, Fritz. (1974). *The Politics of Cultural Despair*. Berkeley, CA, University of California Press.

Stevens, Wallace. (1979). 'The irrational element in poetry', in Gibbons, pp. 48–58.

Stewart, Harold. (1985). 'Changes of inner space', *International Journal of Psychoanalysis*, 68: 255–64.

Stoller, Robert. (1973). *Splitting*. New York, International Universities Press.

—— (1976). *Perversion*. London, Harvester.

Stravinsky, Igor. (1942). *Poetics of Music*. Cambridge, MA, Harvard University Press.

Turco, Lewis. (2000). *The Book of Forms: A Handbook of Poetics*. Hanover and London, University Press of New England.

Valery, Paul. (1952). 'The course in poetics: first lesson', in Ghiselin, pp. 92–106.

—— (1979). 'A poet's notebook', in Gibbons, pp. 170–83.

Vendler, Helen. (1988). *The Music of What Happens*. Cambridge, MA, Harvard University Press.

Waite, Terry. (1993). *Taken on Trust*. London and New York, Hodder & Stoughton.

Winnicott, D. W. (1947). 'Hate in the counter transference', in Winnicott, 1975, pp. 194–203.

—— (1952). 'Anxiety associated with insecurity', in Winnicott, 1975, pp. 97–100.

—— (1958). 'The capacity to be alone', in Winnicott, 1965, pp. 29–36.

—— (1960). 'Ego distortion in terms of true and false self', in Winnicott, 1965, pp. 140–52.

—— (1963a). 'Psychiatric disorder in terms of infantile maturational processes', in Winnicott, 1965, pp. 230–41.

—— (1963b). 'Communicating and not communicating leading to a study of certain opposites', in Winnicott, 1965, pp. 179–92.

—— (1965). *The Maturational Processes and the Facilitating Environment*. London, Hogarth.

—— (1969a). 'The use of an object and relating through identifications', in Winnicott, 1971a, pp. 86–94.

—— (1969b). 'Berlin Walls', in *Home is Where We Start From*. London, Norton, 1986.

—— (1971a). *Playing and Reality*. London, Routledge.

—— (1971b) 'Creativity and its origins', in Winnicott, 1971a, pp. 65–85.

—— (1975). *Through Paediatrics to Psychoanalysis*. London, Hogarth.

Wordsworth, William. (1799). 'The two-part prelude', in *The Pedlar, Tintern Abbey, The Two-Part Prelude*. Cambridge, Cambridge University Press, 1990.

Zibordi, Giovanni. (1983). 'Towards a definition of fascism', in Beetham, pp. 88–96.

Index

Abraham 154
abstract expressionism 196, 197, 205, 206
absurdity 136, 137, 140, 141, 154, 194
abuse: alcohol abuse 27, 30, 114; of the
   analyst, in phantasy 41, 49; child abuse
   57, 65–6, 108, 113–15, 166–7, 168–9;
   emotional 114; movement 120; physical
   114; sexual 113–15, 166–7; and the
   structure of evil 166–9; victimology and
   the trivialising of 166–7; wife battering
   167–9
acceptance, dissociative 91
accident/the accidental 140–1, 146, 196–7;
   accident-prone characters 148
Adam 153
advertising, promise of environmental
   transformation 3
Aeneid (Virgil) 43
aesthetics *see also* art: aesthetic
   intelligence xxii, 240; aesthetic
   moments 3, 11, 12; aesthetic space 11;
   and the creative process 62–4, 67–70, 72
   see also creativity; negative aesthetic
   experience 3–4; personality as an erotic
   aesthetics 60; search for aesthetic
   experience 3–4; surrealism 194–6, 205
aggregation, categorization as 88–9
aggression: aggressive aspect of
   narcissistic self state 82; and omnipotent
   destructiveness 41; reciprocal
   aggression with the object 49; turned
   into humor 90; without persecution
   42–3
Al-Khalil, Samir 172–3
alcohol abuse 114; in normotic breakdown
   27, 30
allegories 176, 177
Allen, Woody 148, 153

Allende, Isabel 200, 203
aloneness: essential 108; isolation *see*
   isolation
alpha elements 26, 226
alpha function 26–7, 55
altered states of consciousness 200, 202
ambivalence 16, 25, 206
amnesia 120
analytic neutrality of expression 7, 233–4
analytic process: breaking up the figurative
   205–6; character reception in 243–4;
   compared with the creative process
   203–4 *see also* psychoanalysis: and
   creativity; countertransference *see*
   countertransference; creativity of 73–4;
   as an elaboration of the true self/idiom
   37–8, 46–50, 53; entering the
   intrinsically traumatic 117; free
   association *see* free association;
   hysterical patients and 9; interpretations
   see interpretations; listening *see*
   listening; obsessional's ritualization of
   9; of reverie 75–6 *see also* reverie; and
   the search for the transformational
   object 7–12; silence in 10, 47, 48, 49,
   76, 137, 182, 188; transference *see*
   transference; working with depression
   and mental interference 182–90
analytic relationship xx, xxv, 40, 47; and
   the analyst's formal effect 247; and the
   experience of the other's character 247;
   the Freudian Pair xxii–xxiv, 229, 255,
   257, 258; patient's unconscious use of
   the analyst 37–43, 46–50; self-
   disclosure in 241; unconscious
   communication in 75, 78, 241
analytic space 7–8, 9, 10, 12, 116,
   243, 245